Henryk Sienkiewicz and his daughter Yadviga.

HANIA.

BY

HENRYK SIENKIEWICZ,

AUTHOR OF "QUO VADIS," "WITH FIRE AND SWORD
"THE DELUGE," "CHILDREN OF THE SOIL," ETC.

TRANSLATED FROM THE POLISH BY

JEREMIAH CURTIN.

**Fredonia Books
Amsterdam, The Netherlands**

Hania

by
Henryk Sienkiewicz

ISBN: 1-58963-647-3

Copyright © 2001 by Fredonia Books

Reprinted from the 1898 edition

Fredonia Books
Amsterdam, The Netherlands
http://www.fredoniabooks.com

All rights reserved, including the right to reproduce this book, or portions thereof, in any form.

In order to make original editions of historical works available to scholars at an economical price, this facsimile of the original edition of 1898 is reproduced from the best available copy and has been digitally enhanced to improve legibility, but the text remains unaltered to retain historical authenticity.

CONTENTS.

	PAGE
PROLOGUE TO HANIA: THE OLD SERVANT	3
HANIA	21
TARTAR CAPTIVITY	171
LET US FOLLOW HIM	219
BE THOU BLESSED	259
AT THE SOURCE	265
CHARCOAL SKETCHES	291
THE ORGANIST OF PONIKLA	375
LUX IN TENEBRIS LUCET	387
ON THE BRIGHT SHORE	401
THAT THIRD WOMAN	483

HANIA

HANIA.

PROLOGUE.

THE OLD SERVANT.

BESIDES old managers, overseers, and foresters there is another type of man which is disappearing more and more from the face of the earth,— the old servant.

During my childhood, as I remember, my parents were served by one of those mammoths. After those mammoths there will soon be only bones in old cemeteries, in strata thickly covered with oblivion; from time to time investigators will dig them out. This old servant was called Mikolai Suhovolski; he was a noble from the noble village of Suha Vola, which he mentioned often in his stories. He came to my father from my grandfather of sacred memory, with whom he was an orderly in the time of the Napoleonic wars. He did not himself remember accurately when he began service with my grandfather; when he was asked for the date, he took snuff, and answered,—

"Yes, I was then without mustaches, and the colonel, God light his soul, was still very young."

In the house of my parents he fulfilled the most varied duties: he was butler; he was body-servant; in summer he went to the harvest fields in the rôle of overseer, in winter to the threshing; he kept the keys of the vodka room, the cellar, the granary; he wound up the clocks; but above all he kept the house in order.

I do not remember this man otherwise than scolding. He scolded my father, he scolded my mother; I feared him as fire, though I liked him. In the kitchen he worked off a whole breviary on the cook, he pulled the pantry boys by the ears through the house, and never was he content with anything. Whenever he got tipsy, which happened once a week, all avoided him, not because he permitted himself to have words with his master or mistress, but because whenever he fastened on any one, he followed that person all day, nagging and scolding without end.

During dinner, he stood behind my father's chair, and, though he did not serve, he watched the man who served, and poisoned life for him with a most particular passion.

"Take care, take care!" muttered he, "or I will take care of thee. Look at him! he cannot serve quickly, but drags his legs after him, like an old cow on the march. Take care again! He does not hear that his master is calling. Change her plate for the lady. Why art thou gaping? Why? Look at him! look at him!"

He interfered in conversation carried on at table, and opposed everything always. Frequently it happened that my father would turn during dinner and say to him, —

"Mikolai, tell Mateush after dinner to harness the horses; we will drive to such and such a place."

"Drive! why not drive? Oi yei! But are not horses for driving? Let the poor horses break their legs on such a road. If there is a visit to be made, it must be made. Of course their lordships are free; do I prevent them? I do not prevent. Why not visit? The ac-

counts can wait, and the threshing can wait. The visit
is more urgent."

"It is a torment with this Mikolai!" shouted my
father sometimes, made impatient.

But Mikolai began again, —

"Do I say that I am not stupid? I know that I am
stupid. The manager has gone to pay court to the
priest's housekeeper in Nyevodov, and why shouldn't
masters go on visits? Is a visit less important than
paying court to a housekeeper? If 't is permitted to the
servant to go, it is permitted to the master."

And thus it went on in a circle without means of
stopping the old grumbler.

We, that is, I and my younger brother, feared him, as
I have said, almost more than our tutor Father Ludvik,
and surely more than our parents. He was more polite
toward my sisters. He said "Panienka"[1] to each of
them, though they were younger than we; but to us he
said "thou" without ceremony. For me he had a
special charm: he always carried gun caps in his pocket.
It happened often that after lessons I would slip into
the pantry, smile as nicely as I could, be as friendly as
possible, and say timidly, —

"Mikolai! A good day to Mikolai. Will Mikolai
clean pistols to-day?"

"What does Henryk want here? I'll get ready a
dish-cloth, that is all."

Then he would mock me, saying, —

"'Mikolai! Mikolai!' When gun caps are wanted,
Mikolai is good, and when not, let the wolves eat him.
Thou wouldst do better to study; thou 'lt never gain
wit from shooting."

"I have finished my lessons," said I, half crying.

"Finished his lessons! Hum! finished. He is studying and studying, but his head is like an empty canister. I won't give caps, and that's the end of it." (While talking, he searched through his pockets.) "But if the cap goes into his eye, Mikolai will catch it. Who is to blame? Mikolai. Who let the boy shoot? Mikolai."

Scolding in this fashion, he went to my father's room, took down the pistols, blew the dust off them, declared a hundred times more that all this was not worth a deuce; then he lighted a candle, put a cap on the nipple of the pistol, and let me aim. Meanwhile I had often to bear heavy crosses.

"How the boy holds the pistol!" said he. "Hum! like a barber. How couldst thou quench a candle, unless as an old man quenches it in church? Thou shouldst be a priest to repeat Hail Marys, and not be a soldier."

In his own way he taught us his military art of other days. Often after dinner I and my brother learned to march under his eye, and with us marched Father Ludvik, who marched very ridiculously.

Then Mikolai looked at him with a frown, and, though he feared the priest more than any one, he could not restrain himself.

"Hei!" said he, "but his grace marches just like an old cow."

I, as the elder, was oftener under his command, so I suffered most. But when I was sent to school old Mikolai cried as if the greatest misfortune had happened. My father and mother said that he became more peevish, and annoyed them two weeks.

"They took the child and carried him away," said he. "And if he dies! Uu! u! But what does he want of schools? Isn't he the heir? Will he study Latin?

They want to turn him into a Solomon. What folly!
The child has gone off, gone off, and crawl, thou old man,
into corners and look for what thou hast not lost. The
deuce knows why 't is done."

I remember when I came home for the first holidays.
All in the house were sleeping yet. It was just dawning;
the morning was cold and snowy. The squeaking of the
well-sweep in the farm-yard and the barking of dogs interrupted the silence. The blinds of the house were
closed, but the windows in the kitchen were gleaming
with a bright light which gave a rosy color to the snow
near the wall. I had come home tired and gloomy with
fear in my soul, since the first rank which I had received
was nothing in particular. This happened because I was
helpless till I had found my place, till I had grown accustomed to routine and school discipline. I feared my
father; I feared the severe, silent face of the priest, who
had brought me from Warsaw. There was no consolation
from any side. At last I saw the door of the kitchen
open and old Mikolai, with his nose red from cold, wading through the snow with pots of steaming cream on
a tray. When he saw me he cried, —

"Oh, golden Panich! my dearest!"

And then he put down the tray quickly, turned over both
pots, caught me around the neck and began to press and
kiss me. Thenceforward he always called me Panich.

For two entire weeks after that he could not forgive
me that cream: "A man is carrying cream for himself
quietly, and the boy comes along. He picked out his
hour accurately," etc.

My father was going to flog me, or at least he promised
to do so, because of the two moderate marks which I had
brought, one for penmanship, the other for German; but
my tears and promises of improvement on one hand, the

intercession of my dear mother on the other, and finally, the troubles raised by Mikolai, prevented it. Mikolai did not know what kind of creature penmanship was, and to punish one for German — that he would not even listen to.

"Well," said he, "is the boy a Lutheran, or some Schwab? Did the lord colonel know how to speak German? or does the lord himself [here he turned to my father] know how to speak it? We met the Germans at — What is the name of the place? At Leipzig, and the devil knows wherever we attacked them we didn't talk German, but they showed us their backs right away."

Old Mikolai had one more peculiarity: he spoke rarely of his former expeditions, but when in moments of special good humor he did so, he lied as if possessed. He did not do this through bad faith; in his old head perhaps facts were mixed up, and grew to fantastic proportions. Whatever military exploits he had heard of during youth he appropriated to himself and my grandfather, his colonel. And he believed sacredly all that he said.

Sometimes in the barn, while overseeing peasants working out their dues in threshing wheat, he would begin to narrate; the men would stop work, and, resting on their flails, listen with lips open in wonderment. Then he would notice them and shout, —

"Why do ye turn mouths on me as big as cannon?"

And again was heard, —

"Lupu! Tsupu! Lupu! Tsupu!"

The sound of flails was heard for some time on the straw, but after a while Mikolai would begin again, —

"My son writes me that he has just been made general by the Queen of Palmyra. He has a good place there, high pay, but there are terrible frosts in that country —" etc.

THE OLD SERVANT.

I may mention that the old man had no success with his children. He had a son, it is true, but a great good-for-nothing, who, when he grew up, made Lord knows what trouble; finally he went into the world and disappeared without trace; and Mikolai's daughter, in her time a wonder of a girl, was giddy with all the officials, as many as there were in the village, and finally died, after giving the world a daughter. That daughter was called Hania. She was about my age, beautiful, but delicate. I remember that often we played soldier. Hania was the drummer, but a nettle to our enemies. She was good and mild as an angel. A grievous fate awaited her in the world, but those are memories which do not concern us at present.

I return to the old man's narratives. Once I heard him tell how on a time the horses of the Uhlans stampeded in Mariampol. Eighteen thousand of them rushed in through the gates of Warsaw. "How many people they trampled to death," said he, "what a day of judgment there was till they were caught, it is easy to imagine." Another time he told, not in the barn, however, but to us all in the mansion, the following, —

"Did we fight well? Why should n't we fight well? I remember once there was war with the Austrians; I was standing in the rank, in the rank, I say, and up to me rides the commander-in-chief, as if to give a message from the Austrians, that is, from the opposite side. 'Ei, thou Suhovolski,' said he, 'I know thee! If we could only catch thee we should finish the whole war.'"

"But did n't he say anything about the colonel?" asked my father.

"Of course! for he said expressly, 'thee and the colonel.'"

Father Ludvik got impatient and said, —

"But thou, Mikolai, tellest lies as if thou wert getting special pay for them."

The old man frowned and would have retorted; but he feared Father Ludvik and respected him, so he said nothing; but after a while, wishing somehow to straighten the affair, he continued, —

"Father Seklutski, our chaplain, told me the same. Once when I got a bayonet thrust from the Austrians under the twelfth, I meant to say the fifth rib, I was in a bad state. Ha! thought I, it is necessary to die, so I confessed all my sins to the Lord God Almighty before Father Seklutski. Father Seklutski listened and listened; at last he said, 'Fear God, Mikolai, thou hast told me all the lies thou knowest.' And I said: 'Maybe, for I don't remember any more.'"

"And they cured thee?"

"Cured! How could they cure me? I cured myself. I mixed right away two charges of powder in a quart of vodka and swallowed it for the night. Next morning I woke up as sound as a fish."

I should have heard more of these narratives and recorded them, but Father Ludvik, I know not why, forbade Mikolai "to turn my head," as he declared, "completely." Poor Father Ludvik, as a priest and a quiet village dweller, did not know first, that every youth whom a storm casts out of his quiet, native corner into the wide arena of the world must have his head turned more than once, and second, that it is not old servants and their narratives that turn them, but some one else.

For that matter the influence of Mikolai on us could not be harmful; on the contrary, the old man watched over us and our conduct very carefully and sternly. He was a conscientious man in the full sense of that word. From his military days one fine characteristic remained with him: conscientiousness and accuracy in carrying out orders.

One winter, as I remember, the wolves inflicted enormous damage; they grew so bold that in the night a few of them came to the village, and then some tens of them. My father, a born hunter, wanted to arrange a great hunt; but since he was anxious that the command of it should be taken by our neighbor, Pan Ustrytski, a renowned destroyer of wolves, he wrote a letter to him, and calling Mikolai said, —

"My tenant is going to the town; let Mikolai go with him, get out on the road near Ustrytsi, and give this letter to Pan Ustrytski. But it is necessary to bring me an answer. Do not come back without an answer."

Mikolai took the letter, got in with the tenant, and they drove off. In the evening the tenant returned; Mikolai was not with him. My father thought that perhaps he would spend the night in Ustrytsi and return in the morning. A day passed, no Mikolai; a second day passed, nothing of him; a third, no sign of him. There was lamentation in the house. My father, fearing that wolves had attacked him on the way home, sent people to search for the man. They searched, but not a trace could they find. They sent to Ustrytsi. In Ustrytsi it was said that he had been there, had not found Pan Ustrytski; that he had inquired where he was, then borrowed four rubles from the lackey and gone, it was unknown whither. What can all this mean? thought we.

Next day messengers came from other villages with information that they had not found him anywhere. We had begun to mourn for him when on the sixth evening my father, who was making dispositions in the chancery, heard all at once, outside the door, the wiping of feet, and hawking and grumbling in a low voice, by which he recognized Mikolai immediately.

In fact, it was Mikolai, chilled through, tired, thin, with icicles hanging from his mustaches, almost unlike himself.

"Mikolai! But fear God! what hast thou been doing all this time?"

"What have I been doing, what have I been doing?" muttered Mikolai. "What was I to do? I did not find Pan Ustrytski at home, I went to Bzin. In Bzin they told me, deuce take it, that Pan Ustrytski had gone to Karalovka. I went there too. He had gone from Karalovka, also. But isn't he free to warm strange corners? Isn't he a lord? Besides, he does not travel on foot. 'Very well,' said I, and from Karalovka I went to the capital, for they said that he was in the district capital. And what business had he in the capital, was he the mayor? He went to the government town. Was I to return? I went to the government town and gave him the letter."

"Well, did he give thee an answer?"

"He did, and he didn't. He gave it, but he laughed so that I could see his back teeth. 'Thy lord,' said he, 'asks me to a hunt on Thursday, and thou givest me this letter on the following Monday. The hunt is over now.' And he laughed again. Here is the letter. Why shouldn't he laugh?"

"But what hast thou eaten all this time?"

"Well, what of it if I haven't eaten anything since yesterday? Do I suffer hunger here? Or are the spoons stingy of food with me? If I haven't eaten, I shall eat."

After that no one gave unconditional commands to Mikolai, but as often as he was sent anywhere we told

THE OLD SERVANT.

him what to do in case he did not find the person at home.

Some months later Mikolai went to a fair at a neighboring town to buy horses, for he knew horses perfectly. In the evening the manager came to say that Mikolai had brought the horses, but had come back beaten and was ashamed to appear. My father went immediately to Mikolai, —

"What is the matter with thee, Mikolai?"

"I had a fight!" he blurted out briefly.

"Be ashamed, old man. Thou wilt pick quarrels in a market? Thou hast no sense. Old, but a fool! Dost thou know that I would discharge another man for such a trick? Be ashamed It must be that thou wert drunk. So thou art spoiling my people, instead of giving an example."

My father was really angry, and when he was angry he did not trifle. But this was the wonder, that Mikolai, who on such occasions did not forget the tongue in his mouth, was as silent as a log this time. Evidently the old man had grown stubborn. Others asked him in vain how it had happened and what was the question. He merely snorted at one, and said not a word to the other.

But they had annoyed him in earnest. Next morning he was so sick that we had to send for the doctor. The doctor was the first man to explain the affair. A week before my father had quarrelled with his overseer; the man ran away on the following day. He betook himself to a certain Pan Zoll, a German, a great enemy of my father, and took service. At the fair were Pan Zoll, our former overseer, and Pan Zoll's servants, who had driven fat cattle to the fair to be sold.

Pan Zoll saw Mikolai first; he approached his wagon

and fell to abusing my father. Mikolai called him a traitor, and when Pan Zoll uttered new outrages against my father, Mikolai retorted with the handle of his whip. Then the overseer and Zoll's servants rushed at Mikolai and beat him till he was bloody.

When my father heard this story tears came to his eyes. He could not forgive himself for having scolded Mikolai, who had been silent about the whole affair purposely.

When Mikolai recovered my father went to reproach him. The old man at first would not confess anything, and grumbled according to his habit; but afterward he grew tender, and he and my father cried like two beavers. Next my father challenged Zoll for the affair, and a duel was fought which that German remembered for many a day.

But had it not been for the doctor, Mikolai's devotion would have remained unknown. Mikolai had hated that doctor for a long time. The cause was as follows: —

I had a beautiful and youthful aunt, my father's sister, who lived with us. I loved her greatly, for she was as good as she was beautiful, and it did not astonish me that all loved her, and among others the doctor, a man who was young, wise, and exceedingly respected in that whole region. At first Mikolai liked the doctor, said that he was a clever fellow and rode well; but when the doctor began to visit us with evident intentions regarding Aunt Marynia, Mikolai's feelings toward him changed beyond recognition. He began to be polite, but cold to him as to a man utterly strange. Formerly he would scold even him When on some occasion he had sat too long with us, Mikolai when preparing him for the road grumbled: "What is the good of knocking around in the night? That serves nothing. Has any one ever seen the like!" Now he ceased to scold, and was as silent as if turned to stone. The honest doctor understood soon what it meant, and, though he smiled kindly as before at the old man, still, I think that in his soul it must have annoyed him.

Happily for the young Esculapius Aunt Marynia cherished for him feelings directly opposite those of Mikolai. On a certain evening, when the moon was lighting the hall very nicely, the odor of jasmine came in through the open window. Aunt Marynia was singing at the piano "Io questa notte sogno." Doctor Stanislav approached and asked in a quivering voice, if she thought that he could live without her. Evidently aunt expressed her doubts on this subject; then followed mutual vows, the calling of the moon to witness, and all things of that sort, which are done usually in such cases.

Unfortunately Mikolai came in just that moment to call them to tea. When he saw what was happening, he ran at once to my father, and since my father was not at the house, for he was walking around the buildings of the estate, he went to my mother, who with her usual kindly smile prayed him not to interfere in the matter.

The confused Mikolai was silent, gnawing himself internally during the rest of the evening; but when my father before going to bed went once more to the chancery to write some letters, Mikolai followed him, and stopping at the door began to cough significantly and knock his feet together.

"What does Mikolai wish?" asked my father.

"But that — What do they call it? — I wanted to ask if it is true that our young lady is going to take — a wife — I wanted to say going to take a husband?"

"Yes. What of it?"

"But it cannot be true that the young lady is going to marry that — barber?"

"What barber? Has Mikolai gone mad?— And must he push in his three coppers everywhere?"

"But the young lady, is she not our young lady; is she not the daughter of the lord colonel? The lord colonel would never have permitted this. Is not the young lady worthy of an heir and a lord of lords? But the doctor, with permission, who is he? The young lady will expose herself to the ridicule of people."

"The doctor is a wise man."

"Wise or not wise, is it few doctors that I have seen? They used to go through the camp and circle around in the army staff; but when it came to anything, a battle, for instance, they were not there. Didn't the lord colonel call them 'lancet fellows'? While a man is well the doctor won't touch him, but when he is lying half alive, then the doctor will go at him with his lancet. It is no trick to cut up a man when he cannot defend himself, for he has nothing in his hand. But try to cut him when he is well, and has a gun. Oi yei! A great thing to go over people's bones with a knife! There is no good in that! But the lord colonel would rise out of his grave if he knew of this. What kind of a soldier is a doctor? Or is such a man an heir? This cannot be! The young lady will not marry him. That's not according to command. Who is he to aspire to the young lady?"

Unfortunately for Mikolai the doctor not only aspired to the young lady, but even got her. Half a year later the wedding took place, and the colonel's daughter, covered with floods of her relatives' tears, and tears of the house-servants in general, but of Mikolai in particular, went away to share the fate of the doctor.

Mikolai did not cherish any feeling of offence against her, for he could not, since he loved her so much; but he would not forgive the doctor. He hardly ever mentioned

his name, and in general tried not to speak of him. I
may say in passing that Aunt Marynia was most happy
with Doctor Stanislav.

After a year God gave them a beautiful boy, after
another year a girl, and so on in turn, as if it had been
written down. Mikolai loved those children as his own;
he carried them in his arms, fondled them, kissed them,
but that there was a certain vexation in his heart because
of the *mésalliance* of Aunt Marynia I noticed more than
once.

We had assembled one Christmas eve, when suddenly
the rumble of a carriage was heard on the road. We
always looked for a number of relatives, therefore my
father said, —

"Let Mikolai look out and see who is coming."

Mikolai went out, and returned soon with delight in
his face.

"The young lady is coming!" cried he, from a distance.

"Who is that?" inquired my father, though he knew
whom Mikolai meant.

"The young lady."

"What young lady?"

"Our young lady."

She was a sight, that young lady, when she came into
the room with three children. A pretty young lady! But
the old man in his fashion called her "the young lady"
and nothing else.

At last his repugnance to Doctor Stanislav came to an
end. Hania fell terribly ill of typhus. That for me too
was a great affliction, since Hania was about my age and
my only playmate, and I loved her almost as a sister.
Doctor Stanislav hardly left her room for three days. The
old man, who loved Hania with all the strength of his soul,
went around during the time of her illness as if poisoned;

he neither ate nor drank, he just sat at the door of her room. To her bed no one was permitted to go except my mother. The old man chewed the hard iron pain which was tearing his breast. His was a soul of strong temper, as well for bodily toil as for blows of misfortune; still it almost bent under the weight of despair near the bed of that single grandchild. At last, after many days of mortal fear, Doctor Stanislav opened the door of the sick girl's room quietly, and with a face beaming with happiness, whispered to those waiting his sentence in the next room, one little phrase: "Saved." The old man could not endure; he bellowed like a bison and threw himself at the doctor's feet, merely repeating with sobs: "Benefactor, my benefactor!"

Hania recovered quickly. After that it was clear that Doctor Stanislav had become an eye in the old man's head.

"A clever man!" repeated he, stroking his mustaches, "a clever man. And sits well on horseback. Without him, Hania— Oh! I will not even mention it— A charm on a dog!"

In a year or so after this event the old man began to fail. His straight and powerful figure bent. He became very decrepit, he ceased to grumble and lie. At last, when he had reached almost ninety years he became perfectly childish. All he did was to make snares for birds; he kept a number of birds in his room, especially titmice.

Some days before death he did not recognize people; but on the very day of his decease the dying lamp of his mind gleamed up once more with bright light. I remember this because my parents were abroad then, for my mother's health. On a certain evening I was sitting before the fire with my younger brother, Kazio, and the priest, who had also grown old. The winter wind with clouds of snow was striking at the window. Father Ludvik was praying; I, with Kazio's help, was preparing weapons for the morrow's hunt on fresh snow. All at once they told us that old Mikolai was dying. Father Ludvik went immediately to the domestic chapel for the sacrament. I hurried with all speed to the old man. He was lying on the bed, very pale, yellow, and almost stiffening, but calm and with presence of mind.

That bald head was beautiful, adorned with two scars: the head of an old soldier and an honest man. The candle cast a funereal gleam on the walls of the room. In the corners chirped tame titmice. With one hand the old man pressed the crucifix to his breast; his other was held by Hania, who was as pale as a lily, and she covered it with kisses.

Father Ludvik came in and the confession began; then the dying man asked for me.

"My master is not here, nor my beloved mistress," whispered he, "therefore it is grievous for me to die. But you, my golden Panich, the heir — be a guardian to this orphan — God will reward you. Be not angry — If I have offended — forgive me. I was bitter, but I was faithful."

Roused again suddenly he called in a strange voice, and in haste, as if breath failed him, —

"Pan! — Heir! — my orphan! — O God — into Thy —"

"Hands I commend the soul of this valiant soldier, this faithful servant and honest man!" said Father Ludvik, solemnly.

The old man was no longer alive.

We knelt down, and the priest began to repeat prayers for the dead, aloud.

Nearly twenty years have passed since that time.

On the tomb of the honest servant the heather of the cemetery has grown vigorously.

Gloomy times came. A storm swept away the sacred and quiet fire of my village. To-day Father Ludvik is in the grave, Aunt Marynia is in the grave; I earn with the pen my bitter daily bread, and Hania —

Hei! tears are flowing!

HANIA.

CHAPTER I.

WHEN old Mikolai on his death-bed left Hania to my guardianship and conscience, I was sixteen years of age; she was younger by almost a year, and was also just emerging from childhood.

I had to lead her from the bed of her dead grandfather almost by force, and we both went to my father's domestic chapel. The doors of the chapel were open, and before the old Byzantine image of the Mother of God two candles were burning. The gleam of these lighted but faintly the darkness on the altar. We knelt down, one at the side of the other. She, broken by sorrow, wearied by sobbing, sleeplessness, and grief, rested her poor little head on my arm, and so we remained there in silence The hour was late; in the hall adjoining the chapel, the cuckoo called hoarsely on the old Dantiz clock the second hour after midnight. Deep silence everywhere, broken only by the painful sighs of Hania, and by the distant sound of the snow-bearing wind, which at times shook the leaden window-sash in the chapel. I did not dare to speak one word of solace; I merely drew her toward me, as her guardian, or her elder brother. But I could not pray; a thousand impressions and feelings shook my heart and head, various images swept before my eyes, but gradually out of that whirlpool one thought and one feeling emerged, — namely, that this pale face with closed eyes, this defenceless, poor little creature resting on my arm, had become to me now a dear sister for whose sake I would give my life, and for whose sake, should the need come, I would throw down the gauntlet to the whole world.

My brother, Kazio, appeared now and knelt down behind us, next Father Ludvik and a few of the servants. We said our evening prayers, according to daily custom: Father Ludvik read the prayers aloud, we repeated them, or answered the litany; the dark face of the Mother of God, with two sabre-cuts on her cheek, looked at us kindly. She seemed to take part in our family cares and afflictions, in our happiness or misfortune, and bless all who were assembled at her feet.

During prayers, when Father Ludvik began to commemorate the dead, for whom we repeated usually "Eternal rest," and connected with them the name of Mikolai, Hania sobbed aloud again; and I made a vow in my soul, that I would accomplish sacredly the duties which the deceased had imposed on me, even had I to accomplish them at the cost of the greatest sacrifice.

This was the vow of a young enthusiast who did not understand yet either the possible greatness of the sacrifices or the responsibility, but who was not without noble impulses and sensitive transports of soul.

After evening prayer we parted to go to rest. On the old housekeeper, Vengrosia, I imposed the duty of conducting Hania to the chamber which she was to occupy in future, — not to the wardrobe chamber, as hitherto, — and to stay the whole night with her. Kissing the orphan affectionately, I went to the business house, where I, Kazio, and Father Ludvik had rooms, and which in the main house we called the station. I undressed and lay down in bed. In spite of my grief for Mikolai, whom I had loved sincerely, I felt proud and almost happy in my rôle of guardian. It raised me in my own eyes, that I, a boy of sixteen, was to be the support of a weak and helpless being. I felt full grown. "Thou wert not mistaken, thou honest old soldier," thought I, "in thy young lord and the heir; in good hands hast thou placed the future of thy grandchild, and thou mayst rest quietly in thy grave."

In truth, I was at peace touching Hania's future. The thought that she would grow up in time, and that I should have to give her in marriage, did not come to my head then. I thought that she would stay with me always, surrounded with attention as a sister, beloved as a sister, sad perhaps, but in peace. According to ancient custom the first son received more than five times as much property as younger members of the family. The younger sons and daughters on their part respected this custom, and never rebelled against it. Though in our family there was no legal primogeniture, I was the first son of the family, and therefore the greater part of the property would be mine; hence, though only a student yet, I looked on the property as my own. My father was among the richest proprietors of that region. Our family was not distinguished, it is true, by the wealth of magnates, but by that large oldtime nobility-wealth which gave bread to be waded through; a calm life and plenty in the native nest until death. I was to be comparatively wealthy, hence I looked with calmness both on my future and Hania's, knowing that whatever fate was awaiting her she would always find refuge and support with me whenever she needed them.

I fell asleep with these thoughts. On the following morning I began to give effect to the guardianship. But in what a ridiculous and childish manner I did it! Still when I recall the whole matter to-day I cannot resist a certain feeling of tenderness.

When Kazio and I came to breakfast we found at table Father Ludvik, Madame d'Yves, our governess, and also my two little sisters, who were sitting on high cane chairs as usual, swinging their feet and prattling joyously.

I sat down with uncommon dignity in my father's arm-chair, and casting the eye of a dictator on the table I turned to the serving lad and said in a sharp, commanding tone, —

"Bring a plate for Panna Hania."

The word "Panna" I emphasized purposely. This had never happened before. Hania ate usually in the wardrobe chamber, for though my mother wished her to sit with us, old Mikolai would never permit it, saying: "What good in that? Let her have respect for lordship. What more does she need?" Now I introduced a new custom. The honest Father Ludvik smiled, covering his smile with a pinch of snuff and a silk handkerchief; Pani d'Yves made a grimace, for in spite of her good heart, she was an inveterate aristocrat, being a descendant of an ancient noble family of France. The serving boy, Franek, opened his mouth widely and gazed at me with astonishment.

"A plate for Panna Hania! Hast thou heard?" repeated I.

"I obey, great mighty lord," answered Franek, who was impressed evidently by the tone in which I spoke.

To-day I confess that the great mighty lord was barely able to suppress the smile of satisfaction called to his lips by that title, given him for the first time in life. Dignity, however, did not permit the great mighty lord to smile.

Meanwhile the plate was ready. In a moment the door opened and Hania entered, dressed in a black robe, which the maid-servant and housekeeper had prepared for her during the night. She was pale, with traces of tears in her eyes; her long golden tresses flowed down over her dress and ended in ribbons of black crape entwined among the strands of hair.

I rose, and hastening to the orphan conducted her to the table. My efforts and all that splendor seemed to embarrass her, confusing and tormenting the child; but I did not understand then that in time of grief a quiet, lonely, uninhabited corner with rest are worth more than the noisy ovations of friends, even if they come from the kindest heart. So in best faith I was tormenting Hania with my guardianship, thinking that I was carrying out my task perfectly. Hania was silent, and only from time to time did she answer my questions as to what she would eat and drink.

"Nothing, I beg the favor of the lord's son."

I was pained by that "I beg the favor of the lord's son," all the more, that Hania had been more confidential with me and had called me simply Panich (lord's son). But just the rôle which I had played since yesterday, and the changed relations in which I had placed her, made Hania more timid and submissive

Immediately after breakfast I took her aside.

"Hania, remember that hereafter thou art my sister. Never say to me, 'I beg the favor of the lord's son.'"

"I will not; I beg the fa — I will not, Panich."

I was in a strange position. I walked through the room with her, and did not know what to say. Gladly would I have consoled her, but to do that I should have to mention Mikolai and his death of the day before; that would have brought Hania to tears, and would have been merely a renewal of her suffering. So I finished with this, that we sat down on a low sofa at the end of the room, the child rested her head on my shoulder, and I began to stroke her golden hair.

She nestled up to me really as to a brother, and perhaps that sweet feeling of trust which rose in her heart called fresh tears to her eyes. She wept bitterly; I consoled her as best I could.

"Thou art weeping again, Hania," said I. "Thy grandfather is in heaven, and I shall try—"

I could not continue, for tears gathered in my eyes.

"Panich, may I go to grandfather?" whispered she.

I knew that the coffin had been brought, and that just in that moment they were placing Mikolai's corpse in it. I did not wish Hania to approach the body till all had been arranged. I went alone.

On the way I met Pani d'Yves, whom I begged to wait for me, as I wished to speak with her a moment. After I had given final orders touching the burial, and had prayed before the remains of Mikolai, I returned to the French woman, and after a few introductory words asked her if in a certain time, when the first weeks of mourning had passed, she would give Hania lessons in French and music.

"Monsieur Henri," answered Pani d'Yves, who evidently was angry because I was ordering everything, like a gray goose in the sky, "I would most willingly, for I love that maiden much; but I do not know whether it lies within the designs of your parents, as also I do not know whether they will consent to the position which you are trying, of your own will, to give this little girl in your family. Not too much zeal, Monsieur Henri."

"She is under my guardianship," said I, haughtily, "and I am answerable for her."

"But I am not under your guardianship, therefore you will permit me to wait till your parents return."

The French woman's resistance angered me, but I succeeded incomparably better with Father Ludvik. The honest priest, who earlier had been teaching Hania, not only favored her further and broader education, but moreover praised me for my zeal.

"I see," said he, "that thou art putting thyself sincerely to thy task, though thou art young and a child yet. This is to thy praise; only remember to be as persistent as thou art zealous."

And I saw that the priest was satisfied with me. The rôle of lord of the house, which I had taken, amused rather than angered him. The old man saw that there was much childishness in my conduct, but that the motives were honest; hence he was proud of me, and gratified that the seed which he had cast into my soul had not been lost. Moreover, the old priest loved me greatly. As to me, on approaching manhood I won him as much as I had feared him during childhood. He had a weakness for me, hence he let himself be led. Hania too he loved, and he was glad to improve her condition in so far as it lay in his power. From him, therefore, I met not the least opposition.

Pani d'Yves had really a good heart, and also met Hania with tenderness, though she was a little angry with me. Indeed, the orphan had no cause to complain of the lack of loving hearts. Our servants began to treat her differently, not as an associate, but as a young lady. The will of the first son in the family, even if a child, was greatly respected among us. This my father exacted. From the will of the first son there was a right of appeal to the old lord and lady, but no one dared to oppose this will without being authorized It was also not in order to address the first son otherwise than as "Panich" (lord's son) from his earliest years. The servants, as well as the younger members of the family, were trained in respect for the Panich, and this respect remained with him during life. "The family is upheld by this," said my father; and in fact because of this respect the voluntary constitution of the family, by virtue of which the eldest son had more property than the younger, was kept up from of old, though not resting on law. That was a family tradition, passing from generation to generation. People were accustomed to look on me as their future lord; and even old Mikolai, to whom everything was permitted, and who alone called me by name, could not resist this feeling to a certain extent.

My mother had a medicine room in the house, and visited the sick herself. In time of cholera she passed whole nights in cottages in company with the doctor, exposing herself to death; but my father, who trembled for her, did not prohibit her, repeating, "Duty, duty." Moreover, my father himself, though exacting, gave assistance. More than once he remitted arrears of labor; notwithstanding his innate impulsiveness, he forgave faults easily; frequently he paid debts for villagers, conducted weddings, was godfather to children; he commanded us to respect the peasants; to old tenants he answered with his hat, — nay, more, he called for their advice frequently. It is not possible to tell how attached the peasants were to our whole family; of this they gave convincing proofs afterward.

I mention these things, first, to show exactly how we live and lived; second, to show that in making Hania a lady I did not meet much difficulty. The greatest passive resistance I met in herself, for the child was too timid, and reared in excessive respect for the "lordships" by Mikolai himself, to be reconciled easily with her fate.

CHAPTER II.

MIKOLAI'S funeral took place three days after his death. Our neighbors appeared in rather large numbers, wishing to honor the memory of the old man, who, though a servant, was respected and loved universally. We buried him in our family vault, and his coffin was placed near the coffin of my grandfather, the colonel. During the ceremony I did not leave Hania for an instant. She had come with me in the sleigh, and I wished that she should return with me; but Father Ludvik sent me to invite the neighbors from the cemetery to our house to warm and strengthen themselves. Meanwhile my comrade and friend, Mirza Selim Davidovich, occupied himself with Hania. He was the son of Mirza Davidovich, a neighbor of my father; he was of Tartar origin and a Mohammedan, but his ancestors had lived in our neighborhood from remote times and enjoyed citizenship and nobility. I had to sit with the Ustrytskis; Hania went with Pani d'Yves and Selim to another sleigh. I saw the honest young fellow cover her with his own fur, then take the reins from the driver and shout at the horses; they flew on like a whirlwind.

On returning to the house Hania went to weep in her grandfather's chamber. I could not hurry after her, for I had to receive the guests in company with Father Ludvik.

Finally all went away except Selim; he was to pass with us the rest of the Christmas holidays, study with me a little, — for we were both in the seventh class, and the examination of *maturitas* was waiting for us, — but still more to ride, to shoot at a mark with pistols, to fence and to hunt, occupations which we both much preferred to translating the Annals of Tacitus or the Cyropedaia of Xenophon.

This Selim was a joyous fellow, a rogue and very mischievous; passionate as a spark, but sympathetic in the highest degree. All in the house loved him greatly except my father, who was angry because the young Tartar shot and fenced better than I. But Pani d'Yves lost her head over him because he spoke French like a Parisian. His mouth was never shut; he retailed gossip and witticisms, and amused the French woman better than any of us.

Father Ludvik had some hope of converting him to the Catholic faith, all the more since the boy jested sometimes about Mohammed, and would beyond doubt have rejected the Koran had it not been that he feared his father, who, out of respect for family traditions, held with both hands to Mohammed, considering that as a noble of long standing he preferred to be an oldtime Mohammedan to a newly made Catholic. Old Davidovich, however, had no other Turkish or Tartar sympathies. His ancestors had settled in Lithuania during the time, perhaps, of Vitold. That was, moreover, a very wealthy nobility, living from of old in the same place. The property which they possessed had been given by Yan Sobieski to Mirza Davidovich, a colonel of light horse, who performed wonders at Vienna, and whose portrait was hanging then in Horeli.

I remember that portrait as making a wonderful impression on me. The colonel was a terrible person; his face was written over by God knows what sabres, as if with mystic letters of the Koran. He had a swarthy complexion, prominent cheek-bones, slanting eyes with a wonderfully gloomy glitter; they had this peculiarity, that they looked at you out of the portrait always, whether you stood straight in front or at either side.

But my comrade, Selim, resembled his ancestors in nothing. His mother, whom old Davidovich married in the Crimea, was not a Tartar, — she came from the Caucasus. I did not remember her, but people said that she was a beauty of beauties, and that young Selim resembled her as much as one drop of water resembles another.

Ah! he was a wonderful fellow, that Selim! His eyes had a scarcely discernible slant; they were not Tartar eyes, though, but the great, dark, pensive, moist eyes for which Georgian women have gained such renown. Eyes with such inexpressible sweetness when calm I had never seen in life, and shall never see again. He had regular features, as noble as if they had come from the chisel of a sculptor, a dark but delicate complexion, lips a trifle full, but red as raspberries, a sweet smile, and teeth like pearls.

When Selim was fighting with a comrade, for example, and this happened often enough, his sweetness vanished like a deceptive nightmare: he became almost terrible; his eyes seemed to swell out slantingly and gleam like the eyes of a wolf; the veins in his face distended; his complexion grew dark; and for a moment the real Tartar was roused in him, just such a Tartar as those with whom our ancestors went dancing. This transformation was short-lived. After a while Selim wept, begged pardon, kissed, and was forgiven usually. He had the best of hearts and a great inclination to noble impulses. He was heedless, however, somewhat frivolous, and a frolicker of unrestrained temperament. He rode, shot, and fenced like a master; he had medium success in learning, for in spite of great gifts he was rather lazy. We loved each other like brothers, quarrelled frequently, made peace as often, and our friendship continued unbroken. In vacation and on all holidays either I spent half the time in Horeli, or he with us.

And now on his return from Mikolai's funeral, Selim was to stay with us to the end of the Christmas holidays.

When the guests took leave after dinner, it was perhaps four o'clock in the afternoon. The short winter day was near its end; the great evening twilight looked in through the windows; on trees standing near the house, and hidden with snow covered with a ruddy gleam, the crows began to caw and flutter. Through the windows we could see whole flocks of them flying across the pond from the forest and floating in the evening light. In the room to which we passed after dinner, silence prevailed. Pani d'Yves went to her chamber to tell fortunes by cards, as her habit was; Father Ludvik walked up and down the room and took snuff; my two little sisters, butting heads, tangled each other's golden curls; Hania, Selim, and I were sitting under the window, on a sofa, looking at the pond on the garden side, on the forest beyond the pond, and on the vanishing daylight.

Soon it became entirely dark. Father Ludvik went out to evening prayers; one of my little sisters chased the other to an adjoining room; we were left alone. Selim had begun to say something when Hania pushed up to me all at once and whispered, —

"Panich, something terrifies me. I am afraid."

"Fear not, Haniulka," answered I, drawing her toward me. "Nestle up to me, this way. Whilst thou art near me, nothing evil can happen to thee. See, I am not afraid of anything, and I shall always be able to protect thee."

That was not true, for whether because of the gloom which filled the hall, or Hania's words, or the recent death of Mikolai, I, too, was under some strange impression.

"Perhaps thou wilt ask to have a light brought?" said I.

"Yes, Panich."

"Selim, ask Franek to bring a light."

Selim sprang from the sofa, and soon we heard an uncommon trampling and noise outside the door. The door opened with a slam; in rushed Franek like a whirlwind, and behind, grasping his arm, was Selim. Franek had a stupid and terrified face, for Selim, holding the boy by the shoulder, was spinning him like a top and turning round with him. Advancing with that motion to the sofa, Selim halted, and said, —

"Thy lord commands thee to bring a light, for the young lady is afraid. Dost wish to bring the light, or shall I twist thy head off?"

Franek went for the lamp and returned with it in a moment; but it seemed that the light injured Hania's eyes, which were red from crying, so Selim quenched it. We were again in mysterious darkness, and again silence reigned among us. Soon the moon cast bright silver light through the window. Evidently Hania was afraid, for she nestled up to me still more closely, and I had to hold her hand besides. Selim sat opposite us in an armchair, and, as his custom was, passed from a noisy mood into thoughtfulness, and after a while fell to imagining. Great silence was among us; we were a little afraid: but it was pleasant there.

"Let Selim tell us some story," said I, "he tells stories so well. Shall he, Hania?"

"Let him."

Selim raised his eyes and thought awhile. The moon lighted clearly his handsome profile. After a time he began to speak in a quivering, sympathetic, and lowered voice: —

"Beyond forests, beyond mountains, lived in the Crimea a certain kind woman named Lala, who could soothsay. Once the Sultan was passing her cottage. This Sultan, who was called Harun, was very rich; he had a palace of coral with columns of diamonds; the roof of that palace was of pearls. The palace was so large that it took a year to go from one end of it to the other. The Sultan himself wore genuine stars in his turban. The turban was of sun-rays, and on top of it was a crescent, which a certain enchanter had cut from the moon and bestowed on the Sultan. That Sultan was passing near Lala's cottage, and weeping; he was weeping so, and weeping, that his tears fell on the road, and wherever a tear fell a white lily sprang up right away.

"'Why art thou weeping, O Sultan Harun?' asked Lala.

"'Why should I not weep,' replied Sultan Harun, 'when I have only one daughter, beautiful as the morning dawn, and I must give her to a black Div with fiery eyes, who every ye—'"

Selim stopped suddenly and was silent.

"Is Hania asleep?" whispered he to me.

"No; she is not asleep," answered the girl, with drowsy voice.

"'How should I not weep,' said Harun the Sultan to her [continued Selim], 'when I have only one daughter, and I must give her to the Div?'

"'Do not weep, O Sultan,' says Lala; 'sit on the winged horse and ride to the grotto of Borah. Evil clouds will chase thee on the road, but throw thou these poppy seeds at them and directly the clouds will fall asleep.'"

And so Selim went on, and then he stopped a second time and looked at Hania. The child was now asleep really. She was very tired and pained, and was sleeping soundly. Selim and I scarcely dared to breathe lest we might waken her. Her breathing was even, peaceful, interrupted only at times by deep sighs. Selim rested his forehead on his hand and fell into serious thought. I raised my eyes toward the sky, and it seemed to me that I was flying away on the wings of angels into heavenly space. I cannot tell the sweetness which penetrated me, for I felt that that dear little being was sleeping calmly and with all confidence on my breast. Some kind of quiver passed through my whole body, — something not of earth; new and unknown voices of happiness were born in my soul, and began to sing and to play like an orchestra. Oh, how I loved Hania! How I loved her, as a brother and a guardian yet, but beyond bound and measure.

I approached my lips to Hania's hair and kissed it. There was nothing earthly in that, for I and the kiss were yet equally innocent.

Selim shivered all at once and woke up from his pensiveness.

"How happy thou art, Henryk!" whispered he.

"Yes, Selim."

But we could not stay there in that way.

"Let us not wake her, but carry her to her room," said Selim.

"I will carry her alone, and do thou just open the door," answered I.

I drew my arm carefully from under the head of the sleeping girl, and laid her on the sofa. Then I took her carefully in my arms. I was still a youth, but I came of uncommonly strong stock; the child was small, frail, and I carried her like a feather. Selim opened the door to the adjoining chamber, which was lighted, and in that way we reached the green chamber, which I had destined to be Hania's room. The bed was already prepared. In the chimney a good fire was crackling; and near the chimney, poking the coals, sat old Vengrosia, who, when she saw me burdened as I was, exclaimed, —

"Ah, for God's sake! and so the Panich is carrying the little maid. Wasn't it possible to wake her, and let her come herself?"

"Let Vengrosia be silent!" said I, angrily. "A young lady, not 'a maid,' only a young lady; does Vengrosia hear? The young lady is tired. I beg not to wake her. Undress her and put her to bed quietly. Let Vengrosia remember that this is an orphan, and that we must comfort her with kindness for the loss of her grandfather."

"An orphan, the poor little thing; an orphan, indeed," repeated the honest Vengrosia, with emotion.

Selim kissed the old woman for this, then he returned for tea.

Selim forgot everything and became frolicsome at tea; I did not follow his example, however, first, because I was sad, and second, I judged that it did not become a serious man, already a guardian, to appear like a child. That evening Selim raised another storm; this time with Father Ludvik, because when we were at evening prayers in the chapel, he flew out to the yard, climbed onto the low roof of the ice-house, and began to howl. The dogs of the yard rushed together from all sides and made such an uproar while accompanying Selim that we could not say our prayers.

"Have you gone mad, Selim?" asked Father Ludvik.

"Pardon me, Father, I was praying in Mohammedan fashion."

"Do not make sport of any religion, thou rascal!"

"But if I, begging your attention, want to become a Catholic, only I am afraid of my father, what can I do with Mohammed?"

The priest, attacked on his weak side, was silent, and we went to bed. Selim and I had a room together, for the priest knew that we liked to talk, and did not wish to hinder us. When I had undressed and saw that Selim was doing the same without praying, I inquired, —

"But really, Selim, dost thou never pray?"

"Of course I do. If thou wish, I will begin right away."

And standing in the window he raised his eyes to the moon, stretched his hands toward it, and began to cry in a singing voice, —

"Oh, Allah! Akbar Allah! Allah Kerim!"

Dressed only in white, with his face raised toward the sky, he was so beautiful that I could not take my eyes from him.

Then he began to explain, —

"What shall I do? I do not believe in this prophet of ours, who would let others have only one wife, but had as many himself as he pleased. Besides, I tell thee that I like wine. I am not free to be anything except a Mohammedan, but I believe in God, and often I pray as I know how. But do I know anything? I know that there is a Lord God, and that is the end of the question."

After a while he continued, —

"Knowest what, Henryk?"

"What?"

"I have splendid cigars. We are children no longer; let us smoke."

Selim sprang out of bed and got a package of cigars. We each lighted one, then lay down and smoked in silence, spitting out of the bed in secret from each other.

"Knowest thou what, Henryk?" said Selim after a while. "How I envy thee! Thou art really grown up now."

"I hope so."

"For thou art a guardian already. Oh, if some one would leave me such a ward to care for!"

"That is not so easy, and, besides, where could another Hania be found in the world? But knowest what?" continued I, in the tone of a mature wise man. "I hope that soon I shall not go to school. A man who has such obligations at home cannot go to school."

"And — thou art raving! What! thou wilt not learn any more? But school is the main thing."

"Thou knowest that I like to study, but duty before all. Unless my father and mother send Hania to Warsaw with me."

"They won't even dream of it."

"While I am in the classes, surely not; but when I am in the University they will. Well, dost thou not know what a student means?"

"Yes, yes! That may happen. Thou wilt be her guardian, and thou wilt marry her."

I sat up in bed.

"Selim, art thou mad?"

"Why shouldst thou not marry her? In school one is not free to marry; but a student may not only have a wife, he may have even children," said Selim.

At that moment all the University prerogatives and

privileges did not concern me in the least. Selim's question illuminated, as with a lightning flash, those sides of my heart which to me were still dark. A thousand thoughts, like a thousand birds, flew through my head all at once. To marry my dear, beloved orphan! Yes; that was the lightning flash, the new flash of thought and feelings. It seemed to me that suddenly into the darkness of my heart some one had brought light. Love, deep, but brotherly hitherto, had grown rosy on a sudden from that light and was heated through it by an unknown warmth. To marry Hania, that bright-haired angel, my dearest, most beloved Hania. With a weak voice now and lower, I repeated like an echo, —

"Selim, art mad?"

"I would lay a wager that thou art in love with her already," said Selim.

I made no answer; I quenched the light, then seized a corner of the pillow and began to kiss it.

Yes; I loved her already.

CHAPTER III.

ON the second or third day after the funeral, my father came, summoned by a telegram. I trembled lest he should recall my dispositions touching Hania, and my forebodings were real to a certain degree. My father praised me and embraced me for my zeal and conscientiousness in fulfilling duties; that pleased him evidently. He repeated even a number of times, "Our blood!" which he did only when he was much pleased with me. He did not divine to what extent that zeal was interested, but my dispositions had not pleased him overmuch. It may be that the exaggerated statements of Pani d'Yves moved him toward this a little, though really in the days following that night in which my feelings rose to consciousness I made Hania the first person in the house.

He was not pleased by my project to educate her in the same way as my sisters.

"I recall and withdraw nothing," said he. "That is the affair of thy mother. She will determine what she likes; that is her department. But it is worth while to think over this: What is best for the girl herself."

"Education, father, will never harm. I have heard that from thy own mouth more than once."

"True, in the case of a man," answered he, "for the education of a man gives position, but with a woman it is different. A woman's education should be in accord with the position which she is to occupy in life. Such a girl does not need more than a medium education; she has no need of French, music, and the like. With a medium education Hania will find more easily an honest official for a husband—"

"Father!"

He looked at me with astonishment.

"What is the matter?"

I was as red as a beet. The blood almost spurted through my face. In my eyes it grew dark. To compare Hania with an official seemed such blasphemy before my world of imagining that I could not withhold a cry of indignation. And that blasphemy pained me the more since it came from the lips of my father. That was the first cold water thrown by reality on the burning faith of youth, the first blow aimed by life into the fairy castle of illusions, the first deceit and disenchantment from the bitterness of which we defend ourselves with pessimism and unbelief. But as red-hot iron, when a drop of cold water falls on it, merely hisses and turns the water into steam, so the burning soul of a man under the influence of its first contact with the cold palm of reality, hisses, it is true, from pain, but soon warms reality itself with its own heat.

My father's words wounded me at once, therefore, and wounded me in a wonderful manner, for under their influence I had a feeling of offence not against my father, but, as it were, against Hania. In virtue, however, of that internal resistance which exists only in youth, I soon threw it as far from my soul as possible, and forever. My father understood nothing of my enthusiasm, and ascribed it to excessive devotion to the duties confided to me, which, moreover, was natural at my time of life, and which, instead of angering, simply flattered him and weakened his dislike to the higher education of Hania. I promised him to write a letter to my mother, who was to remain abroad a good while yet, and beg her to make final arrangements in this regard. I do not remember that I have ever written so long and so heartfelt a letter. I described the death of old Mikolai, his last words, my desires, fears, and hopes; I moved vigorously the chord of compassion which was always quivering in my mother's heart; I depicted the disquiet of conscience which would await me beyond doubt, if we should not do for Hania all that lay in our power, — in a word, according to my opinion at that time, my letter was of its kind a real masterpiece, which must produce its effect. Pacified somewhat by this, I waited patiently for an answer, which came in two letters, — one to me, the other to Pani d'Yves. I had won the battle at all points. My mother not only agreed to the higher education of Hania, but enjoined it most emphatically.

"I should wish," wrote my kind mother, "in case it agrees with the will of thy father, that Hania be considered in every way as belonging to our family. We owe this to the memory of old Mikolai, to his devotion and faithfulness."

My triumph then was as great as it was complete, and Selim shared it with me heartily, — Selim, whom everything which touched Hania concerned as much as if he himself had been her guardian.

It is true that the sympathy which he felt, and the tenderness which he exhibited for the orphan, began to anger me a little, all the more since my own relations with Hania had changed greatly since that memorable night when I had become conscious of my feelings. When with her I felt as if convicted; the former heartiness and childlike intimacy had vanished on my side completely. Barely a few days before the girl had fallen asleep quietly on my breast; now at the mere thought of this the hair rose on my head. A few days before at good-morning and goodnight I kissed her pale lips as a brother would; now the touch of her hand burned me, or pierced me with a delicious quiver. I began to honor her as the object of first love is honored usually; and when the innocent girl, neither divining nor knowing anything, nestled up to me as formerly, I was angry in my soul, though not at her; I looked on myself as sacrilegious.

Love had brought me unknown happiness, but also unknown suffering. If I had had some one to whom I could confide my suffering; if I had been able at times to weep on some one's breast, an act for which I had often a wonderful desire, — I should have removed half the weight, beyond doubt, from my soul. I might have confessed all to Selim, but I feared his disposition. I knew that he would feel my words heartily at the first moment; but

who could assure me that next day he would not ridicule
me with the cynicism peculiar to him, and with frivolous
words defile my ideal, which I dared not touch with any
giddy thought? My character had at all times been well
locked up in me; besides, there was one great difference
between me and Selim. I had always been somewhat
sentimental; Selim had not sentiment to the value of a
copper. I could fall in love only when sad, Selim only
when joyous. I concealed my love from every one,
almost from myself, and really no one discovered it. In
a few days, without ever having seen any models, I had
learned instinctively to hide all indications of that love,
such as the confusion which often came on me, and the
blushes with which I was covered when Hania was
mentioned in my presence, — in a word, I developed
immense cunning, that cunning by the aid of which a
boy sixteen years old will often deceive the most careful eye watching him. I had not the least design of
confessing my feelings to Hania. I loved her, and that
was sufficient. Only at times, when we were alone, something urged me to kneel before her and kiss the hem of
her dress.

Selim meanwhile played his mad pranks, laughed, was
witty and joyous for both of us. He was the first to bring
a smile to Hania's face, when once at breakfast he proposed to Father Ludvik to turn Mohammedan and marry
Pani d'Yves. Neither the French woman, who was rather
easily offended, nor the priest, could get angry with him;
with her he had made himself such a favorite that when
he made eyes at her and laughed, all ended in a slight
scolding and in general merriment. In his treatment of
Hania a certain tenderness and care were evident, but in
this relation too his innate joyousness conquered everything. He was more confidential with her than I. It was

evident that Hania liked him much, for whenever he entered the room she was more cheerful. He made continual sport of me, or rather of my sadness, taking it for the artificial dignity of one who wishes to be grown up in a hurry.

"Look, all of you, he will end by becoming a priest," said he.

Then I dropped the first thing I could, so as to bend down for it and hide the blush which covered my face; but Father Ludvik took snuff and answered, —

"To the honor of God! to the honor of God!"

Meanwhile the Christmas holidays were over. My faint hope of remaining at home was not justified in the least. On a certain evening it was announced to the great guardian that next morning early he must be ready for the road. There was need of starting early, for we had to turn in at Horeli, where Selim was to take farewell of his father. So we rose at six o'clock in the dark. Ah! my soul was as gloomy as that cold wintry, windy morning. Selim was in the worst humor also. As soon as he had crept out of bed, he declared that the world was stupid, and most wretchedly ordered; I agreed with this perfectly. When we had dressed we went from the station to the house for breakfast. It was dark in the yard; small flakes of sharp snow, whirled by the wind, struck our faces. The windows of the dining-room were lighted. Before the entrance stood the sleigh, in which our things were packed already; the horses were shaking the bells; dogs were barking around the sleigh. All this, taken together, formed, at least for us, a picture so gloomy that the heart was straitened at sight of it.

On entering the dining-room we found my father and the priest pacing up and down with serious faces. Hania was not there. I looked with a throbbing heart toward the door of the green chamber. Would she come, or was I to go away without farewell?

Meanwhile my father and the priest fell to giving us advice and detailing morality. Both began with this, that at our age there was no need to repeat to us what labor and learning meant; still both spoke of nothing else. I listened to everything without the least attention, chewing toasted bread and swallowing with straitened throat the heated wine.

All at once my heart beat so powerfully that I could hardly sit in my chair, for in Hania's room I heard rustling. The door opened, and out came Pani d'Yves, in a wrapper, her hair in papers; she pressed my hand warmly. For the disappointment which she had caused me I wanted to throw the glass of wine at her head. She expressed the hope that such good youths would surely learn perfectly; to this Selim answered that the memory of the papers in her hair would give him strength and endurance in study. Hania did not show herself.

It was not destined me, however, to drain the bitter cup. When we rose from the table Hania came out, looking drowsy, yet all rosy and with ruffled hair. When I pressed her hand while wishing good-morning, it was hot. Immediately it occurred to me that she had a fever because of my departure, and I played a tender scene in spirit, but her fever was simply the warmth of sleep. After a while my father and the priest went for letters to be delivered in Warsaw. Selim rode out through the door on an immense dog which had entered the room a moment earlier. I was left alone with Hania. Tears were coming to my eyes; from my lips tender and warm words were rushing forth. I had no intention to confess that I loved her; but I was urged to say something like this, My dear, my beloved Hania! and to kiss her hands at the same time. That was the only convenient moment for such an outburst, though I might give way to it before people without drawing the attention of any one; still I did not dare. I wasted that moment most shamefully. I drew near to her and stretched out my hand, but I did so awkwardly, somehow, and unnaturally. "Hania," said I, with a voice so foreign to me that I drew back at once and was silent. I had the wish to kiss her cheek; meanwhile she herself began, —

"My God! how sad it will be without the Panich!"

"I will come at Easter," said I, in a low, strange bass.

"But it is a long time till Easter."

"Not at all long," muttered I.

At that moment Selim rushed in, and after him came my father, the priest, Pani d'Yves, and some servants. The words, "To the sleigh! to the sleigh!" sounded in my ears. We all went to the porch; there my father and the priest embraced me. When the time came to take leave of Hania, I had an almost irrestrainable wish to seize her in my arms and kiss her as of old; but I could not bring myself to it.

"Farewell, Hania," said I, giving her my hand, but in my soul a hundred voices were weeping, a hundred most tender and fondling expressions were on my lips.

I saw on a sudden that the girl was shedding tears, and with equal suddenness was heard that stubborn Satan within, that irresistible wish to tear open my own wounds, which later in life I felt more than once; so, though my heart was bursting into bits, I said in a cold and rough voice, —

"Do not cry without reason, my Hania." Then I sat down in the sleigh.

Meanwhile Selim took farewell of all. Running up to Hania he seized her two hands, and, though the girl tried to pull them away, he kissed them wildly, first one and then the other. Oh, what a wish I had to beat him off at that moment! When he had kissed Hania, he sprang into the sleigh. "Move on!" cried my father. The priest blessed us with the cross for the road. The driver called "Hetta! ho!" to the horses, the bells sounded, the snow squeaked under the runners, and we moved over the road.

"Scoundrel! robber!" said I in my soul. "That is how thou didst take farewell of thy Hania! Thou wert disagreeable to her, scolded her for tears of which thou wert unworthy, tears of an orphan."

I raised the collar of my fur and cried like a little child in silence, for I was afraid lest Selim should detect me in tears. It appeared, however, that Selim saw everything perfectly; but he himself was moved, hence he said nothing at first. But we had not gone so far as Horeli when he called, —

"Henryk!"

"What?"

"Thou art blubbering?"

"Let me alone."

Again there was silence between us. But after a while Selim again said, —

"Henryk!"

"What?"

"Thou art blubbering?"

I made no answer; suddenly Selim bent down, took a handful of snow, raised my cap, spread the snow on my head, and covered it again, saying, —

"That will cool thee!"

CHAPTER IV.

I DID not go home at Easter, for the approaching examination for *maturitas* stood in the way. Besides, my father wished me to pass the preliminary examination before the beginning of the University year. He knew that I would not like to work in vacation, and that beyond doubt I should forget at least one half of what I had learned in school, so I worked very vigorously. Besides the ordinary lessons in the gymnasium and the work for the examination, Selim and I took private lessons from a student who, as he had entered the University not long before, knew best what we needed.

This for me was a memorable time, for in it fell the whole structure of my thoughts and imagining, reared so laboriously by Father Ludvik, my father, and the whole atmosphere of our quiet house.

The young student was a radical in every regard. While explaining the history of Rome, he knew so well how to explain his disgust and contempt for the great oligarchy during the reforms of the Gracchi that my arch-noble convictions were swept away like smoke. With what profound faith my young teacher declared, for example, that a man who was soon to occupy the powerful and in every sense influential position of student at the University should be free from all "prejudices," and not look on anything save with the compassion of a genuine philosopher.

In general he was of opinion that for the regulation of the world, and for the exercise of a mighty influence on all people, a man is best between the eighteenth and twenty-third year of his life, for later he becomes gradually an idiot or a conservative.

Of those who were neither students nor professors of the University, he spoke with compassion; but he had ideals, which never left his lips. From him I learned for the first time of the existence of Moleschotte and Büchner, — two men of science whom he cited oftenest. One should hear with what ardor our preceptor spoke of the conquests of science in recent times, of great truths which the blind superstitious past had avoided, and which the most recent scholars had raised "from the dust of oblivion" and announced to the world with unparalleled courage.

While uttering these opinions he shook his thick, curly foretop, and smoked an incredible number of cigarettes, assuring us that he was so trained that it was all one to him whether he let the smoke out through his mouth or his nostrils, and that there was not in Warsaw another man who could smoke in that fashion. Then he rose usually, put on his cloak, which lacked more than half its buttons, and declared that he must hurry, for he had another "little meeting." Saying this, he winked mysteriously and added that Selim's age and mine did not permit him to communicate to us nearer information about this "little meeting," but that later and without his explanation we should understand its meaning.

Notwithstanding all this which would not have pleased our parents much, the young student had his really good sides. He understood well what he was teaching us, and besides he was a real fanatic of science. He wore boots with holes in them, a threadbare coat, a cap which was like an old nest; he never had a copper on his person; but his mind never dwelt on his personal cares, poverty, want almost. He lived through a passion for science; of a joyous life for himself he had no thought.

Selim and I looked on him as some higher supernatural personage, as an ocean of wisdom, as an immovable weight. We believed sacredly that if any one could save humanity in case of danger, it was surely he, that imposing genius, who, beyond doubt, was of this opinion himself. But we clung to his convictions as to bird-lime.

As to me, I went farther, perhaps, than even my master. That was the natural reaction against my previous education; and, besides, the student had really opened before me gates to new worlds of knowledge, in comparison with which the circle of my ideas was very narrow. Dazzled by these new truths, I had not many thoughts and fancies to devote to Hania. At first, and immediately after coming, I did not part with my ideal. The letters which I received from her fed that fire on the altar of my heart; but, compared with the ocean of ideas of the young student, all our village world, so calm and quiet, began at once to grow little and diminish in my eyes. Hania's form did not vanish, it is true, but was enwrapped, as it were, in a light mist.

As to Selim, he advanced also by the earthly road of violent reforms; but of Hania he thought less, since opposite our quarters was a window in which sat a schoolgirl named Yozia. Indeed, Selim began to sigh at her, and for whole days they looked at each other from the two windows, like two birds in two cages. Selim repeated with unshaken certainty, "this one or none." Frequently it happened that he would lie face and hands on the bed and study, then throw his book on the floor, spring up, seize me, and cry, laughing like a madman, —

"Oh, my Yozia! how I love thee!"

"Go to the plague, Selim!" I would say to him.

"Oh, it is thou, not Yozia," he would answer roguishly, and return to his book.

At last came the days of examination. Selim and I passed both the final examination of the gymnasium and the one for entrance to the University very favorably; after that we were as free as birds, but we stayed three days longer in Warsaw. We used that time for getting students' uniforms, and for a solemnity which our master considered indispensable; that is, a feast for three in the first winecellar that we came to.

After the second bottle, when Selim's head and mine were turning, and when to the cheeks of our master, now a comrade, a flush came, we were seized by a sudden and uncommon tenderness, combined with an inclination to confessions of the heart.

"Well, ye have come out among people, my boys," said the master, "and the world stands open before you. Ye can amuse yourselves now, throw away money, play the lord, fall in love; but I tell you that these are follies. A life on the surface, without an idea for which a man lives, toils, and struggles, is folly. But to live wisely or to live reasonably, and to struggle wisely, one should look on things soberly. As to me, I think that I look on them soberly. I believe in nothing which I cannot touch myself, and I advise the same to you. God knows there are so many ways of living and thinking in the world, and all in such confusion, that one needs the devil knows what kind of head to avoid error. But I hold fast to science, and that's the end of it. They will not entrap me with trifles. That life is foolish, over this theme I shall not break a bottle on any man's head; but we have science. Had we not, I would shoot myself. Every one has the right to do that, as I think; and I will shoot myself surely if I grow bankrupt to that degree. But on my

foundation one will not be bankrupt. Thou wilt be
deceived in everything: fall in love, the woman will
deceive thee; have religion, the moment of doubt will
come; but thou mayst sit quietly till death investigat-
ing the canal of the nutritive infusoria, and wilt
not even notice how on a certain day the world will
stupidly grow somehow and somehow dark to thee, and
then the end, — the water clock, the portrait in the illustrated paper, the more or less dull biography, and the
comedy will be over! After that there will be nothing.
I can give you my word on that, my little fellows. Ye
may be bold in believing in no nonsense. Science is my
fiddle-bow; Science is the foundation. Meanwhile all this
has the good side, — that if thou occupy thyself with such
things, thou mayst go about in broken boots boldly and
sleep on a hay-loft. It will make no difference to thee.
Do ye understand?"

"To the health and honor of science!" cried Selim,
whose eyes were gleaming like coals.

Our master pushed back his immense woolly forelock,
emptied his goblet, then inhaling smoke he let two
enormous currents of it out through his nostrils, and
continued, —

"Besides exact sciences — Selim, thou art drunk! — besides exact sciences there is philosophy, and there are ideas.
With these life is filled to the brim. But I prefer exact
sciences. Philosophy, and especialy ideal-real philosophy,
I tell you that I revile it. It is guess-work. A man is
pursuing truth, as it were, but pursuing it as a dog pur-
sues his own tail. In general I cannot endure guess-work.
I love facts. Thou canst not squeeze whey out of water.
As to ideas, that is another thing. For them it is worth
while to lay down one's head; but ye and your fathers travel
by stupid ways. I tell you that. Long life to ideas!"

We emptied our goblets again. Our forelocks were steaming. The dark room of the cellar seemed still darker; the candles on the table burned with a faint light; smoke hid the pictures on the walls. Outside the window in the yard an old beggar was singing the pious hymn, "Holy, heavenly, angelic Lady!" and in the pauses he played a plaintive minstrel melody on a fiddle. Wonderful feelings filled my breast. I believed the words of the master, but I felt that he had not told everything yet which could fill out one's life. Something was lacking. A species of melancholy possessed me in spite of myself; so under the influence of imagination, wine, and momentary enthusiasm I said in a low voice, —

"But women, gentlemen! a loving woman, devoted, who stops at nothing in life?"

Selim began to sing, —

> "Woman is changeable:
> Stupid the man who believes in her!"

Our master looked at me with a peculiar expression. He was thinking of something else, but soon he shook himself and said, —

"Oh, ho! thou hast shown the tip of the sentimental ear. Knowest thou, that Selim will go much farther in the world than thou. The deuce will take thee. Guard thyself, guard thyself, I say, lest some petticoat crawl into thy path and spoil thy life. Woman! woman!" (here the master blinked according to his custom), "I know that ware somewhat. I cannot complain; God knows I cannot. But I know this too, that thou must not give thy finger to the devil, for right away he will take thy whole hand. Woman! love! all our misfortune is in this, that we make great things out of nonsense. If thou wish to amuse thyself as I do, amuse thyself, but don't put thy life in it. Have reason at once, and do not pay good coin for false goods. Do ye think that I complain of women? I do not even dream of doing so. On the contrary, I love them; but I do not let myself be taken by chaff of my own imagining. I remember when I fell in love the first time with a certain Lola, I thought, for example, that her dress was sacred, but it was calico. That's the point. Was it her fault that she walked in mud instead of flying through the heavens? No! it was I who was stupid, through putting wings on her by force. Man is rather a limited beast. One or another of us carries God knows what ideal in his heart, and therewith feels a need of loving; hence on seeing the first little goose that he meets, he says to himself, 'That is she.' Afterward he finds out that he has made a mistake, and because of that small mistake the devil takes him, or he lives an idiot all his life."

"But you will acknowledge," said I, "that a man feels the need of loving, and surely you feel that need as well as others."

A scarcely discernible smile shot across his lips.

"Every necessity may be satisfied," answered he, "in various ways. I help myself in my own way. I have said that I do not look on stupid things as great. I am sober, God knows, more sober than at this moment. But I have seen many men who have broken their lives, or snarled them up, like a thread, for one woman; so I say that it is not worth while to put all one's life in that. I say that there are better things, loftier objects, and that love is a trifling matter. To the health of sobriety!"

"To the health of women!" shouted Selim.

"Very good; let us have that," answered our master. "They are agreeable creatures, only take them not too seriously. To the health of women!"

"To the health of Yozia!" cried I, touching Selim's glass.

"Wait! Now is my turn," answered he. "To the health of thy Hania! one deserves the other."

The blood began to play in me, and sparks flashed from my eyes.

"Be silent, Selim," cried I. "Do not mention that name before me in this shop!"

Then I threw my glass to the floor, and it broke into a thousand bits.

"Hast gone mad?" cried our master.

I had not gone mad at all, but anger had sprung up in me and was blazing like a flame. I could listen to everything which the master said about women; I could even take pleasure in it; I could ridicule them with others. I could do that because I did not connect the words and the ridicule with any one of my own, and because it did not even come to my mind that the general theory was to be applied to persons dear to me. But when I heard the name of my purest orphan bandied about frivolously in that room, amid smoke, dirt, empty bottles, corks, and cynical conversation, I thought that I had heard some abominable sacrilege, some defilement, some wrong wrought against Hania, and from anger I almost lost self-control.

Selim looked at me for a moment with astonishment, and then his face began to grow dark quickly, his eyes shot sparks, on his forehead came out knots of veins, his features extended and became sharp as those of a real Tartar.

"Thou dost forbid me to say what I please?" cried he, in a deep voice, broken by panting breath.

Luckily the master rushed between us at this moment.

"Ye are not worthy of the uniforms which ye wear! What is this? Ye will fight, or pull each other by the ears, like school-boys? Yes, philosophers who break glasses on each other's heads. Be ashamed of yourselves! Ye are persons with whom to talk touching universal questions! Be ashamed of yourselves! From the war of ideas to a war of fists. Stop! But I will say that I proposed a toast in honor of universities; and that ye are drones if ye will not make peace, and if ye leave even a drop in the glasses."

We recovered. But Selim, though more drunk, recovered first.

"I implore thy pardon," said he, in a tender voice. "I am a fool."

We embraced heartily, and emptied the glasses to the bottom to the honor of universities. Then our master intoned *Gaudeamus*. Through the glass doors leading to the cellar, merchants began to look in. It was growing dark outside. We were all what is called tipsy. Our joyfulness rose to the zenith and then descended gradually. Our master was the first who fell into meditation, and after a while he said, —

"All this is well, but, taking everything together, life is stupid. These are all artificial means; but as to what happens in the soul, that is another thing. To-morrow will be like to-day: the same misery, four naked walls, the hay-loft, broken boots, and — so on without end. Labor and labor, but happiness? A man deceives himself as best he can and deadens — Farewell!"

So saying, he put his cap with broken crown on his head, executed a few mechanical motions which had for object the buttoning of his coat with buttons which did not exist, lighted his cigarette, and waving his hand said, —

"But do ye pay here, for I am naked, and be in good health. Ye may remember me or not, — all one to me. I am not sentimental. Be in good health, my honest boys — "

He uttered the last words in a low and emotional voice, as if to contradict the statement that he was not sentimental. The poor heart needed love, and was as capable of it as any other heart; but misfortune from years of childhood, poverty, and the indifference of people had taught that heart to withdraw into itself. His soul was a proud one, though ardent, hence always full of fear of being rejected should it incline first to some person too cordially.

We remained alone for a while, and under the influence of a certain sadness. Those were perhaps gloomy forebodings, for we were not to see our poor master again in life. Neither he nor we divined that in his breast had been inherent for a long time elements of mortal disease, from which there was no rescue. Misery, too much exertion, feverish labor over books, sleepless nights, and hunger had hastened the crisis.

In the autumn, at the beginning of October, our master died of consumption. Not many comrades followed his coffin, for it was the time of vacation; but his poor mother, a dealer in wax candles and holy images under the Dominican church, wept aloud for the son whom often she had not understood during life, though, like a mother, she loved him.

CHAPTER V.

THE next day after that feast, horses came from the old Mirza in Horeli, and we set out for home on the following morning. We had two long days' ride before us, so we started at dawn. In our stone house everything was asleep yet; but in the place opposite Yozia's face gleamed in the window, amid geraniums, yellow violets, and fuchsias. Selim, when he had put on his travelling bag and student's cap, stood in the window, ready for the road, to announce that he was going; to this an answer was given from among the geraniums by a melancholy glance. But when he placed one hand on his heart and sent a kiss with the other, the face between the flowers grew red and pushed back quickly into the dark interior of the room.

Below, on the pavement of the yard, a brichka, drawn by four sturdy horses, rolled in. It was time to take farewell and sit in the wagon; but Selim waited, and stood in the window persistently, hoping to see something more. Hope deceived him, however; the window remained empty. Only when we had descended and were passing the dark entrance of the building opposite, did we see on the steps two white stockings, a nut-colored dress, a bosom bent forward, and two bright eyes shaded by a hand; the eyes were looking out of darkness into daylight.

Selim rushed at once to the entrance. I took my seat in the brichka right there close by; I heard whispers and certain sounds very similar to the sound of kisses. Then Selim came out blushing, half laughing, half moved, and sat by my side. The driver struck the horses. Selim and I looked involuntarily toward the window. Yozia's face was among the flowers again; a moment more and a hand holding a white handkerchief was thrust forth; one more sign of farewell, and the brichka rolled out onto the street, taking with it me and the beautiful ideal of poor Yozia.

It was very early in the morning. The city was in slumber; the rosy light of dawn passed along the windows of the sleeping houses. Only here and there an early bird, a passer-by, roused with his steps a drowsy echo; here and there a guard was sweeping the street; sometimes a cart was heard coming from some village to the city market. Beyond this it was noiseless, but clear and breezy, as is usual on a summer morning.

Our light brichka, drawn by four horses, bounded along the pavement, like a nutshell pulled by a string. Soon the cool breath of the river surrounded our faces; the bridge resounded under the hoofs of our horses; and half an hour later we were beyond the barriers among broad fields, and wheat, and forests.

Our breasts breathed deeply of the splendid morning air, and our eyes feasted on the region about. The earth had wakened from sleep; pearly dew was hanging on the wet leaves of the trees and glittering on every ear of wheat. In the hedges the birds moved about joyously with noisy chirping and twittering, greeting the beautiful day. The forests and meadows were coming out of the mist of morning, as if out of swathing bands. Here and there on the meadows, water was gleaming; through this storks waded among the golden flowers of the water-lily. Rosy smoke went straight up from the chimneys of village cottages; a light breeze bent in waves the yellow fields of ripening wheat, and shook the dampness of night from them. Joy was poured out everywhere; it seemed that all was waking, living; that the whole region around was singing, —

> "When the morning dawn arises,
> To thee the land, to thee the sea — "

What was taking place then in our hearts every one will understand easily who remembers how in youth he returned home on such a wonderful summer morning.

The years of childhood and the subjection of school were behind us; the age of youth was spread out broadly, as a rich, flowery steppe, with an endless horizon, — a curious and unknown land into which we had started on a journey with good omens, youthful, strong, almost with wings on our shoulders, like young eagles. Of earthly treasures the greatest is youth, and of that treasure with all its wealth we had not spent yet a single copper.

We passed the road quickly, for at the chief stopping-places relays of horses were waiting for us. Toward evening of the second day, after riding all night, we drove out of a forest and saw Horeli, or rather the pointed summit of the domestic minaret, shining in the rays of the setting sun. Soon we came out onto a dam, bordered with willows and privet, on both sides of which were two immense ponds with grist-mills and saw-mills. We were accompanied by the drowsy croaking of frogs, swimming in water warmed by the heat of the sun and along banks overgrown with grass. It was clear that the day was inclining to its rest. Herds of cattle and flocks of sheep, hidden in clouds of dust, were returning by the dam to the buildings of the farmyard. Here and there crowds of people with sickles, scythes, and rakes on their shoulders were hurrying homeward, singing, "Dana, oi dana!" Those honest toilers stopped the brichka, kissed Selim's hands, and greeted him warmly.

Soon the sun inclined still more toward setting and hid half its bright shield behind the reeds. Only one broad golden line of light was reflected yet on the middle of the ponds, on the banks of which the trees looked into the smooth surface. We turned to the right a little; and soon, amid lindens, poplars, firs, and ash-trees, shone the white walls of the mansion of Horeli.

HANIA. 61

In the yard was heard the bell calling workmen to supper; and from the minaret came the pensive voice of the domestic muezzin, announcing that starry night was falling from the sky to the earth, and that Allah is great. As if to accompany the muezzin, a stork, standing, like an Etruscan vase, in a nest on the top of a tree above the roof of the mansion, issued for a while from his statuesque repose, raised to the sky a bill which was like a bronze arrow, then dropped it on his breast and rattled, shaking his head as if in greeting.

I looked at Selim. There were tears in his eyes, and his face shone with a sweetness beyond compare, peculiar to him alone. We drove into the yard.

Before the windowed porch sat the old Mirza, drawing blue smoke from his pipe; he was looking with a joyful eye at the calm and industrious life moving on that charming landscape. When he saw his son he sprang up quickly, caught him in his arms, and pressed him long to his breast, for though he was stern to the boy he loved him beyond everything. He asked at once about his examination; then followed new embraces. All the numerous servants ran in then to meet the Panich, and the dogs sprang joyously around him. A tame she-wolf, a favorite of the old Mirza, jumped from the porch. " Zula ! Zula!" called Selim, and she put her great paws on his shoulders, licked his face, and then ran around him as if mad, whining and showing her terrible teeth from delight.

Now we went to the dining-room. I looked at Horeli and everything in it, like a man thirsting for novelty. Nothing in it had been modified; the portraits of Selim's ancestors, captains, bannerets, hung on the walls. The terrible Mirza, Sobieski's colonel of light horse, looked on me as before with his ominous, slanting eyes; but his countenance, slashed with sabres, looked still uglier and very terrible. Selim's father had changed most. From being black, his forelock had grown iron gray, his thick mustache had become almost white, and the Tartar type appeared with increasing distinctness in his features. Ah, what a difference between the father and the son, between that bony face, stern, even harsh, and that face simply angelic, resembling a flower, fresh and sweet! But it is difficult for me to describe that love with which the old man looked upon Selim, and with which his eyes followed every movement of his son.

Not wishing to interrupt them, I remained at one side; but the old man, as hospitable as a genuine Polish noble, seized me at once, embraced me, and tried to detain me for the night. I would not pass the night there, for I was in a hurry to reach home, but I had to stay for supper.

I left Horeli late in the evening, and when I was near home the triangle had risen in the sky; that meant that it was midnight. Windows in the village were not lighted; fire in a tar-pit near the forest was visible from a distance. Dogs were barking at the cottages. In the alley of linden-trees, which extended to our house, it was dark; even strain out thine eyes thou couldst see nothing. A man passed at one side humming a song in low tones, but I did not see his face. I reached the porch; the windows were dark. Clearly all were asleep; but dogs, dashing out from all sides, began to bark round the brichka in gladness. I sprang down and knocked at the door; I could not make any one hear for a long time. At last this became disagreeable; I had thought that they would be waiting for me. Only after a time did a light begin to flit here and there past the window-panes, and then a drowsy voice, which I recognized as Franek's, inquired,—

HANIA.   63

"Who is there?"

I answered. Franek opened the door and fell to kissing my hands at once.

" Are all well?" I asked.

" Well," answered Franek; " but the old lord has gone to the city, and will return only to-morrow."

Thus speaking, he conducted me to the dining-room, lighted a hanging lamp over the table, and went to make tea. I was alone for a while with my thoughts, and with my heart beating quickly. But that while was of short duration, for Father Ludvik ran in, in a dressing-gown; the honest Pani d'Yves, dressed also in white, with her usual papers and in a cap; and Kazio, who had come from school for vacation a month earlier. The honest hearts greeted me with feeling, admired my growth; the priest insisted that I had grown manly, Pani d'Yves that I had grown comely.

Father Ludvik, poor man, inquired only after some time, and then timidly, about examination and my school diploma. When he heard of my successes he just wept, taking me in his arms and calling me his dear boy. And now from the chamber came the patter of small naked feet, and my two little sisters ran in, in their night-dresses and little caps, repeating, " Henlis has come! Henlis has come!" and they sprang on my knees. In vain did Pani d'Yves put them to shame, saying that it was an unheard of thing for two young ladies (one was eight, the other nine) to show themselves to people in such "dishabille." The two, without saying a word, put their little arms around my neck and pressed their mouths to my cheeks. After a while I asked timidly about Hania.

"Oh, she has grown!" answered Pani d'Yves. "She will come right away; she is dressing, I think."

In fact, I did not wait long, for five minutes later, perhaps, Hania entered the room. I looked at her; and, oh, what had become in half a year of that slender, thin orphan of sixteen? Before me stood an almost mature, or at least maturing young lady. Her form had grown full, rounded marvellously. She had a delicate but healthy complexion; on her cheeks was ruddiness, as it were, the reflection of the morning dawn. Health, youth, freshness, charm, were radiating from her, as from a rose at its opening. I noticed that she looked at me curiously with her large blue eyes; but I saw also that she must have understood my admiration and the impression which she made on me, for a kind of indescribable smile wandered in the corners of her mouth. In the curiosity with which we looked at each other was hidden the undefined bashfulness of a youth and a maiden. Oh, those simple heartfelt relations of a brother and sister, relations of childhood, had gone somewhere into a forest, to return nevermore.

Ah, how beautiful she was with that smile and that quiet joy in her eyes! Light from the lamp hanging over the table fell on her bright hair. She was dressed in a black robe with something thrown over her which was equally dark. This she held on her breast beneath her white neck with her hand; but in this apparel was evident a certain charming disorder, which arose from the haste with which she had dressed. The warmth of sleep issued from her. When at greeting I touched her hand, it was warm, soft, satin-like, and her touch pierced me with a delightful quiver. Hania had changed as well mentally as physically. When I went away she was a simple maiden, half servant; now she was a young lady, with a noble expression of face and elegant movements, betraying good breeding and the habit of select society.

She was roused morally and mentally; a soul was looking out through her eyes. She had ceased to be a child in every respect; her undefined smile, and a kind of innocent coquetry with which she considered me declared this, and from which it was evident that she understood in how greatly changed relations we stood toward each other. I saw soon that she had a certain superiority over me; for I, though more trained in learning, in reference to life, in reference to understanding every position, every word, was still rather a simple boy. Hania was freer with me than I with her. My dignity of a guardian and lord's son had also gone somewhere into a forest. On the road home I had been arranging with myself how to greet Hania, what to say to her, how to be kind and indulgent, but all these plans tumbled down utterly. The position somehow began to be defined that not I was good and kind to her, but rather that she seemed to be good and kind to me. I could not understand this clearly at first, but I felt the position more than I understood it. I had arranged with myself to ask her what she was studying, what she had learned, how she had passed the time, whether Pani d'Yves and Father Ludvik were satisfied with her; but it was she who always, with that smile in the corners of her mouth, asked me what I had been doing, what I had learned, and what I intended to do in the future. All had come out wonderfully different from what I had intended. Speaking briefly, our relations had changed in a sense directly inverse.

After an hour's conversation we all betook ourselves to rest. I went to my room a little drowsy, a little astonished, a little deceived and downcast, but through various impressions. Love roused again began to push out, like a flame through the cracks of a burning building, and soon covered those impressions completely.

Then simply Hania's form, that maiden figure, rich, full of charms, such as I had seen her, alluring, surrounded with the warmth of sleep, with her white hand holding the disordered dress on her bosom, with her hanging tresses, roused my young imagination, and veiled with itself everything before me.

I fell asleep with her image under my eyelids.

CHAPTER VI.

I ROSE very early next day and ran out to the garden. The morning was beautiful, full of dew and the odor of flowers. I went quickly to the hornbeam picket, for my heart told me that I should find Hania there. But evidently my heart, too receptive of forebodings, had deceived itself. Hania was not there, no trace of her. Only after breakfast did I find myself alone with her. I asked if she would walk in the garden. She consented willingly and ran to her chamber; she returned soon with a large straw hat on her head, which shaded her forehead and eyes, and with a parasol in her hand. She smiled at me roguishly from under the hat, as if to say, "See how this becomes me."

We went to the garden together. I turned toward the hornbeam picket, and on the road thought, how shall I begin conversation, and thought also that Hania, who certainly could begin better than I, had no wish to assist me, but rather amused herself with my perplexity. I walked along at her side in silence, cutting off with my whip flowers growing on the side of the path, till Hania laughed all on a sudden.

"Pan Henryk," said she, catching at the whip, "what have the flowers done to you?"

"Hania, what are the flowers to me? But thou seest that I do not know how to begin talk with thee; thou hast changed much, Hania. Ah, how thou hast changed!"

"Let us suppose that to be true. Does it make you angry?"

"I do not say that it does," answered I, half in sorrow; "but I cannot make myself used to it, for it seems to me that that other little Hania whom I knew before, and thou, are two different beings. That one had grown into my memory, into — my heart, like a sister, Hania, and therefore —"

"And therefore" (here she pointed to herself) "this one is a stranger, is she not?" asked she, in a low voice.

"Hania! Hania! how canst thou even imagine such a thing?"

"Still it is very natural, though perhaps sad," answered she. "You are looking in your heart for the old brotherly feelings, and do not find them, that is all."

"No, I do not look in my heart for the old Hania, for she is there always; but I look for her in thee, and as to my heart —"

"As to your heart," interrupted she, joyously, "I can guess what has become of it. It has stayed somewhere in Warsaw with some other little heart. That is guessed easily!"

I looked deeply into her eyes. I did not know whether she was quizzing me a little or counting on the impression made on me yesterday, and which I was unable to hide, but she was playing with me somewhat cruelly. All at once a wish to resist was roused in me. I thought that I must have a supremely comical face, looking at her with the expression of a mortally wounded deer; so I mastered my feelings and said. —

"If that is true?"

A visible expression of astonishment, and, as it were, of dissatisfaction, came to her face.

"If that is true," answered she, "it is you who have changed, not I."

She frowned a little, and, looking at me from under her forehead, went on some time in silence. I endeavored to hide the glad emotion with which her words penetrated me. "She says," thought I, "that if I love another, it is I who have changed; therefore it is not she who has changed, she —" And from delight I dared not finish this wise inference.

Notwithstanding all this, it was not I, not I, but she who had changed. That little maiden who six months before knew nothing of God's world, to whose mind it had never occurred to mention feelings, and for whom such a conversation would have been as Chinese, carried it on to-day as freely and accurately as if she had been reciting a lesson. How had that child mind developed and become so flexible? But wonderful things take place in girls. More than one falls asleep in the evening a child and wakes up in the morning a woman, with another world of feelings and thoughts. For Hania, with a nature quick, capable, sensitive, the passage of her sixteenth year, another sphere of society, learning, books, read, perhaps, in secret, — all this was more than sufficient.

Meanwhile we walked on side by side in silence which Hania was the first to break.

"Then you are in love, Pan Henryk?"

"Perhaps," answered I, with a smile.

"Then you will be sighing for Warsaw?"

"No, Hania; I should be glad were I never to leave here."

Hania glanced at me quickly. Evidently she wished to say something, but was silent. After a while, however, she struck her skirts lightly with the parasol, and said, as if answering her own thoughts, —

"Ah, what a child I am!"

"Why dost thou say that, Hania?"

"Oh, so — Let us sit on this bench and talk of something else. Is not the view from here beautiful?" asked she, with that well-known smile on her lips.

She seated herself on the bench not far from the paling under an immense linden-tree. From that point the view was very beautiful indeed in the direction of the pond, the dam, and the forest beyond the pond. Hania pointed it out to me with her parasol; but I, though a lover of beautiful views, had not the least desire to look at it, — first, because I knew it perfectly; second, I had before me Hania, a hundred times more beautiful than anything which surrounded her; finally, I was thinking of something else.

"How clearly those trees are reflected in the water!" said she.

"I see that thou art an artist," I answered, not looking at the trees or the water.

"Father Ludvik is teaching me to sketch. Oh, I have learned much while you were gone. I wanted — but what is the matter? Are you angry with me?"

"No, Hania, I am not angry, for I could not be angry with thee; but I see that thou avoidest my questions, and this is the trouble, we are both playing at hide and seek, instead of speaking sincerely and with confidence, as in old times. Maybe thou dost not feel this, but for me it is disagreeable"

These simple words had this effect only, that they brought us into great perplexity. Hania gave me both hands, it is true; I pressed those hands perhaps too vigorously, and, oh, terror! I bent over them quickly and kissed them not at all as befitted a guardian. Then we were confused to the utmost. She blushed to the neck, I also; and finally we were silent, not knowing in any way how to begin that conversation which should be sincere and full of confidence.

Then she looked at me, I at her, and again we hung out red flags on our faces. We sat side by side like two dolls; it seemed to me that I was listening to the hurried beating of my own heart. Our position was unendurable. At times I felt that some hand was seizing me by the collar to throw me at her feet, and another was holding me by the hair and would not let me do so. All at once Hania sprang up and said in a hurried, confused voice, —

"I must go. I have a lesson at this hour with Pani d'Yves. It is nearly eleven."

We returned by the same road to the house, and went on as before in silence. I, as before, kept cutting the heads off the flowers with my whip, but this time she had no compassion for the flowers.

"Our former relations have returned beautifully; there is nothing to be said on that point. Jesus, Mary! what is taking place within me?" thought I, when Hania left me to myself. I was in love so that the hair was rising on my head.

Just then the priest came and took me to look at the management. On the way he told me many things touching our estate; these did not occupy me in the least, though I pretended to listen attentively.

My brother Kazio, who, enjoying his vacation, spent the whole day out of doors, in the stables, in the forest, at shooting, on horseback, or in a boat, was at that particular moment in the farm-yard riding a young horse from the stud. When he saw me and the priest, he galloped up to us on the chestnut, which reared as if mad, and asked us to admire the horse's form, fire, and pace; then he dismounted and went with us. Together we visited the stables, the cow-houses, the barns, and were just going to the fields, when it was announced that my father had come, so we had to go home.

My father greeted me more warmly than ever. When he learned of the examinations, he took me in his arms and declared that thenceforward he would consider me full grown. Indeed, a great change had taken place in him with reference to me. He treated me with more confidence and affection. He began to talk with me at once about property interests; he confided to me his intention of buying one of the neighboring estates, and asked my opinion. I divined that he spoke of that purposely to show me how seriously he looked on my significance as a mature person and the first son in the family. At the same time I noticed how genuinely he was pleased with me and my advance in study. His pride of a parent was flattered immensely by the testimonial which I had brought from the professors. I noticed, meanwhile, that he was testing my character, my style of thought, my ideas touching honor, and that he put various questions purposely to test me with them. It was evident that the parental inspection proved favorable, for though my philosophic and social principles were utterly different from his, I did not bring them forward; in other ideas we could not differ. So my father's severe, lion-like face became more radiant than ever I had seen it. He covered me with gifts that day; he gave me a brace of pistols, with which he had fought a duel not long before with Pan Zoll, and on which were marked a number of other duels which he had fought during youth, while serving in the army. Then I received a splendid horse of Eastern blood, and an ancient sabre handed down from my ancestors; the hilt was set with stones; on the broad Damascus blade was an image of the Mother of God, inlaid with gold in the steel, and the inscription, "Jesus, Mary!" That sabre had become one of our most precious family relics, and for years had been the object of sighs from me and Kazio, for it cut iron as if shavings. My father, when presenting the sabre, unsheathed and whirled it a couple of times so that the air whistled and there was a flash in the room; then he made a cross with it over my head, kissed the image of the Mother of God on the blade, and said, while delivering the weapon into my hands,—

"Into worthy hands! I brought no shame to it; bring thou none!" Then we threw ourselves into each other's arms. Meanwhile Kazio seized the sabre with delight; and though only a lad of fifteen, but uncommonly strong, he began to give blows with an accuracy and with a quickness that would not have shamed any trained master of fencing. My father looked at him with satisfaction, and said,—

"He will be perfect; but thou wilt do what is needed, wilt thou not?"

"I will, father. I should be able to manage Kazio even. Of all the comrades whom I have tried in fencing, only one has surpassed me."

"Who is he?"

"Selim."

My father made a wry face.

"Selim! But thou must be stronger?"

"That is indifferent. What would make me try him? Selim and I will never fight."

"Ai! various things happen," answered my father.

After dinner that day we were all sitting on the broad,

vine-covered porch; from this porch the view was on the immense front yard and in the distance on the shady road bordered by linden-trees. Pani d'Yves was working an altar-cloth for the chapel; my father and the priest were smoking pipes and drinking black coffee. Kazio was circling about in front of the porch, following the turns of swift swallows, at which he wanted to shoot balls; but my father would not let him do that. Hania and I were looking at drawings which I had brought home, and were thinking least of all of the drawings; for me they served only to conceal from others the glances which I cast at Hania.

"Well, and how hast thou found Hania? Does she seem ugly to thee, lord guardian?" asked my father, looking facetiously at the girl.

I began to examine a drawing very carefully, and answered from behind the paper, —

"I will not say, father, that she has grown ugly, but she has grown tall, and has changed."

"Pan Henryk has reproached me already with these changes," put in Hania, with freedom.

I wondered at her daring in presence of my father. I could not have mentioned those reproaches so freely.

"Oh, what matters it whether she has grown old or grown pretty!" said Father Ludvik; "but she learns quickly and well. Let Madame tell how quickly she has learned French."

It should be known that the priest, though highly educated, did not know French and could not learn it, though he had spent a number of years under our roof with Pani d'Yves. The poor man, however, had a weakness for French, and considered a knowledge of it as an indispensable mark of superior education.

"I cannot deny that she learns easily and willingly,"

answered Pani d'Yves, turning to me; "but still I must complain of her."

"Oh, Pani! what new fault have I committed?" cried Hania, crossing her hands.

"What fault? You will explain here right away," answered Pani d'Yves. "Just imagine, this young lady, when she finds a moment of time, takes up a novel immediately; and I have strong reasons for thinking that when she goes to bed, instead of quenching the candle and sleeping, she reads for whole hours."

"She does a very bad thing; but I know from some source that she follows the example of her teacher," said my father, who was fond of teasing Pani d'Yves when he was in good humor.

"I beg your pardon greatly; I am forty-five years of age," answered the French woman.

"Why, just think, I never should have said that," answered my father.

"You are malicious."

"I do not know that; but I know this, that if Hania gets novels from any place, it is not from the library, for Father Ludvik has the key to it. The blame therefore falls on the teacher."

In truth, Pani d'Yves had read novels all her life, and, having a passion to relate them to every one, she must surely have related some to Hania; hence, in the words of my father, which were half in jest, a certain truth lay concealed, which he wished to emphasize purposely.

"Oh, see! Some one is coming!" cried Kazio, suddenly.

We all looked into the shady alley between the linden-trees, and at the other end of it, perhaps a verst away, we saw a cloud of dust, which approached us with uncommon rapidity.

"Who can that be? What speed!" said my father, rising up. "Such a dust one can distinguish nothing."

In fact, the heat was great; no rain had fallen for more than two weeks, so that along the roads clouds of white dust rose at every step. We looked for a while, yet in vain, at the approaching cloud, which was not farther than a few tens of steps from the front yard, when out of the cloud emerged a horse's head with distended, red nostrils, fiery eyes, and flowing mane. The white horse was going at the swiftest gallop; his feet barely touched the earth; and on his back, bent to the horse's neck, in Tartar fashion, was no other than my friend Selim.

"Selim is coming, Selim!" cried Kazio.

"What is that lunatic doing? The gate is closed!" cried I, springing from my place.

There was no time to open the gate, for no one could reach it in season; meanwhile, Selim urged on like a madman, at random, and it was almost certain that he would fall on the gate, more than two ells high, with sharp peaks at the top.

"O God, have mercy on him!" cried the priest.

"The gate! Selim, the gate!" screamed I, as if possessed, waving my handkerchief and running with all my might across the yard.

Something like five yards from the gate, Selim straightened himself in the saddle, and measured the gate with a glance quick as lightning. Next, the scream of women sitting on the porch came to me, the swift trampling of hoofs; the horse rose, suspended his forelegs in the air, and went over the gate at the highest speed without stopping one instant.

When before the porch, Selim reined in his steed so that the beast's hoofs dug into the earth, then snatching the hat from his own head, he waved it like a standard and cried, —

"How are ye, dear beloved lords? How are ye? My respects to the lord benefactor!" cried he, bowing to my father; "my respects to the beloved priest, Pani d'Yves, Panna Hania! We are all together again. Vivat! Vivat!"

Then he sprang from the horse, and throwing the reins to Franek, who had run out of the hall the moment before, he embraced my father, then the priest, and fell to kissing the hands of the ladies.

Pani d'Yves and Hania were pale from terror, and just because of that they greeted Selim as if he had been rescued from death.

"Oh, thou art playing the madman, the madman! What terror thou didst bring on us!" said Father Ludvik. "We thought that it was all over with thee."

"But why so?"

"That gate. How is it possible to race so at random?"

"At random? I saw very well that the gate was closed. Oho! I have my perfect Tartar eyes."

"And thou dost not fear to race so?"

Selim laughed. "Not in the least, Father Ludvik. But for that matter, the merit is my horse's, not mine."

"There is a bold boy for you!" said Pani d'Yves.

"Oh, that is true! Not every man would dare that," added Hania.

"It is thy wish to say," added I, "that not every horse could clear the gate, for more such men could be found."

Hania gazed long at me.

"I would not advise you to try," said she; then she turned toward Selim and her look expressed admiration, for really this daring deed of the Tartar was one of those risks which always please women. One should have

HANIA.

seen him at that moment, his fine, dark hair falling on his forehead, his cheeks flushed from the swift movement, his gleaming eyes, from which shone delight and gladness. As he stood there near Hania, looking her in the eyes with curiosity, no artist could have imagined a more beautiful couple.

But I was touched in the highest degree by her words. It seemed to me that that, "I would not advise thee to try," had been spoken in a voice in which a tone of irony was trembling. I looked with an inquiring glance at my father, who had examined Selim's horse a moment before. I knew his parental ambition; I knew that he was jealous the moment that any one surpassed me in anything, and this had angered him toward Selim for a long time. I concluded, therefore, that he would not oppose in case I wished to show that I was not a worse horseman than Selim.

"That horse gallops well, father," said I.

"Yes, and that Satan sits well," muttered he. "Couldst thou do the same?"

"Hania doubts," answered I, with a certain bitterness. "May I try?"

My father hesitated, looked at the gate, at the horse, at me, and said, —

"Give peace."

"Naturally!" exclaimed I, in sorrow; "it is better for me to be counted an old woman in comparison with Selim."

"Henryk! what art thou saying?" cried Selim, encircling my neck with his arms.

"Gallop! gallop, boy! and do your best," said my father, whose pride was touched.

"Bring the horse here!" called I to Franek, who was leading the tired steed slowly around the yard.

"Pan Henryk!" cried Hania, springing up from her seat, "then I am the cause of this trial. I do not wish it; I do not wish it. Do not do it; do not, for my sake!"

And while speaking, she looked me in the eyes, as if she wished to finish with her eyes that which she could not express in words.

Ah! for that look I would have given the last drop of my blood at that moment; but I could not and would not draw back. My offended pride was stronger just then than aught else; so I mastered myself and answered dryly, —

"Thou art mistaken, Hania, in thinking that thou art the cause. I shall clear the gate to amuse myself."

Thus speaking, in spite of the protests of all save my father, I mounted and moved forward at a walk into the alley of lindens. Franek opened the gate and closed it after me. I had bitterness in my soul, and would have gone over the gate had it been twice as high. When I had ridden about three hundred yards, I turned the horse and began at a trot, which I changed to a gallop immediately.

All at once I noticed that the saddle was moving. One of two things had happened, — either the girth had stretched during the former leap, or Franek had loosened it to let the horse breathe, and through stupidity, or perhaps forgetfulness, had not informed me.

Now it was too late. The horse was approaching the gate at the highest speed, and I did not wish to stop him. "If I kill myself, I shall kill myself," thought I. I pressed the sides of the horse convulsively. The air whistled in my ears. Suddenly the points of the gate gleamed before my eyes. I waved my whip, felt myself borne through air, a scream from the porch struck my ears, it grew dark in my eyes — and after a while I recovered from a faint.

I sprang to my feet.

"What has happened?" cried I. "Was I thrown? I fainted."

Near me were my father, the priest, Pani d'Yves, Selim, Kazio, and Hania white as linen, with tears in her eyes.

"What is the matter? What is the matter?" was the cry on all sides.

"Nothing at all. I was thrown, but that was not my fault. The girth was stretched."

In fact, after the momentary faint I felt perfectly well, only breath lacked me a little. My father fell to touching my hands, feet, shoulders.

"It does not hurt?" inquired he.

"No; I am perfectly well."

My breath too returned to me. But I was angry, for I thought that I seemed ridiculous, — that I must seem ridiculous. In falling from the horse, I was thrown with violence across the whole width of the road, which passed near a grass-plot, and fell on the grass; because of this the elbows and knees of my clean clothing were stained green, my dress and hair disordered. But still the unfortunate outcome had rendered me a service. A moment before, Selim was the object of general attention in our circle, as a guest, and as a guest just arrived; now I had taken from him that palm of victory at the cost of my knees and elbows. Hania, thinking herself all the time, and justly, the cause of this hazardous trial which for me might have ended badly, tried to make up for her hastiness with kindness and sweetness. Under such influence I soon recovered my joyousness, which was communicated to all the society which a moment before had been terrified. We amused ourselves perfectly.

Lunch was served, at which Hania was the mistress, and then we went to the garden. In the garden Selim became as full of pranks as a little boy; he laughed, frolicked, and Hania helped him with all her soul. Finally he said, —

"Oh, how we shall amuse ourselves this time, all three of us!"

"I am curious to know," said Hania, "who is the most joyous!"

"Oh, surely I," answered Selim.

"But perhaps it is I. I am gladsome by nature."

"But the least gladsome is Henryk," added Selim. "He is naturally dignified, and a little sad. If he had lived in the Middle Ages, he would have been a knight-errant and a troubadour, only he cannot sing. But we," continued he, turning to Hania, "have looked for the poppy and found it."

"I cannot agree to that," answered I. "For any given disposition I prefer the opposite, since in this case one has the qualities which are lacking the other."

"Thanks," replied Selim; "I admit that thou art by nature fond of weeping, and Panna Hania of laughing. Well, let it be that: get married, you two —"

"Selim!"

Selim looked at me and began to laugh.

"Well, young man? Ha! ha! Dost remember the oration of Cicero, 'commoveri videtur juvenis,' which in Polish means: the young man seems confused. But that signifies nothing, for without cause even thou canst blush gloriously. Panna Hania, he cooks crawfish [1] gloriously, and now he has blushed for himself and you."

"Selim!"

"Nothing, nothing! I return to my subject. Thou, sir, art a man of weeping, and thou, young lady, art a

---

[1] To cook crawfish, to blush.

lady of laughing; get married. What will happen? He will begin to blubber, and you to laugh; you will never understand each other, never agree, different always; and what do I care for chosen natures? Oh, with me it would be different: we should simply laugh all our lives, and that would be the whole story."

"What are you saying?" answered Hania, and then both laughed heartily.

As to me, I had not the least desire to laugh. Selim did not know what injustice he did me in persuading Hania of the difference between her disposition and mine. I was angry in the highest degree, and answered Selim with sarcasm, —

"Thou hast a strange view, and it astonishes me all the more, since I have noticed that thou hast a weakness for melancholy persons."

"I?" said he, with unfeigned astonishment.

"Yes. I will merely remind thee of a certain maiden, some fuchsias, and a little face between them. I give thee my word that I do not know such a melancholy face."

Hania clapped her hands.

"Oho! I am learning something new!" cried she, laughing. "Is she pretty, Pan Selim; is she pretty?"

I thought that Selim would grow confused and lose his boldness; but he merely said, —

"Henryk?"

"What?"

"Dost thou know what I do with those whose tongues are too long?" And he laughed.

Hania insisted on his telling her even the name of this chosen one; without thinking long, he said, —

"Yozia."

But if he had been what he pretended he would have

paid dearly for his sincerity, for Hania gave him no peace from that hour till evening.

"Is she pretty?"

"Oh, so."

"What kind of hair has she, and eyes?"

"Nice ones, but not such as please me more than all others."

"And what kind please you?"

"Bright hair, and eyes, if they are kind, blue, like those into which I am looking at this moment."

"Oo, Pan Selim!"

And Hania frowned; but Selim, putting his palms together, made himself pleasant with that incomparable sweetness in his eyes, and began, —

"Panna Hania, be not angry. What has the poor little Tartar done? Be not angry! Let the lady laugh."

Hania looked at him, and as she looked the cloud vanished from her forehead. He simply enchanted her. A smile wandered in the corners of her mouth; her eyes grew bright, her face radiant; and at last she answered in a soft, mild voice, —

"Very well, I will not be angry; but I beg you to be nice."

"I will, as I love Mohammed, I will."

"And do you love your Mohammed much?"

"As dogs a beggar."

And then both laughed again.

"But now tell me whom does Pan Henryk love? I asked him, but he would not tell me."

"Henryk? Do you know" (here he looked at me askance) "he is not in love with any one yet, perhaps, but he will love. Oh, I know perfectly whom! and as to me —"

"As to you, what?" inquired Hania, trying to conceal her confusion.

"I would do the very same — but wait a bit; he may be in love already."

"I beg thee to stop, Selim."

"Thou, my honest boy," said Selim, putting his arm around my neck — "Ah, if you knew how honest he is."

"Oh, I know that," said Hania; "I remember what he was to me after my grandfather's death."

A cloud of sadness flew between us then.

"I will tell you," said Selim, wishing to change the subject, "that after examination we had a little feast with our master —"

"And drank?"

"Yes. Oh, that is the custom which one cannot avoid. So while we were drinking, I, being, as you know, a giddy fellow, raised a toast to you. I acted unwisely, but Henryk sprang up: 'How dare you mention Hania in such a place as this?' said he to me; for that was a wine-cellar. We came near fighting. But he will not let any one offend you, no, no —"

Hania gave me her hand. "How good you are, Pan Henryk!"

"Well," answered I, carried away by Selim's words, "say thyself, Hania, is not Selim just as honest, since he tells this?"

"Oh, what great honesty!" said Selim, laughing.

"But it is," answered Hania; "you are worthy of each other, and we shall have such a pleasant time in company."

"You will be our queen!" cried Selim, with enthusiasm.

"Gentlemen! Hania! we invite you to tea," called Pani d'Yves from the garden veranda.

We went to tea, all three of us in the very best feeling.
The table was set under the veranda; the lights, shielded
by glass tubes, burned brightly, and moths in a swarm
circled around them; they butted against the glass walls
of the tubes; the leaves of wild grapevines rustled, moved
by the warm night air; and beyond the poplars rose a
great golden moon. The last conversation between Hania,
Selim, and myself had brought us to a wonderfully mild,
friendly tone. That calm and quiet evening acted also
on the older persons. My father's face and the priest's
were as serene as the sky.

After tea Pani d'Yves began to play solitaire; my
father fell into perfect humor, for he commenced to tell
of old times, which with him was always a sign of good
feeling.

"I remember," said he, "we halted once not far from a
village in Krasnostav. The night was dark; even strain
your eyes out, you could not see anything" (here he
drew smoke from his pipe and let it go above the light).
"People were as tired as a Jew's nag. We were standing
silently, and then —"

Here began a narrative of wonderful and most wonderful happenings. The priest, who had listened to this
more than once, still stopped smoking and listened more
attentively; he raised his spectacles to his forehead,
and, nodding, repeated "Uhum! Uhum!" or called out,
"Jesus, Mary! well, and what?"

Selim and I, leaning against each other, with eyes fixed
on my father, caught his words eagerly. On no face was
the expression depicted so definitely as on Selim's. His
eyes were gleaming like coals; a flush covered his face; his
hot Eastern nature came to the surface like oil Hardly
could he sit in one place. Pani d'Yves smiled as she
looked at him, and showed him to Hania with her eyes;

then both began to observe him, for they were entertained by that face, which was like a mirror or the surface of water, in which everything is reflected that comes near its transparency.

To-day, when I recall evenings like that, I cannot resist my emotion. Many waves on the water, many clouds in the sky, have passed since that time; but still winged memory pushes before my eyes continually similar pictures of the village mansion, the summer night, and that family, harmonious, loving, happy, — a gray veteran telling former adventures of his life; youths with fire in their eyes; farther on a face like a field flower — Ei! Many waves on the water and clouds in the sky have passed since that time.

Meanwhile the clock struck ten. Selim sprang up, for he had received the command to return that same night. The whole company decided to go with him as far as the cross at the end of the lindens near the second gate, I on horseback farther, as far as the meadows. We started then, all of us except Kazio, who had fallen asleep in the best fashion.

Hania, Selim, and I pushed on ahead, we two leading our horses by the bridles, Hania between us. The three old people walked behind. It was dark in the alley; the moon, merely breaking through the dense foliage, marked the dark road with silver spots.

"Let us sing something," said Selim, "some song, old and good; for example, the song about Filon."

"No one sings that," answered Hania. "I know another: 'Oh, autumn, autumn, the leaf is withering on the tree!'"

We agreed at last to begin with "Filon," which the priest and my father liked much, for it reminded them of old times, and then sing "Oh, autumn, autumn!" Hania

placed her white hand on the mane of Selim's horse and
began to sing, —

> "The moon has gone down, the dogs are all sleeping;
> But some one is clapping beyond the pine wood.
> Surely, Filon, my darling, is watching,
> Awaiting me under the favorite maple."

When we finished, the voices of the old people were
heard behind us in the darkness: "Bravo! bravo! sing
something more." I accompanied as best I could, but I
did not sing well; while Hania and Selim had beautiful
voices, especially Selim. Sometimes, when I went too far
beyond the notes, they both laughed at me. Then they
hummed some other songs, during which I thought, "Why
does Hania hold the mane of Selim's horse, and not
the mane of mine?" That horse pleased her peculiarly.
Sometimes she nestled up to its neck, or, patting it, repeated, "My steed, mine!" and the gentle beast snorted
and stretched out its open nostrils toward her hand, as if
looking for sugar. All this caused me to grow sad again,
and I looked at nothing save that hand, which continued
to rest on the horse's mane.

Meanwhile we reached the cross at the end of the linden-trees. Selim bade good-night to all: he kissed the
hands of Pani d'Yves and wished to kiss Hania's; but she
would not consent, and looked at me as if afraid. But as
a recompense, when he was on horseback she approached
him and spoke. In the light of the moon, unobstructed
in that place, I saw her eyes raised to Selim's, and the
sweet expression of her face.

"Do not forget Pan Henryk. We shall always amuse
ourselves and sing together, and now good-night!" said
she, giving him her hand.

Hania and the older people went toward the house,

Selim and I toward the meadows. We rode on some time in silence by an open road without trees. Round about it was so bright that one might count the needle-like leaves on the low juniper bushes growing by the road. From time to time the horses snorted, or a stirrup struck against a stirrup. I looked at Selim; he was thoughtful and turned his eyes to the depths of night. I had an overpowering desire to speak of Hania. I felt the need of confessing to some one the impressions of the day, of telling every word of hers, but not a movement could I make; I knew not how to begin that conversation. Selim began it first, for suddenly, neither from one reason nor another, he bent toward me, and embracing my neck kissed me on the cheek, and cried, —

"Ah, my Henryk! how beautiful and charming thy Hania is! Let the devil take Yozia!"

This exclamation chilled me like a sudden breath of wintry wind. I made no answer, but removed Selim's arm from my neck, and, pushing him away, rode on in silence. I saw that he was greatly confused, and had grown silent also; after a while, turning to me, he said,—

"Art thou angry about something?"

"Thou art a child!"

"Perhaps thou art jealous?"

I reined in my horse.

"Good-night to thee, Selim."

It was evident that he had no desire to take further farewell, but he stretched out his hand mechanically for pressure. Then he opened his lips as if to say something; but I turned my horse quickly, and trotted toward home.

"Good-night!" cried Selim.

He stood a while yet on the same spot, then rode slowly toward Horeli.

Lessening my speed, I rode at a walk. The night was beautiful, calm, warm; the meadows, covered with dew, seemed like broad lakes. From those meadows came the voices of land rails; bitterns were calling in the distant reeds. I raised my eyes to the starry immensity; I wanted to pray and to cry.

Suddenly I heard the tramp of a horse behind me. I looked around; it was Selim. He had caught up, and, coming before me in the road, said with a voice full of emotion, —

"Henryk! I have come back because something is the matter with thee. At first I thought: 'if he is angry, let him be angry!' But afterward I grew sorry for thee. I could not restrain myself. Tell me what the matter is. Perhaps I have spoken too much with Hania? Perhaps thou art in love with her, Henryk?"

Tears stopped my throat, and I could answer nothing at once. If I had followed my first inspiration, thrown myself on Selim's honest breast, cried there, and confessed all! Ah! I remember that whenever I met an outpouring of the heart in another, and opened my own heart affectionately in response, a kind of irresistible, rebellious pride, which should have been broken as a stone with a pickaxe, froze my heart and bound the words on my lips. How many times has my happiness been ruined by that pride, and always have I regretted it later! Still at the first moment I could never resist it

"I was sorry for thee," continued Selim.

So he had compassion on me; that was sufficient to shut my mouth. I was silent. He gazed at me with his angelic eyes; he spoke with an accent of entreaty and repentance in his voice, —

"Henryk! Perhaps thou lovest her? She, as thou seest, has pleased me, but let this be the end. If thou wish, I will not say another word to her. Tell me: perhaps thou art in love with her already? What hast thou against me?"

"I do not love her, and I have nothing against thee. I am a little weak. I was thrown from the horse; I got shaken. I am not at all in love; I only fell from the horse. Good-night to thee!"

"Henryk! Henryk!"

"I repeat to thee, I was thrown from the horse."

We parted again. Selim kissed me in farewell, and rode away more calmly; for, in truth, it might be supposed that the fall had had that effect on me. I remained alone, with a straitened heart, in a kind of deep sorrow, in tears which stopped my throat, moved by Selim's kindness, angry with myself, and cursing my conduct in having repulsed him. I let the horse go at a gallop, and soon I was before the mansion.

The windows of the drawing-room were lighted; the sound of the piano came through them. I gave the horse to Franek, and entered. Hania was playing some song which I did not know; she was playing for herself, falsifying the melody with all a dilettante's confidence, for it was not long since she had begun to learn, but it was more than sufficient to enchant my spirit, which was much more in love than it was musical. When I entered, she smiled at me without ceasing to play. I threw myself into an armchair standing opposite, and looked at her. Over the music-rack her clear, serene forehead was visible, and her brows, outlined symmetrically. Her eyelashes were downcast, for she was looking at the keys. She played some time yet, then stopped, and, raising her eyes on me, said in a fondling, soft voice, —

"Pan Henryk?"

"What, Hania?"

"I wanted to ask something — Ah! Have you invited Selim for to-morrow?"

"No. Father wishes us to go to Ustrytsi to-morrow, for a package has come from mother for Pani Ustrytski."

Hania was silent, and struck a few soft notes; but it was evident that she did so only mechanically, while thinking of something else, for after a while she raised her eyes and said, —

"Pan Henryk?"

"What, Hania?"

"I wanted to ask you about something — Ah! here it is! Is that Yozia in Warsaw very pretty?"

That was too much; anger, mixed with vexation, pressed my heart. I approached the piano quickly; my lips were trembling when I answered, —

"Not prettier than thou. Be at rest. Thou mayst try thy charms boldly on Selim."

Hania rose from the piano stool; a burning blush of offence covered her face.

"Pan Henryk! what do you say?"

"That which thou wert aiming at."

I seized my hat, bowed to her, and left the room.

CHAPTER VII.

IT is easy to divine how I passed the night after those vexations of a whole day. When I had lain down, I asked myself first of all what had happened, and why I had had such adventures. The answer was easy: Nothing had happened; that is, I could not reproach either Selim or Hania with anything which might not be explained by the friendliness which bound us all equally, or by curiosity, or by mutual sympathy. That Selim

pleased Hania, and she him, was more than certain; but
what right had I to be angered because of that, and destroy
every one's peace? Not they were at fault, but I.
This thought should have calmed me, but the opposite
happened. No matter how I explained their mutual
relations, though I saw that I had caused many vexations
unjustly to both, still, I felt that a certain unspeakable
danger was impending in the future; this consideration,
that the danger was not tangible, that it could not be
put in the form of a reproach against Selim or Hania,
made it felt all the more keenly by me. Besides this, I
thought of one other thing; namely, that not having the
right to reproach them, I had still sufficient reason for
alarm. These were all subtleties of the case, almost impossible
to be seized, in which my mind, still unsophisticated,
was entangled and tortured as if amid snares and
darkness. I felt simply wearied and broken, like a man
who has made a long journey; and still one other thought,
bitter and painful, came back to my head without ceasing;
namely, this, that it was I, expressly I, who by jealousy
and awkwardness, was impelling those two persons
toward each other. Oh, how much knowledge had I
been acquiring, though I had no knowledge whatever!
Such things are divined. What is more, I knew that,
amid all these wrong paths, I should go, not where I
wished to go, but where I should be urged by feelings
and circumstances, not infrequently temporary and insufficient,
but which are somehow important and on which
happiness often depends. I was very unhappy; and
though those vexations of mine might seem foolish to
some persons, I will say this, that the greatness of any
misfortune depends not on what it is in itself, but on how
one feels it.

And still nothing had happened. Lying in bed, I

repeated these words to myself, till gradually my thoughts began to grow dim, to scatter, and to fall into the usual disorder of sleep. Various strange elements pushed themselves into this disorder. My father's narratives, persons and events in those narratives, were joined then with Selim, Hania, and my love. Perhaps I had some fever, all the more since I had fallen. The wick of the burnt candle dropped all at once into the candlestick; it grew dark, then blue flame flickered up, then less of it, and still less, till at last the expiring light shone brightly and died. It must have been late; the cocks were crowing outside the window. I fell into an oppressive, unhealthy sleep, out of which I rose not very quickly.

Next morning it appeared that I had slept past the breakfast hour, and past the chance of seeing Hania before dinner, for she had lessons till two with Pani d'Yves. But after a long sleep I took courage, and did not look on the world as so black. "I will be kind and cordial to Hania, and thus make amends for yesterday's peevishness," thought I.

Meanwhile, I had not foreseen one circumstance; namely, that my last words had not only annoyed, but offended her. When she came in with Pani d'Yves to dinner, I hurried toward her quickly; and all at once, as if some one had poured water on me, I withdrew again into myself with my cordiality, not because I wished to do so, but because I was repulsed. Hania answered very politely, "Good-day," but so coldly that all wish for heartfelt effusions deserted me. I sat down near Pani d'Yves, and during the whole dinner Hania seemed not to take note of my existence. I confess that that existence appeared then so empty and pitiful in my eyes that if any man had offered three coppers for it I would have told him to deliver the money. What was I to do? The desire for resistance was roused in me, and I determined to pay Hania in the same coin. That was a wonderful rôle regarding a person whom one loves above everything. I could say truly, " Lips abuse thee, though the heart weeps!" During the whole dinner we did not speak once directly, only through the medium of others. When Hania said, for example, that there would be rain toward the evening, I turned to Pani d'Yves, and told her, and not Hania, that there would be no rain. This pouting and bickering had a certain exciting charm for me. "I am curious to know, my young lady, how we shall get on in Ustrytsi, for we must go there," thought I. "In Ustrytsi, I will ask her something purposely in the presence of others; she must answer then, and so the ice will be broken." I promised myself much from that visit. True, I had to go with Pani d'Yves; but how would that harm me? At present I cared much more for this, that no one at the table should take note of our anger. Should any one notice it, thought I, that one would ask if we were angry; then all would be discovered, all would come out. At the very thought of this, a blush came to my face, and fear pressed my heart. But, oh, wonder! I saw that Hania feared this much less than I; besides, she saw my fear, and in her soul was amused at it. In turn, I felt overcome; but for the moment there was nothing to be done. Ustrytsi was waiting for me, so I caught at that thought as a plank of salvation.

Hania was thinking too of it, for after dinner, when she brought black coffee to my father, she kissed his hand and said, —

"I beg not to go to Ustrytsi."

"Ah, what a rogue, what a rogue, that dear Hania!" thought I, in my soul.

My father, who was a little deaf, did not hear at once. Kissing her on the forehead, he asked, —

"What dost thou wish, little woman?"

"I have one prayer."

"What is it?"

"That I may not go to Ustrytsi."

"But why, art thou ill?"

"If she says that she is ill," thought I, "all is lost, the more since my father is in good humor."

But Hania never lied, even innocently; therefore, instead of masking the lack of wish as a headache, she answered, —

"I am well, but I do not like to go."

"Ah! then thou wilt go to Ustrytsi, for there is need of thy going"

Hania courtesied and went away without saying a word. Had it been proper, I should have gladly shown her zyg, zyg, zyg, on my fingers.

After a while I asked my father why he ordered Hania to go.

"I wish the neighbors to see in her our relative, and grow familiar with that position. Hania in going to Ustrytsi goes there, so to speak, in the name of thy mother; dost understand?"

Not only did I understand, but I wanted to kiss my honest father for that thought.

We were to start at five o'clock. Hania and Pani d'Yves were then dressing upstairs. I gave orders to bring out a light carriage for two persons, since I intended to go myself on horseback. It was three miles to Ustrytsi, so with good weather we had a very pleasant drive before us. Hania came down dressed in black, it is true, but with care and even elegance, for such was my father's desire. I could not take my eyes from her. She looked so beautiful that I felt my heart soften immediately; the desire for resistance and the artificial coldness flew away somewhere beyond the ninth boundary. But my queen passed me in real queenly fashion; she did not even look at me, though I had arrayed myself as best I knew how. I may add in passing that she was somewhat displeased, for really she had no desire to go, though that was not from a wish to annoy me, but from more reasonable causes which I discovered later.

At five o'clock punctually the ladies took their seats in the carriage, and I mounted my horse; we started together. On the road I held aside from Hania, wishing by all means to arrest her attention. In fact, she looked at me once when my horse reared, measured me with calm eye from foot to head, even smiled, I thought, though slightly, which gave me comfort at once; but she turned quickly to Pani d'Yves and began to talk with her in such a way that I could not take part in the conversation.

We came at last to Ustrytsi. Selim had preceded us. Pani Ustrytski was not there. We found at home only Pan Ustrytski, the two governesses, one French, the other German, and Pan Ustrytski's daughters, — the elder Lola, a rather coquettish, pretty, chestnut-haired person of the same age as Hania, and the younger, Marynia, a child yet.

After the first greeting the ladies went at once to the garden for strawberries; but Pan Ustrytski took Selim and me to show us his new weapons, and his new dogs for hunting wild boars; these dogs he had brought at great cost from Vrotslavie. I have mentioned already that Pan Ustrytski was the most passionate hunter in that whole region, and moreover a very honorable and kind man, as active as he was rich. He had only one fault,

which made him annoying to me: he laughed all the
time; every few words he slapped his stomach, repeating,
"A farce, gracious benefactor! What is it called?" For
this reason people spoke of him as "Neighbor Farce," or
"Neighbor What-is-it-called."

Well, Neighbor Farce took us to the kennel, not considering that perhaps we preferred a hundred times to be
with the ladies in the garden. We listened for a while
to his narratives, till at last I remembered something I
had to say to Pani d'Yves, and Selim said right out, —

"All this is very well, lord benefactor. The dogs are
beautiful; but what is to be done if we both have a
greater wish to go to the young ladies?"

"Ah, a farce, gracious benefactor! What is it called?
Well, go then; I will go with you."

And we went. Soon, however, it appeared that I had
nothing to wish for so greatly. Hania, who somehow
kept apart from her companions, did not cease to ignore
me, and occupied herself with Selim perhaps purposely.
It fell to my lot, moreover, to amuse Panna Lola. What
I talked of, how I avoided talking nonsense, how I answered her friendly questions, I know not; for I followed
Selim and Hania incessantly, catching their words, observing their looks and movements. Selim did not notice
me; but Hania did, and lowered her voice designedly, or
looked with a certain coquettishness on her companion,
who permitted himself to be borne away by that flood of
favor. "Wait, Hania," thought I; "thou art acting thus
to torment me; I will treat thee in the same way." And
taking things in that fashion, I turned to Panna Lola.
I have forgotten to say that this young person had a special
weakness for me, and showed it too plainly. I began to
pay court to her. I flattered her, and laughed, though I
had a greater wish to cry; but Lola looked at me, radiant,

with her moist, dark blue eyes, and fell into a romantic frame of mind.

Ah, if she had known how I hated her at that moment! But I was so absorbed in my rôle that I even did something dishonorable. When Panna Lola, in the course of conversation, made some malicious remark about Selim and Hania, though in my soul I was quivering with anger, I did not answer her as I should have done, but merely smiled rather stupidly and passed it over in silence.

We spent about an hour in this way; then lunch was served under a weeping chestnut, which touched the earth with the tips of its branches and formed a green dome above our heads. Then I first learned that Hania's repugnance to visiting Ustrytsi did not regard me; she had better reasons.

The matter stood simply in this way: Pani d'Yves, as a descendant of an ancient noble French house, and, besides, better educated than other governesses, thought herself somewhat superior to the French woman at Ustrytsi, but especially superior to the German; while those two in their turn thought themselves better than Hania, because her grandfather had been a servant. The wellbred Pani d' Yves did not let them know her feelings, but they slighted Hania even to rudeness. Those were common feminine quarrels and ambitions; still I could not permit my dear Hania, who alone was worth a hundred times more than all Ustrytsi, to be their victim. Hania endured the slight with tact and sweetness which did honor to her character, but still such treatment was bitter to her. Had Pani Ustrytski been present, nothing of the kind would have happened, but at that moment both governesses took advantage of the favorable occasion. As soon as Selim sat near Hania, whispers and jests began, in which even Panna

Lola took some part, because she was jealous of Hania's beauty. I rebuffed those taunts a number of times sharply, perhaps even too sharply; but soon Selim took my place in spite of me. I saw a flash of anger shoot across his brows; but he bethought himself quickly and turned a calm, sneering glance on the governesses. Incisive, witty, and eloquent as few persons at his age, he soon confused them so much that they knew not where to take refuge. Pani d'Yves, with her dignity, aided him, and also I, who would have driven out the two foreign women. Panna Lola, not wishing to offend me, came over also to our side, and, though insincerely, showed Hania a kindness twofold greater than usual. In a word, our victory was perfect, but unfortunately, and to my great vexation, the chief merit this time fell also to Selim. Hania, who, notwithstanding all her tact, hardly restrained tears from suffusing her eyes, looked at Selim as her savior, with thankfulness and homage. So when we rose from the table and began to walk again through the garden in couples, I saw her incline toward Selim, and heard her whisper, —

"Pan Selim! I am very — "

Then she stopped suddenly, for she was afraid of weeping; emotion was uppermost in spite of her.

"Panna Hania, do not mention that. Do not mind it; do not be troubled."

"You see how difficult it is for me to speak of this matter, but I wished to thank you."

"For what, Panna Hania? For what? I cannot endure tears in your eyes. For you I would gladly — "

Now in his turn he did not finish, for he could not find the expression; and perhaps he noticed in season that he had let the feelings with which his breast was filled go too far, so he turned away his face not to let his emotion be seen, and was silent.

Hania looked at him with eyes bright from tears, and I then did not ask what had happened.

I loved Hania with all the power of a youthful soul; I deified her; I loved her with the love which is only in heaven. I loved her form, her eyes, every hair of her head, the sound of her words. I loved every bit of her dress. I loved the air which she breathed; that love pervaded me through and through, and was not only in my heart, but in my whole being. I lived only in her and through her; that love flowed in me as my blood; it radiated from me as the warmth of my body. For others something besides love might exist; for me the whole world existed in love; there was nothing beyond it. To the world I was blind, deaf, and indifferent, for my reason and senses were held by that single feeling. I felt that I was blazing like a lighted torch, that that flame was devouring me, that I was dying. What was that love? A mighty voice, a mighty calling of one soul to another, "My deified, my sacred one, my love, hear me!" I did not inquire what had happened, for I understood that not to me, not to me, was Hania answering that heart question. In the midst of indifferent people, a man thirsting for love wanders as in a forest, and he shouts and calls as in a forest, waiting to learn if some voice of sympathy will answer him; so now I did not ask any longer what had happened, for beside my own love and my own useless shouting, I felt and overheard two voices in sympathy, the voices of Selim and Hania. They were calling to each other mutually with the voices of hearts; they were calling unfortunately for me, and they themselves did not know that. One was to the other as a forest echo, and one followed the other as the echo follows the voice. And what could I do against this necessity which they could call happiness, but which I must call misfortune? What could avail against that order of nature, against that fatal logic of things? How win Hania's heart when some irresistible power was impelling it in another direction?

I separated from the company and sat on a bench of the garden, and thoughts like these were sounding in my head, like flocks of frightened birds. A madness of despair and suffering seized me. I felt that in the midst of my family, in the midst of well-wishing hearts, I was lonely. To me the whole world seemed a desert, seemed orphaned; the heaven above me was so indifferent to the wrong done by people that in spite of me one thought beyond others mastered me, swallowed everything, and covered me with its gloomy peace. The name of it was death. And then, an escape from that vicious circle, an end to sufferings, an end of all that sad comedy, a cutting of all the painful knots binding the soul, and repose after torture, — ah! that repose, for which I was so thirsty, that dark repose, that repose of nothingness, but calm and eternal.

I was one exhausted by tears, by suffering and drowsiness. Oh, to sleep! to sleep at any price, even at the price of life. Then from the calm immense blue of heaven to which my former faith of childhood had fled, one thought flew to me like a bird and sat in my brain. That thought was in the brief words: but if —

That was a new circle in which I was involved by the force of implacable necessity. Oh, I suffered greatly, but there from the neighboring alley joyous words came to me, or low, half-audible whispers of conversation. Around me was the odor of flowers; on the trees twittering birds were settling themselves to rest; above me hung the calm sky, ruddy with the evening twilight. All was peaceful, all happy; amidst that bloom of life, in pain and with set teeth, I alone desired to die. Suddenly I trembled; before me rustled the dress of a woman.

I looked; it was Panna Lola. She was calm and mild; she looked at me with sympathy, and perhaps with more than sympathy. Amidst the light of evening and the shadows cast by the trees, she seemed pale; her abundant tresses, unwound as if by chance, fell upon her shoulders.

At that moment I did not feel any hatred toward her. "Oh, thou single compassionate soul!" thought I, "dost thou come to console me?"

"Pan Henryk, you are somehow sad, perhaps suffering?"

"Oh, yes, suffering," cried I, with an outburst; and seizing her hand I placed it against my burning forehead, then I kissed it quickly and ran off.

"Pan Henryk!" cried she after me, in a low voice.

But at that moment, at the crossing of the paths, appeared Selim and Hania. Both had seen my outburst, had seen me kiss and press Lola's hand to my forehead, so smiling, they exchanged glances, as if saying to each other, "We understand what that means."

But soon it was time to go home. Immediately beyond the gate Selim's road lay in another direction, but I was afraid that he might wish to conduct us. I mounted in haste, and said aloud that it was late, and time for Selim and me. When parting, I received from Panna Lola a wonderfully warm pressure of the hand, to which I gave no response.

Selim turned immediately beyond the gate; for the first time he kissed Hania's hand for good-night, and she did not forbid.

She ceased to ignore me. She was in too mild a mood to remember the morning anger, but I interpreted that mood of mind in the worst sense possible. Pani d'Yves fell asleep after a few moments, and began to nod in all directions. I looked at Hania. She was not asleep; her eyes, opened widely, were bright as if from happiness. She did not break the silence; she was evidently too much occupied with her own thoughts. Only when near the house did she look at me, and, seeing that I was so meditative, she asked, —

"Of what are you thinking? Is it of Lola?"

I did not answer a word; I only gritted my teeth. Tear, tear me, if that gives thee pleasure; from me thou wilt not get one groan.

Hania in reality had not even dreamed of tearing me. She asked, for she had a right to ask. Astonished at my silence, she repeated the question. Again I gave no answer. She thought, therefore, that it was pouting continued since morning, and so was silent.

CHAPTER VIII.

ONE morning, some days later, the first ruddy light of early dawn came in through a heart cut in the window-shutter, and roused me from sleep. Soon after, some one knocked on the shutter; and in the rosy opening appeared, not the face of Mitskewich's Zosia, who in a similar manner roused Tadeush, nor of my Hania either, but the mustached face of Vah, the forester, and his deep voice cried, —

"Panich!"

"What?"

"Wolves are following a wolf bitch in the Pohorovy woods. Shall we go to lure them?"

"Right away!"

I dressed, took my gun and hunter's knife, and went out. Vah was all wet from the morning dew; on his shoulder was a single-barrelled gun, long and rusty, but he never missed aim with this piece. It was early; the sun had not risen yet. People had not gone to their work, nor cattle to pasture. The sky was only colored blue, rosy and golden on the east; on the west it was sombre. The old man hurried in his fashion.

"I have a horse and cart. Let us ride to the Pits," said he.

We took our seats and drove on. Just beyond the granaries a hare, or rabbit, sprang out of the oats, ran across the road and into the meadow, marking with a darker trace the surface silvered over by dew.

"A cat crosses the road!" said the forester; "a charm on a dog!" Then added: "It is late already. The earth will soon get a shadow."

This meant that the sun would rise before long, for with the light of dawn bodies cast no shadow.

"But is it bad hunting when there are shadows?" asked I.

"With long shadows it is passable, but with short ones useless work."

In hunter's language this meant that the later the hour, the worse the hunting, for, as is known, the nearer midday the shorter the shadows.

"Where shall we begin?" asked I.

"At the Pits in the Pohorovy woods."

The Pohorovy woods were a part of the forest which was very dense, — that part where "the Pits" were; that is, holes made by the roots of old trees thrown down by storms.

"And do you think that luring will succeed?"

"I will begin to play as a wolf bitch, perhaps some wolf will come."

"But he may not."

"Ei! he will come."

When we reached Vah's cottage we left the horse and cart, and went forward on foot. After half an hour's walk, when the sun had begun to rise, we sat down in a pit.

Round about us was a thicket of impenetrable small growth; only here and there were enormous trees. The pit was so deep that even our heads were concealed in it.

"Now back to back!" muttered Vah.

We sat back to back; above the surface of the ground appeared only the crowns of our heads and the gun-barrels.

"Listen!" said Vah. "I will play."

Putting two fingers in his mouth and modulating his drawling voice with them, he began to imitate a wolf bitch; that is, to howl like a she-wolf when she entices he-wolves.

"Listen!"

And he placed his ear to the ground.

I heard nothing, but Vah took his face from the earth and whispered, —

"Oh, there is sport, but far away, two miles."

Then he waited a quarter of an hour; again he put his fingers to his mouth and howled. The doleful, ominous sound passed through the thicket; and far, far away it flew over the damp earth, rebounding from pine to pine. Vah put his ear to the ground again.

"They are playing, but not farther than a mile away."

Indeed, I heard then, as it were a distant echo of howling, very far away yet, barely audible.

"Where will it come out?" asked I.

"On you, Panich."

Vah howled a third time; a howling answered quite near now. I grasped the gun more firmly, and we held the breath in our breasts. The silence was absolute; a breeze merely shook from hazel-nut bushes dewdrops, which fell pattering on the leaves. From afar, from the other edge of the forest, came the calling of wood grouse.

Suddenly, some three hundred yards distant, something shook in the forest. The juniper bushes moved quickly, and from the midst of the dark needle-like leaves emerged a triangular head, gray, with pointed ears and red eyes. I could not shoot, for the head was too far away, so I waited patiently, though with beating heart. Soon the whole beast came out of the junipers, and with a few short springs ran up toward the pit, smelling carefully on every side. At one hundred and fifty yards the wolf halted and listened, as if foreboding something. I saw that he would not come nearer, and drew the trigger.

The report of the gun was mingled with the painful cry of the wolf. I sprang out of the pit, Vah after me, but we did not find the wolf at the place. Vah, however, examined the spot carefully where the dew was wiped away on the ground, and said, —

"He colors!"

Indeed, there were traces of blood on the grass.

"You haven't missed, though far. He is coloring. Oh, he is coloring! We must follow."

And so we went. Here and there we came upon trampled grass and more traces of blood. The wounded wolf rested from time to time; that was evident. Meanwhile an hour passed in woods and thickets, then a second. The sun was now high; we had gone over an immense piece of road without finding a thing except traces, which at times disappeared altogether. Then we came to the corner of the forest; traces continued for about two versts more through a field toward the pond, and were lost at last in swampy ground covered with reeds and sweet flag. It was impossible to go farther without a dog.

"He will stay there; I shall find him to-morrow," said Vah, and we turned toward home.

Soon I ceased to think of Vah's wolf and the result of the hunt, which was rather unfortunate. I returned to my usual circle of suffering. When we were approaching the forest, a hare sprang up almost from under my feet; instead of shooting it, I trembled, as if roused from sleep.

"Ah!" cried Vah, in indignation, "I would shoot my own brother if he jumped up in that way."

I only laughed and went on in silence. When crossing the so-called "forest road" which led to the highway of Horeli, I saw fresh tracks of a horse wearing shoes.

"Do you know, Vah, what tracks these are?"

"It seems to me that they are made by the young Panich from Horeli, on his way to the mansion."

"Then I will go to the mansion. Farewell, Vah."

Vah begged me timidly to go to his cottage, which was not far, to refresh myself a little. I saw that in case of refusal I should cause him great pain; still I refused, but promised to come next morning. I did not wish to leave Selim and Hania together long without me.

During the five days which had passed since the visit to Ustrytsi Selim had come almost daily. But I guarded them like the eye in my head, and to-day for the first time came the chance that they could be alone. "Now," thought I, "it will come to a confession between them," and I felt that I was growing as pale as he who loses hope of hope.

I feared this as a misfortune, an unavoidable sentence of death, which we know to be coming, but which we delay as long as possible.

On reaching home, I met Father Ludvik in front of the mansion, with a bag on his head, and a wire net over his face; he was going to the beehives.

"Is Selim here, Father Ludvik?" asked I.

"He is; he came about an hour and a half ago."

"Where shall I find him?"

"He went to the pond with Hania and Evunia."

I ran to the garden quickly, then to the brink of the pond where the boats were. One of the largest was missing. I looked out over the pond, but at first could see nothing. I guessed that Selim must have turned to the right toward the alders; in this way the boat and those in it were concealed by the reeds on the bank. I seized an oar, sprang into a one-seated boat, pushed out quietly, kept among the reeds, did not leave them. There I could see without being visible.

In fact, I soon saw them. On a broad part of the pond, free of reeds, was a motionless boat, the oars hanging. At one end was sitting my little sister, Evunia, turned away from Hania and Selim; at the other end were the two. Evunia, bending over the boat, struck the water joyously with her little hands, and was occupied entirely with this amusement; but Selim and Hania, almost leaning against each other, seemed absorbed in conversation. Not the least breath of wind wrinkled the transparent blue surface; the boat, Hania, Evunia, and Selim were reflected in it as in a mirror, calm, motionless.

That was a very beautiful picture, perhaps, but at sight of it the blood rushed to my head; I understood everything. They had taken Evunia, for the child could not be in their way or understand their confessions. They took her for appearance' sake. "All is over," thought I. "All is over!" sounded the reeds. "All is over!" blurted out the ripple, striking the side of my boat; and it grew dark in my eyes. I felt cold and hot. I felt that pallor was covering my face. "Thou hast lost Hania! thou hast lost her!" cried voices above me and in me. Then I heard, as it were, the same voices crying, "Jesus, Mary!" and then these continued, "Push up nearer; hide in the reeds; thou wilt see more!" I obeyed, and pushed on with the boat as silently as a cat. But at that distance I could not hear conversation; I only saw more distinctly that they were sitting side by side on one bench, not holding each other's hands, but Selim was turned toward Hania. It seemed to me after a while that he was kneeling before her, but it only seemed so. He was turned toward her and was looking at her entreatingly; she was not looking at him, but seemed to glance on every side and unquietly; then she raised her eyes. I saw that she was confused; I saw that he was begging for something. I saw finally that he placed his palms together before her, that she turned her head and eyes toward him slowly, that she began to lean toward him, but suddenly recovered herself and pushed back toward the edge of the boat. Then he seized her hand, as though fearing that she might fall into the water. I saw that he did not let the hand go; after that I saw nothing. I let the oar drop, and I fell on the bottom of the boat, for a cloud covered my eyes. "Save! save, O God!" cried I, in spirit; "here they are killing a man!" I felt that breath lacked me. Oh, how I loved her, and how unhappy I was! Lying on the bottom of the boat and tearing my clothing with rage, I felt all the helplessness of that rage. Yes; I was powerless, powerless as an athlete with bound hands, for what could I do? I might kill Selim; I might drive my boat against theirs and sink both in the water; but from Hania's heart I could not tear her love for Selim and take it for myself alone,—that was impossible.

Ah, that feeling of powerless rage, that conviction that there is no help, seemed almost worse at that moment than any other. I had always been ashamed to cry even before myself. If pain pressed tears from my eyes by force, pride kept them back with force not inferior. But now at last burst forth the helpless rage which was rending my breast; and in my loneliness, in presence of that boat with the loving pair reflected in the water, in presence of that calm sky and those reeds rustling plaintively above my head, and in my sadness and misfortune, I burst into measureless sobbing, into one great wave of tears, and, lying on my back with hands clasped above my head, I almost bellowed with mighty, unspeakable sorrow.

Then I grew weak. A numbness came over me. My thinking power almost ceased to act; I felt cold at the points of my fingers and toes. I grew weaker and weaker. I used the remnant of my thought. It seemed that death and a great and icy calm were drawing near. It seemed that that gloomy queen of the grave was taking me into her possession, so I greeted her with a calm, glassy eye. "It is over," thought I, and a great weight, as it were, fell from my breast.

But it was not over. How long I lay thus on the bottom of the boat, I could not tell. Light, downy clouds were moving along the vault of heaven. Lapwings and storks, calling sadly, flew by in succession. The sun had risen high in the heavens and was burning with heat. The breeze had gone down; the motionless reeds had ceased to rustle. I woke, as if from sleep, and looked around. The boat with Hania and Selim was no longer before me. The silence, repose, and delight which reigned in all nature were in wonderful contrast to the torpor in which I had wakened a moment before. Round about all was calm and smiling. Dark sapphire water-grasshoppers were sitting on the edges of the boat and on the leaves of water-lilies which were as flat as shields;

little gray birds were swinging on the reeds, twittering sweetly; here and there buzzed an industrious bee that had wandered in over the water; sometimes from the sweet flag wild ducks were heard; teal escorted their young to the plain of water. Before my eyes, the kingdoms and commonwealths of birds drew aside the curtains concealing their daily life; but I looked at nothing. My torpor had not passed. The day was hot; I felt an unendurable headache. Bending over the boat, I seized water with my hands and drank it with parched lips. That brought back some strength to me. Taking the oar, I moved among reeds toward the landing-place. How late it was! and at home they must have inquired for me.

On the road I tried to calm myself. "If Selim and Hania have confessed that they love each other," thought I, "it may be better that all is passed. At least, the cursed days of uncertainty are over." Misfortune had raised its visor and stood before me with clear face. I knew it, and must struggle with it. Wonderful thing! this thought began to have for me a certain painful charm. But still I was uncertain, and resolved to examine Evunia adroitly, at least in as far as was possible.

I was at home for dinner. I greeted Selim coldly, and sat down at the table in silence. My father looked at me and asked, —

"What is the matter with thee, — art sick?"

"No; I am well, but weary. I rose at three in the morning."

"What for?"

"I went with Vah to hunt wolves. I shot one. Later on I lay down to sleep, and my head aches somewhat."

"But look in the glass, and see what a face thou hast."

Hania stopped eating for a while, and looked at me carefully.

"Perhaps yesterday's visit to Ustrytsi has acted on you, Pan Henryk," said she.

I looked her straight in the eyes and inquired almost sharply,—

"What dost thou mean by that?"

Hania was confused and began to explain something indistinctly. Selim came to her aid,—

"But that is very natural. Whoever is in love grows thin."

I looked now at Hania, now at Selim, and replied slowly, putting a sharp accent on each syllable,—

"I do not see that ye are growing thin, either thou or Hania."

A scarlet flush covered the faces of both. A moment of very awkward silence followed. I myself was uncertain whether I had not gone too far, but fortunately my father had not heard what was said. The priest took it as the usual chaffing of young people.

"Oh, that is a wasp with a sting!" cried he, taking snuff. "He has given it to you. See now, don't tackle him."

O Lord, how little that triumph comforted me, and how gladly I would have transferred it to Selim!

After dinner, in passing through the drawing-room, I looked in the glass. Really, I looked like Piotrovin.[1] It was blue under my eyes; my face was sunk. It seemed to me that I had grown wonderfully ugly, but that was all one to me then. I went to find Evunia. Both my little sisters had dined earlier than we, and were in the garden, where a gymnasium for children had been fixed. Evunia was sitting carelessly on a wooden platform hung by four cords to the crossbeam of a swing. While sitting there, she was talking to herself, shaking the locks of her

---

[1] A man raised from the dead by Saint Stanislav.

golden head from time to time and swinging her feet.
When she saw me she laughed and stretched forth her
little hands. I took her in my arms and went down the
alley with her. Then I sat on a bench, and, putting
Enunia before me, asked, —

"What has Evunia been doing to-day?"

"Evunia went to walk with her husband and Hania,"
answered the little girl, boastingly.

Evunia called Selim her husband.

"And was Evunia polite?"

"She was."

"Ah, that is well, for polite children always listen to
what older people say, and remember that they have
something to learn. But does Evunia remember what
Selim said to Hania?"

"I have forgotten."

"Ei, maybe Evunia remembers a little?"

"I have forgotten."

"Thou art not polite! Let Evunia remember right off,
or I shall not love Evunia."

The little girl began to rub one eye with her fist; and
with the other, which was full of tears, she looked at me
from under her brow, and frowning, as if to cry, her lips
already quivering and in the form of a horseshoe, she
said, —

"I have forgotten."

What could the poor little thing answer? Indeed,
I seemed to myself idiotic, and immediately was ashamed
of having spoken with deceitful tongue to that innocent
little angel, — to ask one thing, wishing to learn another.
Besides Evunia was the pet of the whole house, and my
pet, so I did not wish to torment her any further. I
kissed her, stroked her hair, and let her go. The little
girl ran at once to the swing, and I walked off as wise as

before, but still with the conviction in my heart that a confession had passed between Selim and Hania.

Toward evening Selim said to me, —

"I shall not see thee for a week; I am going on a journey."

"Where?" asked I, with indifference.

"My father commands me to visit his brother in Shumna. I must stay there about a week."

I looked at Hania. That information called out no impression on her face. Evidently Selim had told her of the visit already.

She smiled, raised her eyes from her work, looked at Selim somewhat cunningly, somewhat perversely, and asked, —

"But are you glad to go there?"

"As glad as a mastiff to go to a chain," answered he, quickly; but he restrained himself in time, and seeing that Pani d'Yves, who could not endure anything trivial, was making a wry face, he added, —

"I beg pardon for the expression. I love my uncle; but you see it is pleasanter here for me, near Pani d'Yves." And speaking thus, he cast a sentimental glance at Pani d'Yves, which roused laughter in all, not excluding Pani d'Yves herself, who, though she was easily offended, had a special weakness for Selim. She took him gently by the ear and said with a kindly smile, —

"Young man, I might be thy mother."

Selim kissed her hand, and there was concord; but I thought to myself, what a difference between me and that Selim! If I had Hania's affection, I should merely dream and look toward the sky. What place should I have for jokes! but he laughs, jokes, is joyous as never before. Even when radiant with happiness, he was always joyful. Just before going he said to me, —

"Dost know what I will say? Come with me."

"I will not; I have not the least intention."

The cold tone of the answer struck Selim somewhat.

"Thou hast become strange," said he. "I do not know thee for some time — but —"

"Finish."

"But everything is forgiven those who are in love."

"Unless those who cross our path," answered I, with the voice of the stone Comandore.

Selim struck me with a glance as sharp as lightning, and went to the bottom of my soul.

"What dost thou say?"

"I say that I will not go, and, secondly, that one does not forgive everything!"

Had it not been that all were present at this conversation, Selim certainly would have made the whole question clear at once. But I did not wish to make it clear till I had more positive proof. I saw, however, that my last words had disquieted Selim and alarmed Hania. He loitered yet awhile, putting off his departure under trifling pretexts, and then, choosing the moment, said to me in a low voice, —

"Take a horse and conduct me. I wish to speak to thee."

"Another time," answered I, aloud. "To-day I feel somewhat weak."

CHAPTER IX.

SELIM went really to his uncle and stayed there, not a week, but ten days. For us those days passed in gloom. Hania seemed to avoid me and look on me with concealed fear. I had no intention indeed to speak with her sincerely about anything, for pride tied the words on my lips; and she, I know not why, so arranged affairs that we were never alone for an instant. At last she grew sad, looked wretched and thin. Noting this sadness, I trembled and thought, "Indeed, this is not the passing caprice of a girl; it is a genuine, deep feeling, unfortunately."

I was irritable, gloomy, and sad. In vain did my father, the priest, and Pani d'Yves inquire what the matter was. Was I sick? I answered in the negative; their solicitude simply annoyed me. I passed whole days alone, on horseback; sometimes I was in the woods, sometimes among the reeds in a boat. I lived like a savage. Once I spent a whole night in a forest, with a gun and a dog, before a fire which I had kindled purposely. Sometimes I spent half a day with our shepherd, who was a doctor, and grown wild through continual solitude; he was eternally collecting herbs and testing their properties. This man initiated me into a fantastic world of spells and superstitions.

But would any one believe it, there were moments when I grieved for Selim and my "circles of suffering" as I called them.

Once the idea came to me of visiting Mirza Davidovich in Horeli. The old man was captivated by this, that I visited him for his own sake, and received me with open arms. But I had come with another intent. I wished to look at those eyes in the portrait of Sobieski's terrible colonel of light horse. And when I saw those evil eyes turning everywhere after a man, I remembered my own ancestors, whose counterfeits hung at home in the drawing-room; they were equally stern and iron-like.

My mind, under the influence of such impressions, came to a condition of wonderful exaltation. Loneliness.

the silence of night, life with nature, — all these should have acted on me with soothing effect; but within me I carried, as it were, a poisoned arrow. At times I gave myself up to dreams, which made that condition still worse. More than once, while lying in some remote corner of a pine wood, or in a boat among reeds, I imagined that I was in Hania's apartment at her feet; that I was kissing her hands, her feet, her dress; that I was calling her by the most fondling names, and she, placing her hands on my heated forehead, was saying: "Thou hast suffered enough; let us forget everything! It was a bitter dream. I love thee, Henryk." But then came the awakening and the dull reality, — that future of mine, gloomy as a day of clouds, always without her, to the end of life without her; this future seemed to me all the more terrible. I grew misanthropic, avoided people, even my father, the priest, and Pani d'Yves. Kazio, with his talkativeness of a boy, his curiosity, his eternal laughter and endless tricks, disgusted me to the utmost.

And still those honest people tried to distract me, and suffered in secret over my condition, not knowing how to explain it. Hania, whether she divined something or not, — for she had strong reason to suppose that I was in love with Lola Ustrytski, — did what she could to console me. But I was so harsh even toward her that she could not free herself of a certain dread when talking to me. My father himself, usually severe and unsparing, strove to distract me, turn my attention to something, and meanwhile to test me. More than once, he began conversations which, as he judged, should be of interest. One day after dinner we went out in front of the mansion.

"Does not a certain thing strike thee at times?" asked he, looking at me inquiringly; "I wanted to ask thee about it this good while, — does it not strike thee that Selim is circling a little too much about Hania?"

Judging the case simply, I should have grown confused and let myself be caught, as they say, in the very act. But I was in such a state of mind that I did not betray by one quiver the impression which my father's words made on me, and replied calmly, —

"No; I know that he is not."

It wounded me that my father took part in those questions. I considered that, since the affair touched me alone, I alone should decide it.

"Wilt thou guarantee that?" asked my father.

"I will. Selim is in love with a schoolgirl in Warsaw."

"I say this, for thou art Hania's guardian, and 't is thy duty to watch over her."

I knew that my honest father said this to rouse my ambition, occupy me with something, and snatch my thoughts from that gloomy circle in which I seemed to be turning; but I answered, as if in perverseness, indifferently and gloomily, —

"What sort of guardian am I? Thou wert not here, so old Mikolai left her to me, but I am not the real guardian."

My father frowned; seeing, however, that in this way he could not bring me to terms, he chose another. He smiled under his gray mustache, half closed one eye, in the fashion of a soldier, took me gently by the ear, and asked, as if joking, —

"But has Hania, perhaps, turned thine own head? Speak, my boy."

"Hania? Not in the least. That would amuse thee."

I lied as if possessed; but it passed off more smoothly than I had expected.

"Then has not Lola Ustrytski? Hei?"

"Lola Ustrytski, a coquette!"

My father became impatient.

"Then what the devil is it? If thou art not in love, go as a soldier to the first muster."

"Do I know what the matter is? Nothing is the matter with me."

But I was tormented and made more impatient by questions which in their anxiety neither my father nor the priest spared, nor even Pani d'Yves. At last relations with them became disagreeable. I was carried away by everything and enraged at every trifle. Father Ludvik saw in this certain traits of a despotic character coming to the surface with age, and looking at my father significantly he laughed and said, —

"Topknot chickens by blood!"

But even he lost patience sometimes. Between my father and me there were frequently very disagreeable passages. Once at dinner during a dispute about nobility and democracy I so forgot myself as to declare that I should prefer a hundred times not to be born a noble. My father ordered me to leave the room. The women fell to crying because of this, and the whole house was embittered for two days.

As to me, I was neither an aristocrat nor a democrat; I was simply in love and unhappy. There was no place in me whatever for principles, theories, or social convictions; and if I fought in the name of some against others, I did so only through vexation, to annoy it is unknown whom or why, just as I began religious disputes with Father Ludvik to annoy him. These disputes ended with slamming of doors. In short, I poisoned not the existence of myself only, but that of the whole house; and when after ten days Selim returned, a stone, as it were, fell from every one's breast. When he came I was not at home, for I was racing about through the neighborhood on horseback. I returned only toward evening and went straight to the farm buildings, where a stable-boy said, while taking my horse, —

"The Panich has come from Horeli."

At that moment Kazio came up and repeated the same news.

"I know that already," answered I, harshly. "Where is Selim now?"

"In the garden with Hania, I think. I will go and look for him."

We both went to the garden, but Kazio ran ahead. I, not hurrying purposely with the greeting, had not gone fifty steps when, at the bend of the alley, I saw Kazio hastening back.

Kazio, who was a great rogue and a joker, began from afar to make gestures and grimaces like a monkey. His face was red; he held his finger to his mouth and laughed, stifling laughter at the same time. When he came up to me he called in a low voice, —

"Henryk! He! he! he! Tsss!"

"What art thou doing?" asked I, in ill-humor.

"Tss! as I love mamma! he! he! Selim is kneeling before Hania in the hop arbor. As I love mamma!"

I caught him immediately by the arms and drove my fingers into them.

"Be silent! Stay here! Not a word to anybody, dost understand? Stay here! I will go myself; but be silent, not a word before any one, if thy life is dear to thee."

Kazio, who from the beginning had considered the whole affair on the humorous side, seeing the corpse-like pallor that covered my face, was evidently frightened, and stood on the spot with open mouth; but I ran on, as if mad, toward the arbor.

Crawling forward quickly and silently as a serpent, between the barberry bushes which surrounded the arbor, I worked myself up to the very wall; the wall was made of small short bits of sticks, so I could hear and see everything. The repulsive rôle of a listener did not seem repulsive at all to me. I pushed aside the leaves very delicately and thrust forward my ear.

"There is some one near by!" said the low, suppressed whisper of Hania.

"No; only leaves moving on the branches," answered Selim.

I looked at them through the green veil of the leaves. Selim was not kneeling near Hania now; he was sitting at her side on a low bench. She was as pale as linen; her eyes were closed, her head inclined and resting on his shoulder. He had encircled her waist with his arm, and drawn her toward him with love and delight.

"I love, Hania! I love! I love!" repeated he, whispering passionately; and inclining his head he sought her lips with his. She drew back, as if warding off the kiss, but still their lips met and remained joined in that manner long, long; it seemed to me whole ages.

And then I thought that all which they had wished to say to each other they said in that kiss. Some sort of shame stopped their words They had daring enough for kisses, but not enough for speech. A deathlike silence reigned, and amid that silence there came to me merely their quick and passionate breathing.

I seized the wooden grating of the arbor with my hands, and feared lest I might crush it into bits with that convulsive pressure. It grew dark in my eyes; I felt a turning of the head; the earth flew somewhere from under me into a bottomless pit. But even at the price of my life I wished to hear what they were saying; hence I mastered myself again, and catching the air with parched lips, with forehead pressed to the grating, I listened, counting every breath which they drew.

Silence continued some time yet. At last Hania began in a whisper, —

"Enough, enough! I dare not look you in the eyes. Let us leave this."

And turning her head aside, she tried to tear herself out of his arms.

"Oh, Hania! what is taking place in me? I am so happy!" cried Selim.

"Let us go from here. Some one will come."

Selim sprang up with gleaming eyes and distended nostrils.

"Let the whole world come," said he. "I love, and I will say so in the eyes of all people. I know not how this happened. I struggled with myself; I suffered, for it seemed to me that Henryk loved thee, and thou him. But now I care for nothing. Thou lovest me, and so it is a question of thy happiness. Oh, Hania! Hania!"

And here again was the sound of a kiss; and then Hania began to speak in a soft and, as it were, weakened voice, —

"I believe, I believe, Selim; but I have many things to tell thee. They want to send me abroad to the old lady, I think. Yesterday Pani d'Yves spoke of this to Henryk's father. Pani d'Yves thinks that I am the cause of Pan Henryk's strange conduct. She thinks that he is in love with me. I myself do not know but that is the case. There are times when it seems to me that he is. I do not understand him. I fear him. I feel that he will hinder us, that he will separate us; but I — "

And she finished in a barely audible voice, —

"I love, much, much."

"Listen, Hania. No earthly power shall separate us.

Should Henryk forbid me to come here, I shall write to thee. I have some one who will always bring a letter. I shall come myself too. By the side of the pond after dark. Go always to the garden. But thou wilt not go abroad. If they wish to send thee, I will not permit it, as God is in heaven. Do not say such things, Hania, or I shall go mad. Oh, my beloved, my beloved!"

Seizing her hands, he pressed them passionately to his lips. She sprang up quickly from the bench.

"I hear voices: they are coming," cried she, with fear.

Both went out, though no one was coming and no one came. The evening rays of the sun cast gleams of gold on them, but to me those gleams seemed as red as blood. I too dragged on slowly toward the house. Just at the turning of the alley I met Kazio, who was on the watch.

"They have gone. I saw them," whispered he. "Tell me what I am to do?"

"Shoot him in the head!" cried I, with an outburst.

Kazio flushed like a rose, and his eyes gave out phosphoric light.

"Very good!" said he.

"Stop! Don't be a fool! Do nothing. Meddle in nothing, and on thy honor, Kazio, be silent. Leave everything to me. When thou art needed, I will tell thee; but not a word before any one."

"I'll not even squeak though they kill me."

We went on awhile in silence. Kazio, penetrated with the importance of the question and sniffing some kind of terrible event, toward which his heart was rushing, looked at me with sparkling eyes; then he said, —

"Henryk?"

"What?"

We both whispered, though no one was listening.

"Wilt thou fight with Selim?"

"I know not. Perhaps."

Kazio stopped and suddenly threw his arms around my neck.

"Henryk! my golden brother! My heart! My only one! if thou wish to fight, let me do it. I will manage him. Let me try. Let me, Henryk; let me!"

Kazio was simply dreaming of deeds of knighthood, but I felt the brother in him as never before; therefore I gathered him to my breast with all my strength and said, —

"No, Kazio! I know nothing yet, and, besides, he would not accept thee. I know nothing yet of what will happen. Meanwhile give directions to saddle the horse in good season. I will go in advance, meet him on the road, and speak to him. Meanwhile watch both; but don't let them suspect that thou knowest anything. Have the horse saddled."

"Wilt thou take arms?"

"Phe! Kazio; he has none. No; I only wish to speak with him. Be calm, and go at once to the stable."

Kazio sprang away that moment according to my request. I returned slowly to the house. I was like a man struck on the head with the back of an axe. I have the right to say that I knew not what to do; I knew not how to act. I simply wished to shout.

Until I was perfectly certain that I had lost Hania's heart, I was anxious to be certain. I judged that in every case a stone would then fall from my heart: now misfortune had raised its visor. I was looking at its cold, icy face and stony eyes; but a new uncertainty was born in my heart, — not uncertainty as to my misfortune, but one a hundred times worse, the feeling of my own helplessness, the uncertainty as to how I was to struggle with that feeling.

My heart was filled with gall, bitterness, and rage.
Voices of self-denial, voices of devotion, which at other
times often spoke in my soul, saying, "Renounce Hania
for the sake of her happiness; it is thy duty to think of
that first of all; sacrifice thyself!" Those voices were
perfectly dumb now. The angel of silent sadness, the
angel of devotion and tears, had flown far away from me.
I felt like a worm which had been trampled, but of
which people had forgotten that it possessed a sting. I
had let myself so far be hunted by misfortune as a wolf
by a dog; but, too much despised and pressed upon, I had
begun like a wolf to show my teeth. A new active
power named revenge rose in my heart. I began to feel
a species of hatred for Selim and Hania. "I will lose
life," thought I; "I will lose everything that may be lost
in this world; but I will not permit those two to be
happy." Penetrated by this thought, I grasped it as a
sentenced man grasps a crucifix. I had found a reason
for life; the horizon became bright before me. I drew
in a full breath, broadly and freely, as never before.
My thoughts, which had been scattered and stormed
away, arranged themselves in order and were turned with
all force in one direction ominous for Selim and Hania.
When I reached the house, I was almost calm, and cool.
In the hall were sitting Pani d'Yves, Father Ludvik,
Hania, Selim, and Kazio, who had just returned from the
stable and did not move one step from the two.

"Is there a horse for me?" asked I of Kazio.

"Yes."

"Wilt thou go a part of the way with me?" put in
Selim.

"Yes; I can. I will go to the stacks to see if any
damage is done. Kazio, let me have thy place."

Kazio yielded the place, and I sat down near Selim and

Hania, on a sofa under the window. Involuntarily I remembered how we had sat there immediately after Mikolai's death, when Selim told the Crimean tale about Sultan Harun and the soothsaying Lala. But at that time Hania, still small and with eyes red from weeping, had rested her golden head on my breast and fallen asleep; now that same Hania, taking advantage of the darkness descending into the room, was pressing Selim's hand secretly. In that time the sweet feeling of friendship had joined us all three; now love and hatred were soon to enter into combat. But all was calm apparently: the lovers were smiling at each other; I was more gladsome than usual. No one suspected what kind of gladsomeness that was.

Soon Pani d'Yves begged Selim to play something. He rose, sat at the piano, and began to play Chopin's mazurka. I remained alone for a time on the sofa with Hania. I noticed that she was gazing at Selim as at a rainbow, that she was flying away into the region of fancies on the wings of music, and I determined to bring her back to the earth.

"How many gifts that Selim has, has he not, Hania? He plays and sings."

"Oh, it is true!" said she.

"And, besides, what a beautiful face! Just look at him now."

Hania followed the direction of my eyes. Selim was sitting in the shade; but his head was illuminated by the last light of the evening, and in those gleams he seemed inspired, with his uplifted eyes, — and he was at that moment inspired.

"How beautiful he is, Hania, is he not?" repeated I.

"Are you very fond of him?"

"He cares nothing for my feelings, but women love him. Ah, how that Yozia loved him!"

Alarm was depicted on Hania's smooth forehead.

"And he?" inquired she.

"Ei! he loves one to-day, another to-morrow. He can never love any one long. Such is his nature. If he should ever say that he loves thee do not believe him" (here I began to speak with emphasis); "for him it will be a question of thy kiss, not thy heart, dost understand?"

"Pan Henryk!"

"True! but what do I say? This does not concern thee. And, moreover, thou art so modest, wouldst thou give thy kiss to a stranger, Hania? I beg pardon, for it seems to me that I have offended thee even with the supposition. Thou wouldst never permit that, wouldst thou, Hania, never?"

Hania sprang up to go away, but I seized her by the hand and detained her by force. I tried to be calm, but rage was throttling me, as if with pincers. I felt that I was losing self-control.

"Answer," said I, with repressed excitement, "or I shall not let thee go."

"Pan Henryk! what do you want? What do you say?"

"I say — I say," whispered I, with set teeth, "that thou hast no shame in thy eyes. Hei?"

Hania sat down again on the sofa, helpless. I looked at her; she was pale as linen. But pity for the poor girl had fled from me. I grasped her hand, and squeezing its small fingers, continued, —

"Hear me! I was at thy feet. I loved thee more than the whole world —"

"Pan Henryk!"

"Be silent. I saw and heard everything. Thou art shameless, — thou and he."

"My God! my God!"

"Thou art shameless. I would not have dared to kiss

the hem of thy garment, and he kissed thee on the lips. Thou thyself didst draw him to thy kisses. Hania, I despise thee! I hate thee! I hate thee!"

The voice died in my breast. I began to breathe quickly and catch for air, which was lacking in my breast.

"Thou hast felt," said I, after a while, "that I will separate you. If I had to lose my life, I will separate you, even if I had to kill him, thee, and myself. What I said a moment ago is not true. He loves thee, he would not leave thee; but I will separate you."

"Of what are you talking with so much earnestness?" asked Pani d'Yves, who was sitting at the other end of the room.

There was a moment when I wanted to spring up and tell everything; but I remembered myself, and said in an apparently calm though somewhat broken voice, —

"We were disputing as to which arbor in the garden is the more beautiful, the rose or the hop arbor."

Selim stopped playing suddenly, and looked at us with attention, then he said with the greatest calmness, —

"I would give all others for the hop arbor."

"Thy taste is not bad," answered I. "Hania is of the opposite opinion."

"Is that true, Panna Hania?" asked he.

"Yes," said she, in a low voice.

Again I felt that I could not hold out longer in that conversation. Red circles began to flash before my eyes. I sprang up, and running through several chambers to the dining-room, seized a decanter of water standing on the table, and poured the water on my head. Then, without knowing what I did, I dashed the decanter to the floor, where it broke into a thousand bits, and ran to the entrance.

My horse and Selim's were standing before the porch, saddled. I ran to my room for a moment to wipe the water from my face in some fashion; that done, I returned to the hall. In the hall I found the priest and Selim in the greatest terror.

"What has happened?" asked I.

"Hania has grown weak and fainted."

"What? how?" cried I, grasping the priest by the arm.

"Immediately after thy going she burst into loud weeping, and fainted. Pani d'Yves has taken her to her room."

I flew to Pani d'Yves' chamber without saying a word. Hania had really burst into loud weeping and fainted, but the paroxysm had passed. When I saw her I forgot everything, fell on my knees before her bed like a madman, and, without noticing the presence of Pani d'Yves, cried, —

"Hania, my golden, my love! what is the matter with thee?"

"Nothing, nothing now," answered she, in a weak voice, and she tried to smile. "Nothing now. Really nothing."

I sat a quarter of an hour with her, then I kissed her hand and returned to the hall. It was not true that I hated her; I loved her as never before. But to make up for that, when I saw Selim in the hall I wanted to choke him. Oh, him, him, I hated at that moment from the bottom of my soul. He and the priest ran up to me together.

"Well, how is it there?"

"All is well." And turning to Selim I said in his ear, "Go home. To-morrow we will meet at the Pits near the edge of the forest. I want to speak to thee. I do not wish thee to come here. Our relations must cease."

The blood rushed to his face. "What does this mean?"

"I will tell thee to-morrow. I do not wish to do so to-day. Dost understand? I do not wish. To-morrow morning at six."

When I had said this I went back to Pani d' Yves' chamber. Selim ran some steps after me, but stopped at the door. A few minutes later I looked through the window and saw him ride away.

I sat about an hour in the chamber adjoining that one where Hania was resting. I could not go in, for, weakened by crying, she had fallen asleep. Pani d'Yves and the priest went to hold some consultation with my father. I sat alone till the hour for tea.

During tea I saw that my father, the priest, and Pani d'Yves had faces half mysterious, half severe. I confess that a kind of disquiet seized me. Could they have divined something? That was probable; for in every case between us young people things had happened that day which were quite unnatural.

"To-day," said my father, "I have received a letter from thy mother."

"How is mother's health?"

"Perfectly good. But she is troubled about what is happening here. She wants to return soon, but I will not permit her; she must stay two months longer."

"What is mother alarmed about?"

"It is known to thee that small-pox is in the village; I was so incautious as to inform her."

To tell the truth, I did not know that small-pox was prevalent. It may be that I had heard of it, but of course the information had dropped from my ears, as from a wall.

"Will father go to her?" I asked.

"I shall see. We will talk of that."

"It is now nearly a year that the dear woman has been abroad," said the priest.

"Her health requires it. She will be able to spend the coming winter at home. She writes that she feels much better, but is yearning for us, and is disquieted," said my father. Then, turning to me, he added, "Come to my room after tea. I wish to speak with thee."

"I will, father."

I rose and with all the others went to Hania. She was perfectly well now; she wished even to rise, but my father would not give permission. About ten in the evening a brichka rattled up before the porch, and in it Doctor Stanislav, who had been in peasant cottages since midday. After he had examined Hania carefully, he declared that she was not sick in the least, but needed rest and recreation. He forbade study and prescribed amusement and cheerfulness.

My father asked his advice about taking my little sisters away till the epidemic should pass. The doctor set him at rest by saying that there was no danger, and wrote himself to my mother to be at rest. Then he went to bed, for he was ready to drop from fatigue. I lighted him to the other building, where he was to pass the night with me. I was about to lie down, for I was wearied beyond description by the impressions of the day, when Franek entered and said, —

"The old lord begs the Panich to come."

I went at once. My father was sitting in his room near a desk on which was the letter from my mother. Father Ludvik and Pani d'Yves were present also. My heart fluttered like that of an accused who has to appear before a judgment seat. I felt almost certain that they wished to ask me about Hania. In fact, my father began to speak touching things of great importance. To set my mother at rest, he had determined to send my little sisters with Pani d'Yves to his brother at Kopchan. In that case Hania would be alone with us. This my father did not wish. He knew, he said, that among us young people things were happening which he did not wish to investigate, but for which he had no word of praise; he hoped, however, that the departure of Hania would put an end to them.

Here all looked at me inquiringly, but they were not a little astonished when, instead of opposing Hania's departure desperately, I approved of it gladly. I had calculated simply in this way, that the departure would be equivalent to breaking all relations with Selim. And, besides, a certain hope, like a will o' the wisp, gleamed in my heart, that it was I, and no one else, who would take Hania to my mother. I knew that my father could not leave home, since the harvest was at hand. I knew that Father Ludvik had never been abroad; so I only remained. But this was a faint hope, and soon it was quenched like a will o' the wisp, when my father said that Pani Ustrytski would go abroad for sea baths in a couple of days, and that she had consented to take Hania and accompany her to my mother. The day following the morrow, Hania was to set out in the evening. This saddened me no little, but I preferred that she should go without me rather than stay. Besides, I confess that immense delight rose in my mind when I said to myself, "How will Selim receive this, and what will he do when I tell him about it tomorrow?"

CHAPTER X.

AT six on the following morning I was at the Pits, where Selim was waiting for me. While riding thither, I made a solemn promise to be calm.

"What didst thou wish to say?" inquired Selim.

"I wished to say to thee that I know all. Thou lovest Hania, and she thee. Selim, thou hast acted dishonorably in ensnaring Hania's heart. I wish to tell thee this, first of all."

Selim grew pale, but every element in him was roused. He rode up to me so closely that our horses almost pushed each other, and asked, —

"Why? why? Reckon with thy words."

"First, because as thou art a Mussulman, and she is a Christian, thou canst not marry her."

"I will change my religion."

"Thy father will not permit that."

"Oh, he will permit it."

"In every case, there are obstacles besides that. Even shouldst thou change thy religion, neither I nor my father will give thee Hania, never and never! Dost understand?"

Selim bent toward me from his saddle, and answered, putting emphasis on every word, —

"I shall not ask thee! Dost understand in thy turn?"

I was still calm, for I kept the news of Hania's departure till the last.

"Not only will she not be thine," answered I, with coolness, and with equal emphasis, "but thou wilt not see her again. I know that thou hast in mind to send letters. I declare that I will watch, and for the first one

I will have thy messenger flogged with rods. Thou wilt not come any more to us. I forbid thee."

"Let us see," replied he, panting with rage. "Permit me to speak in my turn. I have not acted dishonorably, but thou hast. Now I see clearly. I asked thee if thou wert in love with her; thy answer was, 'No!' I wanted to withdraw while there was time; thou didst reject the sacrifice. Who is to blame? Thou didst say falsely that thou wert not in love with her. Through vanity, through egotistical pride, thou wert ashamed to confess thy love. Thou didst love in darkness, I in light. Thou didst love secretly, I openly. Thou didst poison her life; I tried to make it happy. Who is to blame? I would have withdrawn; God knows I would. But to-day it is too late. To-day she loves me; and listen to what I say: Ye may forbid me your house, ye may intercept my letters; but I swear that I will not yield up Hania, that I will not forget her, that I will love her always and seek her everywhere. I act directly and honorably; but I love. I love above all things on earth; my whole life is in my love; I should die without it. I do not wish to bring unhappiness into thy house; but remember that there is in me now something of such kind that I myself fear it. I am ready for anything. Oh, if ye work any wrong on Hania —"

He said all this hastily; then he was pale and set his teeth. A mighty love had possessed that fiery Eastern nature, and it radiated from him like heat from a flame; but I paid no heed to that, and answered with icy and cold decision, —

"I have not come here to listen to thy confessions. I jeer at thy threats, and I again repeat : Hania will never be thine."

"Listen once more," said Selim : "I will not try to tell

the greatness of my love for Hania, because I could not express it, and thou couldst not understand it. But I swear to thee that, in spite of all my love, if she loved thee now, I should still find in my soul noble feelings enough to renounce her forever. Henryk, why should we be rivals for Hania? Thou hast always been noble. Listen, then: give her up, and afterward ask even my life of me. Here is my hand, Henryk! The question is of Hania, — Hania, remember."

And he bent toward me with .open arms, but I reined back my horse.

"Leave the care of Hania to me and my father. We have already taken thought for her. I have the honor to inform you that the day after to-morrow Hania will go abroad, and that thou wilt never see her hereafter. Now farewell."

"Ah! in that case we shall meet again."

"We shall!"

I turned my horse and rode home without looking back.

It was gloomy in our house during those two days before Hania's departure. Pani d'Yves and my little sisters went away the day following the conversation with my father. There remained only my father, Kazio, I, the priest, and Hania. The poor girl knew now that she must go, and this news she received with despair. Evidently she thought to seek salvation and the last plank of safety in me; but I, divining this, strove not to be alone with her one moment. I knew myself sufficiently; and I knew that with tears she could do whatever she liked with me, and that I could not refuse her anything. I avoided even her glance, for I could not endure that prayer, as it were, for compassion which was depicted in it whenever she looked at my father or me.

On the other hand, even though I wished to intercede for her, I knew that it would be of no avail, for my father never changed a thing that he had once settled, and withal a certain shame kept me far from Hania. In her presence I was ashamed of my last conversation with Selim, of my recent harshness, of my whole rôle, and finally of this, that without approaching her I still followed her from a distance. But I had reason to follow her. I knew that Selim was circling about our house day and night, like a bird of prey.

On the second day after the conversation I saw Hania hide hastily a written paper, beyond doubt a letter to or from Selim. I divined even that perhaps they would see each other; but though I watched in the gray hour for Selim, I could not catch him.

Meanwhile two days passed quickly, like an arrow through the air. On the eve of the day when she was to pass the night at Ustrytsi, my father went to the next town to buy horses, and took Kazio to try them. Father Ludvik and I were to escort Hania. I noticed that as the decisive moment drew near a wonderful disquiet took possession of her. She changed in the eyes, and her whole body trembled. At moments she shivered as if terrified. At last the sun set in a kind of gloom, behind thick yellowish clouds piled on one another, — clouds that threatened storm and hail. On the western horizon distant thunder-rolls were heard in succession, like the terrible grumbling of a coming tempest. The air was sultry and filled with electricity. The birds had hidden under roofs and trees; only swallows were rushing unquietly through the air. The leaves ceased to rustle on the trees and hung as if they had fainted. From the direction of the farmyard came the plaintive bellowing of cattle, returning from pasture. A species of gloomy unrest pervaded all nature.

Father Ludvik had the windows closed. I wished to reach Ustrytsi before the outbreak of the storm, so I sprang up to go to the stable and hurry the stable-boys. When I was leaving the room Hania stood up, but sat down immediately. I looked at her. She blushed and then turned pale.

"The air oppresses me somehow!" said she; and, sitting near the window, she began to fan herself with a handkerchief.

Her strange disquiet increased evidently.

"We might wait," said the priest; "the storm will burst forth in half an hour or so."

"In half an hour we shall be at Ustrytsi," answered I; "besides, who knows but our fears may be vain." And I ran to the stable.

My horse was saddled already, but there was delay with the carriage, as usual. Half an hour had passed before the coachman drove up to the porch with the carriage. I was behind it on horseback. The storm seemed to be just overhanging, but I did not wish to delay any longer. They brought out Hania's trunks at once and strapped them behind to the carriage. Father Ludvik was waiting on the porch in a white linen coat, a white umbrella in his hand.

"Where is Hania? Is she ready?" asked I.

"She is ready. She went half an hour ago to pray in the chapel."

I went to the chapel, but did not find Hania. I went to the dining-room, from there to the drawing-room,— no Hania in any place.

"Hania! Hania!" I began to call.

No one gave answer. Somewhat alarmed, I went to her room, thinking that she might have grown faint. In her room the old woman Vengrosia was sitting and crying.

"Is it time," asked she, "to take farewell of the young lady?"

"Where is the young lady?" asked I, impatiently.

"She went to the garden."

I ran to the garden immediately.

"Hania! Hania! It is time to go."

Silence.

"Hania! Hania!"

As if in answer to me the leaves began to rustle under the first breath of the tempest; a few large drops of rain fell, and silence set in again.

"What is this?" asked I of myself, and felt that the hair was rising on my head with fright.

"Hania! Hania!"

For a moment it seemed to me that from the other end of the garden I heard an answer. I recovered myself. "Oh, what a fool!" thought I, and ran in the direction whence the voice came. I found nothing and nobody.

On that side the garden ended at a paling; beyond that was a road toward a sheepfold in the field. I seized hold of the paling and looked on the road. It was empty; but Ignas, a farm-boy, was herding geese in a ditch near the paling.

"Ignas!"

Ignas took off his cap and ran toward the paling.

"Hast thou seen the young lady?"

"I saw the young lady when she was going away."

"How? when she was going away?"

"Toward the forest with the Panich from Horeli. Oh, they went, how they went, as fast as ever the horses could gallop!"

Jesus, Mary! Hania had fled with Selim.

It grew dark in my eyes, and then a lightning-flash, as it were, flew through my head. I remembered Hania's disquiet; that letter which I had seen in her hand. Then all had been arranged. Selim had written to her and had seen her. They had chosen the moment before our departure, for they knew that all would be occupied then. Jesus, Mary! A cold sweat covered me. I do not remember when I stood on the porch.

"The horse! the horse!" shouted I, in a terrible voice.

"What has happened? What has happened?" cried the priest.

He was answered only by a roar of thunder, which was heard at that moment. The wind whistled in my ears from the mad rush of my horse. Dashing into the alley of lime-trees, I crossed it in going toward the road which they had taken; I rushed across one field, then another, and hurried on. The traces were evident. Meanwhile the storm had begun; it grew dark. On the black piles of clouds fiery zigzags of lightning began to define themselves. At times the whole sky was one blaze; then a still denser darkness came down; rain poured in one torrent. The trees swayed and bent on the roadside. My horse, struck by the mad blows of my whip and pressed by spurs, was snorting and groaning, and I also snorted from rage. Bent over the neck of the horse, I watched the tracks on the road, not seeing aught else and not thinking of it. In this mood I rushed into the forest. At that moment the storm became still more intense. A kind of rage seized the earth and the sky. The forest bent like wheat in a field, and brandished around its dark branches; the echoes of thunder spread from pine-tree to pine-tree in the gloom; the roar of thunder, the sound of trees, the crash of breaking limbs, were all mingled in a kind of hellish concert. I could not see traces now, but I flew onward like a whirlwind. Only beyond the forest, by the glare of lightning, did I recognize tracks again; but I noticed with terror that the snorting of my horse grew more and more violent, while his speed became less. I redoubled the blows of the whip.

Just beyond the forest began a real sea of sand which I could avoid by going to one side, while Selim had to pass through it. That must delay his flight.

I raised my eyes. "O God! bring it about that I overtake them, and then kill me, if 't is Thy will!" cried I, in despair. And my prayer was heard. All at once ruddy lightning rent the darkness, and in its bloody glare I saw an escaping brichka. I could not distinguish the faces of the fleeing, but I felt sure that they were Selim and Hania. They were less than one third of a mile ahead, but were not going very swiftly; for because of the darkness and the floods, which the rain had raised, Selim was forced to drive cautiously. I uttered a cry of rage and delight. Now they could not escape me.

Selim looked around, shouted too, and fell to beating the frightened horses with a cane. By the gleam of lightning Hania too recognized me. I saw that she grasped Selim in despair, and he told her something. In a few seconds I was so near that I could hear Selim's voice.

"I have weapons!" cried he, in the dark. "Do not come near; I shall shoot."

But I cared for nothing. I pushed on and on.

"Halt!" cried Selim; "halt!"

I was scarcely fifteen yards away, but the road began now to be better, and Selim urged his horses into a full gallop. The distance between us increased for a moment, but again I began to overtake them. Selim turned then and aimed his pistol. He was terrible, but he aimed coolly. Another moment, and I might have touched the carriage with my hand. Suddenly the report of a pistol was heard. My horse threw himself to one side, sprang still a number of times, then sank to his knees. I raised him; he reared on his hind legs, and, snorting heavily, rolled on the ground with me.

I sprang up at once and ran with all the strength left in me, but that was a vain effort. Soon the brichka went farther and farther from me; then I saw it only when lightning rent the clouds. I tried to shout. I could not; breath failed in my breast. The rattle of the brichka came to me fainter and fainter; at last I stumbled against a stone and fell.

In a moment I rose again. "They have gone! they have gone! they have vanished!" repeated I, aloud, and do not remember what happened to me. I was helpless, alone in the tempest and the night. That Satan of a Selim had conquered me. But if Kazio had not gone with my father, we should have pursued them together; and then what would have happened?

"What will happen now?" screamed I, loudly, so as to hear my own voice and not go mad. And it seemed to me that the whirlwind was jeering at me, and whistling: "Sit there at the roadside, without a horse, while he is off there with her." And thus the wind howled and laughed and roared. I went back slowly to my horse. From his nostrils flowed a stream of dark stiffening blood, but he was alive yet; he panted and turned his dying eyes toward me. I sat near him, rested my head on his side, and it seemed to me that I too was dying. But meanwhile the wind whistled above my head and laughed and cried, "He is there with her!" It seemed to me at times that I heard the hellish rattle of that brichka, flying off in the night with my happiness. And the whirlwind whistled, "He is there with her!"

A marvellous stupefaction seized hold of me. How long it lasted I cannot tell. When I recovered, the tempest had passed. Along the sky bright flocks of light, whitish clouds were moving; in the intervals between them the blue of heaven was visible, and the moon was shining brightly. From the field a mist was rising. My horse, already cold, reminded me of what had passed. I looked around to see where I was. On the right I perceived distant lights in windows, so I hurried toward them. It turned out that I was right near Ustrytsi.

I resolved to go to the mansion and see Pan Ustrytski, which I could do the more easily since he lived not in the mansion itself, but had his own little house; in this he slept and spent his time usually. The light was shining yet in his window. I knocked at the door. He opened it himself, and started back frightened.

"Farce!" cried he; "what a look thou hast, Henryk!"

"Lightning killed my horse out there on the road; I had nothing to do but to come here."

"In the name of the Father and Son! But thou art wet through, cold. It is late. Farce! I will have something to eat brought in, and dry clothes for thee."

"No, no; I wish to go home at once, nothing more."

"But why did not Hania come? My wife will start at two in the morning. We thought that you would bring her to spend the night."

I resolved at once to tell him all, for I needed his assistance.

"A misfortune has happened," said I. "I reckon on this, that you will not mention the matter to any one, neither to your wife, nor your daughters, nor the governesses. The honor of our house is at stake here."

I knew that he would tell no one, but I had little hope

that the affair would be concealed; therefore I preferred to anticipate, so that in a given event he could explain what had happened. And I told him all, declaring that I was in love with Hania.

"But thou must fight with Selim, I suppose? Farce! what —" said he, listening to the end.

"Yes; I wish to fight with him to-morrow. But to-day I must pursue them, and therefore I beg you to give me your best horse immediately."

"Thou hast no need to pursue them. They have not gone far. They took various roads and returned to Horeli. Where could they go? Farce! They returned to Horeli, and fell at the feet of the old Mirza. They had no other escape. The old Mirza confined Selim in the granary, and the young lady he will take back to thy house. A farce, is it! But Hania! Hania! well!"

"Pan Ustrytski!"

"Well, well, my child, be not angry. I do not take this ill of her. My women, that is different. But why lose time?"

"That is true; let us not lose time."

Pan Ustrytski stopped for a moment. "I know now what to do. I will go straightway to Horeli, and do thou go home, or better wait here. If Hania is in Horeli, I will take her and go to thy house. Thou thinkest they may not give her to me? Farce! But I prefer to be with the old Mirza when we take her, for thy father is quick-tempered, ready to challenge the old man, but the old man is not to blame. Is he?"

"My father is not at home."

"So much the better!"

Pan Ustrytski slapped his hands.

"Yanek!"

The servant entered.

"Horses and a brichka for me in ten minutes. Dost understand?"

"And horses for me?" said I.

"And horses for this gentleman! Farce! lord benefactor."

We were silent for a time.

"Will you permit me to write a letter to Selim?" asked I. "I wish to challenge him by letter."

"Why?"

"I am afraid that the old man will not let him fight. He will confine him a time and think that sufficient. But for me that is little, little! If Selim is in prison already, you will not see him; that cannot be brought about through the old man; but a letter may be left for any one. Besides, I shall not tell my father that I am going to fight. He might challenge the old Mirza, and the old Mirza is not to blame. But if Selim and I fight to begin with, there will be no reason for their fighting. Indeed, you said yourself that I must fight with him."

"I thought this way: fight, fight! That is always the best way for a noble; whether old or young, it is one. For some one else, a farce! but not for a noble. Well, write; thou art correct."

I sat down and wrote as follows: "Thou art contemptible. With this letter I slap thee in the face. If thou wilt not appear to-morrow near Vah's cottage with pistols or with swords, thou wilt be the last of cowards, which very likely thou art."

I sealed the letter and gave it to Pan Ustrytski. Then we went out; the brichkas had come already. Before sitting in mine, one terrifying thought came to my head.

"But," said I to Pan Ustrytski, "if Selim took Hania not to Horeli?"

"If not to Horeli, then he has gained time. It is night; there are fifty roads in every direction, and — look for a wind in the fields. But where could he have taken her?"

"To the town of N."

"Sixteen miles with the same horses. Then be at rest. A farce! is n't it? I will go to N. to-morrow, to-day even, but first to Horeli. I repeat to thee, be at rest."

An hour later I was at home. It was late at night, very late even, but lights were gleaming everywhere in the windows. Soon people were running with candles through various rooms. When my brichka stopped before the porch, the doors squeaked, and Father Ludvik came out with a lamp in his hand.

"Be quiet!" whispered he, putting his finger to his mouth.

"But Hania?" inquired I, feverishly.

"Hania is here already. The old Mirza brought her back. Come to my room. I will tell thee all."

I went to the priest's room.

"What happened to thee?"

"I pursued them. Selim shot my horse. Is father here?"

"He came just after the old Mirza had gone. Oh, misfortune! misfortune! The doctor is with him now. We were afraid that he would have an apoplectic stroke. He wanted to go and challenge the old Mirza immediately. Don't go to thy father, for it might harm him. To-morrow beg him not to challenge the Mirza. That would be a grievous sin, and, besides, the old man is not to blame. He beat Selim and confined him; Hania he brought home himself. He enjoined silence on his servants. It is fortunate that he did not find thy father."

It turned out that Pan Ustrytski had foreseen everything perfectly.

"How is Hania?"

"Every thread on her was wet. She has a fever. Thy father gave her a dreadful scolding. The poor child!"

"Did Doctor Stanislav see her?"

"He did, and commanded her to go to bed without delay. Old Vengrosia is sitting near her. Wait here for me. I will go to thy father and tell him that thou hast come. He sent horsemen after thee in every direction. Kazio too is not at home, for he has gone to look for thee. O God! O God, Thou Almighty, what has happened here!"

So saying, the priest went to my father. But I could not wait in his room. I ran to Hania. I did not wish to see her, oh, no! that would cost her too much. I wished rather to be sure that she had really returned, that she was again out of danger, under our roof, near me, sheltered from the tempest and the terrible events of that day.

Wonderful feelings shook me when I approached her room. Not anger, not hatred, did I feel in my heart, but a great and deep sorrow, an inexpressible compassion for that poor unfortunate victim of Selim's madness. I thought of her as of a dove, which a falcon had swept away. Ah! how much humiliation the poor thing must have felt, through what shame she must have passed in Horeli, in presence of the old Mirza! I swore to myself that I would not reproach her to-day or ever, and would act with her as if nothing had happened.

At the moment when I reached the chamber door, it opened; old Vengrosia came out. I stopped her and inquired, —

"Is the young lady sleeping?"

"She is not; she is not," repeated the old woman. "Oh, my golden young master, if you had seen what was here! When the old lord bellowed at the young lady, I thought the poor dear would die on the spot. And she was terrified and wet through. O Jesus! Jesus!"

"But now how is she?"

"You will see that she is sick altogether. It is lucky that the doctor is here."

I commanded Vengrosia to return at once to Hania, and not to shut the door; for I wished to look at her from a distance. In fact, looking from the dark chamber through the open door, I saw her sitting on the bed, dressed in night-clothing. A deep flush was on her face; her eyes were gleaming. I saw besides that she was breathing quickly; evidently she had a fever.

I hesitated for a time whether to go in or not; but at that moment Father Ludvik touched my shoulder.

"Thy father calls thee," said he.

"Father Ludvik, she is sick!"

"The doctor will come at once. Meanwhile thou wilt talk to thy father. Go, go; it is late."

"What o'clock?"

"One in the morning."

I struck my forehead with my hand. But I had to fight with Selim at five in the morning.

CHAPTER XI.

AFTER a talk with my father which lasted half an hour, I returned to the station, but did not lie down. I calculated that to reach Vah's at five I must leave the house by four at least, therefore I had not quite three hours before me. Soon after, Father Ludvik came to see if I were not ill after that mad ride, and if I had changed clothing properly after being wet; but for me to be wet was the same as not to be wet. The priest urged me to go to bed at once; meanwhile he forgot himself in talk, and so an hour passed.

He narrated in detail all that the old Mirza had said. It seemed that Selim had simply committed an act of madness; but, as he told his father, he saw no other method. It seemed to him that after the flight, his father would have no escape but to bless him, and we none but to give him Hania. It was also disclosed that after talking with me not only did he write to Hania, but he had a meeting with her; and it was then that he persuaded her to flee with him. The girl, though she did not comprehend the results of this step, resisted instinctively with all her might; but Selim involved her with his prayers and his love. He represented to her that the flight was simply a drive to Horeli, after which they would be united forever and be happy. He assured her that afterward he would bring her to us, but as his betrothed; that my father would agree to everything; that I must agree, and, what was more, I would console myself easily with Lola Ustrytski. Finally, he implored, entreated, and begged Hania. He said that for her he would sacrifice everything, even life; that he could not survive separation; that he would drown, shoot, or poison himself. And then he cast himself at her feet and so persuaded her that she agreed to everything. But when the flight began, and they had started, Hania grew terrified and begged him with tears to return; but he would not, for, as he told his father, he forgot the whole world then.

This was what the old Mirza told Father Ludvik, and he

told it, perhaps, to show that though Selim ventured on a mad deed he had done so in good faith. Taking everything into consideration, Father Ludvik did not share the anger of my father, who was indignant at Hania's ingratitude. According to the priest Hania was not ungrateful; she was simply led astray by sinful worldly love. For that reason the priest gave me some edifying instruction about worldly feelings, but I did not take it ill at all of Hania that her love was worldly; I would have been willing to pay with my life had that love been differently directed. I felt the greatest compassion for Hania, and moreover my heart had so grown to her that, had I wished to tear it away, I should have had to tear it asunder. Therefore I begged Father Ludvik to take her part before my father, and to explain to him her act as he had to me. I took farewell of him then, for I wished to be alone.

After the priest had gone, I took down that famous old sabre, given me by my father, and the pistols, to prepare for the meeting of the morning. Of that meeting I had had neither the time nor the wish to think hitherto. I wished to fight for life and death; that was all. As to Selim, I was convinced that he would not disappoint me. I wiped my sabre carefully with soft cotton along its broad blue blade. In spite of something like two hundred years, it had not one dent, though in its day it had opened not a few helmets and breastplates, and drunk no little Swedish, Tartar, and Turkish blood. The golden inscription, "Jesus, Mary," shone distinctly. I tried the edge; it was as fine as the edge of a satin ribbon. The blue turquoises on the hilt seemed to smile, as if begging for a hand to grasp and warm them.

Having finished with the sabre, I took the pistols, for I knew not what weapons Selim might choose. I dropped olive oil on the locks, put bits of linen cloth around the bullets, and loaded both carefully. They were ready now. It was three o'clock. When I had finished the work, I threw myself into an armchair and began to meditate. From the course of events, and from what Father Ludvik had told me, one point became more and more evident: that I was to blame not a little for all that had happened. I asked myself if I had fulfilled properly the duty of guardian which old Mikolai had imposed on me, and I answered, No. Had I thought of Hania, and not of myself? I answered, No! Of whom had I been thinking in all this affair? Directly of myself. And meanwhile Hania, that mild, defenceless creature, was among us, like a dove among birds of prey. I could not stifle in myself the immensely bitter thought that Selim and I had torn her like a tempting booty; and in that struggle, during which the robber actors were thinking mainly of themselves, she had suffered most who was least to blame. Now in a couple of hours we were to have our last battle concerning her.

These thoughts were bitter and grievous. It turned out that this whole world of nobles was too rude for Hania. Unfortunately my mother had not been at home for a long time, and we men had hands that were too rough; we had crushed between them the delicate flower thrown among us by fate. Blame hung over our whole house, and this blame must be effaced with my blood or Selim's. I was ready for either event.

Meanwhile the light of day had begun to look in with increasing force through my window. I quenched the candles burning on the table; it was almost daylight. Half-past four struck clearly in the hall of the house.

"Well, it is time!" thought I; and, throwing a cloak over my shoulders to hide the weapons in case some one met me, I went out of the station.

While passing near the house, I noticed that the main door in the entrance, which was fastened at night usually by the jaws of an iron lion, was open. Evidently some one had gone out; hence I needed to take every precaution not to meet that person. Stealing along silently by the side of the front yard toward the linden-trees, I looked carefully on all sides, but it seemed to me as if everything round about were sleeping calmly. Only in the alley did I raise my head boldly, feeling sure that they would not see me now from the mansion. The morning was very clear and beautiful after yesterday's tempest. The sweet odor of wet lindens met me with great freshness in the alley. I turned on the left toward the forge, the mill, and the dam; that was the road to Vah's cottage. Sleep and weariness fled far away from me under the influence of the fresh morning and fine weather. I was full of a certain good hope; some internal forewarning told me that in that struggle which was to come, I should conquer. Selim used pistols like a master, but I was not inferior as a shot; in handling a sabre he surpassed me in skill, it is true, but to make up I was far stronger than he, to that degree stronger that he could hardly endure my strokes on his sabre. "And, moreover, come what may," thought I, "this is the end; and if it is not the solution, it will be the cutting of the Gordian knot which has bound me and stifled me so long. Besides, in good or bad faith, Selim has wrought great injustice on Hania, and he must atone for it."

Thus meditating, I reached the bank of the pond. Mist and steam had dropped from the air onto the water. Daylight had painted the blue surface of the pond with the colors of dawn. Early morning had only just begun. The air was growing more and more transparent; it was fresh everywhere, calm, rosy, quiet; only from the reeds came to my ears the quacking of wild ducks. I was near the sluices and bridge, when I stopped on a sudden, as if driven into the earth.

On the bridge stood my father, with his arms behind him and a quenched pipe in one hand. Leaning on the railing of the bridge, he was looking thoughtfully at the water and the morning dawn. It was evident that he as well as I had been unable to sleep, and he had gone out to breathe the morning air, or perhaps to look here and there at the management.

I did not see him at once, for I was walking at the side of the road, so the willows hid the railing of the bridge from me; but I was not more than ten yards away. I hid behind the willows, not knowing at the moment what to do.

But my father stood in the same place all the time. I looked at him. Sleeplessness and anxiety were apparent on his face. He cast his eyes at the pond and muttered the morning prayer.

To my ears came the words, —

"Hail, Mary, full of grace! The Lord be with Thee!" Here he whispered the continuation, and again aloud, —

"And blessed be the fruit of Thy womb. Amen!"

I was impatient at standing behind the willows, and I determined to slip by quietly over the bridge. I could do that, for my father was turned toward the water; and, besides, he was a little deaf, as I have mentioned, for during his time in the army he had been deafened by the excessive roar of artillery. Stepping along cautiously, I was passing the bridge beyond the willows, but unfortunately a badly fastened plank moved. My father looked around.

"What art thou doing here?" asked he.

"Oh, to walk, father, — I am going to walk only," answered I, growing as red as a beet.

My father approached me, and opening slightly the cloak with which I had covered myself carefully, he pointed to the sabre and pistols.

"What is this?" asked he.

There was no help for it; I had to confess.

"I will tell father everything," I said; "I am going to fight with Selim."

I thought that he would burst out in anger, but beyond my expectation he only asked, —

"Who was the challenger?"

"I."

"Without consulting thy father, without saying a word."

"I challenged him yesterday in Ustrytsi, immediately after the pursuit. I could not ask about anything, father, and, besides, I was afraid that thou wouldst forbid me."

"Thou hast guessed right. Go home. Leave the whole affair to me."

My heart was straitened in me with such pain and despair as never before.

"Father, I entreat thee by all that is holy, by the memory of my grandfather, do not forbid me to fight with the Tartar. I remember how thou didst call me a democrat, and wert angry with me Now I remember that thy blood as well as grandfather's is flowing in me. Father, he injured Hania! is that to go unpunished? Give not people the chance to say that our family let an orphan be wronged, or would not avenge her. I am greatly to blame. I loved her, and did not tell thee; but I swear that even if I had not loved, I would for the sake of her orphanhood, our house, and our name do what I am doing now. Conscience tells me that this is noble; and do thou, father, not oppose me; for if what I say is true, then I do not believe that thou wouldst forbid me to be noble. I do not! I do not! Remember, father, that

Hania is wronged; and I challenged, I gave my word. I know that I am not mature yet; but have not the immature just the same feelings and the same honor as grown persons? I have challenged; I have given my word; and thou hast taught me more than once that honor is the first right of nobles. I gave my word, father; Hania was wronged; there is a spot on our house, and I have given my word. Father, father!"

And pressing my lips to his hand, I wept like a beaver; I prayed almost to my father; but in proportion as I spoke, his severe face became gentle, milder and milder; he raised his eyes, and a large heavy tear, really a parental one, fell on my forehead. He fought a grievous battle with himself, for I was the sight of his eyes, and he loved me above all things on earth; therefore he trembled for me; but at last he inclined his iron-gray head and said in a low, barely audible voice, —

"May the God of thy fathers conduct thee! Go, my son, go to fight with the Tartar."

We fell into each other's arms. My father pressed me long; long did he hold me to his breast. But at last he shook himself out of his emotion, and said with strength and more joyously, —

"Now then, fight, my son, till thy battle is heard in the sky!"

I kissed his hand, and he asked, —

"With swords or pistols?"

"He will choose."

"And the seconds?"

"Without seconds. I trust him; he trusts me. Why do we need seconds?"

Again I threw myself on his neck, for it was time to go. I looked back when I had gone about a third of a mile. My father was on the bridge yet, and blessed me from afar with the holy cross. The first rays of the rising sun fell on his lofty figure, encircling it with a kind of aureole. And thus in the light, with upraised hands, that veteran seemed to me like an old eagle blessing from afar its young for such a high-sounding and winged life as he himself had admired on a time.

Ah, how the heart rose in me then! I had so much confidence and faith and courage that if not one, but ten Selims had been waiting for me at Vah's cottage, I should have challenged all ten of them immediately.

I came at last to the cottage. Selim was waiting for me at the edge of the forest. I confess that when I saw him I felt in my heart something like that which a wolf feels when he sees his prey. We looked each other in the eyes threateningly, and with curiosity. Selim had changed in those two days; he had grown thin and ugly, but maybe it only seemed to me that he had grown ugly, his eyes gleamed feverishly, the corners of his mouth quivered.

We went immediately to the depth of the forest, but we did not speak a word the whole way.

At last, when I found a little opening among the pines, I stopped, and asked,—

"Here. Agreed?"

He nodded his head and began to unbutton his coat, so as to take it off before the duel.

"Choose!" said I, pointing to the pistols and the sabre.

He pointed to a sabre which he had with him: it was Turkish. a Damascus blade, much curved toward the point.

Meanwhile I threw off my coat; he followed my example, but first he took a letter from his pocket and said,—

"If I die, I beg to give this to Panna Hania."

"I will not receive it."

"This is not a confession; it is an explanation."

"Agreed! I will take it."

Thus speaking, we rolled up our shirt-sleeves. Only now did my heart begin to beat more vigorously. At last Selim seized the hilt of his sabre, straightened himself, took the position of a fencer, challenging, proud, and holding the sabre higher than his head, said briefly, —

"I am ready."

I struck on him at once, and so impetuously that he had to retreat a number of steps, and he received my blows on his sabre with difficulty; he answered, however, each blow with a blow, and with such swiftness that stroke and answer were heard almost simultaneously. A flush covered his face; his nostrils distended; his eyes stared out slantingly in Tartar fashion, and began to cast lightning.

For a while there was nothing to be heard but the clink of blades, the dry sound of steel, and the whistling breath of our breasts.

Selim soon understood that if the struggle was to continue, he must fall, for neither his lungs nor his strength would hold out. Large drops of sweat came out on his forehead; his breath grew hoarser and hoarser. But also a certain rage possessed him, a certain madness of battle. His hair, tossed around by the movement, fell on his forehead, and in his open mouth shone his white teeth. You would have said that the Tartar nature had become roused in him and grown wild when he felt the sabre in his hand and smelt blood. Still I had the advantage of equal fury with greater strength. Once he could not withstand the blow, and blood trickled from his left arm. After a few seconds, the very point of my sabre touched his forehead. He was terrible then, with that red ribbon of blood mixed with sweat and trickling down to his mouth and chin. It seemed to rouse him. He sprang up to me and sprang away like a wounded tiger. The point of his sabre circled with the terrible swiftness of a fiery thunderbolt, around my head, arms, and breast. I caught those mad blows with difficulty, all the more since I was thinking rather of giving than taking. At times we came so near each other that breast almost struck breast.

All at once, Selim sprang away; his sabre whistled right near my temple; but I warded it off with such strength that his head was for a moment undefended. I aimed a blow capable of splitting it in two, and — a thunderbolt, as it were, struck my head suddenly. I cried, "Jesus, Mary!" the sabre dropped from my hand, and I fell with my face to the earth.

CHAPTER XII.

WHAT happened to me during a long time, I do not remember, nor do I know. When I woke, I was lying on my back in a chamber and on my father's bed. My father was sitting near me in an armchair, with his head bent back, pale, and with closed eyes. The blinds were shut; lights were burning on the table; and in the great stillness of the chamber, I heard only the ticking of the clock. I stared for some time at the ceiling vacantly, and was summoning my thoughts sluggishly; then I tried to move, but unendurable pain in my head prevented me. This pain reminded me a little of all that had happened, so I called in a low, weak voice, —

"Father!"

My father quivered and bent over me. Joy and tenderness were expressed on his face, and he said, —

"O God! thanks to Thee! He has recovered consciousness. What son? what?"

"Father, I fought with Selim."

"Yes, my love! Do not think of that."

Silence continued for a while, then I asked, —

"Father, but who brought me to this room from the forest?"

"I brought thee in my arms; but do not say anything, do not torment thyself."

Not five minutes had passed when I inquired again. I spoke very slowly, —

"Father?"

"What, my child?"

"But what happened to Selim?"

"He fainted also from loss of blood. I had him carried to Horeli."

I wanted to inquire about Hania and my mother, but I felt that consciousness was leaving me again. I thought that black and yellow dogs were dancing on their hind legs around my bed, and I looked at them. Then again I seemed to hear the sounds of village fifes; at moments, instead of the clock which hung opposite my bed, I saw a face look out of the wall and draw back again. That was not a condition of complete unconsciousness, but of fever and a scattering of thought; but it must have lasted rather long.

At times I was a little better, and then I half recognized the faces around my bed, — now my father, now the priest, now Kazio, now Doctor Stanislav. I remember that among those faces was lacking one. I could not make out which; but I know that I felt that lack, and I sought that face instinctively.

One night when I had slept very soundly, I woke toward morning. The lights were burning on the table.

I was very, very weak. All at once I discerned a person bent over the bed whom I did not know at first, but at sight of whom I felt as well as if I had died and was taken into heaven. That was a kind of angelic face; but so angelic, so sacred, kind, with tears flowing out of its eyes, that I felt as though I were preparing to weep. Then a spark of consciousness returned to me; it grew bright in my eyes; and I called weakly in a low voice, —

"Mamma!"

The angelic face bent to my emaciated hand, lying motionless on the coverlet, and pressed lips to it. I tried to raise myself, but felt pain again in my temples; hence I exclaimed only, —

"Mamma! it pains!"

My mother, for it was she, had begun to change the bandages with ice, which were on my head. That process had caused me no little suffering; but now those sweet, beloved hands with careful delicacy began to move around my poor slashed head, so that, not feeling the least pain, I whispered, —

"Pleasant! Oh, pleasant!"

Thenceforward I had more consciousness; only toward evening I fell into a fever; then I saw Hania, though when I was conscious I never saw her near me. But I saw her always in some danger. At one time a wolf with red eyes was rushing at her; again some one was carrying her away, — as it were, Selim, as it were, not Selim, but with a face grown over with black bristles and with horns on his head. Then I cried out sometimes; and sometimes I begged that wolf, or that horned one, very politely and humbly, not to carry her away. At those moments my mother placed her hands on my forehead, and the evil visions vanished immediately.

At last the fever left me for good. I regained perfect

consciousness. That did not mean that I was in better health. Some other kind of sickness attached itself, a certain unheard of weakness, under the influence of which I was evidently sinking.

During whole days and nights I looked at one point in the ceiling. I was as if conscious, but indifferent to all things; I cared not for life, nor death, nor the persons watching over my bed. I received impressions, saw everything that was passing around me, remembered everything, but I had not strength to collect my thoughts, I had not strength to feel.

One evening it seemed evident that I was dying. A great yellow candle was placed near my bed; then I saw Father Ludvik in his vestments. He gave me the sacrament, then he put the holy oil on me, and after that he sobbed so that he came near losing consciousness. They carried my mother out in a faint. Kazio was howling at the wall and tearing his hair. My father was sitting with clasped hands; he was just as if petrified. I saw all of this perfectly, but was perfectly indifferent; and I looked as usual with dead, glassy eyes on the ceiling, on the edge of the bed or the foot of it, or at the window, through which were coming in milky and silvery bundles of moonlight.

Then, through all doors, the servants began to push into the room, crying, sobbing, and howling. Kazio led them in, and they filled the whole room; but my father sat there as stony as before. At last when all had knelt down, the priest began the Litany, but stopped, for he could not go on from tears. My father sprang up suddenly, and bellowing, "O Jesus! O Jesus!" threw himself his whole length on the floor.

At that moment I felt that the points of my toes and my feet were beginning to grow cold; a certain wonderful drowsiness seized me, and a yawning. "Ah! now I am dying!" thought I, and fell asleep.

But instead of dying I fell asleep really, and slept so well that I did not wake till twenty-four hours later, and so greatly strengthened that I was unable to understand what had happened. My indifference had vanished; my powerful young constitution had conquered death itself, and was roused to new life and new forces. Now again there were such scenes of delight at my bed that I shall not attempt to describe them. Kazio was simply frantic from happiness.

They told me later that immediately after the duel, when my father carried me wounded to the house, and the doctor could not answer for my life, they had to shut up the honest Kazio, for he was simply hunting Selim like a wild beast, and he swore that if I died he would shoot the Tartar at sight. Fortunately Selim too was wounded somewhat, and had to lie a time in bed.

But now every day brought me new solace. My desire for life returned. My father, my mother, the priest, and Kazio watched day and night above my bed How I loved them then; how I yearned for them when they left the room! But with life the old feeling for Hania began to speak in my heart again. When I woke from that sleep which all had considered at first an eternal one, I asked straightway for Hania. My father answered that she was well; but that she had gone with Pani d'Yves and my little sisters to his brother's, for the small-pox was increasing in the village. He told me, moreover, that he had forgiven her, that he had forgotten everything, and asked me to be quiet.

I spoke frequently of her afterward with mother, who, seeing that that subject occupied me more than all others. began herself a conversation, and finished it with the kindly though indefinite words that when I got well she would speak with my father of many things which to me would be very agreeable, but that I must be quiet and try to recover as quickly as possible.

While saying this, she smiled sadly, but I wished to weep from delight. Once something happened in the house which disturbed my peace, and even filled me with fear. In the evening, when my mother was sitting near me, the serving-man Franek came in and asked her to Hania's room.

I sat up immediately in bed. "Has Hania come?" I asked.

"No!" answered my mother. "She has not come. He asks me to Hania's room, for they are painting there and putting on new paper."

At times it seemed to me that a heavy cloud and an ill-concealed sadness lay on the foreheads of the persons surrounding me. I had no knowledge of what was passing, and my inquiries were set aside somehow. I asked Kazio; he answered as did others, that in the house all was well; that our little sisters, Pani d'Yves, and Hania would return soon; and, finally, that I must be quiet.

"But where does this sadness come from?" asked I.

"Seest thou, I will tell thee all. Selim and the old Mirza come here every day. Selim is in despair whole days. He cries; he wants absolutely to see thee; and our mother and father are afraid that this visit would harm thee."

"Wise Selim," said I, smiling, "he came near splitting my skull, and now he is crying for me. Well, is he thinking of Hania all the time?"

"How could he have Hania in his head? I know not. For that matter, I did not ask; but I think that he has renounced her altogether."

"That is a question."

"In every case some one else will get her; be at rest on that point."

Here Kazio made a wry face, student fashion, and added with the mien of a rogue, —

"I know even who. God grant only that —"

"That what?"

"That she return as soon as possible," added he, hurriedly.

These words pacified me completely. A couple of days later, in the evening, my father was sitting near me with my mother. He and I began to play chess. After a while mother went out, leaving the door open. Through the door a whole row of rooms was visible; at the end of this row was Hania's room. I looked at it, but I could not see anything, for mine was the only room lighted. Hania's door, so far as I could see in the darkness, was closed.

Then some one went in, as it were Doctor Stanislav, and did not shut the door.

My heart beat unquietly. There was light in Hania's room.

The light fell in a bright column to the dark neighboring hall; and on the background of that clear column it seemed to me that I saw a delicate line of smoke, curling as dust curls in sunlight.

Gradually an indefinable odor struck my nostrils, but an odor which became stronger and stronger every moment. Suddenly the hair rose on my head. I recognized the odor of juniper.

"Father! what is that?" cried I, throwing the chessmen and chess-board on the floor.

My father jumped up, confused, perceiving also that cursed odor of the juniper, and closed the door of the room as quickly as possible.

"That is nothing," said he, hurriedly.

But I was already on my feet; and though I staggered, I pushed quickly toward the door.

"They are burning juniper!" cried I. "I want to go there."

My father caught me by the waist.

"Do not go! do not go! I forbid thee."

Despair seized me; so grasping the bandages around my head, I cried, —

"Well, I swear then that I will tear off these bandages, and open my wounds with my own hands. Hania is dead! I want to see her."

"Hania is not dead. I give thee my word!" cried my father, seizing my hands and struggling with me. "She was sick, but she is better. Calm thyself! Calm thyself! Have we not had misfortune enough already? I will tell thee everything, but lie down. Thou canst not go to her. Thou wouldst destroy her. But lie down; I swear to thee that she is better."

My strength failed me, and I fell on the bed, repeating only, —

"My God! My God!"

"Henryk, come to thyself! Art thou a woman? Be a man. She is no longer in danger. I have promised to tell thee everything, and I will tell it, but on condition that thou collect thy strength. Lay thy head on the pillow. That way. Cover thyself, and be quiet."

I was obedient.

"I am quiet; but more quickly, father, more quickly! Let me know everything right away. Is she really better? What was the matter with her?"

"Listen, then: that night in which Selim took her away there was a storm. Hania wore only a thin dress which got wet to the last thread. Besides, that mad step cost her not a little. In Horeli, where Selim took her, she had no change of clothes, so she returned in that same little wet dress. That very night she got a chill and a violent fever. The next day old Vengrosia could not hold her tongue, and told her about thy trouble. She even said that thou wert killed. Evidently that hurt her. In the evening she was unconscious. The doctor did not know for a long time what the matter was Thou knowest that small-pox was in the village; it is here yet. Hania caught the small-pox."

I closed my eyes, for it seemed that I was losing consciousness; at last I said, —

"Go on, father, for I am calm."

"There were moments of great danger," continued he. "That same day on which we looked on thee as lost, she too was almost dying. But to both of you a lucky crisis came. To-day she is recovering, as well as thou. In a week or so she will be perfectly well."

"But what happened in the house? Oh, what happened?"

My father was silent and looked at me carefully, as if in fear that his words might have shocked my still feeble mind. I was lying motionless. Silence continued a long time. I was collecting my thoughts and was looking at the new misfortune. My father rose and began to walk with long strides through the room, looking at me from time to time.

"Father," said I, after a long silence.

"What, my boy?"

"Is she — is she — greatly marked?"

My voice was calm and low, but my heart was beating audibly in expectation of the answer.

"Yes," answered my father. "As usual after the small-pox. Maybe there will be no marks. There are marks, now; but they will disappear, of course."

I turned to the wall. I felt that something worse than usual was happening to me.

A week later, however, I was on my feet, and in two weeks I saw Hania. Ah! I will not even attempt to describe what had become of that beautiful, ideal face. When the poor girl came out of her room, and I saw her for the first time, though I had sworn to myself previously that I would not show the least emotion, I became weak and fell into a dead faint. Oh, how terribly marked she was!

When they brought me out of the faint, Hania was weeping aloud, certainly over herself and me, for I too was more like a shadow than a man.

"I am the cause of all this!" repeated she, sobbing; "I am the cause."

"Hania, my dear sister, do not weep; I will love thee always!" and I seized her hands to raise them to my lips as before. Suddenly I shivered and drew back my lips. Those hands, once so white, delicate, and beautiful, were dreadful. They were covered with black spots, and were rough, almost repulsive.

"I will always love thee!" repeated I, with an effort.

I lied. I had immense compassion in my heart, and the tearful love of a brother; but the old feeling had flown away, as a bird flies, without leaving a trace.

I went to the garden; and in that same hop arbor where the first confession had taken place between Selim and Hania, I cried, as after the death of some dear one. In truth, the former Hania had died for me, or rather, my love had died; and in my heart there remained merely emptiness and pain, as if from an incurable wound, and a memory that presses tears from the eyes.

I sat long and long. The quiet autumn evening began to flush in the twilight on the tree-tops. They looked for me in the house; at last my father entered the hop arbor. He looked at me and respected my sorrow.

"Poor boy!" said he, "God has visited thee grievously; trust in Him. He knows always what He does."

I rested my head on my father's breast, and for some time we were both silent.

"Thou wert greatly attached to her," said my father, after a while. "So tell me, if I were to say to thee, Give her thy hand for a lifetime, what wouldst thou answer?"

"Father," replied I, "love may fly from me, but honor never. I am ready."

My father kissed me heartily, and said, —

"May God bless thee! I recognize thee, but it is not thy duty, not thy obligation; it is Selim's."

"Will he come here?"

"He will come with his father. His father knows everything now."

In fact, Selim came about dusk. When he saw Hania, he grew red, and then as pale as linen. For a while a great struggle between his heart and his conscience was evident on his face. It was clear that from him too that winged bird, whose name is love, had flown.

But the noble youth conquered himself. He rose, stretched out his arms, fell on his knees before Hania, and cried, —

"My Hania! I am always the same; I will never desert thee, — never, never!"

Abundant tears were flowing down Hania's face; but she pushed Selim away gently.

"I do not believe, I do not believe that it is possible to love me now," said she; then covering her face with her hands, she cried, —

"Oh, how kind and noble you all are! I alone am

less noble, more sinful; but now all is ended. I am another person."

And in spite of the insistence of the old Mirza, in spite of Selim's prayers, she refused her hand.

The first storm of life had broken that beautiful flower when it had barely opened. Poor girl! She needed now after the tempest some holy and peaceful harbor, where she could pacify her conscience, and bring her heart to rest.

She found that quiet and holy harbor. She became a Sister of Charity.

Later on, new events and one terrible storm caused me for a long time to lose sight of her. But after a number of years I saw her unexpectedly. Peace and calm were depicted on those angelic features; all traces of the terrible disease had disappeared. In the black robe and white head-dress of the cloister she was beautiful as never before; but it was a beauty not of earth, beauty more angelic than human.

TARTAR CAPTIVITY

TARTAR CAPTIVITY.

FRAGMENTS FROM THE CHRONICLE OF A NOBLE, ALEXIS ZDANOBARSKI.

CHAPTER I.

MY attendant, riding in advance, or following, thrummed on his teorban, while sorrow and longing for Marysia pressed my heart; and the farther I went the more ardently I loved her. Then came to my mind the words, *post equitem sedet atra cura* (behind the horseman sits dark care). But if in the great decrease of my fortune I had spoken with his serene great mightiness, Pan Tvoryanski, I dared not mention my feelings. Nothing was left me but to win a fortune with my sword, and when I had adorned myself with military glory to stand before him. Neither God nor my Marysia could take it ill of me that I did not make the confession to Pan Tvoryanski. If Marysia had commanded me to spring into fire, or into water, or simply to shed my blood, Thou, O Jesus Christ, who lookest into my heart, seest that I would have done so. There was one thing, however, which I could not sacrifice, even for my charming maiden, and that was the honor of a noble. My fortune was nothing; but the dignity of blood is great, and from my ancestors I had received a command, sacred as a last will, to remember ever that my life was my own, that I might expose it to peril, but *integra rodu*[1] *dignitas* was an inheritance from my ancestors, which I was bound to hand down as I had received it, that is, *integram*. O God, grant eternal rest to my ancestors, and may eternal light shine on them for the ages of ages! Even had his serene great mightiness, Tvoryanski, consented to give me his daughter, I had no place to which I might conduct her. If, considering the scantiness of my fortune, he, in his pride, had called me a pauper, or simply a homespun, I, knowing the excellence of my family, should have been insulted and forced to take revenge on him, which may God not permit, since he is the father of my Marysia.

Nothing remained but to go to the frontier. Of trappings, girdles, and what was best after my ancestors, some I pawned, others I sold and received three hundred weighty ducats, which I gave to Tvoryanski on interest; then, taking farewell of Marysia with tears and deep sighing, I prepared for the road during the night, and next morning I and my attendant turned our horses' heads eastward.

The journey was through Zaslav and Bar to Haysynie. Stopping now at a castle, now at a mansion, now at an inn, we came at last to Uman, beyond which the steppe was open before us, level, rich, silent. My attendant, riding in advance, played on the teorban and sang songs. He seemed as if flying before me, the bird, as it were, which I was pursuing, namely, glory; and behind me followed another bird; this was grief. We were going to the stanitsa called Mohylna, where in his day my serene, great, mighty father stood on guard as colonel of an

---

[1] This word is the genitive of the Polish word *rod*, "stock," or "ancestry." *Integra rodu dignitas* means "the unspotted dignity of ancestry."

TARTAR CAPTIVITY.

armored squadron which he at his own cost had mounted for war with the Bisurmans.[1]

It was very far to Mohylna, for, praise be to God, the Commonwealth has spread itself over the earth widely; and, besides, we had to travel through steppes, on which Tartars and various other ruffians were prowling night and day; a man had to guard his life carefully.

Along the road I marvelled at everything. Since that was my first time in the Ukraine, I saw the strangest deeds and strangest things. That country is warlike; there the common man too is more resolute and daring than with us, and in peasants there is courage of which a noble would not be ashamed. When you pass through a settlement, though people know you to be a man of birth, they hardly raise a cap, and look you straight in the eyes. In every cottage there is a sabre and a musket, and more than one peasant has a hatchet-headed staff in his hand, like a noble in another place. There is a daring nature in these people. They even make small account of commissioners of the Commonwealth; for this the sabre has punished them already, and will punish them more in the future. The vicinity of pagans, and continual readiness for warfare, has developed their courage. They cultivate the earth not too willingly; and if any one wins profit from tillage, he prefers to settle on his own fields rather than on those of a master. On the other hand, they join escorts of nobles, or light squadrons of the Commonwealth readily, and are excellent warriors, especially in scouting and skirmishing, though in battle *non cunctant* (they are not slow). They raise shouts, and go at the enemy as if they were smoke, cutting and thrusting. Each of their settlements is more like a tabor than a village; they keep multitudes of horses, which feed win-

---
[1] Mussulmans.

ter and summer in the steppes, and are as swift as those of the Tartars. Many of these people betake themselves also to the islands of the Dnieper, and there at the Saitch lead a life in the fashion of monks, but military and quite robber-like. From these uncontrolled actions our dear country has suffered much, and will suffer much more in the future, till it tames them. It would be difficult for a noble, or even a great lord, to keep them in one place; for time after time they break away to empty steppes, of which in those regions there are many; they settle in the steppes and live at their own will. In form of body, and in manners, they are different from our peasants; they are tall and strong, dark in complexion, more like Tartars; their mustaches are black, as with the Wallachians; they shave their heads after the fashion of pagans, leaving on the very crown only a tuft, thick and long.

Seeing and considering all this, I wondered greatly at that land and at everything in it; and as I have called it warlike, I repeat now, that a country more suited to an armed and mounted people it would be vain to seek throughout the whole earth. When some of these people are killed, others ride in from all sides and along every road, just as if flocks of birds were flying in; and throughout that wild steppe it is easier to hear the sound of muskets, the clatter of sabres, the neighing of horses, the fluttering of flags in the wind, and the shouts of warriors, than the lark in a meadow.

Old minstrels, greatly honored by every one, go about there as in Podolia and Volynia. These, being blind, play on lyres and sing knightly songs; these minstrels cause courage and love of glory to flourish greatly. Warriors in those regions, seeing that they live to-day and to-morrow decay, esteem their own lives as a broken

TARTAR CAPTIVITY. 175

copper, and spend their blood as a magnate spends gold, caring more for a beautiful death than for life and earthly goods. Others love war above everything, and though often of high birth, they become almost wild in continual fighting, and go to battle as if to a wedding, with great rejoicing and songs. In time of peace they are terribly grieved at not finding an outlet for warlike humors, hence they are dangerous to public peace. These men are called "the desperate." When a warrior is killed, all count that an ordinary occurrence, and even his nearest friends do not mourn overmuch for him, saying that it beseems a man more to die in the steppe, than in bed, like a woman.

Indeed, in that land is the best school and practice of knighthood. When a young regiment has passed one year or two in a stanitsa, it becomes as keen as a Turkish sabre, so that neither German cavalry nor Turkish janissaries can stand before its fury when they are equal in numbers; and what must it be for other inferior soldiers, as, for example, the Wallachians, or any kind of hireling? It is easy to quarrel in the steppe; and this should be avoided, for the whole country is swarming with armed men.

Advancing with my attendant, I met household troops of the Pototskis, the Vishnyevetskis, the Kisiels, the Zbaraskis, in various uniforms, black, red, and many-colored, now quota troops of the Commonwealth, now squadrons of the king The horses of these warriors advanced to their bellies in grass, and snorted as if swimming in water; captains managed the squadrons, as shepherd dogs tend their flocks; the Cossacks beat kettle-drums, blew their horn trumpets and fifes, or sang songs, making so tremendous an uproar that when they had passed and disappeared the wind brought back a sound, as it were, of some distant storm. At intervals moved also the wagons of bullock-drivers, which squeaked shrilly; from this squeaking our horses were frightened. Some of those bullock-drivers were bringing salt from the Liman at the Euxine; others were returning from among foul pagans at the Palus Maeotis, or from Moscow; others were taking Moldavian wine to the Saitch; and the wagons moved one after another in the order of storks, forming lines a mile long on the steppe.

We met also herds of oxen, all of one color, gray, with great curving horns. Crowding together, they moved so closely as to form a solid mass, their horned foreheads swaying from side to side.

Beyond the stanitsa Kiselova, one company of an important hussar regiment met us. The men were in full equipment, and a sound went from their wings, as from those of eagles. My attendant and I could not take our eyes from them, though it was difficult to look at the men, for the eye was struck by a terrible glare of sunlight reflected from their weapons; the gleams from their lance-points raised upward were like flames of burning candles suspended in the air. But the hearts rose in us, for those hussars seemed more like a company of kings than common warriors, such was the *auctoritas* (authority) in them, and the majesty of battle.

Beyond the stanitsa the country was wilder. Often in the steppe we saw at night fires of Cossack couriers sent to various stanitsas, or even of peasants who were fleeing to the steppe. We did not approach these, since we made our own fires.

At times strangers came to us, either hungry men, or men gone astray in the steppe; and once came a wonderful person with a face all grown over with hair, like a wolf's face. My attendant began to cry out with fear when he saw him; and I, thinking that I had to do with a werewolf (wolf man), was reaching for my sabre to slash him. When that monster did not howl, but praised God, I would not touch him. The unknown said that he was a Tartar by descent, but a Catholic. I wondered at that, for the Tartars in Lithuania adhere to the Koran. But this man changed his faith for his wife, and, serving later as a flag-bearer in his regiment, was sent by the Lithuanian hetmans with a letter to the horde, because he knew Tartar. Still it was hateful to my man to sleep at one fire with him. More frequently we spent the night sleeping in turns, or not sleeping at all, so as to keep watch of our horses. More than once I stretched on the grass and looked at the twinkling stars of the sky, thinking in my soul that the one which looked on me most lovingly was Marysia. In my grief I had the consolation of knowing that that little star would never shine for another, but would keep faith with me, since it had a heart that was honest, and a soul as pure as a tear dropped in prayer before God.

At times Marysia came to me in sleep, just as if living; and one night when she came she promised to pray for me and to fly after me through the air, like a swallow, and if she grew weary she would rest on my head, and twitter to heaven to obtain for me glory and happiness. Then she vanished like mist; and when I woke I thought that an angel had been near me, and what astonished me also was this, that the horses pricking their ears snorted loudly, as if they had felt some one near them. Considering such apparitions as a mark of God's favor and encouragement in my toil, I vowed to the most Holy Mary and to Saint Alexis, my patron, never to stain myself with mortal sin, so as to retain their favor in the future also. That night I prayed till daylight, or till the time of starting. Generally we were moving on the road before sunrise, which in those regions is altogether more beautiful than with us; for when the first rays shoot along the plain covered with dew from the night cold, the whole steppe, because of the myriads of flowers, looks like brocade interwoven with pearls. From this comes joy to all creatures. Partridges, quails, ptarmigans, and other birds of the steppe, shooting along through the grass, dash those pearls down to the earth.

There are countless myriads of birds in that region. We met every day cunning bustards and slender storks. These last stand on the ground, stretching upward their long necks, like spears, and keep guard in order around the grave mounds; but when they fly through the air, with tremendous outcry, they rise to such heights that the eye cannot follow them. Bullock-drivers respect these birds greatly; for by the order of their flying they bring the holy cross to one's mind. Warriors too, counting them with their sabres, predict fortune from their number; but, according to my reason, this has nothing to do with reality, for whatever the Lord God in His mercy intends for a man, He will give anyhow. Of other birds there are ravens, crows, hawks, and eagles. These creatures at twilight make a great uproar, now sitting in a circle on some mound, now breaking out without cause in a rattling and croaking so immense and complaining that there is need to shut one's ears.

The evening twilights are far redder than with us. The reason of this is that pagans shed much Christian blood there; this blood goes to heaven and is red, crying for vengeance. Grave mounds here cover the whole country, as far as the eye can reach, and in them are lying knights waiting for the day of Judgment. Some say that these knights are only sleeping, and will wake when the campaign shall be heralded of all Christian kings against the pagan. I know not if this be true; but I think that it may happen, for everything is in the power of God.

This is a land of warlike people, a land which Poles, Cossacks, and Tartars, in continual warfare, have trampled with hoofs of horses, one chasing another in arms. And so whole generations are like those figures which appear and disappear in a holiday puppet-show. Many good nobles come here also to live. They bring peasants from the Crown, or, finding them in the place, begin settlements; for though one must lead a life in continual fear of war, the Lord God has given such courage to our people that dangers, instead of frightening them, are rather an enticement. In fact, when a noble youth comes to years, it is difficult to keep him at home, or on the school bench, for he is tearing away, like a falcon, to fly to the border. Many a one loses his life there; but some poor boy comes out a lord, as have many whose children live now in their castles, keep escorts, and enjoy senatorial dignity in the Commonwealth.

It is in accordance with God's thought for a knightly man to become a lord from war and from land, and by settling the steppe to give growth to the Commonwealth. From the Masovians, who are great people to multiply, and who increase like bees in a hive, are descended most of those colonists. They cultivate the steppe with ploughs, and become agriculturists readily; but in time of war they go in a body, one after another, all willing to die.

Thinking over these matters, I rejoiced greatly; for I understood that either I should lie down in battle, — for which a noble, a Christian warrior should always be ready, — and receive a heavenly crown, or, giving notable service to my country, restore to its former splendor my family, and delight my ancestors in paradise. They, too, came to fortune; not by lawsuits at courts, or by uproars at diets, but by blood, the foundation of life; and what they received they received from the Commonwealth, and they did not spare it on behalf of the Commonwealth. Thus my serene, great, mighty grandfather and my father, each of them, fitted out a regiment for war against the Bisurman. May God grant them light eternal in heaven, for it is proper that a fortune which came with the sabre should be spent on the sabre. As to me, though my heart aches for Marysia, and the wind whistles through my purse, I am the heir of a glorious name and great, noble ambition, owing to which I hear at night, as it were, trumpets and voices of some kind, which call to me, "Preserve thy name unspotted; be equal to thy fathers; yield not to evil!" Thou, O God, so bless me, that I shall preserve my name, and be equal to my fathers! I will break before I bend.

And I proposed to myself that if God would grant me to await a time of fortune, and go for Marysia, I would go, not in ticking, but in brocade, not in a torn cap, but in ostrich plumes, not with one attendant, but with an escort and with a baton in my hand, as a lord for a lord's daughter, as a great knight for a senator's child. And then, without detriment to family honor, I would fall at the feet of Tvoryanski, for I should bow to him, not as to a lord for a fortune, but as to a father for his daughter. In poverty I should have consented to yield her, even though my soul were rent; for if through love I hope to make her my wife, I hope in wealth to blow the dust from before her dear feet, not that they should be bare and bleeding on life's thorny path.

Better courage entered my heart in proportion as I let

myself deeper into the steppe with my attendant. It is sad in that steppe, for it is empty; but it is so spacious there that it seems to a man that he is yonder eagle or hawk. The grass comes higher and higher along the sides of the horses, as if it were greeting you with honor; and while making a great rustling it seems to say, "Welcome, O warrior of God!" The farther, however, the more dangerous, for Mohylna is the last Christian watchtower; the warrior there takes holy communion daily, so as to be ready for death at all hours.

The Tartars, now in large parties, now singly, circle around that stanitsa, though when a larger number comes, an experienced man knows it easily, as in the night the wolves howl behind them tremendously; for when a great camp of them moves, whole flocks of wolves follow, knowing that in the track of it they will find carrion enough, both of them and their horses. Others are of opinion, however, that wolves do not eat Tartar flesh, being friends of the Tartars, who, because of their greed and foul paganism, may well be compared with wild beasts.

But while prowling around, dreadful things too meet the Tartars; for when Cossacks stationed near the armored squadron of the stanitsa catch one of those pagans, they have no pity, and commit terrible cruelties.

One night, I saw a great fire in the steppe, and people around it. I went toward the place with my attendant, wishing to see who were there, and if God would grant me to let fly a few arrows among them. But they were only Cossacks from the stanitsa, who had made a great fire, and were throwing bound Tartars into it alive, hurling each one as if he were a sack. The Tartars called on their Allah in vain. From those who were roasted a strong odor went out; and the Cossacks, dancing around the fire like evil spirits, gave themselves up to delight. I gave command at once to leave off this work, and slay the prisoners simply with sabres, as was proper; to this they answered, —

"Be off, or the same thing will happen to thee!"

When they learned that I was a noble, they removed their caps; and hearing that I was going to the colonel to serve, they offered to conduct me to the station. We went, then, for the rest of the night, in their company, and without adventure; but on the road I saw one wonder more. At a certain place the steppe was covered completely with glittering insects, like those which about Saint John's day appear with us, but not in such numbers. These glittered in the darkness throughout the grass as far as the eye could see, so that you might say that a part of the sky with the stars had fallen, and was lying on the earth. Only at dawn did those little stars cease to gleam; it was not far then to the stanitsa, as was shown by the crowing of cocks, of which there are many, for the soldiers love their shrill crowing, and keep a great number of them. Soon after, when the air became clearer, we saw in the morning dawn several wellsweeps; the wind bore to us barking of dogs and neighing of horses. When nearer still to the stockade, I heard the song, "*Salve janua salutis*," which went out over the dew, and was very loud, for three hundred men were singing it, kneeling on the square beneath the open sky.

When I reached the stanitsa, I went at once to the serene, great, mighty Peter Koshyts, a rich nobleman from Lithuania, and a warrior of experience, who was colonel there. He had been so hacked in long campaigning that men said that pagans had written out the whole Koran on his face with their sabres. He was a knight accustomed to every trick of war, and had served the Commonwealth greatly. Having known my father, he received me as if I had been his own son, and inscribed me that very day in the regiment. Others told me later that I had come in good season, for the locusts would soon swarm from the Crimea. In fact, I learned that there was great fear, and the alarm was sounded in every stanitsa; the knighthood was kept in utmost watchfulness.

CHAPTER II.

WE advanced, as usual, without baggage; for a Tartar detachment can be overtaken only in that way. At three in the afternoon, we came to an elevation, called the Pagan Tombs; and by a lucky chance for us, the fog, which since morning had covered all the steppe, dropped down on a sudden. Though we could not see the Tartar camp itself, we knew from noise and the bellowing of cattle which came out of the fog, that it was not far distant. The Cossacks sent forward on reconnoissance, stole up to the very wagons, seized some prisoners with lariats, and brought them in so badly beaten and terrified that, though put to torture at once, blood came from their mouths instead of words. Our voevoda learned from them, however, that that camp was the main one; that the Khan's brother was there present, with many considerable Murzas; and that, excluding Tartars who had care of extra horses, wagons, prisoners, and the wagon train, those who could be employed in battle were only four times greater in number than our troops.

When he had heard this, the voevoda began to draw us up on those heights in order of battle. Delight entered our hearts, for we saw that in the proportion and number of only four to one the Tartars could not withstand our impetus; since the tabor, and the great number of slow cattle, hindered their retreat, they could not flee from our sabres.

They knew too well of our presence, and, having no escape, began also to make ready for battle, in their own way; this we knew at once by the sound of their great drum, which they call "balt," and which they consider sacred, obeying its voice in all things.

All at once the fog thinned so much that most of the horse-tail standards were visible; and next it disappeared altogether. We saw black swarms of pagandom, — horse at the side of horse, and man near man, standing in a dense mass in the form of a sickle. From out this mass skirmishers began to break away in flocks, and race off in various directions. Some of them rushed right up to our squadrons, jeering at us, shouting terribly, waving their hands, and challenging all who were ready for single combat. But the voevoda permitted only Cossacks to go; he wished to bring the line into perfect order, which was done quickly, since he was an old warrior, experienced and very strict.

Standing in readiness for battle, we looked at the skirmishing and the wonderful work of the Cossacks, who know best how to manage duels with those vermin. They chased then for prisoners, and also to kill; but though we watched intently to see the first body fall headlong, we could not distinguish it, for numbers fell together on both sides. The old essaul of the Cossacks dragged to the very feet of the voevoda a Murza; but he was strangled, for he had dragged him six furlongs, and his face was all torn by prickly plants of the steppe. We took that, however, as a good omen; and the voevoda, who was hurried, gave command to strike up with drum and trumpet, and shouted, —

"Begin! begin!"

The horde answered with a tremendous uproar; hearing these sounds, the skirmishers vanished at once from the field, on which the hussars had to meet now, as usual, the entire strength of the enemy.

The whole army stood, as has been said, on the height, ready to rush directly on the pagan; but it pleased the courage of the voevoda to let off in advance, according to old usage, one squadron, like a falcon from the hoop, so that by breaking everything on its path it might spread dismay and disorder in the ranks of the enemy.

We saw that squadron moving under the lead of Babski, as clearly as a thing on the palm of the hand, since in going down gradually from the height it advanced right there close to us. When they had passed the slope, the horses acquired the highest speed, and the ground bent beneath them, the hussars, leaning forward in their saddles, lowered their lances. The air groaned loudly, and such a strong wind from them struck us that the plumes on our helmets were fluttering. So they went forward with a noise from their wings, and the streamers on their lances, just like a storm; and it was clear that whatever opposed them would be rubbed out of existence.

The captains had received command to give no succor till that squadron had cut a road to the rear through the pagans. We gazed on them well, for they ran about five furlongs, and, since they went on grass, the dust was not great. In our squadron, which stood motionless, there was such silence that the buzzing of horse-flies and gnats could be heard. Each man was straining his eyes out after the advancing squadron; at times a horse neighed, or, smelling blood, stretched his neck and, opening his nostrils, groaned plaintively.

In the Tartar camp no small uproar set in among the pagans; they raised the shout, "Allah! Allah!" and soon a cloud of arrows, dense as rain, struck the hussars, rattling on their mail harness. Then came the cry, "Jesus, Mary!" which was a sign that ours would be there soon with their lances. Indeed, with God's help, they arrived and struck with such impetus that the pagans opened in two halves, like a log when a wedge has split it. They went through the middle, as if on a street. Then that street closed behind them, and the throng hid them completely; we saw only a terrible seething, sometimes a helmet gleamed, and sometimes, when a horse reared under a man, we saw an armed hand; then again a streamer flew into the air, like a bird, and dropped down.

On the square of the Tartar camp, where there was no grass, a terrible dust rose, in which there was a struggling and a boiling. The rattle of muskets, the terrible uproar, and the shouts almost split our ears. On our side murmurs began to go about through the squadron, for it was difficult to remain in one place. Men were ready to rush forward; horses were rearing.

We began to repeat the litany for the dying; while doing so, a certain noble youth, instead of saying, "Lord, have mercy on them!" cried, "I see another streamer!" Then the warriors cried in one voice for permission to rush after the others.

A great and unrestrained enthusiasm seized every rank. Sparks flashed from the eyes of some; others, from desire for pagan blood, were as flushed as blushing maidens; still others, who were younger, shed abundant tears, and, stretching their hands upward, cried, "Let us go to help our brothers."

But the colonel commanded great silence threateningly,

and said, "It is not proper for knights to strike without command, like some kind of militia, and spoil the patience of knighthood with too great eagerness. If any man stirs, he'll be dragged at a horse's tail!"

We looked now in silence at those who were perishing, and at the whole Tartar camp, which, like a gigantic serpent with iron in its entrails, was twisting and squirming from pain, wishing to smother that squadron which had fastened into its body.

Meanwhile the sun had gone down; the redness of evening was in the sky. But there was no longer need to await the command, for suddenly the second squadron was sent rushing after the first, carrying with it destruction, after that went the third and the fourth. Under this avalanche of armed men and horses the camp began to waver, and it was clear that the foul Mohammed would fall in the dust at the feet of Mary most pure.

Meanwhile the cannon, of which six pieces were drawn up just behind us, began to act with weight and majesty, breaking the ends of the camp with their balls. The captains on our side, according to old custom, rolled up their sleeves, and shook their batons very fiercely; the rage of battle rose to our heads like wine. One and another man cried out the name of his patron; and we heard continually: "Saint Peter! Saint John! Saint Matthew!" Some, neglecting the saints, shouted, "Strike! kill!" I, sinful servant of God, began an ardent prayer, and when I had finished and raised my thoughts to Mary, a miracle happened to me, for all at once a pretty little swallow, flying around above our heads, settled on mine and, clapping its wings, began to repeat, "Tsivit!" just as if praying for me. Hence such a power entered my bones that the hair was rising under my helmet.

The moment had come! An orderly rushed to us

from the voevoda and waved the bunchuk standard; then the captains hurried to the ranks; the colonel cried, "In God's name, slay the dog-brothers!"

Our horses rose on their haunches, and next moment the wind whistled in our ears.

We struck the pagans fiercely; unable to stop us, they fell, like grain-stalks trampled under hoofs. We overturned men, horses, tents, pickets. The roaring of cannon outsounded the crash of breaking lances. Horses whined. In the crush, after the breaking of the lances, when new legions fell on us, it came to sabres and two-handed swords. More than one man fought with the stump of his sabre, or drove the soul out of a body with armed fist. Feathers flew into the air from the wings and the helmets of hussars. The air, hot from the meeting of men and horses, stopped the breath in the throats of the combatants.

Now hoarse shouts rose, the groan of trampled men, a whining, a whistling of sabres and arrows. The pagans gave a ferocious resistance; but they had become weak; they were falling ever more thickly, and terror began to seize hold of them. In the uproar and in blindness they could not see whither to flee; therefore, howling, and shielding their faces with their arms, they died under sword blows. Horses, with their riders, crushed down in the furious onset, formed quivering piles, and we rushed over those bodies slippery with blood, cutting through the crowd to the wagons, from which were heard the lament of prisoners, the shrill cry of women, and a calling to Heaven.

The slaughter continued in darkness, until a flame rose from wagons, which the Cossacks had fired. Smoke and sparks burst forth in rolls, and in those sparks and that smoke the cattle in the tabor filled the air with sad bellowing. Then, when the tabor was broken, oxen, sheep, goats, riderless horses, and camels, wild from terror, rushed like a hurricane over the steppe.

The greatest disorder rose at the wagons. Some seized plunder in the uproar; others cut the bonds of captives who, feeling their hands free, broke the burning wagons and struck the enemy with flaming brands. The sobbing of women roused greater rage in the soldiers, so that even those who fell on their faces and stretched their hands out for fetters died beneath the sword.

Considerable detachments which could not break from the tabor, though they howled, imploring mercy, were cut to pieces. After those who fled from defeat went pursuers, and with them I hurried forward. Whole crowds fled before one man; hands grew weary with hewing; feet slipped in blood; the breath stopped in the breasts of horses. In the darkness we cut at random. At last the horse under me, throwing blood from his mouth, fell on the grass; next moment a dream, as it were, seized me, for blood gushed from me in a stream. I sat down to commend myself to God, or the most holy Lady, when the steppe went around, the bright stars began to dance in the sky, and I fainted.

CHAPTER III.

A PAGAN, according to our language, is a beast as it were, or an unclean dog; for what is unclean among men is displeasing to God. And though the Bisurmans call themselves better than Christians, in the depth of their conscience they know their uncleanness and strive eagerly to wash it away, pouring water on their members seven times daily; they would have no need to do this, of course, were they less hardened in sin. With no people is captivity so grievous, because of their cruelty, and because there are neither churches nor Catholic priests in the midst of them. If a prisoner falls into mortal sin, being unable to find absolution at death, he may be damned easily. They treat prisoners with cruelty, too, as is shown by what I suffered. They have a festival which they call "Bimekbairon," before which they fast a whole month. To conceal his own vileness with appearances of justice, Mohammed, their prophet, commanded them to shorten on this day the period of captivity for prisoners, to give freedom to those who have served out their time, and declare to all others how long they must serve in the future, and besides keep their promises under oath. The oath must be uttered two hours after midnight, when their priest is on the tower, or, if there is no tower, when he goes out on a mound and begins to cry with his fingers in his ears: Lai Lacha i Lalach Mohammed Rossulach esse de Miellai, Lala i Lalach! They swear then on books called Hamaeli, at the bottom of which is depicted the sabre of Ali, the assistant of Mohammed, — this sabre they call Delfikari. If they swear on one of these volumes to any one, they will keep the oath surely; but they are so skilled in deceit, that they deceive not only their captives but their god, by swearing on books made of Venetian soap. Such an oath, they say, will be washed away by the first rain that comes, hence it is not possible to believe them.

They sell prisoners into Asia, which is quite another part of the world; those who remain behind, they send to herd flocks; when at work they beat these with raw-hides, and kill them with hunger. Being fond of idleness themselves, they barely rise up to perform ablutions; and for the rest of the day sit on horse-skulls covered with carpets, hold their hands idly across their stomachs, bend now to the right, now to the left. But they are very fond of music and the sound of flutes, and sit listening whole days to whistles. Putting two of these whistles in the mouth, they play on them, fingering as on a flute. Besides, they have drums covered with horsehide, cymbals, bronze disks which make a great clatter, and long staffs ornamented with horse manes and covered with little bells. When they play on these instruments, such a din rises that the dogs howl; but they themselves are delighted, and say that sweetness comes to their ears from the noise, and that various diseases fly away before those voices.

There is great drunkenness among the Tartars, for though not free to drink wine, they fill themselves with mare's milk fermented, which goes to the head more than wine. And then being angry and cruel, they kill prisoners, after they have tortured them.

Of Christian nations the Genoese and Venetians visit them in ships, and deal in various places which were built by the ancients, that is, the Greeks. These Christians bring, above all, parchment lamps of various colors, which the Tartars fill with mutton fat; then lighting these lamps, they hang them on graves and mosques in endless number, and burn incense. These lights, white, rosy, green, and blue, seem suspended in the night air, and afford a wonderful spectacle, which, were it turned to God's praise, might delight every eye. But just at that time they permit the greatest vileness.

Their priests are also sorcerers, and communicate with evil spirits. When the Tartars go to rob and plunder, these priests make the nights dark for them, and raise great fogs in the daytime, so that their camp may escape pursuit.

There are not so many people at Perekop, and in the whole Chersonesus, as we in the Commonwealth imagine; but all are employed in warfare, not merely the nobles. They are very enduring of hunger, cold, and toil, for from youth they go naked, from which cause their skin becomes black. In battle, they cannot stand before armed men, therefore their warfare consists more in stratagem than bravery, and in attacking, seizing, and escaping with all speed. Especially at sight of armored men they lose heart, saying that there is no power even in sorcery to stop their impetus. Any hussar squadron will destroy in battle with the Tartars four or five times its own number. They have less fear of death than of captivity among Cossacks; but for them it is easier to meet the Cossack than it is to meet us. I think that the Commonwealth, if so minded, might easily conquer the whole Crimea, if we were in alliance with Venice, which would send its fleet to the Euxine, and thus not let the Turks come with assistance. But there are people, it seems, among us who prefer skirmishing on the steppes to the safety of the Commonwealth; such men would not be glad should this happen. God enlighten them in their blindness.

The mode of living and manners of the Tartars are beastly; and with their management, or rather indolence, they would die of hunger were it not for robbery, which brings them great riches. To robbery they owe the wealth which I saw among them: such as countless herds of cattle, fat sheep, playful goats, swift horses, and camels. Under tents, or in straggling stone villages, some keep their gold brocade, belts, horse trappings, goblets, carpets, inlaid weapons, spices, and perfumes, all piled in heaps, without order. They make no use of these treasures, fearing that they might have

TARTAR CAPTIVITY.

to give the Khan some of them, or some to the Turks to whom they are subject. They go about in coats of sheep-skin with the wool outside. But what any one has he hides, and says that he is rich, for which reason others respect him. Of towns built by them I have not heard; but those which exist are from remote periods. The Chersonesus was densely inhabited of old, until its towns and inhabitants were destroyed by various pagans. Still certain places have remained rather large and very beautiful; but the inhabitants lead a barbarous life, just as in filthy camping places.

They took me, with a number of others, to a certain settlement called Kizlich, at the very shore of the Euxine, where a small salt stream trickles into deep water. Houses there are built from the ruins of a city destroyed, as those people say, by Sauromati. But some of the buildings are beautiful though much broken. In old times there were temples; into these now the Tartars drive sheep and horses at night; only one have they turned into a mosque.

They dig from the ground too at times stone figures formed as skilfully as if they were living. Tartar children sit on the heads of these, or break their limbs with stones. Those children also threw dust and dirt at me, and called me "Gaur! gaur!" But I endured that patiently, all the more since Aga Sukyman, which in our speech means Solomon, is *præfectus* of this town; he it was who found me in a faint and took me captive. At first he treated me decently. He did this because, finding handsome armor on my body, and an inlaid sabre, he considered me a notable person and expected a large ransom.

I, thinking it improper for a noble even in captivity to dissimulate, denied out of hand. I told him that though of distinguished family I had no fortune, and that no one would come for me with ransom. Not believing this, he, in his cunning, said to me in Russian, —

"Oh, you Poles! each man of you calls himself a poor fellow, and does not promise ransom, so that he may be put to death; for this you promise yourselves great delight in heaven from your God."

He did not sell me into Asia, like many others; and having almost perfect liberty, I went daily to the seashore. There, sitting on the rocks, I gazed into the distance of the water, which was as blue as turquoise, and gave rein to my thoughts. Ofttimes I cried bitterly; for well I understood that my fate was settled by misfortune now, and sealed. I could not think of knightly service to the country, nor of glory, nor Marysia. Hence sadness seized my soul; suffering gnawed into my heart; and there came on me terrible yearning for the Commonwealth, and all that I had lost in it. I would rather not have come into the world, I would rather have perished in battle, I would rather Sukyman had given me to torture at once, for then at least I should have received the palm, and seen with the eyes of my spirit that which I yearned for in my body. In pain I saw not the end of my suffering.

Every Friday, which is Sunday for the Tartars, when other prisoners had rest from their labors, we sat at the stream, and, helping one another to weep, we often sang the psalm: *Super flumina Babylonis.* Thus the day passed for us in remembering and speaking of our country, and from this our souls received no little solace. It happened that among the prisoners who bore the yoke of captivity in Kizlich I was the only noble; hence I exercised a certain rule over the others; I strengthened their spirit, so that not one might be found who

TARTAR CAPTIVITY.

should wish to lighten his misfortune by deserting the true faith. In fact, God did not permit that.

Having among the Tartars importance by reason of the expected ransom, I tried to bring some relief to other captives. Sometimes I succeeded in giving part of my food to the hungriest; sometimes I helped them in their labor. I carried water to the thirsty, not making it a discredit to myself; for if the Lord Jesus made common people inferior in birth and blood, He promised them a crown in heaven, and thereby made them our younger brothers, to whom protection and defence is due from the knightly order.

On their part, these captives kissed my hands with humility; and though I told them that I was only a captive like them, and that the hour might come in which they would see me in greater suffering and debasement than they were in at that time, they would not believe this, and said, —

"For God's sake! that will not be."

But I knew that that would be when Sukyman grew tired of waiting in vain for the ransom; and I prepared for the worst that could happen to the body, since the soul, having lost happiness, was in pain and torture already.

In fact, Sukyman came one day to me, and said: "Thou doest ill to repay my favor with ingratitude. I treat thee like a guest, and thou art living in stubbornness; see then lest I bend thee under my knee."

Here he declared his plans at once, and asked me to write to the Commonwealth for a thousand gold ducats, for which I should receive freedom. I could not do this: first, because I had only three hundred, and but little interest had accrued; second, I feared that Pan Tvoryanski might, through his great liberality, pay for me out of his own purse, which was opposed to my ambition. But when the Lord sent terror into my bones in view of Sukyman's anger, I said, so as to put off the time of torment, that I must be obedient to his will. I gave him a letter; but it was to a priest, an acquaintance whom I had near Kamenets. Describing my captivity, I begged him to implore aid for me, which could come from God only.

Delighted in his greed, Sukyman sent that letter by Tartars going to the fair at Suchava, to which place attendants are sent by our magnates for sweetmeats.

Sukyman was more cordial now than before, and invited me to his house, which was the most beautiful in Kizlich. He was a rich pagan, and greatly respected, as well for his bravery as his good fortune, which had withheld favor from him only in one thing, and that was, that from many wives he had no son, but five daughters. The eldest of these, Illa, he loved much for her beauty. I happened often to see her; for the Tartars do not keep their women in seclusion as the Turks do, and do not force them to cover their faces. When Illa came to the table, she looked at me first with fear and curiosity, as at some wonder. Afterward, when her native wildness was tamed, she would put a vessel of fermented milk to my lips without saying a word, or a ball of rice and mutton, as a sign of her favor. Sukyman not only did not oppose this, but did the like himself, for as we met every day he took a great fancy to me, and frequently persuaded me to throw aside sadness. Through my influence, the other prisoners too were more comfortable, since Illa provided all kinds of food for them plentifully.

Therefore they loved her; and when she came to the cistern they kissed her garments, calling her their patroness. That pagan girl had not only a fair countenance' but a tender heart; so that often I was sorry to think that she must be damned for the errors of her faith. To me she showed more and more affection. She would sit crouched in a corner of the room, and, winding a silk cloth around her head, look whole hours at me in silence, her eyes gleaming like a cat's eyes. I asked her one day why she looked at me in that way. Putting her hand to her forehead, her lips, and her breast, she bent to my feet, and replied, —

"Dear one, I wish to be thy captive."

Then she ran away. Sinful desires fell on me, against which I had to seek defence in ardent prayer. That same day Sukyman came and said to me, —

"Thou didst deceive me with thy letter, therefore I ought to kill thee; but since Allah has not blessed me with sons, I take pity on thy youth and thy beauty. Therefore I tell thee that if thou wilt reject the errors of thy faith and receive our Prophet, I will give thee Illa, who loves thee, and will make thee my son; all that I have will be thine."

At first I could not let the breath out of my mouth from mighty astonishment; but when I recovered, I answered that Satan tempted Christ, showing Him various kingdoms from a mountain-top.

Enraged at these words, he roared like a wild beast; he ordered me to take off the clothes which I wore. When I did this, a Kalmuck captive brought a hempen shirt to me, and Sukyman commanded me fiercely to carry water to the cattle.

It was on Monday, I remember, when I had to begin that labor. I went up the stream, which was salt at the seaside; I took leather bags, and drawing water carried it and poured it into a stone cistern. Tartar women, who went to the stream to wash clothes, set dogs at me. In the evening I did not go to the village as formerly, but lay down to sleep among camels. Because I was wearied, God sent me sleep right away; later I woke on a sudden, and saw some slender figure coming toward me in the moonlight. I made the sign of the cross, thinking it a ghost; but it was Illa, who brought a dish of water, and olive oil. Then, washing my feet and anointing them, she sat near by on the straw, and looked as before at me, in silence, while great silver drops were flowing from her eyelids.

"Illa," asked I, "why hast thou come here?"

She whispered quietly, showing her moist lids in the moonlight, —

"Dear one, why hast thou despised me?"

From weeping she could say no more. The heart in me was moved toward that maiden, and I wanted to gather her to my bosom; but white Marysia stood before me, and the sinful thought flew away. I told Illa that I could not be her husband, if only because of her faith, which in my eyes was for the soul of a man what foul rust is for iron; but that I could give her more than anything which might come from others, that is, the holy cross, which would cleanse her from original sin, and secure her salvation. In her blindness she could not find vision; and, seizing her head with both hands, in great despair, she went away as she had come to me.

The next day I returned to my labor, which was the more oppressive because they gave me to eat sparingly. I met Sukyman, also.

"I will bend thee," said he.

"Thou wilt bend only my body," answered I; "for know that, being a noble, I have a soul that is unbending."

When he heard this, he went away gnashing his teeth. Thus did God punish me for that deceitful letter; if I had not written it, I should not have roused Sukyman against me so savagely because I had rejected his daughter.

On Friday the captives came as usual to meditate, to sing mournful songs, and wash their wounds. Seeing me in my debasement, they fell at my feet with earnest weeping, crying that my dignity had been disgraced. But I did not think so; Christ, though of kingly race, suffered still greater contempt, wishing by that to show the estate of nobles that the worth of honorable blood is stained, not by suffering, but by the dread of it. The prisoners, hearing of the conditions which Sukyman offered me, cried, —

"Oh, pretend to receive the Prophet; do so only for appearance' sake, and you will not lose your soul. When son of the powerful Sukyman, you will bring comfort to yourself and to us, for we shall be your captives."

I told them if that was their counsel, they must be near unto dogs, for they were defiling their lips with barking against the Lord God, not understanding that it is improper to incline, even apparently, before the false prophet. Then they said, —

"We shall all lose our lives here;" and they were in despair.

God has refused honor to people without birth, and made them more regardful of temporal profit.

Hearing of this, the præfectus Sukyman became very angry, and determined to bend me with hunger. He did not wish to kill, or to sell me; for he himself had long loved me, and could not kill me because of Illa, who, as I learned afterward, clung to her father's garments when he made threats against my life, and with great entreaties she restrained him, in the hope that my mind would change soon, in accord with her wishes.

Then times of great affliction came to me, and the foreseen hour of suffering struck. But when I thought of my fathers, of the glory and the untarnished name which they left me, great strength entered my heart. I thought only of this, not to bring disgrace by anything in captivity to the order of nobles, the dignity of which I carried there in myself, and which is the foundation of the Commonwealth. Sukyman, wishing that I should degrade myself, said, —

"Thou mayest eat with dogs, and take what is thrown to them."

Unwilling to do that, I ate only locusts, which I found on the sea shore. Frequently also food was placed near me by some unseen hand, in which I suspected Illa. But later on they watched her, and she could not continue; other women, Tartar witches, not only had no compassion for me, but once they so beat me with sticks that my whole body was blue. If locusts were lacking, I suffered hunger. Sometimes the captives brought me figs gathered in the Tartar gardens; but when I saw that they received blows for so doing, I commanded them to stop. They looked at me with tears, repeating, —

"Our lord, to what has it come with thee!"

Slavery, not only my own, but that of others, became more severe; for the Tartars flamed up with great hatred against us. One poor Cossack, named Fedko, was impaled on a stake, where he died on the second day afterward, repeating, "O Christ! O Christ!" In the night we removed him from the stake and buried him in the sand by the sea, begging God for a death equally beautiful. Surely that Father who existed before the ages ennobled Fedko in heaven, covered him with purple, and raised him to the highest glory.

I was thinking to part soon with my earthly covering, for it was a month since I had begun to eat locusts, which now were scarcer and scarcer in the sand. I had grown terribly emaciated and black, and my legs were tottering under me. When I had filled the bags in the stream, I carried them with groaning, until at last, sitting down in the camel yard, next to the garden, I could go no farther. Then those beasts, whose hearts were better than those of the pagans, stretched out their bent necks through the hurdle fence to me, and, snorting, took pity on my suffering.

But once in the night, while half sleeping, I saw Illa again; she brought water and food to me Because of great weakness, I slept in the daytime as well; and God, in His mercy, sent me dreams about my dear country. Marysia came to me too, all in white, with angel's wings on her shoulders; with these she shaded my head from the heat. She came always at midday, in great heat; and toward evening, when I was weakest, I heard singing coming from heaven. I was unconscious perhaps for a time, for I saw not the light of earth; but afterward health returned to me, for I saw again new piles of straw, the enclosure for the camels, and the heads of those beasts raised toward the sky.

A certain time Sukyman, coming near me, said, —

"Learn the power of the servants of the Prophet!"

To which I answered, "Learn that of a servant of Christ."

Meanwhile a festival came. The Tartars, when night fell, took those Venetian lamps which I have mentioned, and ornamented the whole place with them; then each man, holding a light in his hand, went out on the road,

and they marched on in crowds. That was at the time
of the full moon. They cried in loud voices to their God
and Prophet, for they have a custom to walk and pray
the whole night. They gave great alms also on that day;
captives were sitting in rows along the road; and what
any one asked for in food or in clothing he received. The
years of service were shortened for some; and a certain
Essaul, who had dragged a Tartar child out of the water,
received liberty, for it is mean to refuse what is lawful
on that day. Hence there was great joy among the captives, for no one suffered hunger or received blows, or
was punished with death. Sukyman walked past the
straw where I was lying, and at his side went Illa; but
very haughtily, for she did not look at me, but taking a
barley cake from a basket she threw it toward me, while
looking in the opposite direction. A Kalmuck captive,
sitting near, seized the cake. Sukyman thought that I
would ask as well as others, and he would not have refused me. But, though I had not taken anything in my
mouth for a long time, I did not think it befitting a noble
to stretch out his hand with common people, and I chose
to stifle with wind the hunger which was gnawing my
entrails. Sukyman said then to others, —

"Indeed, this captive has an iron soul; we should entreat him to have pity on himself, for he puts his own
pride above everything."

The pagan did not know that just then my soul had
placed itself in the dust, and in the greatest weakness
before the Lord, for my suffering was almost stronger
than I was. But in the night some one placed food near
me again. When I had eaten this eagerly, I felt stronger,
and dragged myself at once from the camel yard; and,
though my hands and feet were trembling, I began to
carry water again to the cistern. Of locusts, too, God

sent an abundance during the days which succeeded. Meanwhile hunger taught me to eat ugly things of the sea, which, though vile in form, are not bad. I lived then like a bird from day to day, and when I walked along the sea shore each wave brought to my feet those poor snails, making a noise with them as with nutshells.

The nights began to be very cold. Other prisoners were permitted to go to the village. I had to sleep on my straw; but the compassionate camels lay around me, warming me with their breath and bodies. I thought that I should not endure the cold, and that was my one hope; I had no other before me. Ah! dear mother, dear country, how I yearned for thee, and for thee, my maiden, whom I did not see, but did not cease to love, and desired all the more, — desired like water in heat, like bread in hunger, like death in torture!

Still Providence watches in many ways over those whom it tries; for had it not been for the misery and contempt in which I was living, Sukyman might have sold me to Tsargrad or Galata, where there are great markets for slaves; but now, because of that misery, no one would take me at any price, as I was more like a dying man, or a Lazarus, than a knight. Not to mention that merely a filthy shirt covered my naked limbs, my leanness had made me a skeleton, and besides abundant hair had grown out on my face and head; the skin which had cracked on all my body was covered with scabs and red spots from the camels. Some thought me a leper, and even among captives I began to rouse disgust. But I offered up for my sins my body, a vain covering, which, like every garment, tears and falls into rags; for only two things are lasting, the immortal soul and honor, which, based upon birth, is its principal quality, just as brightness is that of stars in the sky.

CHAPTER IV.

SPRING came again, and a warmer sun shone on my misery, to which I had become so accustomed that I had almost forgotten that there are happy people on earth. Storks, wagtails, swallows, and larks flew in flocks toward the north; and I said to them, "Free birds, ah, tell the Commonwealth and all estates that I have endured like a patriot noble, and though fastened so firmly to the earth, though trampled by the feet of pagans, I weep only before God, and preserve a proud face toward my enemies, and have not let my soul be conquered."

The end of my misery was still far away; but that spring brought changes, and new omens, it was full of wonderful auguries: In the sky above the Crimea appeared the rod of God's anger, a comet, and blinking with blue eye it shook its tail as a sign of destruction to the Crimea and pagandom. The terrified Tartars, going with shouting at night, and with an uproar and rattling, sent clouds of blazing arrows to the sky to frighten that bird of evil omen. Their priests proclaimed a fast, and their magicians predicted a plague. Fear fell upon the hearts of people; and it was no vain fear, for tidings came that a plague had broken out at the Palus Maeotis. Expeditions were to go that spring to the Commonwealth by two roads; but they did not go. People, standing in crowds on the street, dared not speak aloud, and only turned their eyes to the East, whence was to fly the "Black Div," as they called it. Fresh news was circling continually; till at last it thundered on Kizlich that the plague had appeared in the Khan's capital. The Khan himself fled from his capital. Some said that he would hide with his

TARTAR CAPTIVITY.

wives in the mountains on the south; others that he would come to Kizlich, where sea breezes purify the air.

The Khan, following the advice of soothsayers, came to Kizlich, driving immense herds and flocks in advance, so as to have food for his court. Sukyman received him with great honor; and people fell on their faces before him, for those slaves consider him almost a god and related to the heavenly bodies. He did not bring many of the horde, only his court, a thousand Baskaks, with a few Hadjis, and Agas in yellow coats; for it was feared that the plague would appear more easily in a great concourse of people.

The plague travelled over the Crimea, especially that part called Yenikale. When it attacked a place, it took every one in it, and passed other villages altogether; but wherever it went, even birds fell down dead. The nearest it came to Kizlich was two days' journey. The Khan thanked God for his escape, and made liberal gifts to the soothsayers; he also gave freedom to many captives. But just when others gathered the fruits of his favor, the last trial met me.

A certain time when the Khan was riding past the straw on which I was lying, he came very near, looked at me, and asked Sukyman who that was who seemed to be so miserable. I know not what answer was given; but I saw that they talked long together, and evidently Sukyman was complaining of my ingratitude and stubbornness, for at last he said aloud, "Try him, lord!"

Made curious by this, the Khan turned his horse toward me. That moment two messengers sprang out before him, and shouted, "On thy face, unbelieving dog!" but I did not obey, though they fell to beating me on the head with long reeds. Then the master, approaching, inquired,—

"Why wilt thou not fall on thy face before me?"

I answered, "If it is not befitting a noble to do that before his own king, how dost thou wish me to do it before a stranger and a pagan?"

Here the Khan, turning his face from me, said,—

"Thou didst speak wisely, O Sukyman." And then he said to me, "If I were to offer thee the choice, either to show me honor and fall on thy face before me, for which thou wouldst receive freedom, or die a cruel death, which wouldst thou choose?"

To this I answered that it did not befit a captive to choose; let him, the Khan, do what he liked with me; but let him observe, however, that each man of the lowest station may inflict a cruel death; but the majesty of a monarch, having its source in the will of God, becomes most like the Creator, and shows its power best, when it gives life instead of death. He pondered over my words, and said afterward,—

"If, being a captive, thou wilt not honor or obey me, thou dost act against God, who commands captives to obey."

I answered, "Only my body is in captivity."

Hearing this, the Tartars grew pale; but the Khan was patient, for it was not in vain that they called him discreet. After he had meditated a time, he rode away; but while doing so, he said to the Agas and to his messengers, "When ye fall into captivity among unbelievers, be like this man."

Now I had rest for two days, and they brought food to me. Some even came to me saying, "Our lord will not forget thee; but when he brings thee into favor, do not forget us."

Captivity had so debased the hearts of those people that, foreseeing a change in my fortune, they were seeking favors with me while I was still lying in filth. I rejoiced in soul, for I thought that I should receive freedom, and perhaps with it find happiness. After two days, the Khan, in passing, turned his horse to me a second time.

"I have weighed," said he, "thy words in my wisdom, and I put them on the scales of justice. Thou hast found favor with me for thy courage; say then what thou dost wish that I should do for thee?"

I answered that for one born in a free condition, freedom was the dearest fruit of his favor.

"And if I refuse it?" asked he.

"Then give me death."

He stopped again; he desired so much that all should admire and praise his wisdom that he undertook nothing without meditation. During this time the heart was beating in me like a hammer. After he had thought a while, he said, —

"Do not draw the bow too far lest it break and wound thy hands; therefore I tell thee my last words: I will give thee a yellow coat, take thee to my court, reward thee with riches, and make thee my equerry, will not extort change of faith from thee, if thou wilt promise to serve me with good will."

My heart quivered at once with great joy, but suddenly I thought that those were temptations of Satan, and besides what should I say to my fathers in answer to their question, "What wert thou on earth?" Could I say to those knights who had fallen in battle, "I was of my own choice a Tartar equerry"? And a terrible fear seized me before that question of my fathers, a fear greater than torture and death; stretching out my hands to the Khan then, I cried, "Oh, lord, do not ask my will, for the will comes from the soul; the soul is not only mindful of faith, but of the condition in which it entered the world; and receiving that condition from my fathers, I must bear it back to them unspotted."

"Captive, thou hast broken the bow," said the Khan.

I saw that the hour had come, for anger began to appear on his face; but he recollected himself and spoke these words to Sukyman, —

"Wise Sukyman, indeed, I have gone too far in kindness to this dog, and now I command thee to break him without fail; but before thou takest his life, bring him by torture to this, that he shall crawl in obedience even at thy feet."

Then he rode away; Kalmucks took me and bound me to a stake, at command of Sukyman. All the people and captives that were there ran together to see what tortures would be given me. Directing my soul to God with all the strength that was in me, I implored this of Him most, to give me fortitude, and not let me debase myself. All at once I felt that my prayer was heard, for a strong spirit breathed on me. I thought that I represented the power of that cross which never will perish; that I was there as an envoy of the Commonwealth, a delegate from the estates to be tortured; that I was there a soldier, to die at command of Christ, called to testify with my blood the foundation of my life, to testify to the soul, which, like a heavenly fire, does not perish.

And thinking thus, though wretched, weak, covered with dust, emaciated by hunger, I felt immeasurable majesty within myself, as if I had been looking from some height on this world. The Kalmucks began to lash me with rawhides, and soon I was swimming in blood.

"Wilt thou fall on thy face?" asked they.

"I am a Polish noble." I answered.

Then they lashed me again; others lighted slow fires at my feet, so that, while burning, I should cry the sooner for mercy. In fact, I began to yield, but not in soul, only in body, for great weakness passed through my bones, and the light of day paled before my eyes. Seeing that death was approaching, I raised my head with the remnant of my strength, and cried in the direction of the Commonwealth, "Dost thou see me; dost thou hear me?"

Then suddenly, as it were, across all the steppe and through Perekop, came to me the voice, "I see." In the distance something began to seem hazy; the heavens and the air ran together; out of this came a woman with a sweet face and stood near me. The fire ceased to burn me; the rawhide whistled above me no more, and I felt that I was flying, borne on the hand of that woman. With her was a legion of angels singing, "Not in a kontush and with a sabre, but in wounds, O knight, knight manful in battle, enduring in torture! O Paladin of Christ, faithful son of the bloody land! Welcome to peace! welcome to happiness! welcome to joy!" And so we flew onward to heaven, and what I saw there my sinful lips cannot utter to mortal ears.

CHAPTER V.

A WAGON squeaks under me, and a fresh, cool breeze blows around. I open my eyes; I see not Kizlich, but a steppe, — a steppe like the sea. Then I close my lids, thinking that a dream is presenting some puppet-show before me. I look again; I see the old face of Kimek, Pan Tvoryanski's house-steward, and behind him a number of attendants.

"Praise be to God," he says, "you have recovered!"
I ask whither I am going.
"To the Commonwealth."
"I am free?"
"Free."
"Who ransomed me?"
"The young lady."

When he said "young lady," something like an immense weeping burst forth from my breast. I stretched out my hands; I fainted.

When I came to myself a day later, a wagon was squeaking beneath me, and Kimek told all. Behold, Pan Tvoryanski had been transferred from this wretched world to a better one, leaving Marysia his heiress; she was living with her uncle, a bishop. Tidings of my misery, my torments and tortures, reached them; then she, falling at her uncle's feet, acknowledged her love, and, with his permission, ransomed me from Sukyman's power.

Kimek did not find the Khan in Kizlich. When the plague passed he went to a place called Eupatoria; and Sukyman, thinking me dead, sold what was left of me for three hundred gold ducats.

Kimek also thought that he would be more likely to take me home dead, for I took no note of God's world for two weeks; still the Lord restored life to me.

Hearing all this, and understanding that I was ransomed from pagan captivity at the instance of my maiden, I wept earnestly, and made this vow in my soul to love that compassionate maiden and guard her during my lifetime. It seemed to me then that my stay in the Crimea, my captivity with Sukyman, and the tortures which I had suffered were a dream. Providence so orders the things of this life that in time everything passes and remains only in memory, with this difference, however, that the harsher the happenings the pleasanter it is to remember them. So that not only past labors, but sorrows become joyous.

If God sometimes tries a man of knightly station severely, He adds strength to him; and if He takes his life, He rewards him even in that way. He sent me a saving angel in my Marysia, and did not let me disgrace myself in time of trials.

When I woke in the night, or when the morning dawned and I waked after sleep, I repeated that I was going to my birthplace, and would see Marysia. Thinking thus, I wished to sit on horseback immediately; but Kimek would not permit that, as there was no strength in me. I lay on my back in the wagon, like some bag, and in that way we went to Mohylna. There, when my old comrades saw me, they rushed out like bees from a hive, crying, "We know of thee, we know! we know! Welcome, dear comrade!" and looking at my feet, into which burnt coals had settled thickly, they covered themselves with tears, and one repeated to another, "Bend the head before him, for he is the truest knight among all!" Then they began to give me what each owned or had acquired from plunder: hence, horses with trappings silk tents, sabres set with precious stones, Italian sequins, Turkish cloth, holsters, rich daggers, vessels of silver or of pure gold, sable furs; one man would give a handful of turquoises or rubies, another a diamond clasp or pin, so that they threw down before me treasures worth thousands of gold ducats which I had to carry in five wagons. This they did with good heart, but the more easily since they were going on a war against the Cossacks; for Loboda and Nalevaika had begun their movement in the Ukraine, for which they were crushed by Jolkevski.

Then we went farther. Frequently various detachments of warriors met us, and some warriors, when approaching, inquired: "Whom are ye carrying?" To which Kimek answered, "A noble cut to pieces in captivity." After these words each not only left us in quiet, but besides gave what he could. Beyond Kieff, we met Jolkevski himself, who, feigning a march on Pereyaslav, wanted to cross the Dnieper. When that famous warrior heard what had met me in captivity, he said, "They reward men of less value with starostaships; I will write to the king of this." He gave me a costly ring, which I wear on my finger till now. My heart rose at sight of his warriors, who, though not numerous, and fatigued by continual pursuing, were so trained and so willing that in no battle could an enemy hold the field before them.

Looking at those men, black from the wind, men who slept on the grass of the steppe, ate nothing for two days and three, removed not their armor at night even, who stanched their wounds with powder, and who withal had the courage of heroes, I felt humble, and thought it not well to be elated and think much of my services, when those made naught of enduring such hardships and were singing in gladness, as if not understanding that they were heroes. Oh, how sorry I was not to be able to mount a horse, wear armor, carry a lance, and go with them! I had to stay behind, and besides pull out dead coals from my skin.

There were great delights at that time in the Ukraine for all valiant souls. Every night flames could be seen, and battle trumpets heard.

Pan Pototski, voevoda of Kamenyets, with Jolkevski, whirled around the steppes like an eagle. Prince Rojinski was victorious near Pavolochy; Yazlovetski was skirmishing; Nalevaika, Loboda and Sasko, with the rabble, rushed away through ravines like fleeing wolves.

Once peasants drunk on Moldavian wine met us. Kimek told them, as he had others, that he was taking home a wounded noble. They lighted many torches to recognize me in the night; then they moved on, taking me to Kremski. When torches were lighted in Kremski's camp I was recognized by that Cossack Essaul who had been with me in the Crimea and was liberated for saving a child. This Cossack began to cry, "O lord! O lord!" and afterward, while saying, "That Pole they are taking is a saint!" he fell at my feet. When he told Kremski how I had helped them in captivity, others came to me cap in hand; these I reprimanded at once for not remaining in obedience to the Commonwealth. Kremski not only did not take my life, more than that, he took nothing, but, having made me a present, sent a guard with me. So the enemy is able to honor wounds and bravery in a warrior, for this God certainly rewarded Kremski with salvation; he was not so hostile to the Commonwealth as people imagined.

In the Ukraine, nay, in the whole Commonwealth, it was seething as in a beehive, and God sent many misfortunes on our land; for with war moved also that helldweller, the pestilence. When their minds were occupied with other things, there were few who paid attention to it; but I saw it with my own eyes from the wagon. That pestilence went not in a straight line, but, as in the Crimea, attacked in spots, carrying off single hamlets, villages, and settlements. Here and there also were mayors of the air,[1] so called; and piles of manure were burning

---

[1] Mayors of the air were officials who saw that the air was made offensive to the pestilence. According to popular belief, the pestilence appeared in the form of a woman.

in the villages, smoking abundantly and offensively, the odor of which the pestilence could not endure. In the night tar-makers watched these heaps lest the fire should die out in them. The people, in view of disaster, formed processions, in which banners with death-heads were carried. At the same time God sent down blindness of some sort on men; for there was no agreement among magnates, who, instead of mounting their horses, as they might have done, simply and honestly, disturbed diets with their wrangling. The enemy assembled on the borders, and our forces were wonderfully scattered. In this, our misfortune has ever consisted; for if all the nobles and magnates would rush to battle in harmony, the orb of the earth would tremble before us. I say this, because there are none who can stand before our lances. Later in life I saw Turkish janissaries, Scottish infantry, and Swedish cavalry broken by them; so I assert, that nature endowed us more richly with warlike capacity than others, but we send a thousand men out, where others send ten times as many.

The secret of why this is done must be sought in God's will, for it should seem to each one easier to mount a horse, than disturb with the tongue. Greater glory would result, less error of mind, greater merit, and more certain salvation.

A man passes like a traveller through the world, and should not be concerned for himself, but only for the Commonwealth, which is and must be without end. Amen!

CHAPTER VI.

O GOD, Holy, Almighty, Immortal, be Thou praised in Thy works! Whenever I turn my eyes filled with tears, I see Thee, and when I see Thee I confess Thee.

Thou hast hung the fires of heaven in the firmament. Thou, in commanding the sun to rise from the sea, makest day on the mountains and in the valleys. In Thy praise is the murmur of pine woods and the lowing of flocks in the field. In Thy praise armies ride through the steppes, with the neighing of horses; and every earthly Commonwealth gives Thee honor. And because Thou hast deserted Thy servant and deprived him of happiness, in this too be Thou praised. My life has passed in war, and my hair has grown white in trials. O Lord, I was present where cannon sang Thy majesty with fire, and thundered Thy name in smoke! In Moldavia and Livonia my blood has flowed; and to-day I am old, my dim pupils are turning earthward, and my body desires endless rest. Not earthly goods, not wealth, not honors, not offices do I bear to that world with me, for behold I am poor as at first. But, O Lord, I will show Thee my shield, and I will say: "Behold, it is stainless; that is only my blood! My name I have preserved unspotted; I have not yielded in spirit — though bending from pain, I did not break."

Here ends the fragment from the diary of Alexis Zdanoborski. It appears from this short chronicle that that "unbroken prince," who would not become a Tartar equerry, had a life full of suffering. In accordance with the spirit of the time he was greatly attached to his name. With Marysia, as is evident from the closing commentary, he was separated by fate. It is certain also that he never married. Indeed, it is proper to infer from all, that this noble died without posterity, and was the last of his race.

LET US FOLLOW HIM

LET US FOLLOW HIM.

CHAPTER I.

CAIUS SEPTIMIUS CINNA was a Roman patrician. He had spent his youth in the legions and in severe camp-life. Later he returned to Rome to enjoy glory, luxury, and a great though somewhat shattered fortune. He used and abused at that time everything which the gigantic city could offer.

His nights were spent at feasts in lordly suburban villas; his days in sword practice with fencers, in discussions with rhetors at the baths, where disputes were held, and where the scandal of the city and the world was related, in circuses, at races, at the struggles of gladiators, or among Greek musicians, Thracian soothsayers, and wonderful dancing-girls from the islands of the Archipelago. He inherited from the renowned Lucullus, a relative on the mother's side, a love for exquisite dishes. At his table were served Grecian wines, Neapolitan oysters, Numidian mice, and locust fat preserved in honey from Pontus.

Whatever Rome possessed Cinna must have, beginning with fish of the Red Sea, and ending with white ptarmigans from the banks of the Borysthenes (Dnieper). He made use of things not only as a soldier run riot, but as a patrician who passes the measure. He had instilled into himself, or had perhaps even roused in himself, a love for the beautiful, — a love for statues rescued from the ruins of Corinth, for pitchers from Attica, for Etruscan vases from foggy Sericum, for Roman mosaics, for fabrics brought from the Euphrates, for Arabian perfumes, and for all the peculiar trifles which filled the void of patrician life.

He knew how to talk of these trifles, as a specialist and connoisseur, with toothless old men, who decked out their baldness in wreaths of roses when going to a feast, and who after the feast chewed heliotrope blossoms to make the breath of their lungs odoriferous. He felt also the beauty of Cicero's periods, and of verses of Horace or Ovid.

Educated by an Athenian rhetor, he conversed in Greek fluently; he knew whole pages of the "Iliad" by heart, and during a feast could sing odes of Anacreon till he had grown hoarse or drunk. Through his master and other rhetors he had rubbed against philosophy, and become sufficiently acquainted with it to know the plans of various edifices of thought reared in Hellas and the colonies; he understood too that all these edifices were in ruins. He knew many Stoics personally; for these he cherished dislike, since he looked on them rather as a political party, and, besides, as hypochondriacs, hostile to joyous living. Sceptics had a seat frequently at his table; and during intervals between courses they overturned entire systems, and announced at their cups, filled with wine, that pleasure was vanity, truth something unattainable, and that the object of a sage could be only dead rest.

All this struck Cinna's ears without piercing to the depth. He recognized no principle, and would have none. In Cato he saw the union of great character and great folly. He looked on life as a sea, on which winds blew whithersoever they listed; and wisdom in his eyes was the art of setting sails in such fashion that they would urge one's boat forward. He esteemed his own broad shoulders and sound stomach; he esteemed his own beautiful Roman head, with his aquiline nose and powerful jaws. He was certain that with these he could pass through life somehow.

Though not belonging to the school of Sceptics, he was a practical Sceptic, and hence a lover of pleasure, though he knew that pleasure was not happiness. The genuine teaching of Epicurus he did not know; hence he considered himself an Epicurean. In general he looked on philosophy as mental fencing, as useful as that which was taught by the sword-master. When discourses on it wearied him, he went to the circus to see blood.

He did not believe in the gods any more than in virtue, truth, and happiness. He believed only in soothsaying, and had his own superstitions; moreover, the mysterious beliefs of the Orient roused his curiosity. To slaves he was a good master, unless when occasional tedium brought him to cruelty. He thought life a great amphora, which was the more valuable the better the wine contained in it; hence he tried to fill his own with the best. He did not love any one; but he loved many things, among others his own eagle-like face with splendid skull, and his shapely patrician foot.

In the first years of his frolicking life he loved also to astound Rome, and succeeded a number of times. Later he grew as indifferent to that as to other things.

CHAPTER II.

AT last he ruined himself. His creditors tore his property to pieces, and in place of it there remained to Cinna weariness, as after great toil, satiety, and one more unexpected thing, a certain deep disquiet. He had tried wealth; he had tried love, as that age understood it; he had tried pleasure, military glory, and dangers. He had come to know the limits of human thought more or less; he had come in contact with poetry and art. Hence he might suppose that from life he had taken what it had to give. Now he felt as though he had overlooked something — and that the most important. But he did not know what it was, and tortured his head over this problem in vain. More than once had he striven to shake himself out of these thoughts, and out of this disquiet. He had tried to persuade himself that there was nothing more in life, and could not be; but straightway his disquiet, instead of diminishing, increased quickly to such a degree that it seemed to him that he was disquieted not only for himself, but for all Rome. He envied the Sceptics and also considered them fools, for they insisted that one may fill completely the void with the empty. There existed in him then two men, as it were, one of whom was astonished at the disquiet which he felt, while the other was forced to recognize it as perfectly normal.

Soon after the loss of his property, thanks to great family influence, Cinna was sent to an official post in Alexandria, partly to build up a new fortune in a rich country. His disquiet entered the ship at Brundisium, and sailed across the sea with him. In Alexandria Cinna thought that questions concerning office, new people, another society, new impressions, would relieve him of the intrusive companion. But he was mistaken.

Two months passed, and just as the grain of Demeter, brought from Italy, grew still more luxuriantly in the rich soil of the Delta, so his disquiet from a sturdy twig changed, as it were, into a spreading cedar, and began to cast a still greater shadow on the soul of Cinna.

At first he strove to free himself of this shadow by the same life that he had led in Rome formerly. Alexandria was a place of pleasure, full of Grecian women with golden hair and clear complexions, which the Egyptian sun covered with a transparent, amber lustre. In their society he sought rest.

But when this also proved vain he began to think of suicide. Many of his comrades had freed themselves from life's cares in that manner, and for causes still more foolish than those which Cinna had, — frequently from weariness alone, from the emptiness of life, or a lack of desire to make further use of it. When a slave held a sword adroitly and with sufficient strength, one instant ended all. Cinna caught at this idea; but when he had almost resolved to obey it, a wonderful dream held him back. Behold, it seemed to him that when he was borne across the river [1] he saw on the other bank his disquiet in the form of a wretched slave; it bowed to him, saying, "I have come in advance to receive thee." Cinna was terrified for the first time in life; because he understood that if he could not think of existence beyond the grave without disquiet, then they would both go there.

In this extreme, he resolved to make the acquaintance of sages with whom the Serapeum was crowded, judging that among them perhaps he might find the solution of his riddle. They, it is true, were unable to solve any doubt

[1] Styx.

of his; but to make up they entitled him "of the museum," which title they offered usually to Romans of high birth and position. That was small consolation at first; and the stamp of sage, given a man who could not explain that which concerned him most highly, might seem to Cinna ironical. He supposed, however, that the Serapeum did not reveal all its wisdom at once, perhaps; and he did not lose hope altogether.

The most active sage in Alexandria was the noble Timon of Athens, a man of wealth, and a Roman citizen. He had lived a number of years in Alexandria, whither he had come to sound the depths of Egyptian science. It was said of him that there was no parchment or papyrus in the Library which he had not read, and that he possessed all the wisdom of mankind. He was, moreover, mild and forbearing. Cinna distinguished him at once among the multitude of pedants and commentators with stiffened brains, and soon formed with him an acquaintance which, after a time, was changed into close intimacy, and even into friendship. The young Roman admired the dialectic skill, the eloquence and dignity, with which the old man spoke of lofty themes touching man's destiny, and that of the world. He was struck especially by this, that that dignity was joined to a certain sadness. Later, when they had grown more intimate, Cinna was seized frequently by the wish to inquire of the old sage the cause of that sadness, and to open his own heart to him. In fact, it came to that finally.

CHAPTER III.

A CERTAIN evening, after animated discussions about the transmigration of souls, they remained alone on the terrace, from which the view was toward the sea. Cinna, taking Timon's hand, declared openly what the great torment of his life was, and why he had striven to approach the scholars and philosophers of the Serapeum.

"I have gained this much at least," said he; "I have learned to know you, O Timon, and I understand now that if you cannot solve my life's riddle, no other man can."

Timon gazed for a time at the smooth surface of the sea, in which the new moon was reflected; then he said,—

"Hast thou seen those flocks of birds, Cinna, which fly past here in winter from northern glooms? Dost thou know what they seek in Egypt?"

"I do. Warmth and light."

"Souls of men also seek warmth, which is love, and light, which means truth. The birds know whither they are flying for their good; but souls are flying over roadless places, in wandering, in sadness, and disquiet."

"Why can they not find the road, noble Timon?"

"Once man's repose was in the gods; to-day, faith in the gods is burnt out, like oil in a lamp. Men thought that to souls philosophy would be the light of truth; to-day, as thou knowest best of all, on its ruins in Rome and in the Academy in Athens, and here, sit Sceptics, to whom it seemed that it was bringing in peace, but it brought in disquiet. For to renounce light and heat is to leave the soul in darkness, which is disquiet. Hence, stretching out our hands before us, we seek an exit in groping."

"Hast thou not found it?"

"I have sought, and I have not found it. Thou hast sought it in pleasure, I in thought; and the same mist encircles us. Know then that not thou alone art suffering, but in thee the soul of the world is tortured. Is it long since thou hast ceased to believe in the gods?"

"At Rome they are honored publicly yet, and even new ones are brought from Asia and Egypt; but no one believes in them sincerely, except dealers in vegetables, who come in the morning from the country to the city."

"And these are the only people who live in peace."

"They are like those who bow down here to cats and onions."

"Just like those, who, in the manner of beasts, ask for nothing beyond sleep after eating."

"But is life worth the living in view of this?"

"Do I know what death will bring?"

"What is the difference, then, between thee and the Sceptics?"

"Sceptics are satisfied with darkness, or feign that they are satisfied, but I suffer in it."

"And thou seest no salvation?"

Timon was silent for a moment, and then answered slowly, as if with hesitation, —

"I wait for it."

"Whence?"

"I know not."

Then he rested his head on the palm of his hand; and as if under the influence of that silence which had settled down on the terrace, he began to speak in a low and measured voice, —

"A wonderful thing; but at times it seems to me that if the world contained nothing beyond that which we know, and if we could be nothing more than we are, this disquiet would not exist in us. So in this sickness I find hope of health. Faith in Olympus and philosophy are dead, but health may be some new truth which I know not."

Beyond expectation, that talk brought great solace to Cinna. When he heard that the whole world was sick, and not he alone, he felt as if some one had taken a great weight from him and distributed it on a thousand shoulders.

CHAPTER IV.

FROM that time the friendship uniting Cinna and the old Greek became still more intimate. They visited each other frequently and exchanged thoughts, like bread in time of a banquet. Besides, Cinna, in spite of experience and the weariness which comes of use, had not reached the age yet when life has ceased to contain the charm of unknown things; and just this charm he found in Antea, Timon's only daughter.

Her fame was not less in Alexandria than the fame of her father. Eminent Romans frequenting Timon's house did her homage, Greeks did her homage, philosophers from the Serapeum did her homage, and so did the people. Timon did not restrict her to the gineceum, after the manner of other women; and he tried to transfer to her everything that he himself knew. When she had passed the years of childhood, he read Greek books with her, and even Latin and Hebrew; for, gifted with an uncommon memory, and reared in many-tongued Alexandria, she learned those languages quickly. She was a

companion to him in thoughts; she took frequent part in
the discussions which were held in Timon's house during
Symposiums. Often in the labyrinth of difficult questions, she was able, like Ariadne, to avoid going astray
herself and to extricate others. Her father honored and
admired her. The charm of mystery and almost of
sacredness surrounded her, besides; for she had prophetic
dreams, in which she saw things invisible to common
mortals. The old sage loved her as his own soul, and the
more for this reason, that he was afraid of losing her; for
frequently she said that beings appeared in dreams to
her, — ominous beings, — also a certain divine light, and
she knew not whether this light was the source of life or
death.

Meanwhile she was met only by love. The Egyptians,
who frequented Timon's house, called her the Lotus; perhaps because that flower received divine honor on the
banks of the Nile, and perhaps also because whoever saw
it might forget the whole world besides.

Her beauty was equal to her wisdom. The Egyptian
sun did not darken her face, in which the rosy rays of
light seemed to be enclosed in transparent mother-of-
pearl. Her eyes had the blueness of the Nile, and their
glances flowed from a remoteness as unknown as the
source of that mysterious river. When Cinna saw and
heard her the first time, on returning home, he conceived
the wish to rear an altar to her in the atrium of his house,
and offer a white dove on it. He had met thousands of
women in his life, beginning with virgins from the remote north, with white eyelashes and hair the color of
ripe wheat, and ending with Numidians, black as lava;
but he had not met hitherto such a figure, or such a soul.
And the oftener he saw her, the better he knew her, the
oftener it happened to him to hear her words, the more

did amazement increase in him. Sometimes he, who did not believe in the gods, thought that Antea could not be the daughter of Timon, but of a god, hence only half woman, and therefore half immortal.

And soon he loved her with a love unexpected, immense, irresistible, as different from the feeling which he had known up to that time as Antea was different from other women. He desired to love her only to do her honor. Hence he was willing to give blood to possess her. He felt that he would prefer to be a beggar with her than to be Cæsar without her. And as a whirlpool of the sea sweeps away with irresistible might all that comes within its circle, so Cinna's love swept away his soul, his heart, his thoughts, his days, his nights, and everything out of which life is composed.

Till at last it swept away Antea.

"*Tu felix* (Thou art happy), Cinna!" said his friends.

"*Tu felix*, Cinna," said he to himself; and when at last he married her, when her divine lips uttered the sacramental words, "Where thou art Caius, there am I, Caia," it seemed to him that his felicity was like the sea, — inexhaustible and boundless.

CHAPTER V.

A YEAR passed, and that young wife received at her domestic hearth almost divine honor; to her husband she was the sight of his eyes, love, wisdom, light. But Cinna, comparing his happiness with the sea, forgot that the sea has its ebbs.

After a year Antea fell into an illness cruel and unknown. Her dreams changed into terrible visions, which exhausted her life. In her face the rays of light were quenched; there remained only the paleness of mother-of-pearl. Her hands began to be transparent; her eyes sank deeply under her forehead; and the rosy lotus became more and more a white lotus, white as the face of the dead. It was noticed that falcons began to circle above Cinna's house, which in Egypt was a herald of death. The visions grew more and more terrible.

When at midday the sun filled the world with bright light, and the city was buried in silence, it seemed to Antea that she heard around her the quick steps of invisible beings, and in the depth of the air she saw a dry, yellow, corpse-like face gazing with black eyes at her. Those eyes gazed persistently, as if summoning her to go somewhere into a darkness full of mysteries and dread. Then Antea's body began to tremble, as in a fever; her forehead was covered with pallor, with drops of cold sweat; and that honored priestess of the domestic hearth was changed into a helpless and terrified child, who, hiding on her husband's breast, repeated with pale lips, —

"Save me, O Caius! defend me!"

And Caius would have hurled himself at every spectre which Persephone might send from the nether world, but in vain did he strain his eyes into space round about. As is usual in midday hours, it was lonely. White light filled the city; the sea seemed to burn in the sun, and in the silence was heard only the calling of falcons circling above the house.

The visions grew more and more frequent, and at last they came daily. They pursued Antea in the interior of the house, as well as in the atrium and the chambers. Cinna, by advice of physicians, brought in Egyptian sambuka players, and Bedouins, blowing clay whistles; the noisy music of these was to drown the sound made

LET US FOLLOW HIM.   231

by the invisible beings. But all this proved futile. Antea heard the sound amid the greatest uproar; and when the sun became so high that a man's shadow was near his feet, like a garment hanging from the arm, in the air quivering from heat appeared the face of the corpse, and looking at Antea with glassy eyes it moved away gradually, as if to say, "Follow me!"

Sometimes it seemed to Antea that the lips of the corpse moved slowly; sometimes that black disgusting beetles came out from between them and flew through the air toward her. At the very thought of that vision her eyes were filled with terror, and at last life became such a dreadful torture that she begged Cinna to hold a sword for her, or to let her drink poison.

But he knew that he had not strength for the deed. With that very sword he would have opened his own veins to serve Antea, but he could not take her life. When he imagined that dear face of hers dead, with closed eyes, filled with icy composure, and that breast opened with his sword, he felt that he must go mad before he could kill her.

A certain Greek physician told him that Hecate appeared to Antea, and that those invisible beings whose noise frightened the sick woman were the attendants of the ominous divinity. According to him, there was no salvation for Antea, for whoso has seen Hecate must die.

Then Cinna, who not long before would have laughed at faith in Hecate, sacrificed a hecatomb to her. But the sacrifice was useless, and next day the gloomy eyes were gazing at Antea about midday.

Attendants covered her head; but she saw the face even through the thickest covering. Then they confined her in a dark room; the face looked at her from the walls, illuminating the darkness with its pale gleam of a corpse.

Every evening the sick woman grew better, and fell into such a deep sleep that to Cinna and Timon it seemed more than once as though she would not wake again. Soon she grew so weak that she could not walk without assistance. She was borne about in a litter.

Cinna's former disquiet returned with a hundredfold greater force and took complete possession of him. He was terrified regarding the life of Antea; but there was also a wonderful feeling that her sickness was in some way mysteriously connected with that of which he had spoken in his first conversation with Timon. Perhaps the old sage had the same thought; but Cinna would not ask him, and feared to talk concerning this matter.

Meanwhile the sick woman withered like a flower in whose cup a poisonous spider has settled.

But the despairing Cinna strove against hope to save her. First he took her to the desert near Memphis; but when a stay in the quiet of the pyramids gave no respite from the dreadful visions, he returned to Alexandria and surrounded her with soothsayers, who professed to enchant away diseases. He brought in from every kind of shameless rabble people who exploited the credulity of mankind by marvellous medicines. But he had no choice left, and snatched at every method.

At this time there came from Cæsarea a renowned physician, a Hebrew, Joseph, son of Khuza. Cinna brought him at once to his wife, and for a time hope returned to his heart. Joseph, who had no faith in Greek and Roman gods, rejected contemptuously the opinion about Hecate. He supposed it more likely that demons had entered the sick woman, and advised Cinna to leave Egypt, where, in addition to demons, marshy effluvia of the Delta might injure Antea. He advised also, perhaps because he was a Hebrew, to go to Jerusalem, — a place where demons have no entrance, and where the air is dry and wholesome.

Cinna followed this advice the more willingly, — first, because there was no other, and second, because Jerusalem was governed by an acquaintance of his, a procurator whose ancestors were formerly clients of the house of Cinna.

In fact, when they came, the procurator, Pontius, received them with open arms and gave them as dwelling his own summer residence, which stood near the walls of the city. But Cinna's hope was swept away before his arrival. The corpse-like face looked at Antea even on the deck of the galley; on coming to the city the sick woman waited for midday with the same deathly terror as on a time in Alexandria.

And so their days began to pass in oppression, despair, and fear of death.

CHAPTER VI.

IN the atrium, in spite of the fountain, the shady portico, and the early hour, it was extremely hot, for the marble was heated by the spring sun; but at a distance from the house there grew an old, branching pistachio-tree, which shaded a considerable area round about. As the place was open, the breeze there was far greater than elsewhere; hence Cinna commanded to carry to that spot the litter, decked with hyacinths and apple-blossoms, in which Antea was resting. Then sitting near her, he placed his palm on her hands, which were as pale as alabaster, and asked, —

"Is it pleasant for thee here, carissima?"

"Pleasant," answered she, in a scarcely audible voice.

And she closed her eyes, as if sleep had seized her. Silence followed. Only the breeze moved with a rustling the branches of the pistachio-tree; and on the earth around the litter were quivering golden spots, formed of sun-rays, which broke through between the leaves; locusts were hissing among the rocks.

The sick woman opened her eyes after a moment.

"Caius," said she, "is it true that in this country a philosopher has appeared, who cures the sick?"

"They call such men prophets here," answered Cinna. "I have heard of him, and I wished to bring him to thee, but it turned out that he was a false miracle-worker. Besides, he blasphemed against the sanctuary and the religion of this country; hence the procurator has delivered him to death, and this very day he is to be crucified."

Antea dropped her head.

"Time will cure thee," said Cinna, seeing the sadness reflected on her face.

"Time is at the service of death, not of life," answered she, slowly.

And again silence ensued; round about the golden spots quivered continually; the locusts hissed still more loudly, and from the crannies of the cliff little lizards crept out onto stones, and sought sunny places.

Cinna looked from moment to moment at Antea, and for the thousandth time despairing thoughts flew through his head. He felt that all means of salvation had been spent, that there was no ray of hope, that soon the dear form before him would become a vanishing shadow and a handful of dust in a columbarium.

Even now while lying with closed eyes in the litter decked with flowers, she seemed dead.

"I will follow thee!" said Cinna, in his soul.

Meanwhile steps were heard in the distance. Immediately Antea's face became white as chalk; from between her half-open lips came hurried breathing; her bosom heaved quickly. The ill-fated martyr felt sure that the crowd of invisible beings which preceded the corpse with glassy eyes were drawing near. Cinna seized her hands and strove to pacify her.

"Fear not, Antea; I hear those steps too. That is Pontius, who is coming to visit us," added he, after a while. In fact, the procurator, attended by two slaves, appeared at the turn of the path. He was a man no longer young; he had an oval face carefully shaven, full of assumed dignity, and also of suffering and care.

"A greeting to thee, noble Cinna, and to thee, divine Antea!" said he, as he came under the shade of the pistachio-tree. "After a cold night the day has grown hot. May it favor you both, and may the health of Antea bloom like those hyacinths and those apple-tree twigs, which adorn her litter."

"Peace be with thee, and be greeted!" answered Cinna.

The procurator seated himself on a piece of rock, looked at Antea, frowned imperceptibly, and answered,—

"Loneliness produces sadness and sickness; but in the midst of crowds there is no place for fear, hence I will give one advice to thee. Unfortunately this is neither Antioch nor Cæsarea; there are no games here, no horse-races; and were we to erect a circus, those madmen would tear it down the next day. Here thou wilt hear nothing but this phrase, 'the law,' and everything disturbs that law. I would rather be in Scythia."

"Of what dost thou wish to speak, O Pilate?"

"Indeed, I have wandered from my subject; but cares are the cause of this. I have said that among crowds there is no room for fear. Now ye can have a spectacle to-day. In Jerusalem, ye should be amused with something; above all, Antea should be in the midst of crowds at midday. Three men will die on the cross to-day; that is better than nothing! Because of the Pasch a mob of the strangest ruffians has come from out all this land to the city. Ye can look at those people. I will command to give you a place apart near the crosses. I hope that the condemned will die bravely. One of them is a marvellous person: he calls himself the Son of God; he is as mild as a dove, and has really done nothing to merit death."

"And didst thou condemn him to the cross?"

"I wanted to rid myself of trouble, and also avoid stirring up that nest of hornets that buzz around the temple; even as it is, they send complaints to Rome against me. Besides, the accused is not a Roman citizen."

"The man will not suffer less for that reason."

The procurator made no answer, but after a while he began to speak, as if to himself, —

"There is one thing that I do not like, — exaggeration. Whoever uses that word before me takes away my cheerfulness for the day. The golden mean! that is what wisdom commands us to follow, as I think. And there is not a corner of the world in which that principle is less respected than here. How all this tortures me! how it tortures me! In nothing is there repose, in nothing balance, — neither in men nor in nature. At present, for example, it is spring; the nights are cold; but during the day there is such heat that it is difficult to walk on stones. It is long yet till midday, and see what is happening! Of the people — better not speak! I am here, because I must be here. Never mind that! I might leave my subject a second time. Go to witness the crucifixion. I am convinced that that Nazarene will die valiantly. I gave command to flog him, thinking in that way to save him from death. I am not cruel. When he was lashed he was as patient as a lamb, and he blessed the people. When he was covered with blood, he raised his eyes and prayed. That is the most marvellous person that I have seen in my life. My wife has not given me a moment of peace because of him. 'Permit not the death of that innocent man!' this is what she has been dinning into my ears since daybreak. I wanted to save him. Twice I went to the bema and spoke to those priests and that mangy rabble. They answered in one voice, raising their heads and opening their jaws to the ears, 'Crucify him!'"

"Didst thou yield to them?" asked Cinna.

"I did, for in the city there would be mobs, and I am here to keep peace. I must do my duty. I dislike exaggeration, and, besides, I am mortally wearied; but when I undertake a thing, I do not hesitate to sacrifice the life of one man for the general welfare, especially when he is an unknown person whom no one will mention. All the worse for him that he is not a Roman."

"The sun shines not on Rome alone," whispered Antea.

"Divine Antea," answered the procurator, "I might answer that on the whole round of the earth the sun shines on Roman rule; therefore for the good of that rule it is proper to sacrifice everything, and disturbances undermine our authority. But, above all, I beg of thee not to ask me to change the sentence. Cinna will tell thee that that cannot be, and that, once sentence is pronounced, Cæsar alone can change it. Though I wished, I have not the power to change. Is that not the case, Caius?"

"It is."

But those words caused Antea evident pain, for she said, thinking of herself, perhaps, —

"Then it is possible to suffer and die without being guilty."

"No one is without guilt," answered Pontius. "This Nazarene has committed no crime; hence I, as procurator, washed my hands. But as a man, I condemn his teaching. I conversed with him purposely rather long, wishing to test the man, and convinced myself that he announces monstrous things. The case is difficult! The world must stand on sound sense. Who denies that virtue is needed? Certainly not I. But even the Stoics only teach men to endure opposition with calmness; they do not insist that we should renounce everything, from our property to our dinner. Answer, Cinna, — thou art a man of sound judgment, — what wouldst thou think of me were I, neither from one cause nor another, to bestow this house in which thou art dwelling on those tattered fellows who warm themselves in the sun at the Joppa gate? And he insists on just such things. Besides, he says that we should love all equally: the Jews as well as the Romans themselves, the Romans as the Egyptians, the Egyptians as the Africans, and so on. I confess that I have had enough of this. At the moment when his life is in peril, he bears himself as if the question were of some one else; he teaches — and prays. It is not my duty to save a man who has no care for his own safety. Whoso does not know how to preserve measure in anything is not a man of judgment. Moreover, he calls himself the Son of God, and disturbs the foundations on which society rests, and therefore harms people. Let him think what he likes in his soul, if he will not raise disturbance. As a man, I protest against his teaching. If I do not believe in the gods, let us concede that it is my affair. Still I recognize the use of religion, and I declare so publicly, for I judge that religion is a curb on people. Horses must be harnessed, and harnessed securely. Finally, death should not be terrible to that Nazarene, for he declares that he will rise from the dead."

Cinna and Antea looked at each other with amazement.

"That he will rise from the dead?"

"Neither more nor less; after three days. So at least his disciples declare. I forgot to ask him myself. For that matter, it is all one, since death liberates a man from promises. And even should he not rise from the dead, he will lose nothing, since, according to his teaching, genuine happiness and eternal life begin only after death. He speaks of this, indeed, as a man perfectly certain. In his Hades it is brighter than in the world under the sun, and whoso suffers more in this world will enter that with greater certainty; he must only love, and love, and love."

"A wonderful doctrine," said Antea.

"And these people here cry to thee, 'Crucify him!'?" inquired Cinna.

"And I do not even wonder at this, for hatred is the soul of this people, for what, if not hatred, can demand that love be crucified?"

Antea rubbed her forehead with her emaciated hand.

"And is he certain that it is possible to live and be happy after death?"

"That is why neither the cross nor death terrify him."

"How good that would be, Caius!"

"How does he know this?" inquired she, after a while.

The procurator waved his hand: "He says that he knows it from the Father of all, who for the Jews is the same as Jove for us, with this difference, that, according to the Nazarene, the Father alone is one and merciful."

"How good that would be, Caius!" repeated the sick woman.

Cinna opened his lips as if to make some answer, but remained silent; and the conversation stopped. Evidently Pontius was continuing to think of the strange doctrine of the Nazarene, for he shook his head and shrugged his shoulders repeatedly. At last he rose and began to take leave.

All at once Antea said, —

"Caius, let us go to look at that Nazarene."

"Hasten," said Pilate, as he was going away; "the procession will move soon."

CHAPTER VII.

THE day, hot and bright from early morning, was obscured about midday. From the northeast clouds were rolling up, either dark or copper-colored, not over large, but dense, as if pregnant with a tempest. Between them the deep blue of the sky was still visible, but it was easy to foresee that they would soon pack together and conceal the whole round of the sky. Meanwhile the sun covered the edges of them with fire and gold. Over the city itself and the adjacent hills there extended yet a broad space of clear blue, and in the valley there was no breath of wind.

On the lofty platform of ground called Golgotha stood here and there small groups of people who had preceded the procession which was to move from the city. The sun illuminated broad, stony spaces, which were empty, gloomy, and barren; their monotonous pearl-color was interrupted only by the black net of ravines and gullies, the blacker because the platform itself was covered with light. In the distance were visible more elevated eminences, equally empty, veiled by the blue haze of distance.

LET US FOLLOW HIM. 241

Lower down, between the walls of the city and the platform of Golgotha, lay a plain bordered in places with cliffs less naked. From crannies in which had collected some little fertile earth, fig-trees peeped forth with few and scant leaves. Here and there rose flat-roofed buildings fixed to the cliff-side, like swallows' nests to stone walls, or shining from afar in the sun-rays were sepulchres, painted white. At present, because of the approaching holidays and the concourse of provincials in the capital, multitudes of huts and tents had been raised near the city walls; these formed whole encampments filled with men and camels.

The sun rose ever higher on that expanse of heaven which was still free from clouds. The hours were approaching in which usually deep silence reigned on those heights, for every living creature sought refuge inside the walls or within the ravines. And even at this time, in spite of uncommon animation, there was a certain sadness in that neighborhood in which the dazzling light fell not on green, but on gray stone expanses. The noise of distant voices, coming from the direction of the walls, was changed into the sound of waves, as it were, and seemed to be swallowed by the silence.

The single groups of people waiting on Golgotha since morning turned their faces toward the city, whence the procession might move at any moment. Antea's litter arrived; a few soldiers, sent by the procurator, preceded it. These were to open a way through the multitude, and in case of need restrain from deeds of disrespect the fanatical throng, and those who hated foreigners. At the side of the litter walked Cinna, in company with the centurion Rufilus.

Antea was calmer, less frightened than usual at the approach of midday, and with it the terror of dreadful visions, which had drawn the life out of her. What the procurator had said touching the young Nazarene, had attracted her mind and turned attention from her own misery. For her there was in this something wonderful which she could hardly understand. The world of that time had seen many persons die as calmly as a funeral pile quenches when the fuel in it is consumed. But that was a calmness coming from bravery, or from a philosophic agreement with the implacable necessity of exchanging light for darkness, real life for an existence misty, vanishing, and indefinite. No one up to that time had blessed death; no one had died with unshaken certainty that only after the funeral pyre or the grave would real life begin, — life as mighty and endless as only a being all-powerful and eternal can give.

And he whom they had appointed for crucifixion declared this as an undoubted truth. This teaching not only struck Antea, but seemed to her the only source of consolation. She knew that she must die, and immense regret seized her. For what did death mean for her? It meant to lose Cinna, to lose her father, to lose the world, to lose love, for a cold, empty gloom, which was half nothing. Hence the more desirable it was for her in life, the greater must be her sorrow. If death could be good for anything, or if it were possible to take with her even the remembrance of love, or the memory of happiness, she would be able to gain resignation the more quickly.

Then, while she expected nothing from death, she heard all at once that it could give everything. And who had made that announcement? A certain wonderful man, a teacher, a prophet, a philosopher, who enjoined love as the highest virtue, who blessed people when they were lashing him; and this man they had condemned to the cross. Hence Antea thought: "Why did he teach thus if the cross was his only reward? Others desired power; he did not desire it. Others desired wealth; he remained poor. Others desired palaces, feasts, excesses, purple robes, and chariots inlaid with mother-of-pearl and ivory; he lived like a shepherd. Meanwhile he enjoined love, compassion, poverty; therefore he could not be malicious and deceive people purposely. If he spoke the truth, let death be blessed as the end of earthly misery, as the change from a lower to a loftier happiness, as light for eyes that are quenching, as wings with which one flies away into endless bliss!"

Antea understood then what the promise of resurrection signified. The mind and heart of the poor sick woman cleaved with all their strength to that teaching. She recalled also the words of her father, who had repeated more than once that some new truth might bring the tortured soul of man out of darkness and imprisonment. And here was the new truth! It had conquered death; hence it had brought salvation. Antea sank with her whole being in those thoughts; so that for many and many a day Cinna for the first time failed to find terror in her face at the approach of midday.

The procession moved at last from the city toward Golgotha. From the height where Antea was sitting, it could be seen perfectly. The crowd, though considerable, seemed lost on those stony expanses. Through the open gate of Jerusalem flowed more and more people, and on the way they were joined by those who had been waiting outside the walls. They went at first in a long line, which, as it moved forward, spread like a swollen river. At both sides were running swarms of children.

The procession was made varied and many-colored by the white tunics and the scarlet and blue kerchiefs of women. In the centre were glittering the arms and spears

of Roman soldiers, on which the sun cast fleeting rays, as
it were. The uproar of mingled voices came from afar
and rose with increasing distinctness.

At last the multitude came quite near; the first ranks
began to ascend the height. The throng of people hurried
on so as to occupy the nearest places and see the torment
more clearly; because of this the division of soldiers, conducting the condemned, fell more and more toward the
rear. Children arrived first, mainly boys, half naked,
with cloths fastened around their hips, with shaven heads,
except two tufts of hair near the temple, embrowned, with
eyes almost blue, and harsh voices. In the wild uproar
they fell to pulling out of the crannies bits of stone broken
from the cliffs; these they wished to throw at those who
were to be crucified. Right after them the height swarmed
with a nondescript rabble. Their faces were for the
greater part excited by the movement and by the hope
of a spectacle. On no face was there a sign of compassion. The noise of rasping voices, the endless number of
words thrown out by each mouth, the suddenness of their
movements, astonished Antea, though accustomed in
Alexandria to the word-loving liveliness of Greeks. Before her, people spoke as if they wished to hurl themselves at one another. They screamed as if escaping
death; they resisted as if some one were flaying them.

The centurion Rufilus, approaching the litter, gave
explanations in a calm, official voice. Meanwhile new
waves flowed up from the city. The throng increased
every moment. In the crowd were seen wealthy men of
Jerusalem, dressed in girded tunics, holding themselves
aloof from the wretched rabble of the suburbs. In
numbers also came villagers which the festival had
brought to the city, with their families; field-workers,
with kindly and astonished faces, came, bearing bags at

their girdles; shepherds came, dressed in goat-skins. Crowds of women came with the men; but as wives of the more wealthy citizens did not leave their homes willingly, these women were chiefly of the people. They were villagers, or women of the street; these last dressed gaudily, had dyed hair, brows, and nails; they wore immense ear-rings and coin necklaces, and gave out from a distance the odor of nard.

The Sanhedrim arrived at last; and in the midst of it, Annas, an aged man with the face of a vulture and eyes with red lids; then appeared the unwieldy Caiaphas, wearing a two-horned hat, with a gilded tablet on his breast. With these walked various Pharisees; as, for instance, those who "drag their legs" and strike every obstacle purposely with their feet; Pharisees with "bloody foreheads," who beat those foreheads against the wall, also by design; and Pharisees "bent over," as if to receive the burden of the sins of the whole city on their shoulders. Gloomy importance and cold vindictiveness distinguished them from the noisy rabble.

Cinna looked at this throng of people with the cool, contemptuous visage of a man of the ruling race, Antea with astonishment and fear. Many Jews inhabited Alexandria, but there they were half Hellenized; here for the first time she saw Jews as the procurator had described them, and as they were in their own native nest. Her youthful face, on which death had imprinted its stamp, her form, resembling a shadow, attracted general attention. They stared at her with insolence in so far as the soldiers surrounding her litter permitted them; and so great among them was contempt for foreigners that no compassion was evident in the eyes of any; rather did gladness shine in them because the victim would not escape death. Then the daughter of Timon understood for the first time, and precisely, why those people demanded a cross for the prophet who had proclaimed love.

And all at once that Nazarene appeared to Antea as some one so near that he was almost dear to her. He had to die, and so had she. Nothing could save him now, after the issuing of the sentence, and sentence had fallen also on her; hence it seemed to Antea that the brotherhood of misfortune and death had united them. But he approached the cross with faith in a morrow after death. She had not that faith yet, and had come to obtain it from the sight of him.

Meanwhile from afar was heard an uproar, a whistling, a howling, then all was silent. Next came clatter of weapons and the heavy tread of legionaries. The crowds swayed, opened, and the division conducting the condemned began to push past the litter. In front, at both sides, and behind, advanced soldiers with slow and measured tread. Next were three arms of crosses, which seemed to move of themselves; they were borne by persons bent under the weight of them. It was easy to divine that the Nazarene was not among those three, for two had the insolent faces of thieves. The third was a simple countryman, no longer young; clearly the soldiers had impressed him to do work for another.

The Nazarene walked behind the crosses; two soldiers marched near him. He wore a purple mantle thrown over his garments, and a crown of thorns, from under the points of which drops of blood issued; of these some flowed slowly along his face, others had grown stiff under the crown, in the form of berries of the wild rose, or coral beads. He was pale, and moved forward with slow, unsteady, and weakened step. He advanced amid insults from the multitude, sunk, as it were, in the meditation of another world; he was as if seized away from the earth altogether, as if not caring for the cries of hatred, or as if forgiving beyond the measure of human forgiveness and compassionate beyond the measure of human compassion, for, embraced now by infinity, raised above human estimate, he was exceedingly mild, and was sorrowful only through his measureless sorrow for all men.

"Thou art Truth," whispered Antea, with trembling lips.

The retinue was passing just near the litter. It halted for a moment while soldiers in front were clearing the road of the throng; Antea saw then the Nazarene a few steps away. She saw the breeze move his hair; she saw the ruddy reflection from his mantle on his pallid and almost transparent face. The mob, rushing toward him, surrounded with a dense half-circle the soldiers, who had to resist with spears, to save him from their rage. Everywhere were visible outstretched arms with clinched fists, eyes bursting through their lids, gleaming teeth, beards thrown apart from mad movements, and foaming lips through which came hoarse shouts. But he looked around, as if wishing to ask, "What have I done to you?" then he raised his eyes to heaven and prayed — and forgave.

"Antea! Antea!" cried Cinna at that moment.

But Antea seemed not to hear his cries. Great tears were falling from her eyes; she forgot her sickness, forgot that for many days she had not risen from the litter; and sitting up on a sudden, trembling, half conscious, from pity, compassion, and indignation at the mad shrieks of the multitude, she took hyacinths with apple blossoms and cast them before the feet of the Nazarene.

For a moment there was silence. Amazement seized the crowd at sight of this noble Roman lady giving honor to the condemned. He turned his eyes to her poor sick face, and his lips began to move, as if blessing her.

Antea fell again on the pillow of the litter; she felt that a sea of light, of goodness, of grace, of consolation, of hope, of happiness, was falling on her.

"Thou art Truth," whispered she, a second time.

Then a new wave of tears came to her eyes.

But they pushed him forward to a place a few tens of steps distant from the litter; on that place stood already the uprights of crosses, fixed in a cleft of the rocky platform. The crowd concealed him again; but, since that place was elevated considerably, Antea soon saw his pale face and the crown of thorns. The legionaries turned once more toward the rabble, which they clubbed away, lest it might interrupt the execution. They began then to fasten the two thieves to the side crosses. The third cross stood in the middle; to the top of it was fastened, with a nail, a white card which the growing wind pulled and raised. When soldiers, approaching the Nazarene at last, began to undress him, shouts rose in the crowds: "King! king! do not yield! King, where are thy legions? Defend thyself!" At moments laughter burst forth, — laughter that bore away the multitude till on a sudden the whole stony height resounded with one roar. Then they stretched him face upward on the ground, to nail his hands to the arms of the cross, and raise him afterward with it to the main pillar.

Thereupon some man, in a white tunic, standing not far from the litter, cast himself on the earth suddenly, gathered dust and bits of stone on his head, and cried in a shrill, despairing voice, "I was a leper, and he cured me; why do ye crucify him?"

Antea's face became white as a kerchief.

"He cured that man; dost hear, Caius?" said she.

"Dost wish to return?" asked Cinna.

"No! I will remain here!"

LET US FOLLOW HIM. 249

But a wild and boundless despair seized Cinna because he had not called the Nazarene to his house to cure Antea.

At that moment the soldiers, placing nails at his hands, began to strike. The dull clink of iron against iron was heard; this soon changed into a sound which went farther, for the points of the nails, having passed through flesh, entered the wood. The crowds were silent again, perhaps to enjoy cries which torture might bring from the mouth of the Nazarene. But he remained silent, and on the height was heard only the ominous and dreadful sound of the hammers.

At last they had finished the work, and the crosspiece was drawn up, with the body. The centurion in charge pronounced, or rather sang out monotonously, words of command, in virtue of which a soldier began to nail the feet.

At this moment those clouds, which since morning had been extending on the horizon, hid the sun. The distant hills and cliffs, which had been gleaming in brightness, gleamed no longer. The light turned to darkness. An ominous bronze-colored gloom seized the region about, and, as the sun sank more deeply behind piles of clouds, the gloom became denser. Men might have thought that some being from above was sifting down to the earth lurid darkness. The air now grew sultry.

All at once even those remnants of lurid gleams became black. Clouds, dark as night, rolled and pushed forward, like a gigantic wave, toward the height and the city. A tempest was coming! The world was filled with fear.

"Let us return!" said Cinna again.

"Once more, once more, I wish to see him," answered Antea.

Darkness had concealed the hanging bodies. Cinna

gave command to carry the litter nearer the place of torment. They carried it so near that barely a few steps were between them and the cross. On the dark tree they saw the body of the Crucified, who in that general eclipse seemed made of silver rays of the moon. His breast rose with quick breathing. His face and eyes were turned upward yet.

Then from the rolls of clouds was heard a deep rumbling. Thunder was roused; it rose and rolled with tremendous report from the east to the west, and then falling, as if into a bottomless abyss, was heard farther and farther down, now dying away, and now increasing; at last it roared till the earth shook in its foundations.

A gigantic blue lightning-flash rent the clouds, lighted the sky, the earth, the crosses, the arms of the soldiers, and the mob huddled together, like a flock of sheep, filled with distress and terror.

After the lightning came deeper darkness. Close to the litter was heard the sobbing of women, who also drew near the cross. There was something ominous in this sobbing amid silence. Those who were lost in the multitude began now to cry out. Here and there were heard terrified voices, —

"O Yah! oj lanu! [woe to us]! O Yah! Have they not crucified the Just One?"

"Who gave true testimony! O Yah!"

"Who raised the dead!"

And another voice called, —

"Woe to thee, Jerusalem!"

Still another, —

"The earth trembles!"

A new lightning-flash disclosed the depths of the sky and in them gigantic figures of fire, as it were. The voices were silent, or rather were lost in the whistling of

LET US FOLLOW HIM. 251

the whirlwind, which sprang up all at once with tremendous force; it swept off a multitude of mantles and kerchiefs, and hurled them away over the height.

Voices cried out anew, —

"The earth trembles!"

Some began to flee. Terror nailed others to the spot; and they stood fixed in amazement, without thought, with this dull impression only, — that something awful was happening.

But, on a sudden, the gloom began to be less dense. Wind rolled the clouds over, twisted and tore them like rotten rags; brightness increased gradually. At last the dark ceiling was rent, and through the opening rushed in all at once a torrent of sunlight; presently the heights became visible and with them the crosses and the terrified faces of the people.

The head of the Nazarene had fallen low on his breast; it was as pale as wax; his eyes were closed, his lips blue.

"He is dead," whispered Antea.

"He is dead," repeated Cinna.

At this moment a centurion thrust his spear into the side of the dead. A wonderful thing: the return of light and the sight of that death seemed to appease that crowd. They pushed nearer and nearer, especially since the soldiers did not bar approach. Among the throng were heard voices, —

"Come down from the cross! Come down from the cross!"

Antea cast her eyes once more on that low-hanging head, then she said, as if to herself, —

"Will he rise from the dead?"

In view of death, which had put blue spots on his eyes and mouth, in view of those arms stretched beyond measure, and in view of that motionless body which had settled down with the weight of dead things, her voice trembled with despairing doubt.

Not less was the disappointment rending Cinna's soul. He also believed not that the Nazarene would rise from the dead; but he believed that had he lived, he alone, with his power, good or evil, might have given health to Antea. Meanwhile more numerous voices were calling:

"Come down from the cross! Come down from the cross!"

"Come down!" repeated Cinna, with despair. "Cure her for me; take my life!"

The air became purer and purer. The mountains were still in mist, but above the height and the city the sky had cleared perfectly. "Turris Antonia" glittered in sunlight as bright itself as the sun. The air had become fresh, and was full of swallows. Cinna gave command to return.

It was an afternoon hour. Near the house Antea said, —

"Hecate has not come to-day."

Cinna also was thinking of that.

CHAPTER VIII.

THE vision did not appear the next day. The sick woman was unusually animated, for Timon had come from Cæsarea. Alarmed for the life of his daughter and frightened by Cinna's letters, he had left Alexandria a few days earlier to look once again on his only child before her parting. At Cinna's heart hope began to knock again, as if to give notice to receive it. But he had not courage to open the door to that guest; he did not dare to harbor hope.

In the visions which had been killing Antea, there had been intervals, it is true, not of two days, but of one in Alexandria, and in the desert. The present relief Cinna attributed to Timon's arrival, and her impressions at the cross, which so filled the sick woman's soul that she could talk of nothing else, even with her father.

Timon listened with attention; he did not contradict; he meditated and merely inquired carefully about the doctrine of the Nazarene, of which Antea knew, for that matter, only what the procurator had told her.

In general she felt healthier and somewhat stronger; and when midday had passed and gone, real solace shone in her eyes. She repeated that that was a favorable day, and begged her husband to make note of it.

The day was really sad and gloomy. Rain had begun in the early morning, at first very heavy, then fine and cutting, from low clouds which extended monotonously. Only in the evening did the sky break through, and the great fiery globe of the sun look out of the mists, paint in purple and gold the gray rocks, the white marble porticoes of the villas, and descend with endless gleams toward the Mediterranean.

The next morning was wonderfully beautiful. The weather promised to be warm, but the morning was fresh, the sky without a spot, and the earth so sunk in a blue bath that all objects seemed blue. Antea had given directions to bear her out and place her under the favorite pistachio-tree, so that from the elevation on which the tree stood she might delight herself with the view of the blue and gladsome distance.

Cinna and Timon did not move a step from the litter, and watched the face of the sick woman carefully. There was in it a certain alarm of expectation, but it was not that mortal fear which used to seize her at the approach of midday. Her eyes cast a more lively light, and her cheeks bloomed with a slight flush. Cinna thought indeed at moments that Antea might recover; and at this thought he wanted to throw himself on the ground, to sob from delight, and bless the gods. Then again he feared that that was perhaps the last gleam of the dying lamp. Wishing to gain hope from some source, he glanced every little while at Timon; but similar thoughts must have been passing through his head, for he avoided Cinna's glances. None of the three mentioned by a word that midday was near. But Cinna, casting his eyes every moment at the shadows, saw with beating heart that they were growing shorter and shorter.

And he sat as if sunk in thought. Perhaps the least alarmed was Antea herself. Lying in the open litter, her head rested on a purple pillow; she breathed with delight that pure air which the breeze brought from the west, from the distant sea. But before midday the breeze had ceased to blow. The heat increased; warmed by the sun, the pepperwort of the cliffs and the thickets of nard began to give out a strong and intoxicating odor. Bright butterflies balanced themselves over bunches of anemones. From the crevices of the rocks little lizards, already accustomed to that litter and those people, sprang out, one after the other, confident as usual, and also cautious in every movement. The whole world was enjoying that serene peace, that warmth, that calm sweetness and azure drowsiness.

Timon and Cinna seemed also to dissolve in that sunny rest. The sick woman closed her eyes as if a light sleep had seized her; and nothing interrupted that silence except sighs, which from time to time raised her breast.

Meanwhile Cinna noticed that his shadow had lost its lengthened form and was lying there under his feet.

LET US FOLLOW HIM.

It was midday.

All at once Antea opened her eyes and called out in a kind of strange voice,—

"Caius, give me thy hand."

He sprang up, and all the blood was stiffened to ice in his heart. The hour of terrible visions had come.

Her eyes opened wider and wider.

"Dost thou see," said she, "how light collects there and binds the air; how it trembles, glitters, and approaches me?"

"Antea, look not in that direction!" cried Cinna.

But, oh, wonder! there was no fear on her face. Her lips were parted; her eyes were gazing, and opening wider and wider; a certain immeasurable delight began to brighten her face.

"The pillar of light approaches me," said she. "See! that is he; that is the Nazarene!—he is smiling. O Mild! O Merciful! The transfixed hands he stretches out like a mother to me. Caius, he brings me health, salvation, and calls me to himself."

Cinna grew very pale, and said,—

"Whithersoever he calls us, let us follow him."

A moment later, on the other side, on the stony path leading to the city, appeared Pontius Pilate. Before he had come near, it was evident from his face that he was bringing news, which, as a man of judgment, he considered a fresh, absurd invention of the ignorant and credulous rabble. In fact, while still at some distance, he began to call, wiping perspiration from his brow,—

"Imagine to thyself, they declare that he has risen from the dead!"

BE THOU BLESSED

BE THOU BLESSED.

ONCE on a bright moonlight night the wise and mighty Krishna fell into deep meditation, and said, —

"I thought man the most beautiful creation on earth; but I was mistaken. Here I see the lotus, rocked by the night breeze. Oh, how much more beautiful it is than any living being; its leaves have just opened to the silver light of the moon, and I cannot wrest my eyes from it!

"Among men there is nothing to compare with it," repeated he, sighing.

But after a while he thought, —

"Why should I, a god, not create, by the power of my word, a being who would be among men what the lotus is among flowers? Let it be then to the delight of man and the earth. Lotus, change thou into a living maiden and stand before me."

The water trembled slightly, as if touched by the wings of a swallow; the night grew bright; the moon shone with more power in the sky; the night thrushes sang more distinctly, then stopped on a sudden, and the charm was accomplished: before Krishna stood the lotus in human shape.

The god himself was astonished.

"Thou wert a flower of the lake," said he; "henceforth be the flower of my thought, and speak."

The maiden began to whisper in a voice as low as the sound made by the white leaves of the lotus when kissed by a summer breeze, —

"Lord, thou hast changed me into a living being; where now dost thou command me to dwell? Remember, lord, that when I was a flower I trembled and drew in my leaves at every breath of the wind. I feared heavy rain; I feared storms; I feared thunder and lightning; I feared even the burning rays of the sun. Thou hast commanded me to be the incarnation of the lotus; hence I have kept my former nature, and now I fear the earth and all that is on it. Where dost thou command me to dwell?"

Krishna raised his wise eyes to the stars, meditated a while, and then asked, —

"Dost thou wish to live on the summits of mountains?"

"Snow and cold are there, lord, I am afraid."

"Well, I will build thee a palace of crystal at the bottom of the lake."

"In the depths of the waters move serpents and other monsters; I am afraid, lord."

"Dost thou prefer the boundless steppes?"

"Whirlwinds and tempests rush over the steppes like wild herds."

"What is to be done with thee, incarnate flower? Ha! In the caves of Ellora live holy hermits. Wilt thou dwell far away from the world, in those caves?"

"It is dark there, lord; I am afraid."

Krishna sat on a stone, and rested his head on his hand. The maiden stood before him, trembling and timid.

Meanwhile the dawn began to brighten the sky on the east. The surface of the lake, the palms, and the bamboos were gilded. At the water, rosy herons, blue storks, in the forest, peacocks and bengalee were heard, and these were accompanied by distant sounds of strings stretched over pearl shells, and by words of human song. Krishna awoke from meditation and said, —

"That is Valmiki, the poet, saluting the rising sun."

After a while the curtain of purple flowers covering the climbing plants was pushed aside, and Valmiki appeared at the lake.

When he saw the incarnate lotus the poet ceased to play, the pearl shell fell from his grasp to the earth, his arms dropped at his sides, and he stood dumb, as if the mighty Krishna had made him a tree at the edge of the water.

The god was delighted with this wonder at his work, and said, —

"Awake, Valmiki, and speak."

And Valmiki said, —

"I love!"

This was the only word that he remembered, and the only word that he could utter.

Krishna's face was radiant at once.

"Wonderful maiden, I have found for thee a worthy dwelling-place in the world: thou wilt dwell in the heart of the poet."

Valmiki repeated a second time, —

"I love!"

The will of the mighty Krishna, the will of the deity, began to urge the maiden toward the heart of the poet. The god also made the heart of Valmiki as transparent as crystal.

Calm as a summer day, quiet as the surface of the Ganges, the maiden advanced toward the dwelling prepared for her. But suddenly, when she looked into the heart of Valmiki, her face grew pale, and terror surrounded her, as a winter wind. Krishna was astonished.

"Incarnate flower," inquired he, "dost thou fear even the heart of a poet?"

"O lord," answered the maiden, "where hast thou commanded me to dwell? There in that one heart I see the snowy summits of mountains, the abysses of waters, full of marvellous creatures, the steppe with its whirlwinds and tempests, and the caves of Ellora with their darkness; therefore I am afraid, O lord!"

But the good and wise Krishna replied, —

"Calm thyself, incarnate flower. If in the heart of Valmiki there lie lonely snows, be thou the warm breath of spring, which will melt them; if in it there be the abyss of waters, be thou the pearl in that abyss; if in it there be the desert of the steppe, sow flowers of happiness there; if in it there be the dark caves of Ellora, be thou in that darkness the sun-ray —"

And Valmiki, who during that time had recovered his speech, added, —

"And be thou blessed!"

AT THE SOURCE

AT THE SOURCE.

I AM a student of yesterday; my diploma of doctor of philosophy is not dry yet, — that is true. I have neither wealth nor position. My whole fortune consists of a rather poor little house and a few hundred rubles' income. I can understand, therefore, why Tola's parents refused me her hand; but they did more, — they insulted me.

But why? What have I done? I brought them, as if on the palm of my hand, a very honest heart, and I said: "Give her to me. I will be the best of sons, and till death I shall not cease to repay you; her I will worship; her I will love and protect."

It is true that I said this stupidly, in a strange voice, while stammering and panting. You knew, however, that I was dragging my soul out, that through me was expressed a feeling the equal of which you could not meet in this world every day; and if you had chosen to refuse me, why not refuse like kind people, with some slight compassion in your hearts, but you insulted me.

You who claim to be Christians, and claim to be idealists, how were you to know what I might do on leaving your house after such a refusal? Who told you that I would not put a bullet into my head, — first, because I could not live without her, and second, because I could not understand the contradiction between your pretended principles and the real practice of your life, that phari-

seeism, that falsehood? Why had you no mercy on me
even for a moment? It was not right to trample even me
without cause; trampling inflicts pain. Were it not for
you, I might achieve something in this world. I am
young, little more than a student, without wealth, without position, — that may be! But I have my future; you
spat on it, but, as God lives, I know not why you did so.

Those icy faces! that contemptuous indignation! Two
days ago I could not imagine that those people could be
such. "We thought you a man of honor; but you have
deceived us, you have abused our confidence —" These
are the words with which they slashed me across the
face, as with a whip. A moment before they had congratulated me on my diploma as heartily as if I had been
their son; and only when, pale from emotion, I told
them what had been the greatest spur in my efforts, their
cordiality and smiles were extinguished, their faces grew
rigid, frost breathed from them — and it turned out that
I had "abused their confidence."

They so crushed, dazed, trampled me that after a while
I thought myself that I had done something disgraceful,
that I had really deceived them.

But how? What is the position? Who is the deceiver, who the deceived, who plays the contemptible
rôle? Either I have gone mad altogether, or there is
nothing mean in this, that a man loves honestly and
desires to give his soul, blood, and toil to another. If
your indignation was genuine, who is the fool in this
case?

Ah, Panna Tola! and I was deceived in thee also, — I
who counted on thee with such confidence. "We are sure,"
said they, "that our daughter has never authorized you in
any way to take this step." Of course I did not contradict.
And then that "daughter" appeared with all the un-

speakable coolness of a well-bred young lady, and stammered, with drooping eyes, that she could not understand even how such a thought could occur to me.

Dost thou not understand? Listen, Panna Tola: thou didst not say, "I love;" I admit that. I have not thy bond and signature, but even if I had I would not present them. I will say this much, however: there is justice and there is a tribunal, — all one where they are, whether somewhere beyond the clouds, or in the human conscience; before this tribunal thou must say: I have deceived this man; I have denied him; I have brought him humiliation and misfortune.

I know not which failed thee, heart or courage; but I know that thou hast deceived me horribly. I love thee still. I do not wish to malign thee; but when it is a question of ruining or saving, there is need of courage. Love and honesty must be greater than fear, or the timbers of an edifice raised with great toil will fall on some one's head. They have fallen on mine. I built my whole future on blind faith in thy love; and the result proved that I built on sand, for courage failed thee at the critical moment, since having to choose between the evil humor of thy parents and my misfortune, thou didst choose my misfortune.

If in this wreck thou hadst been what I thought thee, life would be easier for me now; I should have consolation and hope. Dost thou know that everything which I did for some years I did because of thee and for thy sake? I worked like an ox; I did not rest at night; I gained certain medals and diplomas. Through thee I lived; through thee I breathed; of thee I thought. And now there is a desert before me, in which grief is howling, like a dog. Nothing remains to me. I am curious to know if thou wilt think even once of this.

But beyond doubt thy sober-minded parents will explain to their daughter that I am a student, and that this is my stupid exaltation. As to being a student, if I were one yet, I might answer, like Shakespeare's Shylock, Have we not hands, organs, dimensions, senses, affections, passions? If you prick us, do we not bleed? If you wrong us, shall we not revenge? It is not permissible to wrong any man, no matter who he be. My exaltation, stupid or not, gives no man the right to injure me. It is well that this present society of ours, which is like a great soulless edifice composed of stupidity, lies, and hypocrisy, is cracking and falling, since no one can live in it. I have some leisure now; I am a doctor of philosophy. I will dwell as a philosopher on various human relations, which have recoiled on me recently with such effect. For you people of judgment, so called, it is enough if you find a vain word, an empty name for a thing. Let some other man break his neck on the thing itself. Well, never mind. Exaltation! What profit is there for me in the word, if that to which you apply it wrings my entrails? What aid to me is your dictionary? Meanwhile you deny the right of existence to everything which your blunted nerves cannot feel. When the teeth have dropped from your superannuated jaws, you cease to believe in toothache. But rheumatism is serious; rheumatism hurts, while love is only exaltation. When I think of this, two men rise up in me, — one the student of yesterday, who in the name of the present would hammer human dulness with the back of an axe, the other a person deeply injured, who wishes to curse and to sob. It is impossible to live thus. We have had enough of this idealism in words, and utilitarianism in acts. The time is coming when men must fit their deeds to high principles, or have courage to proclaim principles as cynical as their deeds. God alone knows how often I have heard Tola's parents say that wealth does not constitute happiness, that character is worth more than wealth, that peace of conscience is the highest good. Are those statements true? Well, if they are, I have some character, great industry, a calm conscience; I am young and I love. Still, they turned me out of their house. Were I to win half a million in the lottery, they would give me their daughter to-morrow with delight. Her father would come to my room in the morning and open his arms to me — as God is in heaven he would.

If a man wishes to be a merchant, let him know at least how to reckon; but you, though positive, do not know even this. That position of yours and that judgment of yours conduct you to illusions. You do not know how to reckon — do you hear? I do not say this in excitement; there is no exaggeration in my words. Love exists and is real, hence we must recognize it as an actual value. Were a mathematician of genius to appear, he would show you this value in money, and then you would seize your heads and cry, "Oh, what wealth!" Love is just as positive and tangible, just as absolute in life as is money. The reckoning is simple: life has as much value as the happiness contained in it. Love is an enormous capital, an inexhaustible source of happiness, as great as youth and health. But such simple truths as this cannot find room in your heads. I repeat that you know not how to reckon. A million is worth a million and not a copper more; but you think that it is worth as much besides as all the other good in life. Because of this error you are wandering in a world completely artificial, and you deceive yourselves as to values. You are romantic, but your romanticism is paltry, since it is pecuniary, and besides it is harmful, since it breaks and spoils the lives, not only of people who do not concern you, but the lives of your own children also.

Tola would have had a pleasant life with me; she would have been happy. That being true, what more do you wish? Do not answer that she would have refused me. If you had not killed in her, by your teaching, all freedom, will, sincerity, and courage, I should not be sitting alone now, with a head bursting from pain. No one has looked into Tola's eyes as I have; no one knows better what she felt and what she would have been had you not poisoned the soul in her.

But now I have lost Tola, and with her much else, by which one lives as by bread, and without which one dies. Oh, you, my parents, and thou, my lost wife! at times I admit that you are unconscious of what you have done, or you would come to me now. It cannot be that you have no compassion for me...

What use in reproaches? Right is on my side. All that I have written is strict truth, but that truth will not bring Tola back to me.

And here is the gulf; for I cannot comprehend how justice and truth can be useless. All that I have on my side is useless to me, absolutely useless. Still the world must be constructed just as men's minds are; how comes the break, then? If constructed differently, we must continue forever in our vicious circle; I can write no more.

After a long time I turn to my pen again. Let reality speak for itself. I narrate simply that which took place. The explanation came only after a long series of events; therefore I give them in the order of their happening before I could understand the causes myself.

AT THE SOURCE.

On the morning after that day of disaster Tola's father came to me. When I saw him, I grew rigid. There was a moment when all thoughts flew from my head, as a flock of birds fly from a tree. I think that one must feel something similar at the moment of death. But his face was mild, and right on the threshold he began to speak, stretching his hands toward me, —

"Well, we have spent a bad night, have we not? I understand that; I was young myself once."

I made no answer; I understood nothing; I did not believe that I saw him before my face. Meanwhile he shook my hands, forced me to sit down, and, seating himself in front of me, continued, —

"Recover yourself; be calm; let us talk like honest people. My dear sir, do you think that you are the only person who lay awake? We have not slept either. As soon as we recovered a little after you left us, we felt badly enough to be beyond help. We did indeed! When something is sprung on a man suddenly, he loses his head and then passes the measure. We were grieved, and, to tell the truth, ashamed. The child rushed off to her chamber; and the old people, like old people, fell to throwing the blame on each other. Thou art at fault, woman! thou art at fault, man! said we to each other. Such is human nature. But later came reflection and regret. He is young, honorable, capable; he loves our child with his whole heart, it seems; why in God's name were we so stubborn? One thing will explain our feelings. Should you ever be a father, you will understand this, that in parents' eyes nothing is enough for their child. Still it occurred to us that that which seemed little to us might satisfy Tola, so we made up our minds that it was better to inquire what the girl had in her heart, and we called her to counsel. The third counsellor was a good one! there is no denying that. When she fell to embracing our feet, and put her dear head on our knees, in this way — Well, you know parents' hearts — "

Here he was moved himself, and for a time we sat in silence. Everything that I heard seemed to me a dream, a fairy tale, a miracle; my suffering began to change into hope. Tola's father mastered his emotion, and continued, —

"Indeed, thou hast piled mountains on us, but we are people of good will, though quick-tempered; and, in proof of this, I will say that if thou prefer Tola to thy feeling of offence — come — "

And he opened his arms to me. I fell into them, half conscious, half bewildered, happy. I felt that my throat was contracting, that I was fit only to burst into sobbing. I wanted absolutely to say something, but could not. I had in my soul one scream of delight, astonishment, and gratitude. All this had fallen on me at once, like a thunderbolt; neither my head nor my heart could take it in, and I felt pain almost from that excess of change, that excess of thoughts and feelings. Tola's father removed my hands gently from his shoulders, and, kissing me on the forehead, said, —

"That is well now, well! I expected this of thee after thy attachment to her. Forget what has happened, and compose thyself."

Seeing, however, that I could not regain self-control, or master my emotion, he began to scold me good-naturedly, —

"Be a man; control thyself! Thou art trembling as in a fever! Well, but that little boy has struck in deeply under thy rib."

"Oi, deeply!" whispered I, with an effort.

The father smiled and said, —

"Is it possible? but he seemed like still water."

Evidently my immense love for Tola pleased his parental pride, for he was glad, and smiling he repeated continually, —

"That's a tick! that's a tick!"

I felt then that if we remained a quarter of an hour longer in the room something in my head would give way. Under ordinary conditions I can command myself, but this time the transition was too great. I needed to breathe fresh air, to see the movement on the streets; above all, I needed to see Tola, and convince myself that she was really existing, that all this was not a dream, and that they were giving her to me really.

I asked Tola's father then to go to his house with me; he consented with gladness.

"I wished to propose that myself," said he; "for surely some little nose there is flattening itself against a window-pane, and eyes are looking into the street. Thou art not in a condition now to discuss serious matters; we will do that hereafter."

A few moments later we were on the street. At first I looked at people, houses, carriages, as a man who has come out for the first time after a long illness, and feels dizziness of the head. Gradually, however, movement and fresh air restored me. Above all thoughts one was dominant: "Tola loves thee; in a moment thou wilt see her!" I felt a throbbing in my temples as mighty as hammer strokes, and really a good hoop was needed round my head to contain it. An hour before I had thought that I should never see Tola again in life, or should see her sometime in some place the wife of another. And now I was going to her to tell her that she would be mine; and I was going because she had stretched out her hand first. Yesterday I called her a senseless doll, and still she had thrown herself at the feet of her parents, imploring for both of us. My heart was overflowing with sorrow, repentance, tenderness, and a feeling that I was unworthy of Tola; I swore to myself to reward her for this, to pay with attachment and boundless devotion for each tear of hers shed yesterday.

Others grew blind in love; I had no need to grow blind, for deeds were pleading for Tola. She had wrought this miracle. I had done her injustice. I had done her parents injustice as well. Had they been such as I had thought them, they would not have let themselves be persuaded. They would not have reached that simplicity, not merely human, but angelic, with which her father came to me and said: "We were mistaken; take her!" Neither society ceremonial nor vanity had the power to restrain him from this.

I remembered his words: "Indeed, thou didst pile mountains on us, but we are people of good will, though quick-tempered." That simplicity crushed me the more, the greater the mountains which I had piled on them yesterday. Not a word beyond these, no lofty phrases, a playful smile, — that was all. When I thought of this I could not restrain myself longer; I seized his hand, and raised it with reverence to my lips.

He smiled again with that kindly clear smile, and said, —

"My wife and I have said this long time that our son-in-law must love us."

And it happened as they wished, for before I was their son-in-law I loved them as if I had been their own son.

As I was walking very fast, Tola's father began to jest; he puffed, and pretended to be suffering, said that he could not keep pace with me, complained of the heat.

In fact, the winter had broken the day before. A warm breeze wrinkled the water in the city garden, and in the air there was a species of revival, a kind of spring power. At last we were in front of the house. Something vanished from the window and disappeared in the depth of the room; I was not sure that it was Tola. On the steps my heart began to throb again. I feared the mother. When we had passed the dining-hall we found her in the drawing-room. As I entered, she approached me quickly and reached out her hand, which I kissed reverentially and with gratitude, stammering meanwhile, —

"How have I deserved this?"

"Forgive us yesterday's refusal," said she. "We had not thought of this, that Tola could find no greater attachment in the whole world."

"She could not! She could not!" cried I, with ardor.

"And since the happiness of our child is for us beyond everything, we give her to you, and I can only say: God grant you both happiness!"

She pressed my temples then; after that she turned toward the door and called, —

"Tola!"

And my love came in, pale, with reddened eyes, with bits of hair dropping on her forehead, confused, moved just as I was. How it was that nothing in her escaped my attention, I know not. I only know this, I saw tears gathering under her eyelids, her quivering lips, delight breaking through the tears, and a smile under the confusion. She stood for a moment with arms hanging, as if at a loss what to do; then her father, whom, as was evident, humor never deserted, said, shrugging his shoulders, —

"Ha! a hard case to cure! he has grown stubborn, and will not have thee."

She looked at me quickly, threw herself on her father's neck, and called, as if in an outburst, —

"I do not believe it; I do not believe it!"

If I had followed my heart's first impulse, I should have fallen at her feet. I did not do that simply through lack of courage, and because I had lost my head. I had just presence of mind enough to repeat in my soul, "Do not roar out, thou ass!" The honest father came again to our rescue; freeing himself from Tola's embrace, he said, as if angry with her, —

"If thou dost not believe me, then go to him."

And he pushed her toward me. Heaven opened before me at that moment. I seized her hands. I kissed them with delight, and I know not myself how long it was before I could take my lips from them. More than once I had imagined myself kissing her hands, but it is not for imagination to measure itself with reality! My love, so far, had been like a plant shut up in darkness. Now it was carried suddenly into bright air to luxuriate in warmth and in sunlight, hence the measure of my happiness was filled. I drank openly from the source of good and delight. To love and imprison that love in thyself, to love and feel that thou art entering on thy right to love and take possession, — are things entirely different. I not only had not had, but I could not have had, any comprehension of this.

The parents blessed us, and went out on purpose to leave us alone, so that we might tell each other all that we felt. But at first, instead of speaking, I only looked at her with ravishment, and her face changed beneath my gaze. Blushes covered her cheeks; the corners of her mouth quivered with a smile full of timidity and embarrassment; her eyes were mist-covered; her head sank, as it were, between her shoulders: at moments she dropped her eyelids and seemed to wait for my words.

At last, we sat down side by side at the window, each holding the other's hand. Till that day she had been for me, not of flesh and blood, as it were, but an abstraction, a beloved spirit, a precious name, an admired charm rather than a person, when her arm touched mine, however, and I felt the warmth of her face, I could not resist a certain astonishment that she was so real. A beloved woman seems known but not felt till one is near her. Now I looked with as much wonder at her face, her mouth, her eyes, her bright hair, and her still brighter eyelashes, as if I had never seen her till that moment. I was carried away by her. Never had a face so satisfied all my dreams of woman's beauty; no one had ever attracted me so irresistibly as she. And when I thought that all those treasures would be mine, that they belonged to me already, and were my highest good, the whole world whirled around with me.

At last I spoke. I told her feverishly how I had loved her from almost the very first moment, a year and a half before, in Velichka, where I met her by chance in a large society, to me unknown, and where she had grown faint at the bottom of the salt mine; and I ran to the well for water. The next day I paid a visit to her parents; from that visit I came away in love completely.

All this, as I supposed, was perfectly known to her; but she listened with the greatest delight, blushing, and sometimes even asking questions in a low voice. I spoke a long time, and toward the end less stupidly than I had expected. I told how afterward she had been my only strength; how deeply and dreadfully unhappy I was yesterday when I said to myself that all was lost, and that I had lost faith in her also.

"I was just as unhappy," said she. "And it is true that at first I could not stammer out a word, but later I tried to correct everything."

After a while we were both silent. In me there was a struggle between timidity and a wish to kiss her feet; at last, in the most monstrously awkward way possible, and worthy of the last of idiots, I asked her if she loved me even a little.

She strove for a time to give me an answer, but, unable to bring herself to it, she rose and left the room.

She returned quickly with an album in her hand; she sat again at my side and showed me a drawing, my own portrait.

"I sketched this," said she, "from memory."

"Is it possible?"

"But there is something more," added she, putting her finger on the paper.

Then only did I note that at the side near the edge of the paper, were the letters *j. v. a.*, in a very small hand.

"This is read in French," whispered Tola.

"In French?"

And in my boundless simplicity, I could not think what they meant till she began, —

"Je vous —"

And hiding her face in her hands, she bent so low that I saw the short hair on her neck, and her neck itself. Then I guessed at last and said with throbbing heart, —

"Now I may, I may —"

She raised her face, smiling and radiant, —

"And you must," added she, blinking, and, as it were, commanding me for the future.

At that moment they called us to lunch. At that lunch, I might have eaten knives and forks without knowing it.

A man grows accustomed to nothing so easily as to happiness. All that had passed was simply a series of miracles, but two days later it seemed to me perfectly natural that Tola was my betrothed. I thought that it ought to be so, that she was mine; and for this reason solely, that no other man loved her as I did.

Finally, the news of my betrothal went about through the city, and I began to receive congratulations from my comrades. Tola and I drove out beyond the suburbs with her parents, on which occasion many persons saw us together. I remember that drive perfectly. Tola, in a sack trimmed with otter-skin, and a cap trimmed with the same fur, looked like a vision, for her transparent complexion seemed more delicate with the dark bronze color of the trimmings. All turned to look after us, and so admired was she that some of my acquaintances stood as if fixed to the pavement.

Beyond the barriers, when we had passed rows of cottages, each lower than the other, we reached the open country at last. In the fields, between rows of trees, lay clear water, and on this, light in long streaks was shining. The meadows were flooded; the groves had no leaves; but we felt the presence of spring. Then came the moment of darkness, during which there is great calm in the world; such a calm took possession also of us. After the violent impressions of preceding days, I felt a great and sweet calmness. I had before me the dear face of Tola, rosy from the movement of air, but also soothed in that peace and thoughtful. We were both silent, and only looked at each other from moment to moment and smiled. For the first time in life I understood the meaning of undimmed, perfect happiness. As I was very young and had lived through little, I had, in fact, no heavy sins on my conscience, but, like all men, I bore with me my own load of defects, faults, and failures. Behold, at that moment this burden dropped from my shoulders. I felt in my bosom no bitterness. I had not the least dislike for people; I was ready to forgive and help every one. I felt renewed altogether, just as if love had taken the soul out of me and put into my body an angel immediately.

And this had happened because it was permitted me to love, and she, that dear one sitting opposite, had been given to me. What is more, for that very reason the four persons in that carriage were not merely what is called happy; they were better than ever they had been before. All the pettinesses of society, the paltry ambitions, the pitiful views of existence; all that which debases life and makes it repulsive, flat, and deceitful, — we had shaken away, together with the former sorrow and bitterness. Tola's parents had barely opened their house to this blessed guest when we began to live more broadly and loftily than ever before.

Hence I could not understand why people so often reject that which in life is the one, the supreme good. Still oftener do they squander it. I know those petty wise-saws which circulate like counterfeit money: that love withers, grows old, passes away, vanishes, and that finally habit alone is the bond between man and woman. Now I will show that this truth relates solely to stupid or pitiful people. There are chosen souls, who know how to avoid that condition; I have met such in the world, hence I myself have the wish and the will to become one of them. If this flame to-day makes me so happy, my first duty, and the most direct task of selfishness, is that it should not quench, that it should not even decrease in the future. Therefore I will defy that future! it has time on its side. I have my great love and good will. To live with Tola and cease to love her, — we will see about that!

All at once an irresistible desire mastered me to begin that life at the earliest. I knew that society customs did not permit betrothed persons to marry before the end of certain weeks, or months, but I remembered that I had to deal with exceptional people. I was convinced that Tola would aid me, and I determined to involve her in the affair.

On our return home, when they left us alone, I confessed my thoughts to her. She listened with immense delight. I saw that not only the plan itself, but even discussion concerning it, had for her the charm of a lover's conspiracy, and simply carried her away. At moments she had the look of a child to whom people promise some wonderful amusement which is soon to appear, and she could not restrain herself from dancing through the room. We did not mention the matter that evening, however; but at tea I told of my hopes for the future, and the paths which were opening before me. Tola's parents listened as though those hopes had been realized. Could I have supposed those people of dove-like simplicity to be acting through politeness, I should have called that politeness the very wisest, for seeing their faith and confidence I said to myself, Though I were to lay down my head I will not deceive you.

I took leave at a late hour. Tola hastened after me to the entrance, and repeated, in a whisper, —

"Let it be so; let it be so. Why delay? I am not fond of delay! let it be so. Good-night. I fear only mamma, mamma will be thinking of the wedding outfit."

I did not understand very clearly why she should make a wedding outfit, since young ladies, as young ladies, must have at all times a certain supply of dresses. But in its own way every expression of that sort made me happy to a high degree, since it confirmed in some way that I was not dreaming, that in truth I was going to marry Tola. While returning home I repeated involuntarily: Wedding clothes, wedding clothes! I do not foresee that through them any great difficulty can rise. I saw, however, with the eyes of my soul a multitude of dresses, bright, dark, many-colored, and I fell in love with each of them in turn. Then it occurred to me that I must arrange a house in which to receive Tola. I found new delight in this thought. I needed money a little, but determined in spite of that to arrange all at the earliest. I could not sleep in the night, for I had my head full of dresses, tables, cupboards, and armchairs. Some time since I could not sleep because of suffering; later I could not sleep from delight.

Next morning I visited the cabinet-maker. He understood in a flash what I needed. He showed me various pieces of furniture. At sight of these I saw tangibly my future life with Tola, just as if I had known it all, but my heart began to palpitate. The cabinet-maker advised me to paint the walls, as paper would need a long time to dry. The active man promised to undertake that task for a proper reward.

From his place I went to two intimate comrades to invite them as best men; of my own family I had not a living soul. Their congratulations and embraces were mingled with other impressions in my head, and roused there a genuine chaos.

I found Tola in the drawing-room. I had barely kissed her hands when she came to my ear on tiptoe and whispered one sentence, —

"They have permitted!"

The last shadow on my happiness vanished. Tola was as radiant with delight as a burning candle is with fire. We walked hand in hand through the room and conversed. She told me how everything had happened.

"At first mamma said that that was impossible, and then she said: 'Thou dost not even understand how very unbecoming it is for a young lady to hasten her wedding.' Then I answered that we were both hastening it. Mamma raised her eyes to the ceiling, and shrugged her shoulders. Papa laughed, embraced me, kissed me on the forehead, and even on the hand. 'Thou hast always a weakness for her,' said mamma; 'but one must consider society a little.'

"'Society! society!' said papa. 'Society will not give them happiness; they must find happiness for themselves; and as we have done everything just the opposite of society, let it be the same to the end. It is Lent now; but immediately after Easter they can marry, and the wedding outfit may be finished afterward.'

"Mamma yielded, for papa always insists on his point. (I suppose you will be like him too.) Then I embraced mamma; I did not let her speak a word. Only later could she say, 'All is done in mad fashion.' But I carried my point at last. Are you satisfied?"

I had been so much in love, or so timid, that I had never gone so far as to take her in my arms. Then for the first time I wanted to embrace her; but she put me away gently, saying, —

"It is so nice to walk arm in arm, like good children."

And so we walked on. I told her that I had thought of our house, and had given orders to paint the walls, not in oil, for that was very costly, but in some color which dries quickly, and is exactly like oil. Tola repeated,

"Which dries quickly;" and it is unknown why we both began to laugh, likely for the reason that our mutual delight and happiness could not find room in us. We decided that the little drawing-room should be red, for though that color is common, heads appear on a red background perfectly. The dining-room was to be in bright green tiles, the adjoining room in faience; of others we did not talk, for Tola's shoestring was loose, and she went to the next room to tie it.

After a while she returned with her father, who called me a water-burner and a Tartar; but at the same time he promised that the ceremony should take place on Tuesday after the holidays.

During the first days our love was all emotion and had ceaseless tears in its eyes; but afterward it bloomed out in gladness, like a flower in spring, and we laughed then whole days.

Because of the lateness of the holidays, spring was in the world. The trees were in bud. Before Holy Week Tola and I, with her parents, made visits. People looked at us curiously everywhere; at times this was annoying. Some older ladies put glasses on their eyes at sight of me; but I had to pass the ordeal. Tola, joyous and fresh as a bird, rewarded me a hundredfold for those irksome visits.

I looked myself to the painting of the rooms. Because of the weather everything dried in a twinkle. The bedroom I had painted in rose-color.

My love increased daily. I was sure now that even were Tola to change, were she even to grow ugly, I should say to myself, "Misfortune has touched *me;*" but I would not cease to love her. A man in that state yields himself up so completely that he knows not where his own *I* ceases.

We amused ourselves often like children; at times we teased each other. When, for example, I came in the morning and found her alone, I looked through the room, as if not observing her; I looked for her, and asked, "Is there no one here who is loved?" She searched in the corners, shook her bright head, and answered, "No! it seems not."—"But that young lady?"—"Oh, perhaps she is a little!" Then after a while she added in a whisper, "And perhaps greatly."

At that time a new feeling involved itself in my love. Not only did I love Tola, but I liked her beyond everything. I was dying for her companionship. I could pass whole hours with her talking about anything. At times we talked deeply and seriously touching our future, though in general I avoided all discussions and theories on the theme of what marriage should be; for I thought why must I enclose in prearranged formulas that which should develop spontaneously from love itself. There is no need to lay before flowers theories of how they should bloom.

Good Friday passed silently, gloomily. On the streets there was mist, and a light rain was falling. We and Tola's parents went to the cemetery; we put each what we chose on the plates of beggars. Tola, dressed in black, serene, calm, and dignified, appeared beautiful as never before. At moments, in the gloom of the church, or in the light of the candles, her face was perfectly angelic. That day she caught a slight cold; and I raced through all the cellars, looking for old Malaga, which some one had advised her to drink.

I passed Easter at the house of Tola's parents. Not having any one of my own family, I understood for the first time what it is to have persons dear to one, and to be dear to some one else. The next Sunday there was perfect spring.

Before Easter I had brought some sort of order into our house. The garden had begun to grow green, and the old cherry-trees were in blossom.

Just before the holidays, too, came from the press my doctoral essay about the Neoplatonists. Tola undertook to read it. Poor thing! she blinked, broke her little head, but read from a feeling of duty.

And now memories of the wedding — no, rather, pictures of it — crowd into my head, confused, in disorder, filled with single impressions, somewhat feverish. I see the whole place full of flowers; on the stairs, and in the rooms. There is a hurrying in the house, the arrival of guests, a multitude of strange or little known faces. Tola in the drawing-room, arrayed in a white robe, with a veil, was as beautiful as a vision, but somehow different from what she was usually; she appeared more dignified, as it were, less near. The feeling of a certain haste and movement remained with me. Everything that happened after entering the church seems indefinite: the church, the altar, the candles on the altar, at the sides brilliant toilets of ladies, curious eyes, whispers. Tola and I kneeling before the altar took each the other's hand, as if in greeting; and after a time our voices were heard, sounding like strange voices, "I take thee to myself," etc. I hear till this moment the organ and the mighty, resonant hymn, "*Veni Creator*," which broke forth in the choir, as suddenly as a cloud-burst. I have no recollection whatever of leaving the church; of the wedding there is left in my mind the blessing of her parents, and the supper. Tola sat at my side; and I remember that from moment to moment she raised her hands to her cheeks, which were burning. Through the bouquets on the table I saw various faces, which I should not recognize now. Our health was drunk with applause and great clinking of glasses. About midnight I took my wife home.

Of the road there will always remain in my mind the memory of her head resting on my shoulder, and her white veil with the odor of violets.

Next morning I waited for her at tea in the dining-room; meanwhile she, after dressing, went by another door to the garden, for I saw her through the window against the background of the cherry-tree. I ran to her immediately; she turned, pushed her head toward the tree, as if wishing to hide from me.

I thought that she was jesting; so creeping up quietly, I caught her by the waist, and said, —

"Good-morning. But who is hiding from her husband? What art thou doing here?"

Then I saw that she was blushing, that she was avoiding my eyes and turning away from me really.

"What is the matter with thee, Tola?" asked I.

"See," answered she, confused, "the wind is shaking the blossoms from the cherry-trees."

"Let it take them," said I, "if only thou wilt stay with me."

And I bent her head toward mine; but she whispered with closed eyes, —

"Do not look at me; go away—"

But at the same time her lips pushed toward me almost passionately, and I met them with delight.

The breeze began really to cast white blossoms on our heads.

I woke and saw the naked walls of my room.

I had had typhus,—and a very bad typhus; I had lain two weeks unconscious in fever.

But even a fever is sometimes the mercy of God.

When I regained consciousness I learned that Panna Antonina's parents had taken her to Venice.

But I, lonely as before, finish my confession, which is strange, perhaps. I was so immensely happy in my visions that I wrote them down at once, so that life's irony might not be lost. I conclude the above reminiscences without sorrow, and with my former faith, that among all sources of happiness, that from which I drank during the fever is the clearest and best.

A life which love has not visited, even in a dream, is worse than mine.

CHARCOAL SKETCHES

CHARCOAL SKETCHES.

CHAPTER I.

IN WHICH WE MAKE THE ACQUAINTANCE OF THE HEROES, AND BEGIN TO HOPE THAT SOMETHING WILL FOLLOW.

IN Barania-Glova, in the chancery of the village-mayor, it was as calm as in time of sowing poppy-seed. The mayor, a peasant no longer young, whose name was Frantsishek Burak, was sitting at the table, and scribbling something on paper with strained attention; the secretary of the Commune, Pan Zolzik, young and full of hope, was standing at the window defending himself from flies.

There were as many flies in the chancery as in a cow-house. All the walls were spotted from them, and had lost their original color. Spotted in like manner were the glass on the image hanging over the table, the paper, the seal, the crucifix, and the mayor's official books.

The flies lighted on the mayor too, as on an ordinary councilman; but they were attracted particularly by Pan Zolzik's head, which was pomaded, and also perfumed with violet. Over his head a whole swarm was circling; they sat at the parting of his hair and formed black, living, movable spots. Pan Zolzik from time to time raised his hand warily, and then brought it down quickly on his head; the slap of his palm was heard, the swarm flew upward, buzzing, and Pan Zolzik, seizing his hair, picked out the corpses and threw them on the floor.

The hour was four in the afternoon. Silence reigned in the whole village, for the people were at work in the fields; but outside the chancery window a cow was scratching herself against the wall, and at times she showed her puffing nostrils through the window, with saliva hanging from her muzzle.

At moments she threw her heavy head against her back to drive away flies; at moments she grazed the wall with her horn; then Pan Zolzik looked out through the window, and cried, —

"Aa! hei! May the —"

Then he looked at himself in the glass hanging there at the window, and arranged his hair.

At last the mayor broke the silence.

"Pan Zolzik," said he, with a Mazovian accent, "write that *rapurt;* it is somehow awkward for me. Besides, you are the writer [secretary]."

But Pan Zolzik was in bad humor, and whenever he was in bad humor the mayor had to do everything himself.

"Well, what if I am the secretary?" replied he, with contempt. "The secretary is here for the purpose of writing to the chief and the commissioner; but to such a mayor as you are, write yourself." Then he added with majestic contempt, "But what is a mayor to me? What? A peasant, and that is the end of it! Do what you like with a peasant, he will always be a peasant!"

Then he arranged his hair, and looked again in the glass.

The mayor felt touched, and answered, —

"But see here! Haven't I drunk tea with the marshal?"

"A great deal I care about your tea!" said Zolzik, carelessly. "And besides without arrack, I suppose?"

"That is not true! for it was with arrack."

"Well, let it be with arrack; but still I will not write the report!"

"If the gentleman is of such delicate make-up, why did he ask to be secretary?" answered the mayor, in anger.

"But who asked you? I am secretary only through acquaintance with the chief—"

"Oh, great acquaintance, when he comes here you won't let a breath out of your lips!"

"Burak! Burak! I give warning that you are letting your tongue out too much. Your peasant bones are sticking in my throat, together with your office of secretary. A man of education can only grow common among you. If I get angry, I will throw the secretaryship, and you, to the devil—"

"Will you! And what will become of you, then?"

"What? Shall I go to gnawing the rafters without this office? A man with education will take care of himself. Have no fear about a man with education! Only yesterday Stolbitski, the inspector, said to me, 'Ei, Zolzik! thou wouldst be a devil, not a sub-inspector, for thou knowest how grass grows.' Talk to the fool! For me your secretaryship is a thing to be spat upon. A man with education—"

"Oh, but the world will not come to an end if you leave us!"

"The world will not come to an end, but you will dip a dishcloth in a tar bucket, and write in the books with it. It will be pleasant for you till you feel the stick through your velvet."

The mayor began to scratch his head.

"If anything is said you are on your hind-legs right away."

"Well, don't open your lips too much —"

"There it is, there it is!"

Again there was silence, except that the mayor's pen was squeaking slowly on paper. At last the mayor straightened himself, wiped his pen on his coat, and said, —

"Well, now! I have done it, with the help of God."

"Read what you have tacked together."

"What had I to tack? I have written out accurately everything that is needed."

"Read it over, I say."

The mayor took the paper in both hands and began to read: —

"To the Mayor of the Commune of Lipa. In the name of the Father, Son, and Holy Ghost. Amen. The chief commanded that the soldier lists be ready after the Mother of God, and the registers with you in the parish with the priest, and also our men go to you to harvest; do you understand? That they be written out, and the harvesters too, to send before the Mother of God, as eighteen years are finished; for if you do not do this you will catch it on the head, which I wish to myself and you. Amen."

The worthy mayor heard every Sunday how the priest ended his sermon with Amen, so the ending seemed to him as final as it was appropriate to all the demands of polite style; but Zolzik began to laugh. "How is that?" inquired he.

"Well, write better you."

"Certainly I will write, because I blush for all Barania-Glova."

Zolzik sat down, took the pen in his hand, made a

number of circles with it, as if to acquire impetus, and then fell to writing rapidly.

The notice was soon ready; the author straightened his hair, and read as follows:—

"The Mayor of the Commune of Barania-Glova to the Mayor of the Commune of Lipa. As the recruiting lists are to be ready at command of superior authority on such and such a day of such and such a year, the Mayor of the Commune of Lipa is notified that the register of those peasants of Barania-Glova, which is in the chancery of his parish, is to be taken by him from that chancery and sent at the very earliest date to the Commune of Barania-Glova. The peasants of the Commune of Barania-Glova who are at work in Lipa are to be presented in Barania-Glova on the same day as the register."

The mayor caught those sounds with eager ear; and his face expressed an occupation and a concentration of spirit that was well-nigh religious. How beautiful and solemn all that seemed to him; how thoroughly official it was! Take, for example, even that beginning: "As the recruiting lists, etc." The mayor adored that "as;" but he never could learn it, or rather he knew how to begin with it, but not a word farther could he go. From Zolzik's hand that flowed just like water; so that even in the chancery of the district no one wrote better. Next he blackened the seal, struck it on the paper so that the table quivered, and all was there finished!

"Well, that is a head for you, that is a head!" said the mayor.

"Yes," answered Zolzik, mollified; "but then a writer [secretary] is one who writes books —"

"Do you write books too?"

"You ask as if you did not know; but the chancery books, who writes them?"

"True," said the mayor, who added, after a while, "The lists will come now with the speed of a thunderbolt."

"But next do you see to ridding the village of useless people."

"How are you to get rid of them?"

"I tell you that the chief has complained that the people in Barania-Glova are not as they should be. They are always drinking, says he. 'Burak,' says he, 'does not look after the people; so the matter will be ground out on him.'"

"Yes, I know," answered the mayor; "that all is ground out on me. When Rozalka Kovaliha was brought to bed, the court decided to give her twenty-five, so that a second time she should remember. 'Because,' said the court, 'that is not nice for a girl.' Who commanded? Was it I? Not I, but the court. What had I to do with that. Let them all be brought to bed for themselves, if they like. The court directed, and then laid the blame on me."

At this juncture the cow struck the wall with such force that the chancery trembled. The mayor cried out, with a voice full of bitterness, —

"Aa! hei! may all the—"

The secretary, who was sitting at the table, began to look again in the glass.

"Serves you right," said he; "why don't you look out? It will be the same story with this drinking. One mangy sheep will lead a whole flock astray, and he attracts people to the dram-shop."

"Of course, that is well known; but as to drinking, there is need of drink when people have worked in the field."

"But I tell you only this, get rid of Repa, and all will be well."

"What! shall I take his head off?"

"You will not take his head off; but now that they are making the army lists, inscribe him in the list; let him draw the lot, and that is enough."

"But he is married and has a son a year old."

"Who among the higher authorities knows that? He will not go to make a complaint, and if he goes, they will not listen to him. In time of recruiting no one has leisure."

"Oh, lord writer, it must be that for you the question is not of drinking, but of Repa's wife; and that is nothing but a sin against God."

"What is that to you? This is what you will do; you will look out for your son, who is nineteen years of age, and he as well as others must draw."

"I know that; but I won't give him. If there is no other way, I will ransom him."

"Oh! if you are such a rich man — "

"The Lord God has a little copper money in my hands; not much; but perhaps it will hold out."

"You will pay eight hundred rubles of copper money?"

"And if I say that I will pay, I will pay even in copper, and afterward, if the Lord God permits me to remain mayor, with His supreme assistance, the money may come back to me in a couple of years."

"It will come back, or it will not come back. I need some too; I will not give you all. A man with education has always more outgoes than one who is ignorant; if we should enroll Repa in place of your son, it would be a sparing for you; you cannot find eight hundred rubles on the road."

The hope of saving such a large sum began to tickle Burak, and smile at him agreeably.

"Ba!" said he at last, "that is always a very dangerous thing."

"Well, it is not on your head."

"That is just what I am afraid of, that the thing will be done by your head, and ground out on mine."

"As you like; then pay eight hundred rubles."

"I do not say that I am not sorry for the money."

"But since you think that it will come back to you, why are you sorry? Do not count too much on your mayorship, though; they don't know everything about you yet; if they only knew what I know—"

"You take more chancery money than I do."

"I am not speaking of the chancery now, but of times a little earlier."

"Oh, I am not afraid! I did what was commanded."

"Well, you will explain that somewhere else."

After he had said this, the secretary took his cap and went out of the chancery. The sun was very low; people were returning from the field. First, the secretary met five mowers with scythes on their shoulders; they bowed to him, saying, "Praised." The lord secretary nodded to them with his pomaded head, but did not answer, "For the ages," since he judged that it did not become a man with education to do so. That Pan Zolzik had education, all knew; and only those might doubt who were either malicious, or in general of evil thought,— people to whom every personality raising its head above the common level was as salt in the eye, and would not let them sleep.

If we had proper biographies of all our celebrated people, we should read in the life of this uncommon man, that he gained his first knowledge at Oslovitsi, the capital city of the district of Oslovitski, in which district Barania-Glova also is situated. In the seventeenth year of his life, this young Zolzik had advanced as far as the second class; and would have gone higher as promptly, had it not been that, on a sudden, stormy times came, which interrupted forever his career in the exact sciences. Carried away by the usual enthusiasm of youth, Pan Zolzik, who moreover had been persecuted still earlier by unjust professors, stood at the head of the more actively watchful of his colleagues, made cats' music for his persecutors, tore his books, broke his rule and pens, and, rejecting Minerva, entered on a new career. In this new career he arrived at the office of communal secretary; and as we have heard already, was even dreaming of becoming sub-inspector. He did not succeed badly as secretary. Accurate knowledge rouses respect at all times; and since, as I have remarked, my sympathetic hero knew something about almost every inhabitant in the district, all felt for him respect, mingled with a certain caution, lest they might in any way offend an individuality so uncommon. Even persons of "intelligence" bowed to him, and peasants took off their caps at a distance, saying, "Praised."

Here I see, however, that I must explain more clearly why Pan Zolzik did not answer to the "Praised," with the usual "For the ages of ages." I have mentioned already that he considered that as unbecoming in a man of education; but there were other reasons also. Faculties which are thoroughly self-acting are generally bold and radical. Pan Zolzik had arrived at the conviction that "the soul is a breath; and that is the end of the question." Moreover, the secretary was reading "Isabella of Spain, or the Secrets of the Court of Madrid," just then in course of publication by the Warsaw publishing house of Pan Breslauer. This novel, remarkable in every regard, pleased him so much and penetrated him so deeply that on a time he had even a plan to leave all and go to Spain. "Marfori succeeded," thought he; "why should not I also succeed?" He might have gone, indeed, for he was of the opinion that "in his stupid country a man was merely going to loss;" but happily he was detained by circumstances which this *epopaea* will mention further on.

In fact, as a result of reading that "Isabella of Spain," which was issued periodically, to the greater glory of literature, by Pan Breslauer, Pan Zolzik looked very sceptically at the clergy, and therefore at everything connected directly or indirectly with the clergy. This was the reason why he did not give the mowers the usual answer, "For the ages of ages," but went on; he went on and on, till he met girls coming home from the harvest field with sickles on their shoulders. They were just passing a great pool, and went, one after another, goose fashion, raising their skirts behind, and exposing their red legs. Then Pan Zolzik said, —

"How are ye, titmice?" And he stopped on the very path; when any girl passed, he caught her around the waist, kissed her, and then pushed her into the puddle. But that was just for sport, and the girls cried. "Oi! oi!" laughing till their back teeth could be seen. Afterwards, when they had passed, the secretary heard, not without pleasure, how they said, one to another, "But that is a nice cavalier; he is our secretary!" "And he is as blooming as an apple!" The third one said, "And his head has the smell of a rose; so that when he catches you around the waist your head is just dizzy!"

The secretary went forward, full of pleasant thoughts. But farther on, near a cottage, he heard a conversation about himself; and he halted behind the fence. Beyond the fence was a dense cherry orchard, in the orchard bees, and not far from the beehives two women were talking. One had potatoes in her apron, and was peeling them with a small knife, while the other was saying,—

"Oi! my Stahova, I am so afraid that they will take my Franek and make a soldier of him, that my flesh creeps."

"You must go to the secretary," answered the other. "If he cannot help you, no one can help you."

"And what can I take him, my Stahova? It is not possible to go with empty hands to him. The mayor is better; you can take him white crawfish, or butter, or linen under your arm, or a hen; he will take anything without grumbling. But the secretary won't look. Oh, he is terribly proud! For him you must just open your handkerchief, and out with a ruble!'

"Ye'll not wait," muttered the secretary to himself, "till I take eggs or a hen from you. Am I some kind of a bribe-snatcher? But go with your hen to the mayor."

Thus thinking, he pushed apart the branches of the cherry-tree and was going to call to the women, when he heard all at once the sound of a brichka behind him. The secretary turned and looked. In the brichka was sitting Pan Victor, a young student, with his cap on the side of his head, and a cigarette between his teeth; the brichka was driven by that Franek of whom the women were talking a moment before.

The student bent over the side of the brichka, saw Pan Zolzik, waved his hand to him, and cried,—

"How art thou, Pan Zolzik? What news in the village? Dost thou always pomade thy hair two inches deep?"

"The servant of my lord benefactor!" said Zolzik, bowing low. But when the brichka had gone a short distance, he muttered,—

"May thy neck break before the end of the journey!"

The secretary could not endure that student. He was a cousin of the Skorabevskis, and came to visit them every summer. Zolzik not only could not endure the young man, but feared him like fire, for he was always jesting; a great rogue, he made a fool of Zolzik as if purposely, and was the only man in the whole place who made no account of him. Once even Pan Victor had happened in during a session of the communal council, and told Zolzik explicitly that he was an idiot, and the peasants that they had no need to obey him. Zolzik would have been glad to take revenge; but — what could he do to the student? As to others, he knew even something of each one, but of Pan Victor he knew nothing.

The arrival of that student was not to his liking; therefore Pan Zolzik went on with a cloudy brow, and did not halt till he came to a cottage standing a little way in from the road. When he saw it, his forehead grew bright again. That was a cottage poorer, perhaps, than others, but it had a neat look. The space in front was swept clean, and sweet-flag was scattered in the yard. Near the fence lay pieces of wood; in one of them was sticking an axe with its handle erect. A little farther was a barn with open doors; near it a building which was both a shed and a cowhouse; still farther was a field in which a horse was nipping grass, and moving about with fettered feet. Before the shed was a large manure heap on which two pigs were lying. Near this ducks were walking along. Close to the pieces of wood a cock was scratching the ground among chips, and whenever he found a grain, or a worm, he called "Koh! koh! koh!" The hens flew to the call, in hot haste, and seized the dainty, pulling it from one another.

By the door of the cottage a woman was scutching

hemp, and singing, "Oi ta dada! Oi ta dada! da-da-na!" Near her lay a dog with his forelegs stretched out; he was snapping at flies which were lighting on his cut ear.

The woman was young, perhaps twenty, and remarkably handsome.

She wore a white shirt drawn together with red strings, and on her head was the ordinary peasant cap. She was as healthy as a mushroom; she was broad in the shoulders and hips, slender in the waist, active, — in one word, a deer. She had delicate features, a head not large, and a complexion perhaps even pale, but somewhat gilded by sun-rays, very dark eyes, brows as if painted, a small delicate nose, and lips like cherries. Her fine dark hair was dropping out from under the cap.

When the secretary approached, the dog lying near the scutching-bench rose, thrust his tail under him, and began to growl, showing his teeth from moment to moment as if he were laughing.

"Kruchek!" cried the woman, with a thin, resonant voice, "wilt thou lie down! May the worms bite thee!"

"Good-evening," began Zolzik.

"Good-evening, lord secretary!" answered the woman, not ceasing to work.

"Is yours at home?"

"He is at work in the woods."

"But that is too bad; I have an affair with him from the commune."

An affair with the commune for common people always means something evil. The woman stopped working, looked with alarm at the secretary, and inquired with concern, —

"Well, what is it?"

Zolzik meanwhile passed through the gateway and stood near her.

"Let us have a kiss, then I'll tell you."

"Keep away!" said the woman.

But the secretary had succeeded already in putting his arm around her waist, and drawing her toward him.

"I will scream!" said she, pulling away vigorously.

"My pretty one, — Marysia!"

"Oh, this is just an offence against God! Oh!"

She struggled still more vigorously; but Pan Zolzik was so strong that he did not let her go.

At this moment Kruchek came to her aid. He raised the hair on his back, and with furious barking sprang at the secretary; and, since the secretary was dressed in a short coat, Kruchek seized his nankeen trousers, went through the nankeen, caught the skin, went through the skin, and when he felt fulness in his mouth, he began to shake his head madly and tug.

"Jesus! Mary!" cried the lord secretary, forgetting that he belonged to the *esprits forts*.

But Kruchek did not let go his hold till the secretary seized a billet of wood and pounded him uncounted times on the back with it; when Kruchek got a blow on his spine, he sprang away whining piteously. But after a while he jumped at the man again.

"Take off this dog! take off this devil!" cried the secretary, brandishing the stick with desperation.

The woman cried to the dog, and sent him outside the gate. Then she and the secretary gazed at each other in silence.

"Oh, my misfortune! Why did you look at me?" asked Marysia, at length, frightened by the bloody turn of the affair.

"Vengeance on you!" shouted the secretary. "Ven-

CHARCOAL SKETCHES. 305

geance on you! Wait! Repa will be a soldier. I wanted to save him. But now — you will come yourself to me! Vengeance on you!"

The poor woman grew as pale as if some one had struck her on the head with a hatchet; she spread out her hands, opened her mouth, as if she wanted to say something; but meanwhile the secretary raised his cap with green binding from the ground, and went away quickly, brandishing the stick in one hand, and holding his badly torn trousers with the other.

CHAPTER II.

SOME OTHER PERSONS AND DISAGREEABLE VISIONS.

AN hour later, perhaps, Repa came home from the woods with the carpenter Lukash, on the landlord's wagon. Repa was a burly fellow, as tall as a poplar, strong, just hewn out with an axe. He went to the woods every day, for the landlord had sold to Jews all the forest which was free of peasant privileges. Repa received good wages, for he was a good man to work. When he spat on his palm, seized the axe, gave a blow with a grunt and struck, the pine-tree groaned, and chips flew from it half an ell long. In loading timber onto wagons he was also the first man.

The Jews, who went through the woods with measures in their hands and looked at the tops of the pines, as if hunting for crows' nests, were amazed at his strength. Droysla, a rich merchant from Oslovitsi, said to him, —

"Well, Repa! devil take thee! Here are six groshes for vodka. No! here, wait; here are five groshes for vodka!"

But Repa did not care, — he just wielded his axe till the woods thundered; sometimes for amusement he let his voice out through the forest, —

"Hop! Hop!"

His voice flew among the trees, and came back as an echo. And again, nothing was heard but the thunder of Repa's axe; and sometimes the pines too began to talk among their branches with a sound as is usual in a forest.

At times, also, the wood-cutters sang; and at singing, Repa too was the first man. One should have heard how he thundered forth with the wood-cutters a song which he had taught them himself, —

"Something shouted in the woods,
     B-u-u-u-u!
And struck terribly,
     B-u-u-u-u!
That's a mosquito that fell from the oak,
     B-u-u-u-u!
And he broke a bone in his shoulder,
     B-u-u-u-u!
That was an honest mosquito,
     B-u-u-u-u!
He is flying barely alive,
     B-u-u-u-u!
And they asked the mosquito,
     B-u-u-u-u!
Oi, is a doctor not needed?
     B-u u-u!
Or any druggist?
     B-u-u-u!
Only a spade and a pickaxe,
     B-u-u-u-u!"

In the dramshop, too, Repa was first in everything: he loved sivuha; and he was quick at fighting when he had drunk anything. Once he made such a hole in the head of the house-servant, Damaz, that Yozvova, the housekeeper, swore that his soul could be seen through it. Another time, but that was when he was barely seventeen years of age, he fought in the dramshop with soldiers on furlough. Pan Skorabevski, who was mayor at the time, took him to the chancery, and gave him a couple of blows on the head; but for appearance' sake only, then, being satisfied, he inquired, —

"Repa, have the fear of God! How didst thou manage them? There were seven against thee."

"Well, serene heir," answered Repa, "their legs were worn out with marching, and the moment I touched one he fell to the floor."

Pan Skorabevski quashed the affair. For a long time he had been very friendly to Repa. The peasant women even whispered into one another's ears that Repa was his son.

"That can be seen at once," said they; "he has the courage of a noble, the dog blood!"

But this was not true; though everybody knew Repa's mother, no one knew his father. Repa himself paid rent for a cottage and three morgs of land, which became his own afterward. He cultivated his land; and, being a good worker, his affairs went on well. He married, and met such a wife that a better could not be found with a candle; and surely he would have been prosperous, had it not been that he liked vodka a little too well.

But what could be done? If any one mentioned the matter, he answered right off, —

"I drink from my own money, and what's that to you?"

He feared no one in the village; before the secretary alone had he manners. When he saw from a distance the green cap, the stuck-up nose and goatee walking in high boots along the road slowly, he caught at his cap. The secretary knew also some things against Repa. During the insurrection certain papers were given Repa to carry, and he carried them.

When he came that day from the woods to his cottage, Marysia ran to him with great crying, and began to call out, —

"Oh, poor man, my eyes will not look long on thee; oh, I shall not weave clothes for thee, nor cook food long for thee! Thou wilt go to the ends of the earth, poor unfortunate!"

Repa was astonished.

"Hast eaten madwort, woman, or has some beast bitten thee?"

"I have n't eaten madwort, and no beast has bitten me; but the secretary was here, and he said that there was no way for thee to escape from the army. Oi! thou wilt go, thou wilt go to the edge of the world!"

Then he began to question her: how, what? — and she told him everything, only she concealed the tricks of Pan Zolzik; for she was afraid that Repa would say something foolish to the secretary, or, which God keep away! he would attack him, and harm himself in that way.

"Thou foolish woman!" said Repa, at last, "why art thou crying? They will not take me to the army, for I am beyond the years; besides, I have a house, I have land, I have thee, stupid woman, and I have that tormented lobster there too."

While saying that he pointed to the cradle where the "tormented lobster," a sturdy boy a year old, was kicking and screaming to make a man's ears split.

The woman wiped her eyes with her apron, and said. —

"What does this all mean, then? Or does he know of the papers which thou wert carrying from forest to forest?"

Repa began now to scratch his head. "He does indeed!" After a while he added, "I will go and talk with him. Maybe it is nothing terrible."

"Go, go!" said Marysia, "and take a ruble with thee. Don't go near him without a ruble."

Repa took a ruble out of the box, and went to the secretary.

The secretary was a single man, so he had no separate housekeeping, but lived in the house of four tenements standing at the dam, — the so-called "brick house." There he had two rooms, with a separate entrance. In the first room there was nothing but some straw and a pair of gaiters; the second was both a reception and a sleeping room. There was a bed in it, almost never made up; on the bed two pillows without cases, from these pillows feathers were dropping continually; near by was a table, on it an inkstand, pens, chancery books, a few numbers of "Isabella of Spain," published by Pan Breslauer, two dirty collars of English make, a bottle of pomade, paper for cigarettes, and finally a candle in a tin candlestick, with a reddish wick and a fly drowned in the tallow close to the wick.

By the window hung a large looking-glass; opposite the window stood a bureau on which were the very exquisite toilet articles of the secretary, — jackets, vests of fabulous colors, cravats, gloves, patent-leather shoes, and even a cylinder hat which the lord secretary wore whenever he had to visit the district capital of Oslovitsi.

Besides this, at the moment of which we are writing, in an armchair near the bed rested the nankeen trousers of the lord secretary; the lord secretary himself was lying on the bed and reading a number of "Isabella of Spain," published by Pan Breslauer.

His position, not the position of Pan Breslauer, but the secretary, was dreadful, so dreadful, indeed, that one would need the style of Victor Hugo to describe it.

First of all, he feels a raging pain in his wound. That reading of "Isabella," which for him had been always the dearest pleasure and recreation, now increases, not only the pain, but the bitterness which torments him after that adventure with Kruchek. He has a slight fever, and is barely able to collect his thoughts. At times terrible visions come to him. He has just read how young Serrano arrived at the palace of the Escurial covered with wounds after a brilliant victory over the Carlists.

The youthful Isabella, pale with emotion, receives him. The muslin rises in waves above her bosom.

"General, thou art wounded!" says she with trembling voice to Serrano.

Here it seems to the unhappy Zolzik that he is really Serrano.

"Oi! oi! I am wounded!" repeated he, in a stifled voice. "Oh, queen, pardon! But may the most serene — "

"Rest, general! Be seated. Be seated. Relate thy heroic deeds to me."

"Relate them I can, but as to sitting I cannot in any way," cries Serrano, in desperation. "Oi! — Pardon, O queen! That cursed Kruchek! I wish to say Don José — Ai, ai! ai!"

Here pain drives away dreaming. Serrano looks around; the candle is burning on the table and spluttering, for just then it begins to burn the fly which had dropped into the tallow; other flies are crawling along the wall. Oh! this is the house of four tenements, not the palace of the Escurial! There is no Queen Isabella here. Pan Zolzik recovers presence of mind. He rises in the bed, moistens a cloth in a dish of water standing near the bed, and changes the application on his wound.

Then he turns to the wall, dozes, or rather dreams half asleep, half awake, and is going again evidently by extra post to the Escurial.

"Dear Serrano! my love! I will dress thy wounds myself," whispers Queen Isabella.

Then the hair stands on Serrano's head. He feels the whole horror of his position. How is he to refuse obedience to the queen, and how is he in this case to yield himself to the dressing of his wound? Cold sweat is coming out on his forehead, when suddenly — the queen vanishes, the door opens with a rattle, and before him stands neither more nor less than Don José, Serrano's sworn enemy.

"What dost thou wish? Who art thou?" shouts Serrano.

"I am Repa!" answers Don José, gloomily.

Zolzik wakes a second time; the Escurial becomes the brick house again, the candle is burning, the fly is crackling in the wick, and blue drops are scattered; in the door stands Repa, and behind him — but the pen drops from my hand — through the half-open door are thrust in the head and shoulders of Kruchek. The monster holds his eyes fixed on Pan Zolzik, and seems to laugh.

Cold sweat in very truth is coming out on the temples of Pan Zolzik, and through his head flies the thought, "Repa has come to break my bones, and Kruchek to help him."

"What do ye both want here?" cries he, in a terrified voice.

Repa puts the ruble on the table, and answers, —

"Great, mighty lord secretary! I have come about the conscription."

"Out! out! out!" cries Zolzik, into whom courage enters in one instant. And falling into a rage he rises to spring at Repa; but at that moment his wound, received in the Carlist war, pains him so acutely that he drops again on the pillow, giving forth smothered groans.

"Oi! ye!"

CHAPTER III.

MEDITATIONS AND EUREKA.

THE wound became inflamed.

I see how my fair readers will begin to drop tears over my hero, and hence, before any of them faint, I will hasten to add, that my hero did not die of the wound. Long life was predestined to him. For that matter, if he had died, I should have broken my pen and stopped this story; but as he did not die I continue.

In truth, then, the wound grew inflamed, but unexpectedly it turned to profit for the lord secretary of the chancery of Barania-Glova, and turned in this very simple way: The wound drew the humors from Pan Zolzik's head, therefore he began to think more clearly, and saw at once that, up to that time, he had been committing pure folly. For just listen: The secretary had a design, as they say in Warsaw, on Repa's wife, and that is not to be wondered at, for she was a woman whose equal was not to be found in the whole district of Oslovitsi, therefore he wanted to get rid of Repa. If once they took Repa into the army, Pan Zolzik might say to

himself, "Now frolic, my soul, with thy coat off." But
it was not so easy to substitute Repa for the mayor's son.
A secretary is a power. Zolzik was a power among secretaries; there was this misfortune, however, that he was
not the last resort in recruiting. In this case, one had to
do with the district police, with the military commissioner, with the chief of the district, with the commander of the guard. Not all at least of these were
interested in presenting the army and the State with Repa
instead of Burak. "To inscribe him in the recruiting
list, and what further?" asked my sympathetic hero.
"They will verify the list, and it must be compared with
the parish record; and since it will be hard to muzzle
Repa's mouth, they will give a reprimand, and perhaps
throw the secretary out of his office, and thus finish the
matter."

The greatest men have committed follies under the influence of passion, but just in this is their greatness, that
they open their eyes in proper season. Zolzik said to
himself that in promising Burak to inscribe Repa in the
list of recruits he had committed his first stupidity; in
going to Repa's wife and attacking her at the hemp, he
had committed the second; when he frightened her and
her husband with the enrolment, he committed the third
stupidity. Oh, lofty moment! in which a man truly
great says to himself, "I am an ass!" thou didst come
to Barania-Glova, thou didst descend, as if on wings, from
that region where the lofty rests on the sublime, for
Zolzik said to himself plainly, "I am an ass!"

But was he to reject the plan now, when he had shed
his own blood for it (in his enthusiasm he had said, the
blood of his own breast)? Was he to reject the plan when
he had sanctified it by a new pair of trousers, for which
he had not paid Srul, the tailor, and a pair of nankeens,

he did not know himself whether he had worn them twice? — No, and never! On the contrary now, when to his projects against Repa's wife was added a desire for vengeance against both, and Kruchek with them, Zolzik swore to himself that he would be a fool unless he poured tallow into Repa's skin.

He meditated over methods the first day, while changing poultices; he meditated the second day, while changing poultices; he meditated the third day, while changing poultices; and do you know what he thought out? Well, he did n't think out anything!

On the fourth day, the guard brought him diachylum from the apothecary in Oslovitsi; Zolzik spread it on a cloth, applied it, and how wonderful were the effects of this medicament! Almost simultaneously he cried out, "I have found it!" In fact, he had found something.

CHAPTER IV.

WHICH MAY BE ENTITLED: THE BEAST IN THE SNARE.

A FEW days later, I do not know well whether five or six, in a private room of the public-house in Barania-Glova sat Burak the mayor, the councilman Gomula, and young Repa. The mayor took his glass, —

"You might stop quarrelling, when there is nothing to quarrel about."

"But I say that the Frenchman will not give up to the Prussian," replied Gomula, striking the table with his fist.

"The Prussian is cunning, the dog blood!" answered Repa.

"What good is it that he is cunning? The Turk will help the Frenchman, and the Turk is the strongest."

CHARCOAL SKETCHES.

"What do ye know! The strongest is Harubanda [Garibalda]."

"You must have got out of bed shoulders first. But where did you pull out Harubanda?"

"What need had I to pull him out? Have n't people said that he sailed down the Vistula in boats with a great army? But the beer in Warsaw did n't please him, for generally it is better at home, so he went back."

"Don't lie for nothing. Every Schwab [1] is a Jew.

"But Harubanda is no Schwab."

"What is he?"

"Well what? He must be Cæsar and that's the end of it!"

"You are terribly wise!"

"You are not wiser."

"But if you are so wise, then tell what was the surname of our first father?"

"How? Yadam, of course."

"That is a Christian name; but his surname?"

"Do I know?"

"See there! But I do. His surname was Skrushyla."

"You must have the pip."

"If you don't believe, then listen:—

"'Gwiazdo morza, któraś Pana
Mlekiem swojém wykarmiła
Tyś śmierci szczep, który wszczepił
Pierwszy rodzic, skruszyła.'" [2]

[1] A Suabian, a German.
[2] The translation of those four lines is ·—

Star of the sea who nourished
The Lord with thy milk,
The seed of death engrafted by our first father,
Thou didst crush.

The last line in the Polish if taken alone would mean, our first father, Skrushyla, and the wise Gomula takes it alone. Taken in connection with its pronoun and ending the compound Tys, the first word in the third line, it means: Thou hast crushed.

"Well, and is n't it Skrushyla?"

"You are right this time."

"You had better take another drink," said the mayor.

"Your healths, gossips!"

"Your health!"

"Haim!"

"Siulim!"

"God give happiness!"

All three drank; but since that was at the time of the Franco-German War, Councilman Gomula returned again to politics.

"Well, drink again!" said Burak, after a while.

"The Lord God give happiness!"

"The Lord God reward!"

"Well, to your health!"

They drank again, and, since they drank arrack, Repa struck his empty glass on the table, and said,—

"Ei! that was good! good!"

"Well, have another?" asked Burak.

"Pour it out!"

Repa grew still redder; Burak kept filling his glass.

"But you," said he at last to Repa, "though you are able to throw a korzets of peas on your shoulder with one hand, would be afraid to go to the war."

"Why should I be afraid? If to fight, then, fight."

"One man is small, but very brave; another is strong, but cowardly," said Gomula.

"That is not true!" answered Repa. "I am not cowardly."

"Who knows what you are?"

"But I will go," said Repa, showing his fist, which was as big as a loaf of bread. "If I should go into one of you with this fist, you would fly apart like an old barrel."

"But I might not."

"Do you want to try?"

"Be quiet!" interrupted the mayor. "Are you going to fight or what? Let us drink again."

They drank again; but Burak and Gomula merely moistened their lips. Repa emptied a whole glass of arrack, so that his eyes were white.

"Let us kiss now," said the mayor.

Repa burst into tears at the embraces and kisses, which was a sign that he was well drunk; then he fell to complaining, lamenting bitterly over the blue calf which had died two weeks before in his cowhouse at night.

"Oh, what a calf that was which the Lord God took from me!" cried he, piteously.

"Well, don't mourn over the calf!" said Burak. "A writing has come to the secretary from the government, that the landlord's forests will go to the cottagers."

"And in justice!" answered Repa. "Was it the landlord who planted the forest?"

Then again he began to lament, —

"Oi! what a calf that was! When he bunted the cow with his head while sucking, her hind part flew up to the crossbeam."

"The secretary said — "

"What is the secretary to me?" asked Repa, angrily. "The secretary is no more for me, —

"'He is no more for me
Than Ignatsi — '"

"Let us drink again!"

They drank again. Repa grew calm somehow, and sat down on the bench; that moment the door opened, and on the threshold appeared the green cap, the upturned nose, and the goatee of the secretary.

Repa, who had his cap pushed to the back of his head, threw it at once on the floor, stood up and bellowed out:

"Be praised."

"Is the mayor here?" asked the secretary.

"He is!" answered three voices.

The secretary approached, and at the same moment flew up Shmul, the shopkeeper, with a glass of arrack. Zolzik sniffed it, made a wry face, and sat down at the table.

Silence reigned for a moment. At last Gomula began,

"Lord secretary?"

"What?"

"Is that true about this forest?"

"True. But you must write a petition as a whole commune."

"I will not subscribe," said Repa, who had the general peasant aversion to subscribing his name.

"No one will beg of thee. If thou wilt not subscribe, thou wilt not receive. Thy will."

Repa fell to scratching his head; the secretary, turning to the mayor and the councilman, said in an official tone, —

"It is true about the forest; but each one must surround his own part with a fence to avoid disputes."

"That's it; the fence will cost more than the forest is worth," put in Repa.

The secretary paid no attention to him.

"To pay for the fence," said he to the mayor and the councilman, "the government sends money. Every one will receive profit even, for there will be fifty rubles to each man."

Repa's eyes just flashed, though he was drunk.

"If that is so, I will subscribe. But where is the money?"

"I have the money," said the secretary. "And here is the document."

So saying, he took out a paper folded in four, and read something which the peasants did not understand, though they were greatly delighted; but if Repa had been more sober, he would have seen how the mayor muttered to the councilman.

Then, O wonder! The secretary, taking out the money, said,—

"Well, who will write first?"

All subscribed in turn; when Repa took the pen, Zolzik took away the document, and said,—

"Perhaps thou are not willing? All this is of free will."

"Why shouldn't I be willing?"

"Shmul!" called the secretary.

Shmul appeared in the door. "Well, what does the lord secretary wish?"

"Come here as a witness that everything is of free will." Then, turning to Repa, he said, "Perhaps thou art not willing?"

But Repa had subscribed already, and fixed on the paper a jew [1] no worse than Shmul; then he took the money from Zolzik, fifty whole rubles, and, putting them away in his bosom, cried,—

"Now give us some more arrack!"

Shmul brought it. They drank once and a second time; then Repa planted his fists on his knees and began to doze. He nodded once, nodded a second time; at last he dropped from the bench, muttering, "God be merciful to me a sinner," and fell asleep.

Repa's wife did not come for him; she knew that if he were drunk he would abuse her, perhaps. He used to do

[1] A great ink blot.

so. The next day he would beg her pardon, and kiss her hands. When he was sober, he never said an evil word to the woman; but sometimes he attacked her when he was drunk.

So Repa slept all night in the public house. Next morning he woke at sunrise. He looked, stared, saw that it was not his cottage, but the dram-shop, and not the room in which they were sitting the evening before, but the general room, where the counter was.

"In the name of the Father, Son, and Holy Ghost!"

He looked still more carefully; the sun was rising and shining in through the colored window-panes, and at the window was Shmul, dressed in a shroud with a head-band and plate on his forehead; he was standing, nodding and praying aloud.

"Shmul, dog faith!" cried Repa.

But Shmul made no answer. He swayed backward and forward, prayed on.

Then Repa began to feel of himself, as every peasant does who has slept a night in a drinking-house. He felt the money.

"Jesus, Mary! but what is this?"

Meanwhile, Shmul had finished praying; he removed the shroud and cap, put them away in the room, then returned with slow step, important and calm.

"Shmul!"

"Well, what dost thou want?"

"What money is this that I have here?"

"Knowest not, stupid fellow? Thou didst agree last night with the mayor to take the place of his son; thou didst take the money and sign an agreement."

Repa became as pale as a white wall; then he threw his cap on the floor, dropped onto it, and roared till the window-panes rattled.

"Now go out, thou soldier!" said Shmul, phlegmatically.

Half an hour later, Repa was approaching his cottage; his wife, who was cooking breakfast just then, heard him when the gate squeaked, and ran straight from the fire to meet him; she was very angry.

"Thou drunkard!" began she.

But when she looked at the man, she was frightened, for she hardly knew him.

"What is the matter with thee?"

Repa went into the cottage, and at first could not say a word; he only sat on the bench and looked at the floor.

But Marysia began to inquire, and got everything out of him finally.

"They sold me," said he.

Then she in her turn broke into a great lament; he after her; the child in the cradle began to roar; Kruchek, the dog, outside the door howled so piteously that women with spoons in their hands ran among other cottages and inquired one of another, —

"What has happened there at Repa's?"

"It must be that he is beating her, or something."

Meanwhile Repa's wife was lamenting still more than Repa himself, for she loved him, poor woman, above everything in the world.

CHAPTER V.

IN WHICH WE BECOME ACQUAINTED WITH THE JUDICIAL BODY OF BARANIA-GLOVA AND ITS CHIEF REPRESENTATIVES.

NEXT morning there was a session of the communal court. Members from the whole place were assembled, with the exception of the lords, or nobles. Though a few nobles in the district were members, those few, not wishing to differ from their peers, adhered to the policy known in England as non-intervention, a policy so much lauded by that renowned statesman John Bright. This abstention did not exclude, however, the direct influence of the "intelligence" on the fate of the commune. For if any man of the "intelligence" had a case, he invited Pan Zolzik to his house on the eve of the session of the court, vodka was brought to the room of the representative of the "intelligence," and cigars were given; after that the affair was discussed easily, then followed dinner, to which Pan Zolzik was invited with the cordial words, "Well, sit down, Pan Zolzik, sit down!"

Pan Zolzik sat down; and next day he said carelessly to the mayor, "Yesterday I dined with the Zarembas, the Skorabevskis, or the Dovbors. Hm! There is a daughter in the house; we understand what that means!"

During dinner Pan Zolzik tried to maintain good manners, to eat of various problematical dishes in the way that he saw others eat of them, and tried, moreover, not to show that that intimacy with the mansion gave him too much pleasure.

He was a man filled with tact, who knew how to conduct himself everywhere; therefore, not only did he not lose courage on such occasions, but he pushed himself into the conversation, mentioning meanwhile this "honorable commissioner" or that "excellent chief," with whom yesterday, or some other day, he had played a small game at a copeck a point. In one word, he endeavored to show that he was on a footing of close intimacy with the first powers in the district. He noticed, it is true, that during his narratives the company looked somehow strangely into their plates; but he judged that that was the fashion. After dinner it astonished him also more than once, that the noble, without waiting for him to say farewell, clapped him on the shoulder and said, "Well, be in good health, Pan Zolzik;" but again he judged that that was the way in good society. Then, while pressing the host's hand in farewell, he felt in it something that rustled; he bent his fingers, and, pressing the noble's palm, he gathered to himself that something "that rustled," not forgetting to add, however, "Oh, my benefactor! there is no need of this between us. As to your case, you may be at rest, my benefactor."

With such energetic management, and with the native gifts of Pan Zolzik, the affairs of the village would have been conducted in the best manner surely, had it not been for one misfortune; namely, this one, that only in certain cases did Pan Zolzik raise his voice and explain to the court how it should consider an affair from the legal point of view. Other affairs, those not preceded by anything that rustled, were left to the independent action of the court, and during the course of this action he remained speechless, to the great distress of the judges, who then felt simply without a head.

Of the nobles, or more precisely of the lords, only one,

Pan Floss, the tenant of Maly Postempovitsi, sat at first as a judge in the village sessions; and he declared that the "intelligence" should take part in them. But this declaration was received ill everywhere. The nobles said that Pan Floss must be a "red," which for that matter was shown by his name. The peasants, with a democratic feeling of their own separateness, contended that it did not become a lord to sit on a bench with peasants, the best proof of which was contained in this statement, "Those lords do not do that." In general, the peasants reproached Pan Floss with not being a lord among lords. Pan Zolzik, too, did not like him; for Pan Floss had not tried to win his friendship with anything that rustled, and once at a sitting Pan Floss had, as judge, even ordered him to be silent. Discontent with Pan Floss was universal; the result of which was that on a certain fine morning, in the presence of the whole assembly, he heard from the mouth of a judge sitting near him the following, "You are not a lord! Pan Dovbor is a lord; Pan Skorabevski is a lord; but you are not a lord, you are an upstart." Upon hearing this, Pan Floss, who was just about buying Kruha Volya, spat on everything, and left the village to its own devices, as he had formerly left the city. But the nobility said that "he was played out," adding, meanwhile, in defence of the principle of non-intervention, one of those proverbs which form the wisdom of nations; this proverb went to prove that it is not possible to improve peasants. Now the council, untroubled by participation of the "intelligence," deliberated on their own affairs unaided by the superior element, and by means of Barania-Glova reason alone, which, moreover, should suffice, in virtue of the principle that the reason of Paris suffices Paris. Finally, it is certain that practical judgment, or, in other words, the so-called "sound peasant sense," is worth more than any intelligence of another element, and that the inhabitants of a country brought its sound sense by birth into said country. This, it strikes me, needs no demonstration.

And this became evident at once in the village of Barania-Glova, when at the above-mentioned session the question from the government was read, whether the council would repair, at its own cost, the highway in front of the communal land, which highway led to Oslovitsi. In general, the project was exceedingly disagreeable to the assembled *patres conscripti;* therefore one of the local senators gave utterance to the brilliant idea that there was no need to improve the road, for they could go through Pan Skorabevski's meadow. If Pan Skorabevski had been present at the session, he would no doubt have found something to say against this *pro bono publico* amendment; but he was not there, for he adhered to the principle of non-intervention. The project of going through the meadow would have been accepted unanimously had Pan Zolzik not dined at Pan Skorabevski's the day before. During the dinner he related to Panna Yadviga the scene of stifling two Spanish generals in Madrid, which he had read in "Isabella of Spain," published by Pan Breslauer. After dinner, while pressing the hand of Pan Skorabevski, he felt in his palm something that rustled. Now the secretary, instead of recording the decision, laid down his pen, which always meant that he wanted to say something.

"The lord secretary wants to say something," said voices in the assembly.

"I want to say that ye are fools!" answered the lord secretary, phlegmatically.

The power of real parliamentary eloquence, even when concise, is so great that after the above statement, which was a protest against the meadow amendment, and in general against administrative management by the Barania-Glova body, that same body began to look around with disquiet, and to scratch itself on its noble organ of thought, which with that body was an unerring indication of entering into business more profoundly.

At last, after a considerable interval of silence, one of its representatives answered in a tone of inquiry,—

"Why are we fools?"

"Because ye are fools."

"It must be so," said one voice.

"A meadow is a meadow," added a second.

"We cannot pass without it, in spring," finished a third.

To wind up, the amendment proposing Pan Skorabevski's meadow was lost, the official project was accepted, and they apportioned to each man his part in the expense of improving the road according to the estimate sent in. Justice was rooted to that degree in the minds of the legislative body, that it did not occur to any one to wriggle out, with the exception of the mayor and councilman Gomula, who, to make up, took on themselves the burden of seeing that everything was done as quickly as possible.

It should be confessed, however, that such a disinterested sacrifice on the part of the mayor and the councilman, like every virtue which goes beyond the ordinary limit, roused a certain jealousy in the other councillors, and even called forth one voice of protest which sounded angrily, —

"But why do ye not pay?"

"Why should we give money when what ye pay is enough?" answered Gomula.

This was an argument which I hope not only the

sound sense of Barania-Glova, but of every one would have found unanswerable. The voice of the protester was silent for a time, then it said in a tone of conviction, —

"That is true!"

The affair was settled thoroughly, and they would have proceeded without delay to the decision of others, had it not been for the sudden and unexpected invasion of the legislative chamber by two young pigs, which, rushing in as if mad, through the open door, began without any reasonable cause to fly through the room, running between the men's legs, and squealing in sky-piercing voices.

Of course deliberation was interrupted; the legislative body rushed in pursuit of the intruders; and for a time the deputies, with rare unanimity, cried, "Ah sik! ah tsiu!" "May the paralysis take you!" and the like. Meanwhile the pigs ran between Pan Zolzik's legs, and stained, with some green stuff, his sand-colored trousers; this greenness could not be rubbed off, even though Pan Zolzik washed it with glycerine soap and rubbed it with his own toothbrush.

But, thanks to the resolution and energy which never deserted the representatives of the commune, and did not desert them at that time, the pigs were seized by the hind-legs and, in spite of their most vigorous protests, thrown out through the doorway. After this, it was possible to pass to the order of the day.

In this order was found an action brought by a villager named Sroda against Pan Floss. It happened that Sroda's oxen, having filled themselves in the night with Pan Floss's clover, toward morning left this vale of tears and misery, and transferred themselves to a better and an ox world. Sroda, in despair, brought the whole sad case before the court, and implored justice and deliverance.

The court penetrated to the depth of the subject, and, with a quickness peculiar to itself, came to the conviction that, though Sroda had let his cattle into Pan Floss's field intentionally, still, if on that field there had been growing, for example, grass or wheat, not that "vile clover," the oxen would have enjoyed to that moment the best and most desirable health, and certainly would not have experienced those sad attacks of inflation to which they had fallen victims.

Starting from this major premise, and passing by a road, as logical as it was legal, to the minor premise, the court decided that in every case, not Sroda had caused the death of the oxen, but Pan Floss; therefore Pan Floss should pay Sroda for his oxen, and, as a warning for the future, he was to pay into the village treasury five rubles for the support of the chancery. The above-mentioned sum, in case the defendant refused payment, was to be taken from his dairy farmer, Itska Zweinos.

Next were decided several cases of a civil nature, all of which, in so far as they did not touch nearly or remotely the genial Zolzik, were decided with entire independence, and on the scales of pure justice hung on sound Barania-Glova reason.

Thanks, therefore, to the English principle of non-intervention, which was adhered to by the afore-mentioned "intelligence," the general harmony and unanimity was disturbed only by passing remarks touching paralysis, the decaying of intestines, and the plague, which were uttered in the form of wishes by the litigating parties as well as by the judges themselves.

I consider that, thanks also to this priceless principle of non-intervention, all disputes could be decided in this way, that the side gaining, as well as the side losing, paid always a certain sum, relatively rather large, "to the chancery." This insured indirectly that which is so desirable in village institutions, the independence of the mayor and the secretary, and had the virtue to wean the people from litigiousness, and raise the morality of Barania-Glova to a level of which eighteenth-century philosophers dreamed in vain. This also is worthy of attention (we refrain from expressing praise or blame), that Pan Zolzik always entered in his books only one half of the sum destined for the chancery, the other half was set aside for "unforeseen circumstances," in which the secretary, the mayor, and councilman Gomula might find themselves.

Finally, the court proceeded to judge criminal cases; in consequence of this they ordered the village policeman to bring in the prisoners and place them in presence of the court. I need not add that in Barania-Glova the newest system of imprisonment was adopted, — the system most consistent with the demands of civilization, namely, solitary confinement. This cannot be put in doubt by evil tongues. To-day any one may convince himself that in the mayor's pen at Barania-Glova there are as many as four divisions. The prisoners sit in these separately, in company with animals of which a certain zoology, for the use of youth, states, "The pig, an animal justly so called because of its uncleanness, etc," and to which nature has denied horns absolutely, which may also serve as a proof of its wisdom. Here prisoners sat in apartments only with companions, which, as is known, could not hinder them from yielding themselves to reflection, thinking over the evil they had done, and undertaking a change of life.

The policeman went without delay to that prison of

cells, and from those cells brought before the face of the court, not two male criminals, but a man and a woman; from this the reader may infer easily how delicate was the nature, and how psychologically involved were the cases which the court of Barania-Glova had to decide at times. In truth, this affair was very delicate, —

A certain Romeo, otherwise named Vah Rehnio, and a certain Juliet, otherwise called Baska Jabianka, worked together with an agriculturist, one as a serving-man, the other as a maid-servant. And, what is the use of concealment, they fell in love, being unable to live without each other, just as Nevazendeh[1] could not live without Bezevandcha.[1] Soon, however, jealousy crept in between Romeo and Juliet; for the latter once saw Romeo stopping too long with Yagna of the mansion-house Thenceforth, the unfortunate Juliet was merely waiting for her opportunity. So on a certain day, when Romeo came from the field too early, according to Juliet's thinking, and asked for his supper with insistence, matters came to an outburst and explanations on both sides, whereby there was an interchange of some dozens of blows of the fist and of a pot-ladle. The traces of these blows were to be seen in blue spots on the ideal face of Juliet, as well as on the cut forehead of Romeo, which was full of manly pride. The court had to declare on whose side was justice, and which was to pay the other five zlotys, or, speaking more correctly, seventy copecks silver, in compensation for deceit in love, and the results of the outburst

The corrupt breath of the West had not been able yet to embrace the sound mental character of the court; hence, disgusted to the bottom of their souls with eman-

[1] Two pigeons in one of the Persian fables of Bidpay or Pilpay.

cipation of woman, as a thing hostile, and revolting to the more ideal disposition of the Slavs, the judges gave the right of speech, first, to Romeo, who, holding his cut forehead, began, —

"Great, mighty court! But that pig ear has given me no peace this long time. I came home, like any good man, to supper, and she made at me. 'Thou chestnut dog,' says she, 'the master is in the field yet, and thou come now to the house! Thou wilt put thyself behind the stove, and blink at me.' I never scolded her; but when she saw me with Yagna of the mansion, as I helped the girl to draw water out of the well, from that moment she was raging at me. She threw my plate on the table so the food almost flew from it, and then she would n't let me eat it; she gave out her mind at me in this way, 'Thou son of a pagan, thou traitor, thou geometer, thou suffragan!' When she said suffragan, and only then, I gave it to her on the snout, and only so from temper; but she at me then with a pot-ladle on the forehead."

Here the ideal Juliet could not restrain herself; but, clinching her fist and shoving it under Romeo's nose, she cried, with shrieking voice, —

"Not true! not true! not true! Thou liest like a dog!"

Then she burst into weeping with her whole overflowing heart, and, turning to the court, cried, —

"Great, mighty court! I am an unfortunate orphan. Oh, help me, for God's sake! It was not at the well I saw him with Yagna; may they be blind! 'Libertine!' says I, 'are the times few that thou didst say that thy love for me was such that thou didst wish to put a fist under my rib?' May he melt; may his tongue become a stake! Not a pot-ladle should he get on the head, but a maple club. The sun was still high, but he comes from the field and calls for something to put in his stomach. I talk to him as if to some good man, politely, 'Thou scoundrel's picture,' says I, 'the master is in the field yet, and thou art at the house!' But I didn't call him a suffragan; as the Lord God is good to me, I did not! But may he —"

At this point the mayor called the defendant to order, making a remark to her in the form of a question, —

"Thou plague, wilt thou shut that snout of thine?"

A moment of silence followed; the judges began to meditate over the sentence; and what a delicate feeling of the situation! They did not adjudge five zlotys to either side; but, to preserve their own dignity merely, and for a warning to every loving couple in all Barania-Glova, they condemned the two to sit twenty-four hours longer in prison, and to pay a ruble each to the chancery.

"From Vah Rehnio and Baska Jabianka, fifty copecks each for the chancery," noted down Pan Zolzik.

Then the sitting of the court was ended. Pan Zolzik rose; he drew his sand-colored trousers up, and his violet-colored vest down. The councillors, with the intention of separating, had already taken their caps and whips, when all at once the door, which had been closed after the invasion of the pigs, opened half-way, and in it appeared Repa, gloomy as night, and after him his wife, and the dog Kruchek.

The woman was as pale as linen; her comely, delicate features expressed grief and humility, and in her large eyes were tears which afterward flowed down her cheeks.

Repa was going in boldly, with head thrown back; but when he saw the whole court, he lost his attitude at once, and, in rather a low voice, said, —

"May He be praised!"

CHARCOAL SKETCHES. 333

"For the ages of ages!" answered the councilmen, in a chorus.

"And what are ye here for?" asked the mayor, threateningly. The mayor was confused at first, but he recovered himself, "What business have ye? Have ye been fighting, or what?"

"Great, mighty court," began Repa. "But let the most serene — "

"Be quiet! be quiet!" interrupted the woman; "let me speak, and do thou sit quietly."

Then she wiped the tears and her nose with her apron, and began to tell the whole story, with a trembling voice. Ah! but to whom had she come? She had come with a complaint against the mayor and the secretary, to the mayor and the secretary.

"They took him," said she; "they promised him timber if he would write his name; then he wrote his name. They gave him fifty rubles; but he was drunk, and he didn't know that he was selling his life and mine and the little boy's. He was drunk, great, mighty court, as drunk as if he were not a creature of God," continued she, now in tears. "Of course a drunken man does not know what he is doing; so in the court, if any one writes anything when he is drunk, they spare him, for they say that he did not know what he was doing. In God's name, mercy! A sober man would not sell his life for fifty rubles! Have pity on me, and on him, and on the innocent child! What will become of me, the unfortunate, alone, and alone in the world, without him, without my poor fellow! God give you happiness for this, and reward you in the name of the unfortunate!"

Here sobbing interrupted her words. Repa cried, too, and from time to time wiped his nose with his finger. The faces of the councilmen grew long; they looked one at another, and then at the secretary and the mayor, without knowing what to do, until the woman recovered her voice, and began to speak again, —

"The man goes about as if poisoned. 'Thee I will kill,' says he. 'I will destroy the child; I will burn the house; but,' says he, 'I will not go, and I will not go.' How am I to blame, poor woman, or the little boy? He is no longer in the field, at the scythe, or the axe; but he sits in the house and sighs and sighs. But I wait for judgment; so do you men have God in your hearts, and do not let injustice be done. Jesus of Nazareth! O Chenstohova Mother of God! intercede for us, intercede!"

For a time nothing was audible but the sobbing of the woman; at last one old councilman muttered, —

"It is not well to make a man drunk, and then sell him."

"No; it is not well," answered others.

"May God and His Most Holy Mother bless you!" cried the woman, falling on her knees at the threshold.

The mayor was put to shame; no less troubled was the councilman Gomula; so both looked at the secretary, who was silent; but when Repa's wife had finished, he said to the grumbling councilmen, —

"Ye are fools!"

There was silence as when poppy-seed falls.

"It is written expressly," continued the secretary, "that if any one meddles in a voluntary contract he will be judged by a marine court. And do ye know, ye fools, what a marine court is? Ye do not, ye fools; a marine court is —" Here he took out his handkerchief and wiped his nose; then, with a cold and official voice, he continued his speech, "Whichever fool of you does n't know what a marine court is, let him stick his nose into the dish, and he will know what a marine court is till his seventh skin smarts. When a volunteer is found for a man who is conscripted, let one and another of you be careful not to meddle with them. The contract is signed; there are witnesses; and that is the end of the matter! This is understood in jurisprudence; and if any one does n't believe, let him look at procedure and precedents. And if they drink besides, what of that? But don't ye drink, ye fools, always and everywhere?"

If Justice herself, with scales in one hand, and a drawn sword in the other, had stepped out from behind the mayor's stove, and stood suddenly among the councilmen, she would not have frightened them more than that marine court, procedure, and precedents. For a while, there was deep silence; only after a time did Gomula speak in a low voice; all looked around at him, as if astonished at his boldness.

"That is true! A man sells a horse, he drinks; the same if he sells an ox, a pig too. That's the custom."

"That's it; we drink, but according to custom," put in the mayor.

Then the councilmen turned more boldly to Repa, —

"Well, if thou hast brewed beer, drink it."

"Or, art thou six years old, or knowest not what thou art doing?"

"Besides they will not take off thy head."

"And when thou goest to the army, thou canst hire a man; he will take thy place in the house, and with the woman."

Joyfulness began to possess the whole assembly.

All at once the secretary opened his mouth again; all was still.

"But ye do not know," said he, "where to interfere, and what ye should n't touch. That Repa threatened his wife and child, that he promised to burn his own house, with that ye can meddle, and not let such a thing go unpunished. Since the woman has come with a complaint, let her not go away from this court without justice."

"Not true, not true!" cried the woman, in despair. "I have never suffered any wrong from him. O Jesus! O dear wounds of the living God! — has the world come to an end?"

But the court acted, and the direct result was, that Repa and his wife not only effected nothing, but the court, in proper anxiety for the safety of the woman, decided to secure her by confining Repa in the pen for two days. And lest such thoughts should come to his head in future, it was decided also that he should pay two rubles and a half to the chancery.

Repa sprang up like a madman, and shouted that he would not go to the pen, and as to the chancery fine, he would give not two rubles, but the fifty rubles received from the mayor; and he threw them on the floor, crying, —

"Let the man take them who wishes!"

A terrible uproar began. The policeman ran in and fell to dragging Repa; Repa at him with his fist, he at Repa's hair. She screamed till one of the councilmen took her by the neck and pushed her through the doorway, giving her a fist in the back to help her out; others helped the policeman to drag Repa to the pen.

Meanwhile the secretary wrote down, "From Vavron Repa one ruble and twenty-five copecks for the chancery."

Repa's wife went to her empty house almost out of her senses. She saw nothing in front of her, and stumbled against every stone, wringing her hands above her head and crying, "Ooo! oo! oo!"

The mayor had a good heart, therefore, while going slowly with Gomula toward the inn, he said, —

"I am a little sorry for that woman. Shall I give them a quarter of peas, or something?"

CHAPTER VI.

IMOGENE

HERE I hope that the reader has understood sufficiently and estimated the genial plan of my sympathetic hero. Pan Zolzik had, as has been said, checkmated Repa and his wife. To inscribe Repa on the list would have led to nothing. But to make him drunk, and bring it about that he should sign the agreement himself, and take the money, that involved the affair somewhat, and was a clever trick which showed that in a concourse of circumstances Pan Zolzik might play a famous rôle. The mayor, who was ready to ransom his son with eight hundred rubles, that was surely all his "copper," agreed to the plan with delight; all the more since Pan Zolzik was as moderate as he was genial, taking only twenty-five rubles for his part in the affair. But even this money he took without greed, just as he gave part of the chancery money also without greed to Burak. I have to confess that Pan Zolzik was always in debt to Srul, the tailor from Oslovitsi, who furnished the whole region about with "pure Parisian" garments.

And now, since I have come out into the road of confession, I will not conceal the reason why Pan Zolzik dressed so carefully. It flowed, no doubt, from æsthetic causes; but there was also another motive, the following:

Pan Zolzik was in love. Do not think, however, that it was with Repa's wife. He had for the woman, as he expressed himself once, a "little appetite," and that was all. Besides this, Pan Zolzik was capable of a feeling which reached higher and was very complicated. My male, if not female, readers surely divine that the object of these feelings could be no other than Panna Yadviga Skorabevski. More than once when the silver moon had mounted the sky, Pan Zolzik took his harmonium, on which instrument he played with skill, sat on the bench before the house of four tenements, and, looking toward the mansion, sang with melancholy, and sometimes with sighing: —

> "But from the very dawn,
> Till late night, I shed tears;
> In the night I breathe heavy sighs;
> I have lost every hope."

The voice went toward the mansion, amid the poetic stillness of summer nights; and Pan Zolzik added, after a while, —

> "O people, O people, people unfeeling,
> Why have ye poisoned the life of the young man?"

If any man condemns Pan Zolzik for sentimentality, I will answer that he is mistaken. Too sober was the mind of this great official to be sentimental. In his dreams, Panna Yadviga took the place of Isabella of Spain, and he that of Serrano or Marfori. But as reality did not answer to his dreams, this iron personage betrayed himself once in his feelings; namely, when toward evening, he saw, near the woodshed, petticoats drying on a clothes-line; and by the letters Y. S., with a crown near the seam, he recognized that they belonged to Panna Yadviga.

Then tell us, benefactor, who could restrain himself? Pan Zolzik did not restrain himself; he approached and fell to kissing one of these petticoats fervently. Malgoska, the housemaid, seeing this, flew at once to the mansion with her tongue and news that, "The lord secretary was wiping his nose on the young lady's petticoat." Happily, however, no one believed this, and the feelings of the lord secretary were revealed to no person.

But had he hope? Do not take it ill, my benefactors, that he had. As often as he went to the mansion, a certain inner voice, weak it is true, but increasing, whispered in his ear, —

"Well now, Panna Yadviga will press thy foot under the table during dinner to-day." "Hm! never mind the polish," added he, with that grandeur of soul which is peculiar to persons in love.

The reading of books published by Pan Breslauer gave him faith in the possibility of various pressings. But Panna Yadviga not only did not press his foot — who can understand woman? — she looked on him as she would on a fence, or a cat, or a plate, or any such thing. How much he suffered, poor man, to turn her attention to himself! More than once when tying a cravat of unheard of colors, or while putting on some new trousers with fabulous stripes, he thought, "This time she will notice me!" Srul himself, when bringing him the new suit, said, "Well, in such trousers, one might go with proposals even to a countess!"

Of what use is all that to him? He is at the dinner; Panna Yadviga enters, haughty, spotless, serene as a sovereign; her robe rustles with its folds, big and little; she sits down, takes a spoon in her slender fingers, and does not look at him.

"Does she not understand that this is costly!" thought Zolzik, in despair.

Still he did not lose hope.

"If I could only become sub-inspector!" thought he. "A man need not put a foot out of doors. From sub-inspector to inspector is not far; a man would have then a yellow carriage, a pair of horses, and if even then she would press one's hand under the table—" Pan Zolzik permitted himself to go still further into immeasurably remote consequences of this pressure of the hand; but we will not betray his thoughts, since they were too secretly heartfelt.

What a rich nature, however, Pan Zolzik's was is shown by the ease with which, at the side of this ideal feeling for Panna Yadviga, which moreover answered to the aristocratic tendencies of the young man, a place was found in him for the equally important "little appetite," his feeling for Repa's wife. True, Repa's wife was what is called a handsome woman; still it is sure that this Don Juan of Barania-Glova would not have devoted so many steps to her had it not been for the wonderful stubbornness of the woman, which deserved punishment. Stubbornness in a simple woman, and against him, seemed to Pan Zolzik so insolent, so unheard of, that not only did the woman take at once in his eyes the charm of forbidden fruit, but he determined to teach her the lesson which she deserved. The affair with the dog, Kruchek, fixed him still more in his purpose. He knew that the victim would defend herself; hence he invented that voluntary contract of Repa's with the mayor, which gave, at least in appearance, to his mercy, or his enmity, Repa himself and his entire family.

But Repa's wife did not give up the affair as lost after the interview at the mayor's. The next day was Sunday, and she resolved to go as usual to Lipa, and take counsel at once with the priest. There were two priests in Lipa; one the parish priest, Canon Ulanovski, so old that his eyes stared like those of a fish, and his head moved continually, swaying from side to side; not to him did Marysia decide to go, but to the curate, Father Chyzik, who was a very holy man and wise; therefore he could give her good counsel and console her. She wished to go early and talk with him before mass; but she had to do her own work and her husband's also, for he was confined in the pen. Before she had swept the cottage, fed the horse, the pigs, the cow, cooked the breakfast, and carried it to Repa in the pen, the sun was high, and she saw that she could not talk to the priest before mass.

In fact, when she came services had begun. Women, dressed in green jackets, were sitting in the graveyard, and putting on hastily the shoes which they had brought in their hands. Marysia did the same, and went straight into the church.

Father Chyzik was preaching; the canon, wearing his cap, was sitting in an armchair at the side of the altar, his eyes staring and his head shaking as usual. The Gospel had been read. Father Chyzik was preaching, I know not for what reason, of the Albigensian heresy in the Middle Ages, and was explaining to his parishioners in what manner alone they were to consider that heresy, as well as the bull *ex stercore* which was issued against it. Then very eloquently, and with great impressiveness, he warned his flock, as simple people, lowly, like birds of the air, hence dear to God, not to listen to various false sages, and in general to people blinded with Satanic pride who sow tares instead of wheat, or they would gather tears and sin. Here, in passing, he mentioned Condillac, Voltaire, Rousseau, and Ohorovich, without making any distinction between them; and at last he came to a minute description of the various unpleasantnesses to which the damned would be exposed in the next world. And another spirit entered into Repa's wife; for though she did not understand what Father Chyzik was saying, she thought, "He must be speaking beautifully, since he shouts so that he is all in a sweat, and the people are sighing, as if the last breath were going out of them."

The sermon ended and mass continued. Ei! Repa's wife prayed; she prayed as never before in her life; she felt too that it was easier and lighter at her heart.

Finally the solemn moment came. The canon, white as a dove, brought out the most holy sacrament from the ciborium, then turned to the people and holding in his hand the monstrance, which was like the sun, holding it there, with trembling hands, near his face, he remained for a while with closed eyes and inclined head, as if collecting breath; at last he intoned, "Before so great a sacrament!"

The people in a hundred voices roared in response immediately, —

> "We fall on our faces,
>   Let the old law with the testament
>   Give place to the new;
>   Faith will be the supplement
>   To that which agrees not with the senses."

The hymn thundered till the window-panes rattled; the organ groaned; the bells great and small rang; before the church a drum thundered; the censers gave out blue smoke; the sun entered in through the window and illuminated in rainbow tints those rolls of smoke. In the midst of this noise, incense, smoke, and sun-rays, the most holy sacrament glittered on high for an instant, then the priest lowered it, and again he raised it, and that white old man with the monstrance seemed like some heavenly vision, half concealed by the mist of incense, and radiant, from whom came grace and consolation which fell upon all hearts and all pious souls. That grace and that great peace took under the wings of God the suffering soul of Repa's wife also.

"O Jesus, concealed in the most holy sacrament! O Jesus!" cried the unhappy woman, "do not desert me, unfortunate!" And from her eyes flowed tears; they were not such tears as she had shed at the mayor's, but in some sort pleasant tears, though large as Calcutta pearls, yet sweet and peaceful.

The woman fell before the majesty of God, with her face to the floor, and then she knew not what happened. It seemed to her that angels raised her, like a slender leaf, from the earth and bore her to heaven, to eternal happiness, where she saw neither Pan Zolzik, nor the mayor, nor recruiting lists, nothing but brightness, and in that brightness the throne of God, around which was such glory that she had to close her eyes, and whole clouds of angels were there, like birds with white wings.

Repa's wife lay so long that when she rose mass was over; the church was deserted; the incense had risen to the roof; the last of the people were at the door; and at the altar an old man was quenching the candles, — so she rose up and went to the priest's house to speak to the curate.

Father Chyzik was just eating dinner; but he went out at once, when they told him that some weeping woman wished to see him. He was still a young man; his face was pale and serene; he had a white, lofty forehead, and a pleasant smile.

"What do you wish, my woman?" asked he, in a low, but clear voice.

She seized his feet, and then told him the whole story, crying meanwhile and kissing his hand; at last, raising to him humbly her black eyes, she said, —

"Oh, advice, benefactor! advice! I have come to seek advice of you."

"And you are not mistaken, my woman," answered Father Chyzik, mildly. "But I have only one advice, and it is this: Offer to God all your sufferings. God tries His faithful. He tries them as severely as Job, whose wounds were licked by his own dogs, or Azarias, on whom God sent blindness. But God knows what He does, and He will reward those who are faithful. Consider the misfortune which has happened to your husband as a punishment for his grievous sin of drunkenness, and thank God that punishing him during life He may pardon him after death."

The woman looked at the priest with her dark eyes, rose up and went out in silence, without saying one word. But along the road she felt as though something were choking her. She wanted to cry, but she could not.

CHAPTER VII.

ABOUT five o'clock in the afternoon, on the main road between the cottages, gleamed in the distance a blue parasol, a yellow straw hat with blue ribbons, and an almond-colored dress trimmed with blue; that was Panna Yadviga, who had gone out to walk after dinner; at her side was her cousin, Pan Victor.

Panna Yadviga was what is called a pretty young

lady; she had black hair, blue eyes, a complexion like milk, and besides wore a dress made with wonderful care, neat and exquisite; light came from it and added to her beauty. Her maiden form was outlined charmingly, as if floating along in the air. In one hand she held a parasol, in the other her dress, from under which was visible the edge of her white petticoat and her shapely, small feet, enclosed in Hungarian boots.

Pan Victor, who walked at her side, though he had an immense curling forelock of light color, and a beard which he was just letting out, looked also like a picture.

This couple were radiant with youth, health, gladness, happiness; and besides there was evident in both that higher, holiday life, a life of winged flights, not only in the external world, but in the world of thought, the world of broader desires, as well as broader ideas, and at times in the golden and shining paths of imagination.

Among those cabins, and compared with children of the village peasants, and all that common surrounding, they seemed like beings from another planet. It was even pleasant to think that there was no bond, at least no spiritual bond, between that splendid, that developed and poetical couple, and the prosaic life of the village, full of gray reality, and half animal.

They passed on, side by side, and conversed of poetry and literature as ordinarily a polite cavalier and a polite lady do. Those people in homespun, those peasants, those women, did not understand even their words and their language. It was dear to think of it! — confess that to me. O ye petty nobility!

In the conversation of this splendid couple there was nothing which had not been heard a hundred times before. They flitted from book to book, as butterflies flit from one flower to another. But such a conversation does not seem empty and commonplace when one is speaking with a dear little soul; when the conversation is simply the canvas on which that soul fastens the golden flowers of its own thoughts and feelings, and when, from time to time, its interior is disclosed, like the opening interior of a white rose. And, besides, such a conversation flies up in every case, like a bird in the air, to cerulean spheres, attaches itself to the world of mind, and rises like a climbing plant on a pole. There in the village inn, rude people were drinking and talking in peasant words of peasant things; but that couple were sailing in another region, and on a ship which had, as Gounod's song says, —

> "Masts of ivory
> With a banner of satin,
> A rudder of pure ruddy gold."

Moreover, it is proper to add that Panna Yadviga had, for purposes of self-training, turned the head of her cousin. In these conditions poetry is more frequently mentioned.

"Have you read the last edition of Eli?" asked the cavalier.

"You know, Pan Victor, that I am dying about Eli. When I read him, it seems to me that I hear music; and involuntarily I apply to myself that verse of Uyeiski, —

> "'I lie on a cloud,
> Melted in calm,
> With a dreamy tear in my eye:
> I hear no breath.
> A sea of violet odor
> Surrounds me;
> With palm placed in palm,
> I sail — I fly —'

"Ah!" exclaimed she, suddenly, "if I knew him, I am sure that I should be in love with him. We should understand each other to a certainty."

"Happily he is married," answered Pan Victor, dryly.

Panna Yadviga inclined her head a little, repressed a half smile on her lips, till the dimples appeared in her cheeks, and, looking askance at Pan Victor, she inquired, —

"Why do you say, happily?"

"Happily for all those for whom life would have no attraction in the case you have just mentioned."

When he said this, Pan Victor was very tragic.

"Oh, you attribute too much to me!"

Pan Victor passed into lyric poetry, "You are an angel —

"Oh, that is all well enough — but let us talk of something else."

"Then you do not like Eli?"

"A moment ago I began to hate him."

"Oh, you put on ugly faces! I ask you to become serene, and tell me your favorite poet."

"Sovinski," muttered Pan Victor, gloomily.

"But I simply fear him. Irony, blood, fire — wild outbursts."

"Such things do not terrify me at all," said Pan Victor; then he looked so valiant, that a dog, which had run out from a cottage, hid its tail under its belly and withdrew in fright.

Now they arrived at the house of four tenements; in the window appeared an upturned nose, a goatee, and a bright-green cravat; they halted before a pretty cottage covered with wild grapevines, and looking with its rear windows on a pond.

"You see what a nice little house this is; it is the only poetical place in Barania-Glova."

"What house is it?"

"Formerly, it was an asylum. Here village children learned to read, when their parents were in the field. Papa had this house built purposely."

"And what is in it now?"

"Now, kegs of brandy are in it—"

But they did not finish their thoughts, for they came to a great puddle in which lay a number of pigs, "justly so-called for their filth." To pass around that puddle, they had to go near Repa's cottage; so they turned in that direction.

Repa's wife was sitting on a log before the gate, with her elbows on her knees, and her chin on one hand. Her face was pale, and, as it were, turned to stone; her eyes were red; her look dull, and fixed on the distance without thought. She had not even heard the passers-by; but the young woman saw her, and said,—

"Good-evening!"

Marysia stood up, and, approaching, seized the feet of Panna Yadviga and Pan Victor, and began to weep in silence.

"What is the matter?" asked the young lady.

"Oh, thou my golden berry, my dawn! perhaps God has sent thee to me! Take thou my part, our consolation!"

Here the woman narrated the whole affair, interrupting the story with kissing the young lady's hands, or rather her gloves, which she stained with tears; the young lady became greatly confused; anxiety was clearly evident on her pretty, important little face, and she knew not what to say; but at last she said, with hesitation,—

"What can I advise you, my woman? I am very sorry for you. Indeed — what can I advise? — go to papa — maybe papa — But farewell."

Then Panna Yadviga raised her almond-colored robe till the stripes of her blue-and-white stockings were visible above her boots; and she and Pan Victor passed on.

"May God bless thee, most beautiful flower!" called Repa's wife, after her.

Panna Yadviga grew sad; and it seemed to Pan Victor that he saw tears in her eyes; so, to drive away sadness, he began to talk of Krashevski and other smaller fish in the literary sea; and in that conversation, which became gradually more lively, both of them soon forgot that "disagreeable incident."

"To the mansion!" said Repa's wife, meanwhile. "And that is where I ought to have gone first. Ei! I am a stupid woman!"

CHAPTER VIII.

THE mansion had a porch covered with grapevines, and a view on the yard as well as on a road lined with poplars. In summer Pan and Pani Skorabevski drank coffee on this porch after dinner. They were sitting there now, and with them Father Ulanovski, Father Chyzik, and Stolbitski, the inspector of mines. Pan Skorabevski was a man of rather full habit, and ruddy, with large mustaches. He sat in an armchair, smoking a pipe; Pani Skorabevski was pouring tea; the inspector, who was a sceptic, was jesting with the old canon.

"Now, reverend benefactor, just tell us of that famous battle," said he.

The canon put his hand to his ear, and inquired, —

"Hei?"

"Of the battle!" repeated the inspector, more distinctly.

"Ah! of the battle?" said the canon; and, as it were, meditating, he began to whisper to himself, and to gaze upward as though recalling something. The inspector arranged his face ready for laughter; all awaited the narrative, though they had heard it a hundred times; for they always enticed the old man to repeat it.

"Well," began the canon, "I was still a curate, and the parish priest was Father Gladysh — I am right, Father Gladysh. It was he who built over the vestry. But, eternal light to him! — well, once after mass, I say, 'Father Gladysh?' and he asks, 'What?' 'It seems to me that something will come of this,' I say. And he says, 'It seems to me, too, that something will come of it.' We look; from behind the wind-mill come out some men on horses, some on foot, and next banners and cannon. Then at once I think to myself, Oh! from the opposite side I think, sheep are coming? but they are not sheep, only cavalry. The moment these saw those: Stop! and the other side too: Stop! The minute the cavalry rushed out of the woods, these to the right, those to the left, these to the left, those after them. Then they see: Difficult! then on to them. When they began to fire beyond the mountain, something flashed again. 'Do you see, Father Gladysh?' I say, and he says, 'I see.' And there they were, just thundering from cannon and guns; those to the river, these won't let them cross; this that one, that the other one! Then these for a while have the best, again the others have. Roar! smoke! And then to the bayonets! All at once, I think, these are weakening. 'Father Gladysh,' I say, 'those are winning!' And he says, 'It seems to me, too, that they are winning.' The words were hardly out of my mouth when these to their legs! those after them. Then drown, kill, take captive,

and I think, 'It is finishing —' But what finish! that
— I say, just, but! — "

Here the old man waved his hand, and, settling himself more deeply into the chair, fell, as it were, into meditation; but his head shook more than usual, and his eyes stared more.

The inspector was crying from laughter.

"Father Benefactor, who was fighting with whom; where was it, and when?"

The canon put his hand to his ear and said, —

"Hei?"

"I am just dying from laughter," remarked the inspector to Pani Skorabevski.

"Perhaps a cigar?"

"Perhaps coffee?"

"No, I cannot, from laughter."

The Skorabevskis laughed through politeness toward the inspector, though they had to listen to that narrative every Sunday. The joyousness was general; when it was interrupted by a low, timid voice from outside the porch, which said, —

"May He be praised!"

Pan Skorabevski rose at once, passed along the porch, and inquired, —

"But who is there?"

"It is I, Repa's wife?"

"Why?"

The woman bent as low as she could with the child, and seized his feet

"I came for salvation, serene heir, and for mercy."

"My dear woman give me peace, even on a Sunday?" interrupted Pan Skorabevski with as good faith as if the woman had been attacking him every week day. "You see, besides, that I have guests. So I shall not leave them for you."

"I will wait."

"Well, wait, then. Besides, I shall not be broken in two."

Then Pan Skorabevski pushed his bulk back into the porch; the woman withdrew to the garden fence, and stood there in humility. But she had to wait long enough. The lord and lady amused themselves with conversation; and to her ears flew from time to time glad laughter, which gripped her heart wonderfully, for she was not inclined to laughter, poor thing. Later Panna Yadviga and Pan Victor came home; and all entered the house. The sun inclined gradually to its setting. To the porch came out the lackey Yasek, whom Pan Skorabevski always called "one another," and began to lay the table for tea. He changed the cloth, set glasses on the table, and put spoons into them with a rattle. Marysia waited and waited. It came to her head to go back to her cottage and return later; but she was afraid that it might be too late then; so she sat down on the grass near the fence and gave her breast to the child. The child suckled and went to sleep, but with an unhealthy sleep, for since morning he was weak, somehow. She too felt that heat and cold ran through her from foot to head.

At times yawning seized her; but she did not mind that, she just waited patiently By degrees it grew dark, and the moon rose on the dome of the sky. The table was set for tea; lamps were burning on the porch; but the company did not come out, for the young lady was playing on the piano.

Repa's wife repeated the "Angel of the Lord," at the paling; and then she thought how Pan Skorabevski would save her. She did not know well how; she did not understand that he, from his position, was acquainted with the commissioner and with the chief of the district: that if he would only say a word, all would be well, and with God's help the evil would be turned aside. Meanwhile she thought that if Zolzik or the mayor opposed, he would know where to go for justice. "The young lord has always been kind and good to people," thought she, "so he will not desert me." And she was not mistaken, for Pan Skorabevski was really a humane man. She remembered that he had always been kind to Repa; further, that her late mother had nursed Panna Yadviga: so consolation entered her heart. That she had been waiting already a couple of hours seemed so natural that she did not stop to think over it.

Now the company returned to the porch. Marysia saw through the grapevine leaves that the young lady was pouring tea from a silver tea-pot, and, as her mother used to say, such odoriferous water that thou art sweet the whole day from it. All drank tea, conversed and laughed joyously. Only then did it come to Marysia's head that in the condition of lords there is always more happiness than in that of simple people; and she herself did not know why the tears flowed again down her face. But those tears soon gave way to another impression. "One another" brought out steaming dishes; and then she remembered that she was hungry, for she had been unable to take dinner into her mouth, and in the morning she had only drunk a little milk.

"Oh, if they would give me even bones to gnaw!" and she knew they would surely give, not bones alone; but she dared not ask lest she might offend, and intrude before guests; for this Pan Skorabevski might be angry.

At last supper was over; the inspector went away immediately; half an hour later the two priests took their places in the mansion carriage. Marysia saw Pan Skorabevski seat the canon; then she judged that the moment had come, and she drew near the porch.

The carriage moved away; Pan Skorabevski cried to the driver, "If thou turn over the carriage on the embankment, I will turn thee over!" Afterward he looked at the sky wishing to see what kind of weather there would be on the morrow, then he noticed the white shift of the woman in the darkness.

"Who is there?"

"Repa's wife."

"Ah, that is you! Tell me quickly what is needed, for it is late."

She repeated everything again; he listened, puffing his pipe all the time, and then said, —

"My dear, I would help you willingly if I could; but I have promised myself not to mix up in the affairs of the village."

"I know, serene heir," said Marysia, with a quivering voice; "but I thought that perhaps you, serene heir, would take pity on me —" Her voice broke on a sudden.

"All this is very good," answered Pan Skorabevski; "but what can I do? I cannot break my word for you; and to the chief I will not go on your account, for as it is, he says that I annoy him with my own affairs all the time. You have your commune, and if the commune cannot help you, you know the way to the chief of the district as well as I do. What did I wish to say? But go with God, my woman."

"The Lord reward," said Repa's wife, in a dull voice, seizing the feet of the heir.

CHAPTER IX.

REPA on leaving the pig-pen went, not straight to his cottage, but to the inn. It is known that in trouble the peasant takes to drink. From the inn, led by the same thought as his wife, he went to Pan Skorabevski's and committed folly.

A man who is not sober knows not what he says. So Repa was stubborn; and when he heard the same thing that his wife had about the principle of non-intervention, he answered rudely; not only did he not understand that lofty diplomatic principle because of the mental dulness innate in peasants, but he answered with that rudeness which is also special to them, and was thrown out of doors.

When he returned to the cottage, he told his wife himself, "I was at the mansion."

"And thou didst receive nothing."

He struck the table with his fist, "To set fire to them, the dog faiths!"

"Be quiet, thou wretch. What did Pan Skorabevski say?"

"He sent me to the chief of the district. May he be —"

"That is it; we must go to Oslovitsi."

"I will go there," said Repa. "I will show him that I can do without him."

"Thou wilt not go, poor man, thou wilt not go, my dear; but I will go. Thou wouldst drink, become insolent, and only increase the misfortune."

Repa did not wish to give way at first; but in the afternoon he went to the inn to drown the worm, next day the same; his wife inquired no more about anything, she left all to the will of God, and on Wednesday took the child and started for Oslovitsi.

The horse was needed for field work, so she went on foot, and at daylight, for it was fifteen solid miles to Oslovitsi. She thought that perhaps she might meet good people on the road, who would let her sit even on the side of a wagon; but she met no one. About nine in the morning, while sitting wearied at the edge of a forest, she ate a piece of bread and a couple of eggs which she had with her in a basket; then she went on. The sun began to burn; so when she met Hershek, the tenant of Lipa, who was taking geese to the city, she asked him to let her sit in his wagon.

"With God, my woman," said Hershek; "but there is so much sand here that the horse is hardly able to draw me alone. Give a zloty and I'll take you."

Then Marysia remembered that she had only one cheski (three copecks) tied up in a handkerchief. She was ready to give that to the Jew and offered it; but he answered, —

"A cheski? But thou wilt not find a cheski on the ground; a cheski is money, keep it!"

So saying, he lashed his horse and drove on. It became hotter in the world, and sweat flowed in a stream from the woman; but she walked with all her might, and an hour later she was entering Oslovitsi.

Whoever knows geography properly, knows that a person entering Oslovitsi from the direction of Barania-Glova must pass a church built before the Reformation. In this church long ago there was a miracle-working image of the Mother of God; before this church, to the present time, a whole street of beggars sit every Sunday, and call for alms in heaven-piercing voices. Since it was a week-day, there was only one beggar at the paling; but he, stretching from beneath his rags a naked foot without toes, held in his hand the cover of a box of shoe-polish, and sang:

> " Holy, heavenly,
> Angelic lady ! "

Seeing some one passing, he stopped singing, and pushing his foot out still more, began to cry, as if some one were flaying him, —

"Oh, compassionate people! A poor cripple begs charity! May the Lord God, the Merciful, give you every good thing on earth!"

When Repa's wife saw him, she untied the handkerchief, took the cheski, and approaching him said, —

"Have you five groshes?"

She wanted to give him only one grosh; but when the beggar felt the six groshes in his fingers he began to abuse her, " You grudge a cheski to the Lord God, and the Lord God will grudge you assistance. Go to the paralysis, while I am in good humor."

Then the woman said to herself, " Let it be to the glory of God," and went on. When she came to the market square, she was frightened. It was easy to find Oslovitsi; but to go astray in Oslovitsi was still easier, and indeed that place was no joke. Go to a new village, and thou wilt have to inquire where this or that person lives; but what must it be in a place like Oslovitsi !

"I shall go astray here, as in a forest," thought Marysia.

There was no help for it but to inquire of people. It was easy to inquire about the commissioner; but when she went to his house she learned that he had gone to the capital. As to the chief of the district, they told her

that she must look for him at his office. But where was
the office? Ei! stupid, stupid woman, it is in Oslovitsi,
and nowhere else!

She looked and looked in Oslovitsi for the office; at
last she saw a kind of palace, so big that it was a terror,
and before it numberless wagons, carriages, and Jewish
carts. It seemed to Marysia that there was some kind of
festival. "But where here is the office?" asked she of
some one in a frock-coat, seizing him by the leg.

"Thou art standing in front of it, woman."

She plucked up courage, and entered the palace. She
looked again. It was full of corridors, on the right a
door, on the left a door, farther on doors and doors, and
on each letters of some kind. She made the sign of the
cross, and, opening silently and timidly the first door,
found herself in a great room divided into stalls, like a
church. Behind one stall sat a man in a frock-coat with
gilt buttons, a pen over his ear; before the stalls stood a
great number of all sorts of people. The men were paying
and paying, and he of the frock-coat was smoking a
cigarette and writing receipts which he gave to the men.
Whoever took a receipt went out. Then Marysia thought
that it was needful to pay there, and she was sorry for
her cheski, so she walked up with great timidity to the
barrier.

But no one even looked at her. She stood there, stood;
about an hour passed, some came in, others went out;
the clock ticked behind the barrier, and still she stood
there. At last the number decreased somehow, and
finally there was no one. The official sat at the table
and began to write. Then she grew bold to speak, —

"Jesus Christ be praised!"

"Who is there?"

"Serene chief — "

"This is the money department."

"Serene chief!"

"This is the money department, I tell you."

"But where is the chief?"

The official pointed with his pen to a door.

"There!"

She went out again into the corridor. There? but where? There were doors everywhere without number; into which was she to enter? At last she saw, among the various people who were going hither and thither, a peasant standing with a whip in his hand, so she went straight to him.

"Father."

"But what do you want?"

"Where do you come from?"

"From Lipa; but why?"

"Where is the chief here?"

"Do I know?"

Then she asked some one with gilt buttons, but not in a frock-coat, and with holes in his elbows. He would not even listen, he merely answered, —

"I've no time!"

Again the woman went into the first door that she came to; she did not see, poor thing, that there was a notice, "Persons not belonging to the service are forbidden to enter." She did not belong to the service; the notice she did not see, as is said.

The moment she entered she saw an empty room, under the window a bench, on the bench some one sitting and dozing. Farther on a door to another room, in which she saw men walking, they were in frock-coats and in uniforms.

She approached the man who was dozing on the bench, she had some courage in his presence, for he

seemed a peasant, and on the feet stretched out in front
of him were boots with holes in them. She pushed
his arm.

He woke, looked at her, and then shouted, —

"It is forbidden!"

The poor woman took to her legs, and he slammed the
door behind her.

She found herself for the third time in the corridor.
She sat down near some door, and, with a patience truly
peasant-like, determined to sit there even to the end of
time. "And, besides, some one may ask," thought she.
She did not cry; she just rubbed her eyes, for they were
itching, and she felt that the whole corridor, with all its
doors, was beginning to whirl around her.

There were people near her, one to the right, another
to the left. Doors slam! slam! and the people were talking one to another; she could hear, "Haru! haru!" just
as at a fair.

But at last God had pity on her. Out of the door
near where she sat came a stately nobleman whom she
had seen in the church at Lipa; he stumbled against
her, and asked, —

"Why are you sitting here, woman?"

"Waiting for the chief."

"Here is the sheriff, not the chief."

The nobleman pointed to a door down the corridor,
"There, where the green tablet is. But do not go to him,
for he is occupied. Wait here; he must pass."

And the noble went on; but Marysia looked after him
with a glance such as she would give to her guardian
angel. Still she had to wait long enough. At last the
door with the green tablet opened with a clatter; out of
it came a military man no longer young, and he walked
along the corridor hastening greatly. Oi! you could

know at once that he was the chief, for after him flew a number of petitioners, running up now from the right, now from the left, and to Marysia's ears came the exclamations: "One short word, lord chief!" "Gracious chief!"

But he did not listen, and went on. It grew dark in the woman's eyes at sight of him. "Let the will of God be done," shot through her head; she rushed to the middle of the corridor, and, kneeling with upraised hands, barred the way.

He saw her, and stopped; the whole procession halted.

"What is the matter?" inquired he.

"Most holy chief!" And she could go no further; she was so frightened that the voice broke in her throat: her tongue became a stake of wood.

"What is it?"

"Oh, oh! according to the list —"

"What is that? Do they want you in the army? Hei?" asked the chief.

The petitioners immediately fell to laughing in a chorus, to uphold the good humor of the chief; but he said at once to those courtiers, —

"I pray you! I pray you be silent!"

Then he said impatiently to the woman, —

"More quickly! What is it? — for I have no time."

But she had lost her head altogether from the laughter of the audience, and blurted out disconnectedly: "Burak, Repa! Repa! Burak, O!"

"She must be drunk," said one of those nearer.

"She left her tongue in the cottage," added another.

"What do you want?" asked the chief, still more impatiently. "Are you drunk, or what?"

"O Jesus! Mary!" cried the woman, feeling that the

last plank of salvation was going from her hands.
" Most sacred chief — "

But he was really very much occupied, for the levy
had begun already, and there was much business in the
district; besides he could not talk with the woman, so he
waved his hand, and said, —

" Vodka! vodka! And the woman is young and good-
looking."

Then he turned to her with such a voice that she
came near sinking through the floor, —

" When thou art sober, lay the affair before the commune, and let the commune lay it before me."

He went on hurriedly, and the petitioners after him,
repeating, " One short word, lord chief!" " Gracious
chief!"

The corridor was deserted; it was silent there; only
her little boy began to cry. She woke then as if from
sleep, stood up, raised the child, and began to sing in a
voice which seemed not her own.

She went out of the building. The sky was covered
with clouds; on the horizon it was thundering. The air
was sultry.

What was taking place in the woman's soul, as she
passed the old church a second time in returning to
Barania-Glova, I will not undertake to describe. Ah!
if Panna Yadviga had found herself in a similar position,
I might write a sensational novel, in which I would
undertake to convince the most obdurate positivist that
there are ideal beings in this world yet. But in Panna
Yadviga every impression would have risen to self-
consciousness; despairing struggles of the soul would have
expressed themselves in no less despairing, and therefore very dramatic, words and thoughts. That vicious
circle, that deep and painful feeling of helplessness,

weakness, and overpowering opposition, that rôle of a leaf in a storm, the dull knowledge that there is no salvation from any side, neither from earth, nor from heaven, would surely have inspired Panna Yadviga with a monologue no less intense than the terror of her position; this I should need merely to write down to make a reputation.

But Repa's wife? Peasants when they suffer merely suffer, nothing more. This woman in the strong hand of misfortune was simply like a bird tormented by a vicious child. She went forward; the wind drove her; sweat flowed from her forehead; and that was the whole history. At times when the child, who was sick, opened his mouth and began to pant, as if ready to die, she called to him, "Yasek, O Yasek, my heart!" And she pressed her lips of a mother to the heated forehead of the little one. She passed the pre-Reformation church, and went on into the field, till she stopped on a sudden; a drunken peasant was coming toward her.

Clouds were rolling on in the sky, denser and denser, and in them something like a storm was preparing; from time to time there was a flash of lightning; but the peasant did not inquire, he let his coat-skirt to the wind, pulled his cap over his ears, and reeled along, now to the right, now to the left, singing, —

> "To the garden went Dodo,
> He went to buy parsnips,
> But I will give Dodo
> A club on the leg,
> Dodo will run then.
> Uu, du!"

Seeing Repa's wife, he stopped, opened his eyes, and cried, —

> "Oh, let us go to the wheat,
> For 'thou art a kind woman!"

And he tried to seize her by the waist. Frightened for herself and the child, she sprang to one side, the man after her; but, being drunk, he fell. He rose at once, it is true, though he did not pursue her; he only picked up a stone and threw it after the woman with such force that the air whistled.

She felt a pain in her head; it grew dark before her at once; and she knelt down. She remembered only one thing, "the child," and began to flee farther. She stopped under the cross, and, looking around, saw that the man was half a verst distant, staggering along toward the town.

At this moment she felt a certain strange warmth on her neck; she put her hand there, and, looking at her fingers, saw blood.

It grew dark in her eyes; she lost consciousness.

When she recovered, her shoulders were resting against the cross; in the distance a carriage from Dovborko was approaching, and in it young Pan Dovbor, with a governess from the mansion.

Pan Dovbor did not know Repa's wife; but she knew who he was, she had seen him at church; she thought then to hurry to the carriage and beg him, for God's mercy, to take even the child before the storm came; she rose to her feet, but could not advance.

Meanwhile the young man had driven up; and, seeing an unknown woman standing at the cross, he called, —

"Woman! woman! take a seat."

"May the Lord God —"

"But on the ground, on the ground."

That young Dovbor was a jester known in the whole region about; he attacked every one on the road in this fashion, trifled with them, as in this case, and then drove on farther. His laughter and that of the governess came to the ears of Repa's wife; then she saw how they began to kiss, and soon after they disappeared with the carriage in the dark distance.

Repa's wife was left alone. But it is not in vain that people say, "Women and toads thou wilt not kill, even with a scythe." After an hour or so she dragged on again, though the legs were bending under her.

"What is the little child guilty of, the golden fish, O Lord God!" repeated she, cuddling the sick Yasek to her bosom.

And then fever seized her, for she began to mutter, as if drunk.

"In the cottage is an empty cradle, and mine has gone to the war with his gun."

The wind swept the cap from her head; her beautiful hair fell to her shoulders and waved in the wind. All at once lightning flashed; the thunderbolt came so near that the smell of sulphur surrounded her, and she crouched. This brought her to herself, and she cried, "But the Word became flesh!"

She looked at the sky, which was storming, merciless, raging, and she began to sing in a trembling voice, "Whoso puts himself under the care!" A certain ominous, metallic flash fell from the clouds to the earth. She went to a forest at the roadside; but there it was still darker and more terrible. From moment to moment a noise was heard, as if the terrified trees were whispering to one another in an immense whisper, "What will happen! Oh! for God's sake!" Then came silence. Again from the forest depth was heard some voice. Shudders passed through the woman; she thought that perhaps the "evil one" was laughing at the wood devils, or perhaps the host would pass by in a terrible dance at any moment.

"If only out of the forest, if only out of the forest!" thought she; "and there ahead beyond the forest is the mill and the cabin of Yagodzinski's miller." She ran on with the last of her strength, catching at the air with parched lips. Meanwhile the sluices of heaven were opened above her head; rain, mixed with hail, fell as if from a bucket; the wind struck, and with such force that the trees were bent to the earth; the forest was filled with mist, with steam, with waves of rain; the road was not to be seen; trees were bending along the earth and roaring and splitting; around was the breaking of limbs, and then came darkness.

The woman felt weak. "Save me, O people!" cried she, in a faint voice; but no one could hear her. The wind blew the voice back into her throat. Then she understood that she could not go farther.

She took off her head-kerchief, her apron, stripped herself almost to her shift, and wrapped up the child; then, seeing a weeping birch near, she crawled to it almost on her hands and knees, and, putting down the child under the branches, fell herself by his side.

"O God, receive my soul!" cried she, and she closed her eyes.

The storm raged for some time yet, and at last fell away. But night had come; through the intervals between the clouds the stars began to shine. Under the birch was the white, motionless form of the woman.

"Now!" said some voice in the darkness. After a while the noise of a wagon and the splashing of horses' feet in the pools was heard at a distance.

This was Hershek, the cow farmer of Lipa, who had sold his geese in Oslovitsi, and was coming home. Seeing Repa's wife, he came down from his wagon.

CHAPTER X.

THE VICTORY OF GENIUS.

HERSHEK took the woman from under the birch, and would have taken her to Barania-Glova; but on the road he met Repa, who, seeing that a storm was coming, took his wagon and went to meet his wife. She lay all night and the next day in bed; but the following day she got up, for the little boy was sick. Her gossips came and incensed the child with consecrated garlands; and then old Tsisova, the blacksmith's wife, conjured the disease with a sieve in her hands and a black hen. In fact, it helped the child immediately; but the trouble was greater with Repa, who filled himself with vodka beyond measure; it was not possible to agree with him on any point.

Strange thing, when Marysia came to herself and inquired for the child, instead of showing her tenderness, he said gloomily, —

"Thou wilt fly through towns, and the devil will take the child. I would have given it thee, hadst thou lost him!" Only then did the woman feel great pain, at such ingratitude, and with a voice straight from the heart she tried to reproach him; but she could go no further than to cry out, "Vavron!"

And she looked at him through her tears. Repa almost sprang from the trunk on which he was sitting. For a time he was silent, and then said, in a changed voice, "My Marysia, forgive me those words, for I see that I have wronged thee." Then he roared with a great voice, and began to kiss her feet; and she accompanied him with tears. He felt that he was not worthy of such a wife. But that concord did not last long. The grief, which was festering like a wound, began at once to inflame them against each other. When Repa came home, either drunk or sober, he did not speak a word to his wife, but sat on the box and looked at the ground with a wolfish face. He would sit that way whole hours, as if turned into stone. The woman was busy around the room, worked as before, but was silent also. Later, when one wished to speak to the other, it was somehow awkward. So they lived as if in great feeling of offence, and deathlike silence reigned in the cottage. And what had they to say, since both knew that there was no help for them, that their fortune had ended? After a number of days, some evil thoughts began to come to the man's head. He went to confession to Father Chyzik; the priest would not give him absolution, and commanded him to come next day; but on the morrow, Repa, instead of going to the church, went to the inn.

People heard him say, when drunk, that if the Lord God would not help him, he would sell his soul to the devil; and they began to shun him. A curse, as it were, was hanging over the cottage. People scattered reports sharp as beggars' whips, and said that the mayor and the secretary did well, for such a rascal would bring only God's vengeance on all Barania-Glova. And against the woman old gossips began to say uncreated things.

It came about that Repa's well dried up. So Marysia went for water to the well in front of the inn; and on the way she heard boys say to one another, "There goes the soldier's wife!" "Not the soldier's wife, but the devil's wife!"

She went on without speaking a word; but she saw how they made the sign of the cross. She took the jug to go home, and there, before the inn, stood Shmul. When he saw her, he took out the porcelain pipe which hung at his beard, and called to her.

"Marysia!"

She stopped and inquired, "What do you want?"

"Were you at the village court?" asked he.

"I was."

"You were with the priest?"

"I was."

"Were you at the mansion?"

"I was."

"Did you go to the chief?"

"I did."

"And you got nothing?"

She merely sighed, and Shmul continued, —

"Well, you are such fools that in all Barania-Glova there is nothing more foolish. And what did you go for?"

"Where was I to go?"

"Where?" answered the Jew, "and on what is the contract? On paper; if there is no paper, there is no contract; tear the paper, and that is enough."

"Oh, how you talk!" said she, "if I could have got at that paper I should have torn it long ago."

"But don't you know that the secretary has the paper? Well! I know that you can do much with him; he said to me himself, 'Let Repa's wife come and ask me, and I,' said he, 'will tear the paper, and that's the end of it.'"

Marysia said nothing, but took the jug by the ear and went toward the brick house; meanwhile it had grown dark out of doors.

CHAPTER XI.

ENDED MISFORTUNE.

THE Great Bear had gone down already, and the triangle had risen, when the door squeaked in Repa's cottage; his wife came in quietly. She entered and stood as if fixed to the floor, for she thought that her husband would be sleeping as usual in the inn; but he was sitting on the box at the wall, with his fists resting on his knees, and looking at the floor. The coals were burning out in the chimney.

"Where hast thou been?" inquired Repa, gloomily.

Instead of answering, she fell on the floor, and lay before his feet, with great weeping and sobbing. "Vavron! Vavron!" cried she, "for thee it was that I yielded myself to shame. He deceived me, then abused and put me out. Vavron, have pity on me, at least thou, my heart! Vavron! Vavron!"

Repa took his axe out of the box.

"No," said he, with a calm voice; "thy end has come at last, poor woman. Take leave of this world now, for thou shalt see it no more; thou wilt not sit in the cottage any longer, poor woman; thou wilt lie in the churchyard —"

She looked at him with terror.

"Dost wish to kill me?"

"Well, Marysia," said he, "do not lose time for nothing; make the sign of the cross, and then will be the end; thou wilt not even feel it, poor thing."

"Vavron, wilt thou, indeed?"

"Lay thy head on the box."

"Vavron!"

"Lay thy head on the box!" cried he, with foam on his lips.

"Oh, for God's sake, save me! People! sa—"

A dull blow was heard, then a groan, and the blow of a head against the floor; then a second blow, a fainter groan; then a third, a fourth, a fifth, and a sixth blow. On the floor gushed a stream of blood; the coals in the chimney were quenched. A quiver passed through the woman from head to foot; then her body stretched, and was motionless.

Soon after a broad, bloody conflagration rent the darkness; the buildings of the mansion were blazing.

EPILOGUE.

AND now I will whisper something in your ear, reader. They would not have taken Repa to the army. An agreement like the one in the inn was not sufficient. But you see peasants do not know these things; the "intelligence," thanks to neutrality also, not much! therefore Pan Zolzik, who knew a little of this, calculated that in every case the affair would drag on, and fear would throw the woman into his arms.

And that great man was not mistaken. You ask what happened to him? Repa, when he had set fire to the buildings of the mansion, was going to take vengeance on him, but at the cry of "Fire!" the whole village was up, and Zolzik escaped.

He continues in his office of secretary in Barania-Glova, and at present he has the hope of being chosen judge.

He has just finished reading "Barbara Ubryk," and hopes that Panna Yadviga may press his hand any day under the table.

Whether those hopes of the judgeship and the pressure will be justified, the future will show.

THE ORGANIST OF PONIKLA

THE ORGANIST OF PONIKLA.

THE snow was dry, squeaking, and not over deep; but Klen had long legs, therefore he walked briskly over the road from Zagrabie to Ponikla. He went the more briskly because a good frost was coming, and he was dressed scantily in a short coat and a still shorter sheepskin overcoat above it, in black trousers and thin, patched boots. Besides, he had a hautboy in his hand; on his head a cap lined with the wind; in his stomach a couple of glasses of arrack; in his heart delight; and in his soul many causes for the delight.

That morning he had signed a contract with Canon Krayevski, as the future organist of Ponikla. Up to that time he had strolled about like any wretched gypsy, from inn to inn, from wedding to wedding, from fair to fair, from festival to festival, seeking profit with his hautboy, or on the organ, which he played better than any organist in that region. Now he was to settle down at last and have a fixed life beneath his own roof. A house, a garden, a hundred and fifty rubles a year, other earnings on occasions, a personal position, almost half spiritual, an occupation in the service of God, — who would not respect such a station?

Not long since any Matsek in Zagrabie, or Ponikla, if settled on a few morgs of land, looked on Pan Klen as a nobody; now people would take off their hats to him. An organist and, moreover, in such an immense parish

— that was not a bundle of straw! Klen had been sighing this long time for that position; but while old Melnitski lived, it was not to be thought of. The old man's fingers were stiff, and he played badly; but the canon would not send him away for anything, since he had been twenty years with him.

But when the "lysa" struck the old man so badly in the pit of the heart that in three days he died, Pan Klen did not hesitate to ask for the position, and the canon did not hesitate to give it, for a better organist could not be found in that region.

How such skill came to Pan Klen on the hautboy, the organ, and various other instruments which he understood, it was difficult to discover. He had not received the gift from his father, for his father, a man of Zagrabie, served during youth in the army, and did not work in his old age at music; he twisted hemp ropes, and played on no instrument beyond a tobacco-pipe, which was always between his mustaches.

From childhood Klen did nothing but listen wherever there was music. While a stripling, he went to "blow the bellows" for Melnitski at Ponikla. Afterward, when certain musicians came to Zagrabie, he ran away with them. He strolled about whole years with that company. God knows where he played, surely wherever it happened: at fairs, weddings, and in churches; only when the company broke up, or died, did he return to Zagrabie, as poor as a church mouse, haggard, and living like a bird on a branch. He continued to play, sometimes for the public, sometimes for the Lord God.

And, though people reproached him with want of stability, he became famous. They said of him in Zagrabie and in Ponikla, "Klen, just Klen. But when he begins to play it is no offence to the Lord, and it is a delight to man!" Others said to him, "Fear God, Pan Klen, what devil is sitting within thee?"

And in real fact some sort of devil was sitting in that thin wretch with long legs. During the life of Melnitski, whenever he took the old organist's place on great holidays and festivals, he sometimes forgot himself thoroughly at the organ. This would happen, especially in the middle of mass, when people in the church were absorbed in prayer, when the censers had sent incense over the whole nave, and everything living was singing, when Klen had let himself out, and the service, with the ringing of great and little bells, with the odor of myrrh, amber, and fragrant plants, with the gleaming of lights and the glitter of the monstrance, had so elevated every soul that the whole church seemed flying off on wings to the sky. The canon, now raising, now lowering the monstrance, closed his eyes in ecstasy, and Pan Klen did the same in the choir; and it seemed to him that the organ itself was playing; that voices from the tin pipes rose like waves, flowed like rivers, rushed like torrents, gushed like fountains, poured like rain; that they were filling the whole church; that they were under the dome, and before the altar, in the rolls of incense, in the light of the sun, and in the souls of the people, — some awful and majestic like thunder, others like the singing of people, speaking in living words, still others sweet, fine, like falling beads, or the trilling of nightingales. And after mass, Pan Klen came down from the choir dazed, with eyes staring, as if after sleep; but as a simple man, he said, and thought, that he had tired himself out. The canon in the sacristy put some money in his hand, and some praise in his ear; then he went out among the people, who were thronged around the church; and there they raised their hats to him, though he lived as a lodger in Zagrabie; and they admired him beyond measure.

But Pan Klen went in front of the church not to hear, "Hei! See! There goes Klen!" But he went to see that which was dearest to him in Zagrabie, in Ponikla, and in the whole world, Panna Olka, the daughter of the tile-maker of Zagrabie. She fastened into his heart like a wood-tick, with her eyes, which were like star-thistles, with her bright face, and her lips red as cherries.

Pan Klen himself, during the rare moments in which he looked on this world with sound judgment, and in which seeing that the tile-maker would not give him his daughter, thought that it would be better to let her go; but he felt, with terror, that he could not let her go; and with great alarm he repeated to himself, "Hei! she has got in! Thou wilt not pull her out with pincers!"

For her it was surely that he stopped wandering about, for her he lived; and when he played on the organ he thought that she was listening, and therefore he played better.

And she loving, to begin with, his "talent" for music, loved him afterward for himself; and that Pan Klen was for her the dearest of all, though he had a strange, dark face, eyes that were looking somewhere else, a scant coat, a still scanter overcoat, and legs as long and as slim as the legs of a stork.

But "the father," the tile-maker, though he, too, carried air in his pockets for the most part, was unwilling to give Olka to Klen. "Any one will look at the girl," said he; "why should such a fellow as Klen fix her fate?" and he hardly let the man into the house, and sometimes he would not let him in.

But when old Melnitski died, everything changed right away.

Klen, after signing the contract, went with all speed to the tile-maker's.

"I do not say," said the tile-maker to him, "that something must surely happen right away; but an organist is not a tramp." And, inviting him into the house, he treated him to arrack, and feasted him as a guest. And when Olka came in, the father rejoiced with the young people because Klen had become a man; he would have his house, garden, and, next to the canon, would be the great person in Ponikla.

So Klen had sat with them from midday till evening, to his own great delight and to Olka's; and now he was returning by the road to Ponikla, on squeaking snow and in twilight.

It was preparing for frost; but what cared Pan Klen? He merely went faster and faster; and, while going, he thought of that day, thought of Olka, and he was warm. A happier day in his life there had never been.

After an empty, treeless road, through frozen meadows covered with snow, now red and now blue beneath the sky, he carried his gladness like a lantern which he had to light him in the dark. He remembered again and again all that had happened: his conversation with the canon; the signing of the contract; every word with the tile-maker and Panna Olka. When they were alone for a while she said to him, "It was all one to me! I would have gone with you, Anton, without that, even beyond the sea; but for father it is better in this way!" He kissed her on the elbow with great gratitude, saying, "God reward thee, Olka, for the ages of ages, amen!" And now, when he recalled it, he was a little ashamed of himself, for having kissed her on the elbow, and for having said too little to her; for he felt that if the tile-maker would have permitted, she would have gone with him to the edge of the world. Such an honest girl! And then she would have gone with him if necessary along that empty road in the snow. "Oh, thou, my pure gold!" thought Pan Klen, "since it is so, thou wilt be a lady." Then he went still more swiftly, and the snow squeaked more loudly.

Soon he began to think, "Such a woman will not deceive a man." Then great gratitude mastered him. And indeed if Olka had been there with him, he would not have held out; he would have thrown his hautboy on the ground, and pressed her to his bosom with all the strength in his bones. He ought not to have acted differently an hour earlier; but it is always so: wherever a man has to do anything or say anything from the heart, he "becomes a fool, and has a wooden tongue." It is easier to play on the organ.

Meanwhile, the golden and red stripes which were shining on the western sky changed gradually into golden ribbons and golden knots, and finally they vanished. Darkness came; and the stars twinkled in the heavens, looking sharply and dryly on the earth, as is usual in winter. The frost grew severe, and began to bite the ears of the future organist of Ponikla; so, knowing the road perfectly, Pan Klen decided to cut across the field, and reach his own house the more quickly.

After a while he seemed black on the level, snowy expanse, — tall, sticking up ridiculously. It occurred to him that to kill time he might play a little before his fingers got stiff; and as he thought so he did. His voice sounded strangely in the night and on that waste, as if he were frightened a little by that white, melancholy plain; and it sounded all the more strangely that Klen played the most joyous things. He recollected that he had begun to play and sing, after one and another glass at the tile-maker's, that Olka accompanied him gladly with her thin little voice. He wished now to play those same songs, so he began with that with which she had begun:

> "Level, O God, the mountains with the valleys,
>   Let them be very level!
>   Bring, O God, my love,
>   Bring him early!"

But the song did not please the tile-maker, for it seemed to him a "peasant song," and he commanded Klen to sing a "noble song." Then they took up another, which Olka had learned in Zagrabie: —

> "Pan Ludwig went a hunting,
>   He left Helunia like a picture.
>   Pan Ludwig came home, the music was playing.
>   The trumpeters trumpeting, Helunia was sleeping."

This was more to the taste of the tile-maker. But when pleasure seized them they laughed most at the "Green Pitcher." The lady in that song, before she laughed at the end, cried and sang piteously for her broken pitcher:

> "My green pitcher,
>   Oh, the Pan broke it!"

But the Pan falls to consoling her: —

> "Quiet, Panna, weep not,
>   I will pay thee for thy pitcher!"

Olka prolonged as much as possible, "My gre-e-e-en pitcher," and then laughed. Klen took his lips from the hautboy, and answered her as the Pan, with a great flourish: —

> "Quiet, Panna, weep not —"

And now, remembering in the night that gladness of the daytime, he played to himself "My Green Pitcher," and smiled in addition, as much as his lips would allow, employed as they were in blowing the hautboy. But as the frost was violent, and his lip were freezing to the mouthpiece of the instrument, and his fingers were stiff going over the keys, he ceased to play and went on, somewhat panting, and with his face in a mist which rose from his breath.

After a time he got tired, for he had not counted on this, that in fields snow lies more deeply than on a beaten road, and that it is not easy to draw one's legs out of it. Besides, in meadows in some places there are hollows, made even by drifts through which one must wade to the knee. Klen began to regret then that he had left the road, for some wagon might have come along on the way to Ponikla.

The stars twinkled more and more sharply; the frost became more severe, but Pan Klen even sweated; still, when the wind rose at moments, and blew toward the river, he became very cold. He tried to play again, but as he had to keep his mouth closed he tortured himself all the more.

At last a feeling of loneliness seized him. Round about it was so empty, silent, and remote that he was wonder-stricken In Ponikla a warm house was waiting for him; but he preferred to think of Zagrabie, and said to himself, "Olka is going to sleep; but there, praise be to God, it is warm in the house." And at the thought that it was warm and bright there for Olka, Pan Klen's honest heart rejoiced all the more, the colder and darker the way was for him.

The meadows ended at last, and then began pastures grown over here and there with juniper. Pan Klen was so tired now that a great desire seized him to sit down, with his hautboy, under the first sheltered bush, and rest. "But I shall freeze if I do so," thought he, and went on.

THE ORGANIST OF PONIKLA.   383

Unfortunately, among junipers, as along fences, snowdrifts form sometimes. Klen passed through a number of these, and became so exhausted that finally he said to himself, —

"I will sit down. Unless I fall asleep I shall not freeze; and to keep from sleeping, I will play again, 'My Green Pitcher.'"

He sat down, played again, again the vanishing voice of the hautboy was heard in the silence of night, and over the snow. But Klen's eyelids stuck together more and more, and the notes of the "Green Pitcher," growing weaker, and gradually growing silent, were silent altogether at last. Still he struggled against sleep; he was conscious yet; he was thinking still of Olka; but at the same time he felt himself in a greater desert, more and more alone, as if forgotten; and wonderment seized him that she was not there with him in that loneliness and that night.

He murmured, "Olka! where art thou?"

And once more he spoke as if calling her, —

"Olka!"

The hautboy dropped from his stiffened hands.

Next morning the dawn shone on his sitting figure, with the hautboy near his long legs, and his face was blue, astonished as it were, and at the same time fixed in listening to the last note of the song, "My Green Pitcher."

LUX IN TENEBRIS LUCET

LUX IN TENEBRIS LUCET.[1]

SOMETIMES in the autumn, especially in November, such wet and gloomy days come that life becomes repulsive even to a healthy man. From the time that Kamionka had fallen ill and stopped work on his statue of "Compassion," bad weather had caused him more suffering than sickness itself. Every morning, when he had dragged his body out of bed, he rubbed the great sweating window of his studio and looked upward, in the hope that he would see some little strip of blue sky; but every morning disappointment awaited him. An oppressive lead-colored mist hung over the earth; rain was not falling, still the paving stones in the yard looked like sponges soaked in liquid; everything was wet, slippery, penetrated through and through with water, single drops of which falling from the eave-troughs sounded with a peculiar and desperate monotony, as if measuring that sluggish time of sadness.

The window of the studio looked out on a courtyard, which was bounded by a garden. The grass beyond the paling was green yet with a sort of sickly greenness, in which were death and decay; but the trees with their yellow leaves, and their branches black from dampness and also effaced by the mist somewhat, seemed dead altogether. From among those trees came every evening the

[1] Light shineth in the darkness.

cawing of crows, which had flown in from the forests and fields to the city for winter quarters, and which, with a great clattering of wings, settled down for the night on the branches.

The studio in days like this was as gloomy as the place for bones in a cemetery. Marble and plaster of Paris need azure. In that leaden light the whiteness had something sad in it; figures in dark terra-cotta lost all precision of lines and changed into indefinite forms almost terrible.

Dirt and disorder increased the gloom of the studio. On the floor was a thick layer of dust, formed from pieces of dry terra-cotta ground fine from trampling; to this was added mud from the street. The naked walls were merely ornamented here and there with models of hands and feet in plaster of Paris; near the window hung a small mirror, above it a horse skull, and a bouquet of artificial flowers quite black from dust.

In the corner was a bed covered with a quilt, old and rumpled; near the bed a commode; on this an iron candlestick.

Kamionka, through reasons of economy, kept no separate lodging-place; he slept in the studio. Usually the bed was concealed by a screen, but the screen had been removed to let the sick man look out more easily through the window near the foot of his bed, and see if the weather were clearing. Another and larger window placed in the ceiling of the studio was covered with dust on the outside to such a degree that even on bright days a gray and gloomy light passed in through it.

But the weather did not clear. After a number of days of darkness the clouds settled down thoroughly, the air was penetrated to the last degree with a watery, heavy mist, and became still darker. Kamionka, who so far had lain on the bed in his clothing, felt worse, so he undressed and lay down for good.

Speaking precisely, he was not so much sick with any definite disease as he was bowed down, dissatisfied, exhausted, and sad in general. His weakness cut the feet from beneath him. He had no wish to die; but neither did he feel strength to live.

The long hours of the dismal day seemed longer because he had no one for company. His wife had been dead twenty years; his relatives lived in another part of the country; and he did not live with his colleagues. In recent years every acquaintance had withdrawn from him because of his ever-increasing sorrow. At first, his disposition amused people; but later, when he grew stranger and stranger, when every jest roused a permanent feeling of offence in him, even those nearest the man broke off all relations with him.

People took it ill of him also that with age he had grown devout, and his sincerity was suspected. Malicious tongues said that he sat in church only to receive orders from churches through his relations with priests. This was not true. His piety did not flow from deep and calm faith, perhaps, but it was unselfish.

What, however, lent a show of truth to the critics, was the penuriousness which increased more and more in Kamionka. For a number of years he had lived in his studio to lessen expenses; he lived God knows on what food, and injured his health so much that at last his face was as yellow and transparent as if moulded from wax. He avoided people also for this, lest some one might ask of him sometime a favor.

In general, he was a man of broken character, embittered and uncommonly unhappy. Still his was not a common nature at bottom, for even his faults had artistic traits which were special to him. Those who judged that with his penuriousness he must have collected a considerable property were mistaken. In truth, Kamionka was poor; for all that he owned he had spent on engravings of which he had whole portfolios at the bottom of his bureau; these, from time to time, he counted with the greed and the care of a usurer counting his money. He concealed this taste the more carefully, perhaps, because it had grown on the basis of great misfortune and deep feeling.

On a time, a year more or less after the death of his wife, he saw in an antiquarian's collection an old engraving, representing Armida. In the face of this Armida he detected a likeness to the face of his dead one. He bought the engraving immediately, and from that time on he sought copperplates, those at first representing only Armida, then, as the fancy increased, every other.

Those who have lost persons much loved by them are forced to attach life to something, or they could not exist. As to Kamionka, no one would have thought that this rather aged original and egotist had ever loved his wife more than he loved his existence. It is likely, moreover, that had she not died, life would have flowed on for him more broadly, more calmly, and more in human fashion. Be that as it may, love in Kamionka survived his happy days, his youth, and even his talent.

His piety, which in the course of years turned into a custom resting on the preservation of external forms, flowed from this love of his also. Kamionka, without being a man of deep faith, began after the death of his wife to pray for the dead one, since this seemed to him the only thing he could do for her, and thus a kind of thread kept them together.

Natures apparently cold are often able to love with great power and persistently. After the death of his wife,

Kamionka's whole life and all the thoughts that he had, entwined themselves around her memory, and drew food from it, just as plant parasites draw food from the tree on which they are growing. But from memories of that sort the human plant can gain nothing but poisonous juices made up of sorrow and enormous vexation, hence Kamionka too poisoned himself, grew distorted, went to nothing.

Had he not been an artist, he would not have survived, perhaps, but he was saved by his calling. After the death of his wife, he began to make a monument to her. It is useless for the living to say that it is all one to the dead in what graves they are lying. Kamionka wished that it should be beautiful there for his Zosia, and he worked with his heart no less than his hands. This was why he did not become insane the first half year, but grew inured to despair.

The man was out of joint and unhappy; but art saved the artist. From that moment, Kamionka existed by virtue of his calling. People who look at statues and images in galleries do not divine that artists may serve their art honestly or dishonestly. In this regard, Kamionka was without reproach. He had no wings at his shoulders, — he possessed only talent somewhat above the common, and perhaps, therefore, art could not fill out his life, or give him recompense for all losses; but he respected it deeply, and was ever sincere with regard to it. During the long years of his labor, he had never tempted it, and had never committed injustice regarding it, either in view of fame, profit, praise, or blame. He always did that which he felt. During his happy years, when he lived like other men, he was able to say things touching art which were quite uncommon, and after that, when people began to turn aside from him, he thought frequently of this art in his lonely studio, in a manner which was lofty and honest.

He felt greatly abandoned; but in this there was no cause for wonder. People's relations must have a certain medium measure in virtue of which the exceptionally unhappy are cut off from life. For that very reason, they are covered with as much strangeness and as many faults as a stone thrown up from a torrent is covered with moss, when it ceases to rub against others. Now when Kamionka was ill, no living soul looked into his studio, with the exception of a servant-woman, who came twice a day to make tea for him, and serve it. At every visit, her advice was to call in a doctor; but he, fearing the outlay, would not give his consent to this.

At last he became very weak; perhaps for the reason that he took nothing into his mouth except tea. But he had no desire then for anything, either for eating, or work, or life. His thoughts were as if withered like those leaves on which he looked through the window; and those thoughts of his answered perfectly to that autumn, to that drizzle, to that leaden darkness. There are no worse moments in life than those in which a man feels that he has accomplished what he had to accomplish, that he has outlived that which he had to outlive; and that nothing more in this world belongs to him. Kamionka had lived almost fifteen years in continual dread that his talent would exhaust itself; now he was sure that it had, and he thought with bitterness that even art was deserting him. He felt therewith weariness and exhaustion in every bone of his body. He did not expect a sudden death; but he did not believe in a return to health. In general, there was not one spark of hope in him.

If he wished for anything it was only that the weather would brighten, that the sun would shine into his studio.

For he thought that in that case he might gain consolation. He had always been specially sensitive to slush and to darkness; such days had always deepened his sadness and depression, and what must it now be when that "hopeless time," as Kamionka called it, was joined to his sickness!

Every evening when the servant brought tea he inquired: "Is it not clearing on the edge of the sky somewhere?"

"There is such a mist," answered she, "that one man cannot see another."

Kamionka, hearing this answer, closed his eyes and lay motionless a long time.

In the yard it was always quiet save that drops of rain pattered evenly and monotonously in the gutters.

About three o'clock one afternoon it was so dark that Kamionka was forced to light a candle. And he was so weak that he did this with no little difficulty. Before he reached for a match he meditated a long time; then he extended his arm lazily; the thinness of this arm, evident through the shirt sleeve, filled him, as a sculptor, with repugnance and bitterness. When he had lighted the candle he rested again, without moving, till the evening arrival of the servant, listening with closed eyes to the drops sounding in the gutter.

His studio looked strange then. The flame of the candle lighted the bed with Kamionka lying on it, and came to a focus in a shining point on his forehead with its skin dry and yellow as if polished. The rest of the room was sunk in darkness, which grew denser each moment. But as it grew dark outside the statues became more rosy and acquired life. The flame of the candle now sank, now rose, and in that quivering light the statues too seemed to sink and rise exactly as if they were rising on tiptoe to gain a better look at the face of the sculptor, and be convinced that their creator was living.

And indeed there was a certain immobility of death in that countenance. But at times the blue lips of the sick man stirred with a slight movement, as if in prayer, or as if he were cursing his loneliness and those dreadful drops of moisture which measured with even monotony the hours of his sickness.

One evening the woman came a little drunk, therefore more talkative than usual.

"There is so much work on my head that I can barely look in twice a day," said she; "if you would call a religious, a sister of charity costs nothing, and she would be better for a sick man."

This advice pleased Kamionka, but he, like others who are afflicted, had the habit of always opposing whatever advice people gave him; so he would not agree.

But after the woman had gone he began to think thus: "A sister of charity costs nothing, but what aid she might give, and what comfort!" Kamionka, like every sick man left to himself, experienced much suffering and struggled with a thousand petty miseries, which annoyed him as much as they made him impatient. More than once he lay for whole hours with a crooked neck before he would move to arrange his own pillow. Often in the night he was cold and would have given God knows what for a cup of tea; but if it was difficult to light a candle, how was he to think of making tea? A sister of charity would do all this with the mild readiness usual to those sisters. Oh, how much easier to be sick if one had their assistance!

The poor man came at last to think of sickness under such conditions as something desirable and pleasant, and he wondered in his soul if the like happiness were accessible to him even.

LUX IN TENEBRIS LUCET.

It seemed, too, that if a sister were to come and bring with her a little joyousness and solace to the studio, perhaps the weather would clear up outside, and the sounding drops of water cease to pursue him.

He regretted at last that he had not accepted the advice of the woman immediately. Night was approaching, long and gloomy, and the woman was to look in at him only next morning. He understood now that that night would be for him more grievous than all the nights which had ever preceded it.

Then he thought what a Lazarus he was — and in distinction to his present wretchedness his former happy years stood before his eyes as if living. And as a moment before the thought of the sister of charity, so now the remembrance of those years joined itself in the same wonderful manner in his weakened brain, with the understanding of sun and light and fair weather.

He began to think of his dead one, and to speak with her, as he had the habit of doing when he was ill. At last he wearied himself, felt that he was growing weak, and fell asleep.

The candle was burning slowly. Its flame from being rosy was blue, then it gleamed brightly a number of times, and died. Deep darkness embraced the studio.

But meanwhile in the yard drops of rain fell as evenly and gloomily as if by means of them darkness and grief were distilled through all nature.

Kamionka slept long and lightly, but all at once he woke with a certain wonderful impression that something uncommon was happening in the studio. The morning dawn was in the world. The marbles and plasters of Paris began to grow white. The broad Venetian window opposite his bed was penetrated more and more with pale light.

In this light Kamionka saw a figure sitting at his bedside.

He opened his eyes widely and looked at the figure: it was that of a sister of charity.

She was sitting motionless, turned slightly toward the window, with her head inclined. Her hands were laid on her knees,—and she seemed to be praying. The sick man could not see her face, but he saw plainly her white head-dress and the dark outline of her rather frail shoulders.

His heart began to beat somewhat nervously, and these questions flew through his head,—

"When could the servant have brought in this sister of charity; and how did she enter?"

Next he thought that perhaps something seemed to him thus because he was weak, then he closed his eyes. But after a while he opened them again.

The sister of charity was sitting on the same spot, motionless as if sunk in prayer.

A wonderful feeling composed of fear and delight began to raise the hair on the head of the sick man. Something attracted his eyes with incomprehensible power to that figure. It seemed to him that he had seen it somewhere, but where and when he could not remember. An irresistible desire to see her face seized him, but the white head-dress concealed it. Kamionka, without knowing why, did not dare to speak or to move, or hardly to breathe. He felt only that the sensation of fear and delight was possessing him more and more powerfully, and he asked with astonishment, "What is this?"

Meanwhile there was perfect day. And what a marvellous morning that must be outside! Suddenly without any transition there came into the studio a light as powerful, bright, and joyous as if it were springtime and May.

Waves of golden glitter, rising like a flood, began to fill the room, to overflow it so mightily that the marbles were drowned and dissolved in that brightness; the walls were covered with it and then disappeared altogether. Kamionka found himself as it were in some bright space without boundary.

Then he noticed that the covering on the head of the sister began to lose its white stiffness, that it trembled at the edges, melted, dissolved like clear mist, and changed into light.

The sister turned her face slowly toward the sick man, and then the deserted sufferer saw in the bright aureole the well-known hundred times beloved features of his dead wife.

He sprang from the bed, and from his breast came a cry, in which all his years of sorrow, tears, suffering, and despair were united, —

"Zosia! Zosia!"

And seizing her, he drew her to him; she threw her arms around his neck.

More and more light came into the room.

"Thou didst not forget me," said she at last, "hence I have come. I obtained an easy death for thee."

Kamionka held her in his arms all the time, as if in fear that the blessed vision would vanish from him together with the light.

"I am ready to die," answered he, "if thou wilt stay with me."

She smiled at him with her angelic smile, and taking one arm from his neck she pointed downward, and said, —

"Thou art dead already. Look!"

398 LUX IN TENEBRIS LUCET.

He looked in the direction of her hand, and behold, under their feet, he saw through the window in the ceiling of his own gloomy and lonely studio, and there on the bed lay his own corpse, with widely opened mouth, which in the yellow face seemed a dark hole as it were.

And he looked on that emaciated body as something foreign. But after a while all began to vanish from his eyes, for that surrounding brightness, as if urged by a wind from beyond this world, went off somewhere into infinity.

ON THE BRIGHT SHORE

ON THE BRIGHT SHORE.

CHAPTER I.

THE artist was sitting beside Pani Elzen in an open carriage; on the front seat were her sons the twin brothers, Romulus and Remus. He was partly conversing with the lady, partly thinking of a question which required prompt decision, and partly looking at the sea. There was something to look at. They were driving from Nice toward Monte Carlo by the so-called Old Cornice; that is, by a road along impending cliffs, high above the water. On the left, the view was hidden by naked towering rocks, which were gray, with a rosy pearl tinge; on the right was the blue Mediterranean, which appeared to lie immensely low down, thus producing the effect of an abyss and of boundlessness. From the height on which they were moving, the small fishing boats seemed like white spots, so that frequently it was difficult to distinguish a distant sail from a seamew circling above the water.

Pani Elzen had placed her hand on Svirski's arm; her face was that of a woman delighted and forgetful of what she is doing; she gazed with dreamy eyes over the mirror of the sea.

Svirski felt the touch; a quiver of delight ran through him, and he thought that if at that moment Romulus and Remus had not been in front of them, he might have placed his arm around the young woman, perhaps, and pressed her to his bosom.

But straightway a certain fear seized him at the thought that hesitation would then have an end, and the question be settled.

"Stop the carriage, please," said Pani Elzen.

Svirski stopped the carriage, and they were silent a moment.

"How quiet it is here after the bustle of Monte Carlo!" said the young widow.

"I hear only music," answered the artist; "perhaps the bands are playing on the iron-clads in Villa Franca."

In fact, from below came at intervals muffled sounds of music, borne thither by the same breeze which brought the odor of orange-blossoms and heliotropes. Beneath them were visible the roofs of villas, dotting the shore, and almost hidden in groves of eucalyptus, while round about were large white spots formed by blossoming almond-trees, and rosy spots made by peach blossoms. Lower down was the dark-blue sunlit bay of Villa Franca, with crowds of great ships.

The life seething there presented a marvellous contrast to the deep deadness of the naked, barren mountains, above which extended the sky, cloudless and so transparent that it was monotonous and glassy. Everything was dimmed and belittled amid that calm greatness; the carriage with its occupants seemed, as it were, a kind of beetle, clinging to the cliffs along which it was climbing to the summit with insolence.

"Here life ends altogether," said Svirski, looking at the naked cliffs.

Pani Elzen leaned more heavily on his shoulder and answered with a drowsy, drawling voice, —

"But it seems to me that here life begins."

After a moment Svirski answered with a certain emotion, "Perhaps you are right."

And he looked with an inquiring glance at her. Pani Elzen raised her eyes to him in answer, but dropped them quickly, as if confused, and, though her two sons were sitting on the front seat of the carriage, she looked at that moment like a maiden whose eyes could not endure the first ray of love. After that, both were silent; while from below came snatches of music.

Meanwhile, far away at sea, at the very entrance to the bay, appeared a dark pillar of smoke, and the quiet of the company was broken by Remus, who sprang up, and cried, —

"Tiens! le 'Fohmidable'!"

Pani Elzen cast a glance of displeasure at her younger son. She knew the value of that moment, in which every next word might weigh in her fate decisively.

"Remus," said she, "will you be quiet?"

"But, mamma, it is the 'Fohmidable'!"[1]

"What an unendurable boy!"

"Pouhquoi?"[1]

"He is a duhen[1] [duren, a simpleton]; but this time he is right," called out Romulus, quickly; "yesterday we were at Villa Franca,"— here he turned to Svirski. "You saw us go on velocipedes; they told us there that the whole squadron had arrived except the 'Fohmidable,' which was due to-day."

To this Remus answered with a strong accent on every last syllable, —

"Thou art a duhen,[1] thyself!"

The boys fell to punching each other with their elbows.

---

[1] Romulus and Remus lisp or pronounce *r* in the Parisian manner, hence the use of *h* instead of *r* in the above words, both French and Polish.

Pani Elzen, knowing how Svirski disliked her sons' style of speech, and generally the manner in which they were reared, commanded them to be silent.

"I have told you and Pan Kresovich," said she, "not to speak among yourselves in any language but Polish."

Kresovich was a student from Zürich, with incipient lung disease; Pani Elzen had found him on the Riviera, and engaged him as tutor for her sons, after her acquaintance with Svirski, and especially after a public declaration of the malicious and wealthy Pan Vyadrovski, that respectable houses had ceased to rear their sons as commercial travellers.

Meanwhile the unlucky "Formidable" had spoiled the temper of the sensitive artist. After a time, the carriage, gritting along the stones, moved on.

"You took their part, and I brought them," said Pani Elzen, with a sweet voice; "you are too kind to the boys. But one should be here during moonlight. Would you like to come to-night?"

"I like to come always; but to-night there will be no moon, and of course your dinner will end late."

"That is true; but let me know when the next full moon comes. It is a pity that I did not ask you alone to this dinner— With a full moon, it must be beautiful here, though on these heights I have always a throbbing of the heart. If you could see how it throbs at this moment; but look at my pulse, you can see it even through the glove."

She turned her palm, which was confined so tightly in the Danish glove as to be turned almost into a tube, and stretched it to Svirski. He took the hand in both of his, and looked at it.

"No," said he; "I cannot see the pulse clearly, but perhaps I can hear it."

And, inclining his head, he put his ear to the buttons of her glove; for a moment he pressed the glove firmly to his face, then touched it lightly with his lips, and said, —

"In years of childhood I was able sometimes to catch a bird, and its heart beat just this way. The beating here is just as in a captured bird!"

She laughed, almost with melancholy, and repeated, "'As in a captured bird.' But what did you do with the captured birds?"

"I grew attached to them, immensely. But they always flew away."

"Bad birds."

"And thus my life arranged itself," continued the artist, with emotion; "I have sought in vain for something which would consent to stay with me, till at last I have lost even hope."

"Do not lose that; have confidence," answered Pani Elzen.

Svirski thought then to himself, that, since the affair had begun so long before, there was need to end it, and let that come which God permits. He felt at the moment like a man who closes his eyes and ears with his fingers; but he felt also that it was needful to act thus, and that there was no time for hesitation.

"Perhaps it would be better for you to walk a little," said he. "The carriage will follow, and, besides, we shall be able to speak more in freedom."

"Very well," answered Pani Elzen, with a resigned voice.

Svirski punched the driver with his cane; the carriage halted; and they stepped out. Romulus and Remus ran forward at once, and only stopped, when some tens of yards ahead, to look from above at the houses in Eze, and roll stones into the olive-groves growing below. Svirski and Pani Elzen were left alone; but that day some fatality seemed to weigh on them, for before they could use the moment they saw that a horseman, coming from the direction of Monaco, had stopped near Romulus and Remus. Behind him was a groom dressed in the English manner.

"That is De Sinten," said Pani Elzen, with impatience.

"Yes, I recognize him."

In fact, they saw next moment before them a horse's head, and above it the equine face of young De Sinten. He hesitated whether or not to salute and go on, but considering evidently that if they had wanted to be alone they would not have brought the boys, he sprang from the horse, and, beckoning to the groom, began to greet them.

"Good-day," answered Pani Elzen, somewhat dryly. "Is this your hour?"

"It is. Mornings, I shoot at pigeons with Wilkis Bey, so I cannot ride lest I disturb my pulse. I am now seven pigeons ahead of him. Do you know that the 'Formidable' comes to Villa Franca to-day, and to-morrow the admiral will give a ball on deck?"

"We saw it arrive."

"I was just going to Villa Franca to see one of the officers whom I know, but it is late. If you permit, I will go with you to Monte Carlo."

Pani Elzen nodded, and they went on together. De Sinten, since he was a horseman by nature, began at once to speak of the "hunter," on which he had come.

"I bought him from Waxdorf," said he. "Waxdorf lost at *trente et quarante*, and needed money. He bet *inverse*, and hit on a lucky series, but afterward fortune changed." Here he turned to the horse. "He is of pure Irish blood, and I will give my neck that there is not a better hunter on the whole Cornice; but it is difficult to mount him."

"Is he vicious?" inquired Svirski.

"Once you are in the saddle, he is like a child. He is used to me; but you, for instance, could not mount him."

At this Svirski, who in matters of sport was childishly vain, asked at once, —

"How is that?"

"Do not try, especially here above the precipice!" cried Pani Elzen.

But Svirski had his hand on the horse's shoulder already, and a twinkle later was in the saddle, without the least resistance from the horse; perhaps the beast was not at all vicious, and understood, too, that on the edge of a cliff above a precipice it was better not to indulge in pranks.

The rider and the horse disappeared at a slow gallop along the turn of the road.

"He rides very well," said De Sinten; "but he will spoil my horse's feet. There is no road here for riding."

"The horse has turned out perfectly gentle," said Pani Elzen.

"I am greatly pleased at this, for here an accident happens easily — and I was a little afraid."

On his face, however, there was a certain concern; first, because what he had said about the horse's stubbornness at mounting seemed like untruth, and, second, because there existed a secret dislike between him and Svirski. De Sinten had not, it is true, at any time serious designs touching Pani Elzen; but he would have preferred that no one should oppose him in such designs as he had. Besides, some weeks before, he and Svirski had engaged in a rather lively talk. De Sinten, who was an irrepressible aristocrat, had declared, during a dinner at Pani Elzen's, that to his thinking man begins only at the baron. To this Svirski, in a moment of ill-humor, answered with an inquiry, —

"In what direction?" (up or down).

De Sinten took this reply so seriously that he sought advice of Vyadrovski and Councillor Kladzki as to how he ought to act, and learned, with genuine astonishment, that Svirski had a coronet on his shield. A knowledge of the artist's uncommon strength, and his skill in shooting, had a soothing effect, perhaps, on the baron's nerves; it suffices that the negotiation had no result, except to leave in the hearts of both men an indefinite dislike. From the time that Pani Elzen seemed to incline decidedly toward Svirski, the dislike had become quite Platonic.

But this dislike was more decided in the artist than in De Sinten. No one had supposed that the affair of the widow and the artist could end in marriage; but among their acquaintances people had begun to speak of Svirski's feelings toward Pani Elzen, and he had a suspicion that De Sinten and his party were ridiculing him as a man of simple mind. They, it is true, did not betray themselves by the slightest word on any occasion; but in Svirski the conviction was glimmering that his suspicion was justified, and this pained him, specially out of regard for Pani Elzen.

He was glad, therefore, that on this occasion, thanks to the horse's gentleness, De Sinten seemed a person who, without reason, told things which were untrue; hence he said, on returning, —

"A good horse, and specially good because he is as tame as a sheep."

He dismounted, and they walked on together, three of

them, and even five, for Romulus and Remus followed closely. Pani Elzen, to spite De Sinten, and perhaps from a wish to be rid of him, turned the conversation to pictures and art in general, of which the young sportsman had not the faintest idea. But he began to retail gossip from the Casino, and congratulated the young woman on her luck of yesterday; she listened with constraint, being ashamed, in presence of Svirski, of having taken part in play. Her vexation was increased when Romulus called out, —

"Mamma, but did you not tell us that you never play; will you give us a louis d'or for that?"

"I sought Councillor Kladzki, wishing to invite him to dinner to-day; when I found him he and I played a little," answered she, as if speaking to no one in particular.

"Give us a louis d'or apiece," repeated Romulus.

"Or buy us a little roulette table," added Remus.

"Do not annoy me! Let us go to the carriage," said she, turning to Svirski. Then she took farewell of De Sinten.

"At seven, did you say?" inquired he.

"At seven."

They parted; and after a while Svirski found himself again at the side of the beautiful widow. This time they occupied the front seat, since they wished to look at the setting sun.

"People say that Monte Carlo is more sheltered than Mentone," remarked the widow; "but, oh, how it bores me at times! That endless noise, that movement, those acquaintances which one must make, willingly or unwillingly. Sometimes I wish to rush away and spend the rest of the winter in some quiet corner where I should see only those whom I see with pleasure — What place do you like best?"

"I like San Raphael greatly; the pines there go down to the sea."

"True, but it is far from Nice," answered she, in a low voice; "and your studio is in Nice."

A moment of silence followed, after which Pani Elzen inquired, —

"But Antibes?"

"True! I forgot Antibes."

"Besides, it is so near Nice. After dinner you will stop with me a little and talk of a place where one might escape from society."

"Do you wish really to flee from people?"

"Let us talk sincerely; I detect doubt in your question. You suspect me of speaking as I do so as to appear better, or at least less shallow, than I am — And you have a right to your suspicion, since you see me always in the whirl of society. But my answer is this: We move frequently with a force not our own, because once we were impelled in a given direction, and endure now in spite of us the results of previous life. As to me, it may be that this is because of the weakness of woman, who has not strength to free herself without the aid of another — I confess this — But that fact does not save one from yearning greatly and sincerely for some quiet corner and a calmer life. Let people say what they choose, we women are like climbing plants, which creep along the ground when they cannot grow upward. For this reason, people are often mistaken, thinking that we creep of our own choice. By creeping, I understand empty society life, without lofty thought. But how am I, for example, to defend myself against this! Some one begs permission to present an acquaintance; the man presented makes a visit, after that a second, a third, and a tenth — what am I to do? Not permit the presentation? Of course I permit it; even for this reason, that the more people I receive, the more indifferent I am to each, and the more each is prevented from occupying an exceptional position."

"You are right," said Svirski.

"But do you see that in this way is created that current of social life from which I cannot tear myself with my own strength, and which wearies and tortures me to such a degree that at times I could scream out from pain."

"I believe you."

"You ought to believe me; but believe also that I am better and less vain than I seem. When doubts come to you, or when people speak ill of me, think to yourself: She must have her good side. If you will not think thus, I shall be very unhappy."

"I give you my word, that I wish always to think the best of you."

"And you should think so," said she, with a soft voice; "for though everything which is good in me were more stifled than it is, it would bloom out afresh were I near you, so much depends on those with whom one associates — I should like to say something; but I am afraid — "

"Say it."

"You will not think me fanciful, or even worse? I am not fanciful; I talk like a sober-minded woman who states only that which is real, and looks at things coolly. At your side, for example, I should regain my former spirit, as calm and collected as when I was a girl; and now I am almost a grandmother — thirty-five years of age."

Svirski looked at her with a clear face, very nearly in love; then he raised her hand slowly to his lips, and said. —

"Ah! In comparison with me you are really a child. Forty-eight is my age — and that is my picture!" said he, pointing to the setting sun.

She began to gaze at that light which was reflected in her shining eyes, and said, in a low voice, as if to herself, "Great, marvellous, beloved sun!"

Then silence followed. The calm ruddy light was falling on the faces of both. The sun was setting in genuine majesty and grandeur. Beneath it, slender clouds, recently blown asunder, took on the forms of palm lilies, and were gleaming like gold. The sea along the shore was sunk in shadow; farther out, in open spaces, lay a boundless light. In the valley, the motionless cypress-trees were outlined sharply on the lily-colored background of the sky.

CHAPTER II.

THE guests invited by Pani Elzen assembled at the Hôtel de Paris at seven o'clock. A separate room and also a smaller one adjoining, in which coffee was to be served, had been assigned for the dinner. The lady had issued invitations to a dinner "without ceremony;" but the gentlemen, knowing what to understand by this, came in dress-coats and white neckties. Pani Elzen appeared in a pale rose-colored, low-necked dress with a great fold in the back extending from the top of the bodice to the bottom of the skirt. She looked fresh and young. She had a finely cut face, and a small head, by which principally she had charmed Svirski at the beginning of their more intimate acquaintance. Her plump shoulders had, especially at the edge of the dress, the appearance and transparency of mother-of-pearl; but her arms from the elbow to the wrist were slightly reddened, seemingly rough; that, however, merely heightened the impression of their nakedness. In general, she was radiant with gladness, good-humor, and that brilliancy which women have when they are happy.

Among the invited guests, besides Svirski and De Sinten, came the old councillor, Kladzki, with his nephew Sigismund, a young man of no great social experience, but forward, whose eyes gleamed at Pani Elzen too expressively, and who did not know how to conceal what he felt; next, was Prince Valerian Porzetski, a man forty years of age, bald, with a large head coming to a point at the top like that of an Aztec; Pan Vyadrovski, rich and sarcastic, the owner of oil wells in Galicia, a lover of art and a dilettante; finally, Kresovich, a student, the temporary tutor of Romulus and Remus, a man whom Pani Elzen invited because Svirski liked his fanatical face.

The point with the lady was always, and more especially on that day, to have an "intellectual" salon, as she expressed it. She could not, however, turn the conversation at first from local gossip and the happenings of the Casino, which Vyadrovski called the "Slav world,"— more of Slav speech was heard there, he said, than any other. Vyadrovski's life in Monte Carlo was spent generally in ridiculing his fellow-countrymen and the younger Slav brothers. That was a hobby which he mounted gladly, and galloped without rest. So he began at once to relate how, two days before, there remained in the "Cercle de la Méditerranée," at six in the morning, seven persons, all of Slav blood.

"We are born thus," said he, turning to the hostess. "In other countries people count: Nine, ten, eleven, twelve, etc.; but every real Slav says, in spite of himself:

Nine, ten, knave, queen, king— Yes; to the Cornice comes the cream of our society, and here they make cheese of it."

Prince Valerian, of peaked head, announced now, in the tone of a man who is discovering new truths, that every passion which exceeds the measure is ruinous, but that to the "Cercle de la Méditerranée" belonged many foreigners of distinction with whom it was useful and worth while to make acquaintance. It was possible to serve one's country everywhere. For instance, he had met there three days before an Englishman, a friend of Chamberlain, who had inquired of him touching our country; and he described on a visiting-card the economic and political condition in general, and the social aspirations in particular. Beyond doubt, the card would go, if not to Chamberlain, who is not here, to Salisbury, and that would be better Probably, also, he would meet Salisbury at the ball which the French admiral is to give, and during which the whole "Formidable" would be illuminated *à giorno* by electricity.

Kresovich, who was not only a consumptive, but a man of another style of thought, a man who hated that society in which he was forced to appear as the tutor of Romulus and Remus, snorted ironically and as venomously as a hyena when he heard of this visiting-card. Pani Elzen, wishing to turn attention from him, said,—

"But here people are putting forward the wonders of electricity. I have heard that the whole road from Nice to Marseilles will be lighted by electricity."

"An engineer, Ducloz, drew up such a plan," said Svirski; "but he died two months ago. He was such a fanatical electrician that very likely he desired in his will to have his grave lighted by electricity."

ON THE BRIGHT SHORE.

"Then," said Vyadrovski, "he should have on his tomb the inscription, O Lord, grant him eternal rest, and may electric light shine on him for the ages of ages. Amen!"

But Kladzki, the old councillor, attacked Vyadrovski, and said that he was trifling with grave subjects which were beyond witticism; then he attacked the whole Riviera. "All," said he, "from people to things, is simply a show and a jest. Everywhere they pretend to be 'marquises, counts, and viscounts;' but they are really on the watch to snatch away handkerchiefs. As to comfort, it is the same. In my office at Veprkoviski, five rooms could be put, each as large as the little den which they have given me in the hotel. The doctors have sent me to Nice for fresh air; but, as God lives, that *Promenade des Anglais* has the vile odor of a lodging-house in Cracow; my nephew Sigismund can testify to this."

But Sigismund's eyes were crawling out of his head as he looked at Pani Elzen's arms; and he did not hear what his uncle was saying.

"Remove to Bordighieri," said Svirski. "Italian dirt is artistic at least; while French dirt is vile."

"Still you are living in Nice?"

"I am, because I could not find a studio beyond Ventimiglia. Were I to move, I should prefer Antibes, on the other side."

When he had said this, he looked at Pani Elzen. At the corners of her mouth a faint smile appeared, and she dropped her eyes. Next moment, however, wishing, as it seemed, to turn conversation toward art, she spoke of Rumpelmayer's exhibition, and of the new pictures which she had seen two days before, and which the French journalist, Krauss, called impressionist-decadent.

At this Vyadrovski raised his fork, and inquired, in the tones of a Pyrrho, —

"What are the decadents in general?"

"From a certain point of view, they are people who ask of art itself the various sauces with which it is served," answered Svirski.

Prince Valerian, however, felt wounded by what old Kladzki had said of "marquises, counts, and viscounts."

"Even the adventurers who come here," said he, "are high-class adventurers, and are not satisfied with snatching the handkerchief from your nose. Here one meets corsairs of grand style. But besides them come all who are richest, or most exquisite in the world. Here financial magnates meet people of high blood on equal footing; this is especially good, for let the world refine itself! Pan Kladzki should read such a book as the 'Idylle Tragique,' and be convinced that, in addition to suspected people, the highest social spheres come here also — precisely such as we shall meet on the 'Formidable,' which for that occasion is to be lighted *à giorno* by electricity."

Prince Valerian forgot evidently that he had given information already about the lighting of the "Formidable." In fact, it was not the subject of conversation just then; and immediately they began to talk of the "Idylle Tragique." Young Kladzki, mentioning the hero of that novel, said: "It was good enough for such a fellow, since he was dunce enough to give up a woman for a friend; he, Kladzki, would not do that for ten friends, he would not for his born brother, since that was his property, and his own." But Vyadrovski interrupted him; for French novels, with which he was carried away, were another hobby of his on which he cultivated a higher school of galloping over authors and their productions.

"But what enrages me to the utmost," said he, "is this sale of painted foxes for foxes of genuine color. If those gentlemen are realists, let them write the truth. Have you turned attention to their heroines? A tragedy begins, very well! the lady struggles with herself, 'wrestles dreadfully' through half a volume; but, as God lives, I know from the first page what will be, how all will end. What a bore, and how often has it happened before this! I accept those heroines, and their place in literature too; but let no one sell them to me for tragic vestals. What is the tragedy for me, when I know that such rent souls have had lovers before the tragedy, and will have others after it! They will 'struggle' again as they have done already, and everything will end in the same fashion. What a lie, what a loss of moral sense, of truth, what a turning of heads! And to think that among us this stuff is read, this merchandise accepted as genuine; that these drawing-room farces are taken as tragedies, and received as important! In this way, all difference between an honest woman and a harlot is effaced; and a society position is created for puppets without a nest of their own. This French gilding suits our puppets, and they exhibit themselves under the authority of such and such authors. There is no principle in it, no character, no feeling of duty, no moral sense; there is nothing in it but false aspirations, and false posing for a psychological riddle."

Vyadrovski was too intelligent not to understand that by speaking in this fashion he was throwing stones at Pani Elzen; but, being thoroughly malevolent, he spoke so purposely. Pani Elzen listened to his words with all the greater vexation, because there was truth in them. Svirski was burning with a wish to answer rudely; but he knew that he could not take Vyadrovski's words as having any application, so he chose to give a new turn to the conversation.

"In French novels, something else has always struck me," said he; "namely, this, that it is a world of barren women. In other countries, when two people fall in love, either according to law or outside of it, the result is a child; but in French novels, no one has children. How strange this is! It does not seem to occur to those gentlemen who write novels that love cannot remain without results."

"As the society, so the literature," said old Kladzki. "It is known that in France population is decreasing. In the upper society a child — is an exception!"

"Mais c'est plus commode et plus elégant," answered De Sinten.

"The literature of sated idlers who must disappear with it," said Kresovich, who had snorted previously.

"What do you say?" inquired De Sinten.

The student turned his resolute face to the baron, "I say the literature of sated idlers!"

Prince Valerian discovered America a second time. "Every class has its beauties and its pleasures," said he. "I have two passions: politics and photography."

But the dinner was nearing its end; a quarter of an hour later all passed into the adjoining room for coffee. It seemed to Pani Elzen that a certain negligence ought to please Svirski, as he was an artist and somewhat of a gypsy, so she lighted a very slender cigarette, and, leaning on the arm of her easy-chair, crossed her legs. But, being of comparatively low stature, and a trifle broad in the hips, she raised her dress too high by this posture. Young Kladzki dropped his match immediately, and looked for it so long that his uncle punched him slightly in the side, and whispered angrily, —

"What are you thinking of; where are you?"

The young man straightened himself and said in a whisper, "That is what I do not know."

Pani Elzen knew from experience that even well-bred men, when they can take some advantage, become rude in presence of women, especially if those women are unprotected. This time she had not observed young Kladzki's movement; but when she saw the unrestrained and almost cynical smile with which he answered his uncle, she felt convinced that he was talking of her. And in her heart she had a contempt for all that society except Svirski and Kresovich, the tutor, whom she suspected of being in love with her, notwithstanding his hatred for women of her circle.

But that evening Vyadrovski brought her almost to a nervous attack; for it seemed as though for what he had eaten and drunk, he had undertaken to poison every spoonful of her coffee, and every moment of her time. He spoke generally, and as it were objectively, of women, without crossing the bounds of politeness, but at the bottom of his words there was not only cynicism, but a completeness of allusion to Pani Elzen's character and social position, which was simply offensive, and to her, immensely disagreeable, especially before Svirski, who both suffered and was impatient.

A stone fell from her heart, therefore, when at last the guests went away and only the artist remained.

"Aa!" exclaimed she, breathing deeply, "I feel the beginning of neuralgia, and I know not myself what is happening to me."

"They tormented you?"

"Yes, yes — and more than tormented!"

"Why do you invite them?"

She approached him feverishly, as if losing control of her nerves. and said. —

"Sit quietly, do not move! I cannot tell — perhaps I destroy myself in your eyes; but I need this as a medicine. Oh, yes! To remain a moment in this way at the side of an honest man — a moment in this way!"

All at once her eyelids were bedewed abundantly; but she put her finger to her lips time after time as a sign not to speak, and to let her remain silent.

But Svirski was moved, since he had always grown soft as wax at sight of woman's tears. The confidence which she showed him, conquered the man and filled his heart with tenderness. He understood that the decisive moment had come, so, putting his arm around her, he said,—

"Stay with me forever; give me a right to yourself."

Pani Elzen made no answer; great tears were flowing from her eyes, but they were silent tears.

"Be mine," repeated Svirski.

She put her hand on his other shoulder, and nestled up to him as a child to its mother.

Svirski, bending over, kissed her forehead, then he fell to kissing tears from her eyes, and gradually the flame seized him; in a moment he caught her in his athletic arms, pressed her with all his strength to his breast, and sought her lips with his lips. But she defended herself.

"No! no!" said she, with panting voice. "Thou art not like others — later! No! no! Have pity!"

Svirski held her in his embrace; she bent backward; at that moment he was just like other men; happily for Pani Elzen, there was a knock at the door. They sprang apart.

"Who is there?" inquired Pani Elzen, impatiently.

The gloomy head of Kresovich appeared in the doorway.

"Pardon me," said he, in a broken voice. "Romulus is coughing, and perhaps he has a fever; I thought it necessary to inform you."

Svirski stood up.

"Should you not send for a doctor?"

Pani Elzen had recovered her usual self-possession already.

"I thank you," said she; "if necessary, we will send from the hotel; but first I must see the boy. Thank you! but I must go — so till to-morrow! Thank you!"

And she stretched her hand to him, which Svirski raised to his lips.

"Till to-morrow — and every day. Till we meet again!"

Pani Elzen, when alone with Kresovich, looked at him inquiringly, and asked, —

"What is the trouble with Romulus?"

The student grew paler than usual, and answered almost rudely, —

"Nothing."

"What does this mean?" asked she, with a frown.

"It means — dismiss me, otherwise — I shall go mad!" And turning he walked out. Pani Elzen stood for a moment with flashes of anger in her eyes and with wrinkled brows; but her forehead smoothed gradually. She was thirty-five years of age, it is true, but here was a fresh proof that no man had thus far been able to resist her. Next moment she went to the mirror as if to seek in it confirmation of that thought.

Svirski returned to Nice in a car without other passengers; he raised to his face from moment to moment a hand which retained the odor of heliotrope. He felt disturbed, but also happy; and the blood was rushing to his head, for his nostrils were inhaling Pani Elzen's favorite perfume.

CHAPTER III.

NEXT morning the artist woke with a heavy head, as if after a night spent in drinking, and, moreover, with great alarm in his heart. When light falls in the daytime on theatrical decorations, that which seemed magic the night before looks a daub. In life, the same thing takes place. Nothing unexpected had happened to Svirski. He knew that he had been going toward this, that he must go to it; but now, when the latch had fallen, he had a feeling of incomprehensible fear. He understood that as late as yesterday he might have withdrawn; and regret took possession of him. In vain did he repeat to himself that it was not the time for reasoning. Various reproaches which formerly he had made to himself regarding Pani Elzen, and above all regarding marriage with her, returned to him with renewed force. The voice which formerly had whispered unceasingly in his ear, "Do not be a fool!" began to cry, "Thou art a fool!" And he could not put down this voice either by arguments, or by repeating, "It has happened!" for reason told him that the folly had become a fact, and that the cause lay in his own weakness.

At that thought shame possessed him. For had he been young, he would have had youth as his excuse. Had he made the acquaintance of that lady on the Riviera, had he heard nothing of her before, his ignorance of her character and her past would have justified him; but he had met her before. He had seen her rarely, it is true; but he had heard enough, when people in Warsaw spoke more of her than of any one else. She was called there the "Wonder woman," and humorists had sharpened their wits on her, as a knife is sharpened on a grindstone; this, however, had not prevented men from crowding to her salon. Women, though less favorable, received her also out of regard for the remoter or nearer relationship which connected her with the society of the city. Some, especially those whose interest it was that opinion in general should not be too strict, even rose in defence of the beautiful widow. Others, less yielding, still did not dare to close their doors against her, for the reason that they had not courage to take this course earlier than others. Once a local comedy writer, on hearing some one reckon Pani Elzen among the "demi-monde," answered, "She is neither the half world nor the whole world, she is rather three-quarters."

But since everything in great cities is effaced, Pani Elzen's position was effaced in time. Her friends said, "We cannot, of course, ask too much of Helena; but she has her own really good traits" And, without noting it, they conceded greater freedom to her than to other women. At one time it was stated by some one that for a period before the death of her husband, she had not lived with him; at another it was whispered that she was rearing Romulus and Remus like jesters, or that she had no thought for them of any kind; but to such malevolent statements attention would have been turned only if Pani Elzen had been a woman of less beauty and less wealth, or had kept a less hospitable house. Among themselves, men had not been backward in speaking of the "Wonder woman,"—not even those who were in love with her; they talked of her through jealousy; only those were silent who, at the given moment, were fortunate, or who wished to pass as more fortunate than others. In general, malice was such that according to report Pani Helena had one man for the winter in the city, and another for the summer.

Svirski knew all this. He knew it better than other men, for an acquaintance of his in Warsaw, a certain Pani Bronich, a near relative of the beautiful widow, told him of an event painful to Pani Elzen, which ended in a grievous illness. "What that poor Helena suffered, God alone knows; but perhaps in His mercy He brought it about before the time, so as to save her from greater moral suffering." Svirski, however, admitted that this "event before the time" might be a pure invention; still it was less possible for him than for others to be deceived as to Pani Elzen's past, and least of all was it possible for him to believe that she was a woman to whom he could confide his peace with safety.

Still, all these facts roused his curiosity, and drew him to her specially. When he heard of her presence at Monte Carlo, he desired, with intentions not entirely honest, perhaps, to approach her and know her better. He wanted also, as an artist, to analyze the charm exercised on men by that woman, who was talked of everywhere.

But he met only disenchantment from the first. She was beautiful and physically attractive; but he saw that she lacked goodness and kindness toward people. In her eyes a man was of value only in so far as he was useful to her in some way. Beyond that, she was as indifferent as a stone. Svirski did not note in her either any feeling for mental life, art, or literature. She took from them what she needed, giving nothing in return. He, as an artist and a man of thought, understood perfectly that such a relation betrays at the basis of things a nature which, despite all elegant semblances, is vain, rude, and barbarous. But to him women of that kind had been known from of old. He knew that they impose on the world by a certain force which position and a mighty merciless egotism confers. Of that sort of creature, it had been said often in his presence, "A cold, but clever woman." He had always thought of such persons without respect and with contempt. They were to his mind devoid not only of lofty spiritual finish, but of intellect. Beasts have the mind which snatches everything for itself, and leaves nothing to others.

In Pani Elzen, as in Romulus and Remus, he saw a type in which there is no culture below the surface; beneath is an unknown plebeian depth. Beyond that, he was struck by her cosmopolitan character. She was like a coin, so worn that one could hardly discover to what country it belonged. And he was penetrated by disgust, not only as a man of qualities opposite to hers, but also as a man of a society really higher, and who knew that in England, for instance, or France or Italy, people would not deny the soil from which they had grown and would look with contempt on cosmopolitan twigs without a root.

Vyadrovski was right when he said that Romulus and Remus were reared like commercial travellers, or like porters in a great hotel. It was known universally that Pani Elzen's father possessed a title, that was true; but her grandfather was the manager of an estate; and Svirski, who had a high sense of humor, thought it ridiculous that these great-grandsons of a farm bailiff not only did not know Polish well, but like genuine Parisians could not pronounce *r*. They offended him too in his character of an artist. The boys were good-looking, even beautiful; Svirski, however, felt, with his subtle artistic sense, that in those two bird skulls, which resembled each other, and in those faces, the beauty was not inherited through a

series of generations, but was as if by accident, by
physical chance, which had come from their twinship.
In vain did he say to himself that their mother too was
beautiful; the feeling adhered to him always that that
beauty did not belong to the mother or the sons, and that
in this, as in the question of property, they were parvenus.
It was only after long intercourse with them that this
impression was weakened.

Pani Elzen, from the beginning of their acquaintance,
commenced to prefer Svirski and to attract him. He
was of more value to her than the rest of her acquaintances;
he bore a good family name; he had considerable
property and a great reputation. He lacked youth, it is
true; but Pani Elzen herself was thirty-five years of age,
and his form of a Hercules might take the place of
youth. Finally, for a woman who had been mentioned
without respect, to marry him meant the recovery of
honor and position. She might suspect him of other
inclinations and a fickle disposition; but he possessed
kindness and — like every artist — a certain basis of
simplicity in his soul; hence, Pani Elzen thought herself
able to bend him to her will. In the end of ends she was
influenced not by calculation only, but by this too, that
as he let himself be attracted, he attracted her. At last
she said to herself that she loved him, and she even
believed that she did.

With him that happened which happens to many, even
perfectly intelligent people. His reason ceased to act
when his inclinations were roused, or, worse still, it entered
their service; instead of striving to conquer, it
undertook to find arguments to justify them. In this
fashion Svirski, who knew and understood every weak
point, began to make excuses, twisting, mollifying, explaining.
"It is true," thought he, "that neither her nature

nor her conduct, so far, give guarantees; but who can say that she is not tortured by her present life, that she is not yearning with all her soul for another? In her action there is undoubtedly much coquetry; but again who will say that she has not developed that coquetry because she has fallen in love with me sincerely? To imagine that a person, even filled with faults and failings, has no good side, is childish. What a medley is the human soul! There is merely need of proper conditions to develop the good side, and the bad will disappear. Pani Elzen has passed her first youth. What stupidity to suppose that no voice in her is calling for calm, rest, honor, and healing. And just for these reasons perhaps a woman like her values more than others an honest man, who would make her feel certain of all things." This last thought seemed to him uncommonly profound and appropriate. Formerly sound judgment had declared that Pani Elzen wanted to catch him, but now he answered, "She is right; we may say of any woman, even one of the most ideal character, who wishes to unite herself to a man whom she loves, that she wants to catch him." As to the future, the hope also of children quieted him. He thought that he would have something to love, and she would be obliged to break with vain, social life, for she would not have time for it; and before children could grow up, her youth would have passed; after that her house would attract her more than society. Finally, he said, "In every case life must arrange itself; before old age comes I shall live a number of years with an interesting and beautiful woman, near whom every week day will seem a festival."

And those "few years" became in fact the main charm for him. There was something humiliating for Pani Elzen in this, that he feared no extraordinary event for the single **reason** that her youth, and therefore possibilities, must

soon pass. He did not confess this to himself, though
it was the basis of his consolation; and he deceived
himself, as is ever the case with people in whom reason
has become the pander of their wishes.

And now, after the event of the previous evening, he
woke up with immense alarm and disgust. He could not
avoid thinking of two things: first, that if any man had
told him a month before that he would propose to Pani
Elzen, he would have thought that man an idiot;
second, that the charm of relations with her which lay in
uncertainty, in unfinished words, in the mutual divining
of glances and thoughts, in the deferred confessions and in
mutual attractions, was greater than that which flowed
from the present condition. For Svirski it had been
more agreeable to prepare the engagement than to be
engaged; now he was thinking that if in the same
proportion it would be less agreeable to become a husband than to be an affianced, deuce take his fate. At
moments the feeling that he was bound, that he had
no escape, that, whether he wished or not, he must take
Pani Elzen with Romulus and Remus into his life-boat
seemed to him simply unendurable. Not wishing then
as a man of honor to curse Pani Elzen, he cursed Romulus and Remus, with their lisping, their bird-like, narrow
heads and bird-like skulls.

"I have had my cares, but really I have been as
free as a bird, and I could put my whole soul into my
pictures," said he to himself; "now, Satan knows how it
will be!" And the cares of an artist, which he felt at
that moment, spoiled his good-humor, though they turned
his thoughts in another direction. Pani Elzen and the
whole marriage question receded into the second place;
and into the first came his picture, "Sleep and Death,"
on which he had been working for a number of months,

and to which he attributed immense importance. This picture was a protest against the accepted idea of death. Frequently, while talking with artists, Svirski had been indignant at Christianity because it had brought into life and art the representation of death as a skeleton. That seemed to him the greatest injustice. The Greeks had imagined Thanatos [1] as a winged genius; that was correct. What can be more disgusting and frightful than a skeleton? If death be represented in that way, it should not be by Christians, who conceive death as a return to new life. According to Svirski, the present idea was born in the gloomy German soul which created Gothic architecture, — solemn and majestic, but as gloomy as if the church were a passage, not to the glories of heaven, but to underground gulfs. Svirski had marvelled always that the Renaissance had not recreated the symbol of death. Indeed, if Death had not always been silent, and had desired to complain, it would have said, "Why do people depict me as a skeleton? A skeleton is just what I have no wish to be, and will not be!" In Svirski's picture the genius of Sleep was delivering, mildly and quietly, the body of a maiden to the genius of Death, who, bending down, extinguished in silence the flame of a lamp burning at her head.

Svirski when painting had said to himself, "Oh, what wonderful silence there is here!" and he wanted that silence to appear from the lines, the form, the expression, and the color. He thought also that if he could convey that feeling, and if the picture could interpret itself, the work would be both new and uncommon. He had another object also: following the general current of the time, he had convinced himself that painting should avoid literary ideas; but he understood that there was an immense

[1] Death.

difference between renouncing literary ideas, and a passionless reflection of the external world as is shown in photographic plates. Form, color, stain — and nothing more! as if the duty of an artist were to destroy in himself the thinking essence! He recollected that whenever he had seen pictures by English artists, for example, he had been impressed, first of all, by the mental elevation of those artists. It was evident from their canvases that they were masters of a lofty mental culture, greatly developed intellects, thinking deeply, often even learned. In Poles, on the contrary, he saw always something which was directly the opposite. With the exception of a few, or at best of a small number, the generality was composed of men capable, but lacking thought, men of uncommonly small development, and devoid of all culture. They lived, nourished somewhat by crumbs of doctrines falling from the French table, and crumbs which had lost much of their savor. These artists did not admit for a moment that it was possible to think out anything original touching art, and especially to produce original creations in a Polish style. To Svirski, it was clear, also, that a doctrine which enjoins absence of thought must please their hearts. To bear the title of artist, and at the same time be mentally a minor, is convenient. To read, know, think — deuce take such toil!

Svirski thought that if even a landscape is simply a state of soul, that soul should be capable not only of the moods of a Matsek (a peasant), but should be subtle, sensitive, developed, and expanded. He had quarrelled about this with his comrades, and had discussed with them passionately. "I do not require you," said he, "to paint as well as the French, the English, or the Spanish — I demand that you paint better! Above all, that you paint in your own style; whoso does not strive for this should make copper kettles." He showed, therefore, that if a picture represents a stack of hay, or hens scratching in a yard, or a potato field, or horses at pasture, or a corner of sleeping water in a pond, there should, above all, be a soul in it; hence he put into his pictures as much of his own self as he could, and besides he "confessed himself" in other pictures, the last of which was to be Hypnos and Thanatos (Sleep and Death).

The two geniuses were almost finished; but he had no success with the head of the maiden. Svirski understood that she must be not only beautiful, but possess great individuality. Models came who were really good, but not sufficiently individual Madame Lageat, at whose house the artist had taken his studio, and who was an old acquaintance, had promised to find him one, but the work advanced slowly. Some new model was to appear that morning; but she had not come, though it was eleven o'clock.

All this, combined with his yesterday's proposal, caused Svirski to be in doubt touching not only his own peace of mind, but his artistic future in general, and his picture in particular. Hypnos seemed to him at that moment somewhat heavy, Thanatos somewhat stupid. Finally, he thought that since he could not work, he would better stroll to the shore, where a sight of the sea might clear mind and soul.

Just at the moment when he was ready to go, the bell sounded in the entrance, and next appeared in the studio two Scottish plaids, two heads of hair, and the two bird faces of Romulus and Remus; after them came Kresovich, paler than usual and gloomier than ever.

"Good-day, sir! Good-day, sir!" cried the two boys. "Mamma sends these roses and invites you to lunch."

While speaking, they shook bunches of tea and moss

roses, then handed them to Svirski, and began to run about and look at the studio. They wondered especially at the sketches representing naked bodies, and were stopped by them, for they stood before these sketches, and, punching each other with their elbows, said, —

"Tiens!"

"Regarde!"

Svirski, who was angered by this, looked at his watch and said, —

"If we are to be in time for lunch, we must go at once." He took his hat, and they went out. There were no carriages near the studio, so they walked. The artist passed on with Kresovich, and inquired, —

"Well, how are your pupils?"

Kresovich, turning to him his malignant, sneering face, answered, —

"My pupils? Oh, nothing! They are as healthy as fish, and are comfortable in their Scottish dresses. There will be fun with them; but not for me."

"Why so?"

"Because I am going to-morrow."

"Why so?" asked Svirski, with astonishment. "I knew nothing of this; no one mentioned it. I am sorry!"

"They are not sorry," answered Kresovich.

"Perhaps they do not understand."

"They will never understand. Neither to-day, nor at any time in their lives! Never!"

"I hope that you are mistaken," said Svirski, dryly; "but in every case it is unpleasant for me to hear this."

"Yes!" continued the student, as if speaking to himself. "A pity, but a pity for time lost. What do they care for me, or I for them? It is even better that they should be as they will be. A man who wishes to sow wheat must plough in the grass; and the weaker it is, the easier it is to plough it in. Much might be said of this matter; but it is not worth while, especially not for me. The microbes are eating me, anyhow."

"Consumption has never threatened you. Before Pani Elzen asked you to teach, she questioned the doctor about your health — and you should not wonder at that, for she was anxious about her children. The doctor assured her that there was no danger."

"Of course not. I have discovered a certain remedy against microbes."

"What is the remedy?"

"It will be announced in the papers. Such discoveries as that are never hidden under a bushel."

Svirski glanced at Kresovich, as if to convince himself that the man was not speaking in a fever; meanwhile they reached the station, which was swarming with people.

The visitors at Nice were going as usual in the morning to Monte Carlo. At the moment when Svirski was buying a ticket, Vyadrovski saw him.

"Good-morning," said he, coming up; "you are going to the Mountain?"

"Yes. Have you a ticket?"

"I have a monthly one. The train will be crowded."

"We can stand in a passage."

"This is a genuine Exodus, is it not? And each one carries his mite to the widow. Good-morning, Pan Kresovich! What say you of life in this place? Make some remark from the point of view of your party."

Kresovich blinked as if unable to understand what was asked of him, then answered, —

"I enroll myself in the party of the silent."

"I know, I know! — a strong party: it is either silent or explosive," and he laughed.

Meanwhile the bell rang, and there was need of haste. From the platform came the call, "En voiture! en voiture!" The next moment Svirski, Kresovich, Vyadrovski, and the two boys were in the passage of a car.

"With my sciatica this is pleasant!" said Vyadrovski. "See what is going on. Useless to think of a seat. A regular migration of nations!"

Not only the seats, but the passages were crowded with people of every nationality. Poles, Russians, English, French, Germans, all going with a rush to break the bank, which daily repulsed and broke them, as a cliff jutting out from the shore breaks a wave of the sea. Women were crowding up to the windows, — women from whom came the odor of iris and heliotrope. The sun shone on the artificial flowers in their hats, on satin, on lace, on false and genuine diamond ear-rings, on jet glittering like armor on projecting bosoms increased with india-rubber, on blackened brows, and on faces covered with powder or rouge, and excited with the hope of amusement and play. The most practised eye could not distinguish the demi-monde who pretended to be women of society, from women of society who pretended to be of the demi-monde. Men with violets in their buttonholes examined that crowd of women with inquiring and insolent gaze, inspecting their dresses, their faces, their arms, and their hips, with as cool minuteness as if they were inspecting, for example, objects set out for sale. There was in that throng a kind of disorder of the market-place, and a species of haste. One moment the train rushed into the darkness of tunnels, again the sun glittered in the windows, the sky, the sea, palm groves, olive groves, villas, the white almond-trees, and a moment later night embraced all again. Station appeared after station. New crowds thronged into the cars, elegant, exquisite, hurrying on, as it were, to a great, glad festival.

"What a true picture of a breakneck life!" said Vyadrovski.

"What is this true picture?"

"This train. I might philosophize till lunch-time; but since I prefer to philosophize after lunch, perhaps you would consent to lunch with me?"

"Excuse me," answered Svirski; "I am invited by Pani Elzen."

"In that case I withdraw!" And he smiled.

The supposition that Svirski was to marry Pani Elzen had not entered his head for an instant. He felt even certain that the artist was concerned in the same way as others; but, being an admirer of artists in general, and of Svirski in particular, he felt glad that Svirski was beating his opponents.

"I represent property," thought he; "Prince Valerian a title; young Kladzki youth; and De Sinten the world of fashionable fools. All these, especially here, possess no small value, and still the Wonder woman took Svirski. She is surely a person of taste." And looking at the artist he began to mutter, "Jo triumpe, tu moraris aureos currus —"

"What do you say?" inquired Svirski, who had not heard because of the noise of the train.

"Nothing! A hiccough from Horace. I will say that since you refuse me, I will give a breakfast of condolence to myself, De Sinten, Prince Valerian, and Kladzki."

"Indeed! why do you wish to condole?" asked Svirski, pushing forward suddenly, and looking into his eyes almost threateningly.

"For the loss of your society," answered Vyadrovski, coolly. "But, my dear sir, what cause have you in mind?"

Svirski shut his lips and gave no answer; but he thought, "His cap burns the head of a criminal. Were I to marry any ordinary girl of the country, the idea would never have come to my head that any man could have me in mind when speaking with irony and malice."

Pani Elzen, freshened, young, and comely, was waiting for them at the station. It was evident that she had come only the moment before, for she breathed hurriedly, and there was a flush on her face which might be taken for emotion. When she gave Svirski both hands at greeting, Vyadrovski thought, —

"Yes, he has beaten us all by seven lengths. She seems really in love."

And he glanced at her almost favorably. In a white flannel robe, with sailor collar, and with gleaming eyes, she seemed to him, in spite of slight traces of powder on her face, younger and more enchanting than ever. For a moment he was sorry that he was not the happy man whom she had come to greet, and he thought that the method by which he had sought her favor, through relying on the utterance of stinging words, was stupid. But he comforted himself with the thought of how he would sneer at De Sinten and the other "distanced men."

After the greeting, Svirski thanked her for the roses; and she listened with a certain vexation, glancing momentarily at Vyadrovski, as if ashamed that he was a witness of those thanks.

On his part, Vyadrovski understood that he would do better to leave them. But all went together again in a lift up the mountain on which was the Casino and the garden. On the way, Pani Elzen recovered self-control thoroughly.

"To lunch at once! to lunch!" said she, joyously. "I have an appetite like a whale!"

Vyadrovski muttered to himself that he would like, God knows, to be Jonah; but he did not say this aloud, thinking that were Svirski to take him by the collar and throw him out of the lift, as he deserved for his joke, he would fall too far.

In the garden he took leave of them at once, and went his way; but he looked around and saw Pani Elzen lean on Svirski's arm and whisper something in his ear.

"They are talking of the dessert after lunch," thought he.

But he was mistaken, for, turning her charming head to the artist, she whispered, —

"Does Vyadrovski know?"

"He does not," answered Svirski. "I met him only at the train."

When he had said this he felt a certain fear at the thought that Pani Elzen mentioned the betrothal as a fixed fact, and that he would have to announce it to every one; but the proximity of Pani Elzen, her beauty and her charms, so acted on him that he grew serene and took courage.

The lunch was eaten with Romulus, Remus, and Kresovich, who, during a whole hour, said not one word. After black coffee, Pani Elzen permitted her boys to go toward Rocca Brune under guidance of their tutor; then she asked Svirski, —

"Which do you prefer, to ride or to walk?"

"If you are not tired, I would rather walk," answered he.

"Very well. I am not tired at all. But where shall we go? Would you look at the pigeon-shooting?"

"Willingly, but we shall not be alone there. De Sinten and young Kladzki will be sure to exercise after lunch."

"Yes; but they will not trouble us. When pigeons are the question, these two young men grow deaf and blind to all else that happens around them. For that matter, let them see me with my great man!"

And, turning her head, she looked with a smile into his eyes: —

"Doesn't the great man wish that himself?"

"Of course, let them see us!" answered Svirski, raising her hand to his lips.

"Then we will go down; I like well enough to see the shooting."

"Let us go."

And after a while they were on the great steps leading to the shooting gallery.

"How bright it is here! How pleasant and how happy I am!" said Pani Elzen.

Then, though there was no one near them, she asked in a whisper, "But you?"

"My light is with me!" answered he, pressing her arm to his breast.

And they began to descend. The day was uncommonly bright, the air golden and azure; the sea was dark in the distance.

"We will stay here awhile," said Pani Elzen. "The cages are perfectly visible from this spot."

Beneath them was a green half-circle covered with grass, extending far into the sea. In this half-circle were placed, in a curving line on the ground, cages containing pigeons. Moment after moment, some one of those cages was opened suddenly, and a frightened bird rushed through the air; then a shot was heard, and the pigeon fell to the ground, or even into the sea, where boats were rocking with fishermen in them waiting for their prey.

Sometimes it happened, however, that the shot missed. Then the pigeon flew toward the sea, and afterward, moving in a circle, returned to seek refuge in the cornice of the Casino.

"From here we do not see the marksmen, and do not know who fires," said Pani Elzen, joyously, "so we will guess; if the first pigeon falls, we will remain in Monte Carlo; if it escapes, we will go to Italy."

"Agreed. Let us look! Out it comes!"

A cage fell open that instant, but the bird, as if dazed, remained on the spot. They frightened the pigeon by rolling a wooden ball toward it; next a shot thundered. The bird did not fall at once, however; it made straight for the sea, coming down gradually to the surface, as if wounded; but at last it vanished completely in the brightness of the sun.

"Maybe it fell, maybe it did not fall! The future is uncertain," said Svirski, laughing.

"It is that unendurable De Sinten," said Pani Elzen, pouting like an angry child. "I will bet that is he! Let us go down."

And they went farther down toward the shooting, among cactuses, sunflowers, and goat grass clinging to the walls. Pani Elzen stopped at every report of a gun, and in her white robe, on the great steps, against the green background, she looked like a statue.

"There is nothing after all which drops into such splendid folds as flannel," said Svirski.

"Oh, you artist!" exclaimed the young widow. And there was irony in her voice, for she felt a little angered that Svirski at that moment was thinking not of her, but of the folds into which various kinds of cloth fall.

"Let us go."

A few minutes later they were under the roof of the shooting gallery. Of acquaintances they found only De Sinten, who was shooting on a bet with a Hungarian count. The two men were dressed in reddish English costume with caps of the same material buttoned down on the visor, and barred stockings, both very distinguished, both with witless faces. But, as Pani Elzen had foreseen, De Sinten was so occupied with shooting that he did not notice the widow and the artist at first, and only after a time did he come and greet them.

"How are you succeeding?" inquired the lady.

"I am victorious! I am almost sure of a great winning." Here he turned to Svirski. "But do you shoot?"

"Of course; but not to-day."

"And I," continued De Sinten, looking significantly at Pani Elzen, "am to-day lucky in play."

They called him just then to the shooting.

"He wanted to say that he is unlucky in love," said Svirski.

"Imbecile! Could it be otherwise?"

But in spite of these words of blame, it was evident by the face of the beautiful lady that she was not angry that testimony was given in presence of Svirski of how enchanting she was, and how much desired by all, — and that was not to be the last testimony of the day.

"I wanted to ask you about something," said the artist, after a moment of silence; "but I could not ask during lunch in presence of the boys and Kresovich. Kresovich told me on the way that he was leaving you, or, at least, that he is the tutor of the boys for the last day. Is this true, and why is it?"

"It is true. First of all, I am not sure of his health. A few days since I sent him to the doctor. The doctor declared again that he is not threatened with consumption, otherwise I should not have kept him an hour; but in every case he looks worse and worse; he is peculiar, excitable, often he is unendurable. That is the first reason. And, then, do you know his opinions? They will not be accepted by Romulus and Remus. The boys are reared in such fashion that those opinions cannot take root in them. Besides, I do not wish them in childhood to know of such things, to meet with such an erratic spirit, with such ill-will toward that sphere of society to which my sons belong. You wished them to speak with some one in their own language; that was sufficient for me; that was for me a command. This is the kind of person that I am, and such shall I remain. I understood, too, that they ought to know their own language somewhat. At present great attention is given to this subject, and I confess that people are right. But even in this regard Kresovich is too erratic."

"I am sorry for him. There are certain wrinkles in the corners of his eyes which show him to be a fanatic. His face is a strange one, and really he is a curious man."

"Again art is speaking through you," said Pani Elzen, smiling. But after a moment she grew serious, and on her face even anxiety appeared.

"I have another reason," said she. "It is difficult for me to speak of it; but still I will tell you, for with whom am I to be outspoken if not with my great man? — such a loved one, and so honest, who is able to understand everything. You see I have noticed that Kresovich has lost his head, and fallen in love with me to madness; under these conditions he could not remain near — "

"How is that, and he too?"

"Yes," answered she, with downcast eyes.

And she struggled to pretend that the confession caused her pain; but just as a moment before after the words of De Sinten, there flew across her mouth a smile of flattered self-love and feminine vanity. Svirski took note of that smile, and a bitter, angry feeling straitened his heart.

"I have succumbed to the epidemic," said he.

She looked at him a moment, and asked in a low voice, —

"Was that said by a jealous man, or by an ungrateful one?"

"You are right," answered he, evasively. "If that be the position, Kresovich should go."

"I will settle with him to-day, and that will be the end."

They ceased talking; nothing was heard save the shots of De Sinten and the Hungarian. Svirski, however, could not forgive her that smile which he had caught on the wing. He said to himself, it is true, that Pani Elzen was obliged to act with Kresovich as she had acted, that there was nothing over which to be angry — still he felt rising vexation in his soul. On a time, at the beginning of his acquaintance with Pani Elzen, he saw her riding; she was some yards ahead; after her hurried De Sinten, young Kladzki, Prince Valerian, Wilkis Bey, and Waxford. On Svirski, the group produced the fatal impression at the moment, that it was a kind of chase after a woman. At present the picture stood in memory before him so vividly and with such sharpness that his artistic nature suffered really.

"It is absolutely true," said he to himself, "that all are running after her, and if I had been thrown in clearing some obstacle, the next man behind would have caught her."

But further meditation was stopped by Pani Elzen,

who declared that she was growing cold in the shade, and wished to warm herself a trifle in the sun.

"Let us go to your rooms, and do you get a wrap," said Svirski, rising.

They set out for the upper terrace, but halfway on the steps she stopped all at once and said, —

"You are dissatisfied with me. In what have I offended; have I not done what was proper?"

Svirski, whose discontent had calmed somewhat on the way, and who was touched by her alarm, said, —

"Pardon an old original; I beg you to do so."

Pani Elzen wanted absolutely to find out what had made him gloomy, but in no way could she get an answer. Then, half jesting, half sad, she fell to complaining of artists. How unendurable, how strange they are, men whom any little thing offends, any little thing pains; they shut themselves up at once in themselves and then run to their lonely studios! To-day, for instance, she had noted three times, she said, how the artist was in him. That was bad! Let this wicked artist as punishment stay for dinner, then stay till evening.

But Svirski declared that he must return to his studio; then he confided to her his anxieties of an artist, his trouble in finding a model for "Sleep and Death," and finally the hope which he connected with that picture.

"I see from all this," answered the young widow, smiling, "that I shall have one terrible, permanent rival, art."

"That is not a rival," answered Svirski; "it is a divinity which you will serve in my company."

At this the symmetrical brows of the beautiful lady frowned for an instant; but meanwhile they reached the hotel. That day Svirski became convinced that Paradise would open to him only by marriage. And on the train he was thankful to Pani Elzen for that conviction.

CHAPTER IV.

PANI ELZEN, before beginning her toilet for dinner, summoned Kresovich so as to pay him. She summoned him with a certain curiosity in her soul as to what their parting would be. During life, she had seen so many people fashioned, as it were, by a single cutter on one common pattern, that this young original had held her attention for some time; and now, when he was to leave in a little while, and take a broken heart with him, he occupied her still more. She felt sure that his passion would betray itself in some way, and she had even a slightly concealed wish that it should betray itself, promising, not altogether sincerely, that she would restrain it by one look or one word, should it dream of surpassing a certain measure.

Kresovich, however, came in cool, with a face rather ominous than loving. Pani Elzen, when she looked at him, thought that Svirski, as an artist, could not help noting that head, for there was in it something quite exceptional. Those features were as if of iron, — features in which will surpassed intelligence, giving them an expression which to a certain degree was dull, but also implacable. Svirski had divined long before that Kresovich was one of those men who, once seized by a given idea, have a faith which no breath of doubt can ever dim. Doubt never undermines the capacity for action in men like him, for the reason that a persistent and powerful character is joined to a certain narrowness of thought. Fanaticism flourishes on this soil alone. Pani Elzen, in spite of her society understanding, was too frivolous to grasp this. Kresovich would have attracted her attention only had he been an exceptionally handsome fellow; but since he was not, she met the man the first time she saw him as she would a thing; and it was only Svirski's unconscious teaching which brought her to turn attention to the student. At present she received him politely, and, after paying what she owed, in a voice cold, it is true, and indifferent as usual, but with words which were very polite, expressed sorrow that her intended departure from Monte Carlo, soon to take place, was a hindrance to further relations between them. Kresovich, putting the money into his pocket mechanically, answered, —

"I informed you yesterday that I could teach Romulus and Remus no longer."

"It is just that which pleases me," answered she, raising her head.

Evidently she wished, at least at first, to keep the conversation in a ceremonial tone, and impose that tone on Kresovich. But it was enough to look at him to see that he had the unbending determination to say all that he had resolved in his mind to say.

"You have paid me in genuine money," said he; "do not then give me counterfeit coin for the road."

"What do you mean?"

"I mean this," said he, with emphasis; "that you do not part with me because of your journey, nor have I thanked you for the service. There is another cause, and what that is you know as well as I do."

"If I know, perhaps I do not wish to hear of it, nor to mention it," answered Pani Elzen, haughtily.

He approached one step toward her, putting his hands behind him, and rearing his head almost threateningly.

"But it is unavoidable," said he: "first, because in a moment I shall go away, and, second, for other reasons too, of which you will know to-morrow."

Pani Elzen rose with frowning brow and somewhat with the theatrical posture of an offended queen.

"What does this mean?"

He drew still nearer, so that his mouth was barely a few inches from her face, and began to speak with concentrated energy.

"This means that I ought to have hated you and all your circle; but I have fallen in love with you. This means that for your sake I have degraded myself in my own conscience; for this cause I shall mete out my own punishment to myself. But precisely for this reason I have nothing to lose, and you must pay me for my iniquity, otherwise there will be a catastrophe!"

Pani Elzen was not frightened, for in general she had no fear of men. She did not fear Kresovich's consumption either, since the local physician had quieted her perfectly on that point. Her astonishment alone was real; anger and fear were merely apparent. Amazement sprang up in her heart at once, "But he is a bird of prey, ready to tear me to pieces." For her nature, wrapped up as it was in corruption and fond of novelty, every adventure, especially when it flattered her female vanity, had an unspeakable charm. For this cause her moral sense was astonished at nothing. If Kresovich had implored her for one moment of delight, for the right to kiss the hem of her garment with humility, and on his knees, she would have given command to throw him out of doors. But this man, terrible, almost wild, this representative of a sect of whose tremendous energy fabulous tales were related in her social circle, seemed demonic, so different from all men whom she had seen up to that time that she was seized with ecstasy. Her nerves were greedy of novelty. She thought, too, that in case of resistance, the adventure might take on proportions altogether unforeseen, and turn into a scandal; for that lunatic was really ready for anything.

But Kresovich continued, covering her face with his burning breath, —

"I love, and I have nothing to lose. I have lost health, I have destroyed my future, and have demeaned myself! — I have nothing to lose! Do you understand? To me it is all one whether at your call ten men run in here or a hundred; for you it is not all one! Afterward I shall go; and the secret will be lost — I swear!"

Pani Elzen cared only for preserving appearances, which the hypocritical woman always tries to preserve and to deceive herself.

Turning her eyes, filled with feigned terror, to his face, which was really like the face of a madman, she asked, —

"Do you want to kill me?"

"I want pay — not in money!" answered he, in a stifled voice. Then growing paler yet, he seized her in his arms; and she began to defend herself. But she did so like a fainting woman whom terror deprives of strength and consciousness.

CHAPTER V.

SVIRSKI, on arriving at Villa Franca, got out and went to the harbor; for it occurred to him that he might return to Nice by boat. He found, just at the edge of the harbor, a fisherman, an old acquaintance, who, pleased at the sight of a liberal customer, undertook with usual Ligurian boastfulness to take him "even to Corsica though the Sirocco were to turn the sea bottom upward."

But the question was only of a short trip, all the easier because there was not the slightest breeze. Svirski took his place at the stern, and they moved over the smooth sea. After a time, when they had passed the luxurious private yachts, they approached ironclads, whose calm, black immensities were outlined firmly and distinctly in the afternoon sunlight. The deck of the "Formidable" was garlanded already with lamps of various colors, for the ball of the following evening, to which Svirski was to receive an invitation. At the bulwarks were sailors, who, seen from below, looked like pygmies when compared with the ship. The iron walls of the vessel, the smoke-stacks, the masts, the rigging, were reflected in the transparent water as in a mirror. From time to time among the ironclads pushed a boat, which from a distance seemed a black beetle, moving its row of legs symmetrically. Beyond the vessels began empty space, in which the sea surface, as is usual when anything leaves the harbor, rose and fell, though there was no wind, now raising, now letting down Svirski's boat, with a movement at once broad and agreeable. Soon they were approaching lofty cliffs, on the right side of the harbor, along which extended a gray, dusty road; lower down was a parade-ground, where

ON THE BRIGHT SHORE. 449

soldiers were practising on trumpets. At last, when they had turned the promontory, against which waves were rolling, they sailed into deep water.

Beyond the harbor there is always some breeze, therefore the fisherman hoisted his sails. Svirski, instead of steering toward Nice, turned to the open sea.

They went straight ahead, rocked by the swell. The sun was lowering toward evening. The rocky cliffs and the sea had grown purple; everything round about was calm, quiet, and so immense that, in spite of himself, Svirski thought how contemptible and petty life was in view of those elements which surrounded him at that moment. Suddenly he felt as if his own affairs, and those of other men, had gone somewhere very far off. Pani Elzen, Romulus, Remus, and all his acquaintances along the shore, all that swarm of people filled with fever, unrest, paltry ambitions, and wretched desires, were belittled in his eyes. As a man accustomed to analyze what happens within him, he was frightened at that impression; for he considered that if he loved Pani Elzen really, her portrait would not be covered by anything, would not be dimmed, would not be decreased, would not disappear. Such had been the case with him formerly. Svirski remembered that when a woman whom he loved got married, he went on a journey. At that time he learned first to know Italy, Rome, Sicily, and the sea, and the coast of Africa; and no impression dimmed in his mind the memory of the beloved woman. In the galleries of Florence and Rome, on the sea and in the desert, she was with him; through her he received every impression, and everywhere he said to her, as if present, "Look at this!" The difference between those distant years and to-day filled him with sadness.

But the calm of the sea acted on him in a manner that

was healing. They had sailed out so far that the shores began to be concealed. Then the sun went down; one star twinkled, and then another. The dolphins, which in the evening twilight passed before the boat with the motion of waves, disturbing the calm surface with their sharp backs, sank in the depth, and from no point came an echo. The surface of the water had grown so smooth that at moments the sails became limp. Finally, the moon rose from beyond the mountains, pouring a greenish light over the sea and illuminating it far off to the limit of the horizon.

A southern night began, as mild as it was silent. Svirski sheltered himself in the coat lent him by the fisherman, and meditated: "All that surrounds me is not only beauty, but truth as well. The life of man, if it is to be normal, should be ingrafted on the trunk of nature, grow out of it, as a branch grows out of a tree, and exist in virtue of those same laws. Then it will be truthful and besides moral, for morality is at bottom nothing else than the agreement of life with the universal law of nature. For instance, simplicity and calm surrounds me; I understand this, and I feel it is as an artist; but I have n't it in myself as a man, for my life, and the life of these people among whom I live, has departed from nature, it has ceased to fit itself to that law, to be its result, and has made itself a lie. Everything in us is artificial, even the feeling of natural laws has perished in us. Our relations are founded on falsehood. Our senses are crooked; our souls and our impulses sick. We deceive one another and even ourselves, till at last no man is sure that he wishes really that toward which he is striving, or that he will strive toward that which he wishes."

And there, in presence of that night, of that infinity of

the sea, of the stars, of all nature, of its calmness, its simplicity, its immensity, he was seized by a feeling of the gigantic falsehood of the relations between men. False seemed to him his love for Pani Elzen; false her relation to him, to her children, to other men, to society; false the life on that bright shore; false their present and false their future. "I am encircled, as if by a net," thought he; "and I know not how to tear myself out of it." And indeed that was true. For if all life is a falsehood, what is to be done in face of that fact? Return to nature? Begin some sort of life half savage, half peasant? Break with people and become a reformer right away? Svirski felt too old for this, and too sceptical. For such a course one needs to have the dogmatism of Kresovich, and to feel evil as a spur to battle and reform, not as a mere impression which may grow faint to-morrow! But another thought came to Svirski's mind as a recompense. The man who does not feel in himself power to reform the world, may flee from it, for a time, at least, and draw breath. For instance, he could go to Marseilles the next day, and a couple of days later somewhere else, out on the open ocean, hundreds of miles from the shore, from sickly life, from lies and deceptions. In this way all would be settled immediately, or rather cut off as if with a knife.

And in one moment he was seized by such a desire to turn that idea into action that he gave command to return to Nice.

"The wild beast, which feels itself in a net," thought he, "tries first of all to get out. That is its first right — and just that is in accord with nature, hence it is moral. The net around me is not Pani Elzen alone, but all things taken together. I feel perfectly that in marrying her I shall marry a life of lies. That might happen even without her fault, and through the necessity of things — from such a complication one is always free to escape."

And now he pictured other scenes to himself, — scenes which he might see in his flight: broad deserts with water and with sand, unknown lands and people, the sincerity and truth of their primitive life, and finally the variety of events, and all the difference between days to come and the present.

"I ought to have done this long since," said he to himself.

Then a thought entered his mind which could come only to an artist, that if he should leave his betrothed suddenly and go to Paris, for example, the act would belong to "vile literature;" but should he shoot off beyond the equator, to the land where pepper grows, the fact of leaving her would be diminished in view of the distance, the affair would make another impression, would appear more original, and, for that very reason, in better taste.

"But I," thought he, "will go devilish far!"

Meanwhile from a distance Nice rose before him in the form of a bundle of lights. In the middle of that bundle was the building called "Jetée Promenade," which gleamed in the form of a gigantic lighthouse. As the boat, urged by a strong breeze, approached the harbor, every one of those lights changed, as it were, into a pillar of fire, which quivered on the moving water near the shore. The sight of these gleams sobered Svirski.

"The city! — and life!" thought he.

And at once his former plans began to fall apart like dream-visions born of night and emptiness. That which a moment earlier he thought justifiable, necessary, and easy of accomplishment, seemed a whim devoid of the essence of reality, and in part dishonest. "With life, whatever it be, one must reckon. Whoso has lived under its laws the years that I have, must feel responsible to it. It is no great thing to say to one's self: I used them as long as they were pleasant, but the moment they were painful I went back to nature."

Then he fell to thinking more connectedly, not of general theories, but of Pani Elzen.

"By what right could I leave her? If her life has been artificial and false, if her past is not clear, I, who knew that, might have refrained from proposing. At present I could have the right to break with her only in case I discovered in her evil which she concealed, or if she committed some fault touching me. But she has committed no fault of that sort. She has been honest and sincere with me. Besides, there is something in her which attracts me; if not, I should not have proposed. At moments I feel that I love her; and because doubt comes at times on me, must she be the sufferer? My flight would in every case be an injustice to the woman, and who knows that it would not be a blow."

He understood now, that to think of flight and permit it are, for a decent man, two opposite poles. He could only think of it. He could appear before the eyes of Pani Elzen more easily, and ask her to return his word to him; but to flee from danger was a thing directly opposed to his personal nature and the character of his stock, which was thoroughly civilized. Besides, at the very thought of doing injustice to a woman, the heart quivered in him; and Pani Elzen grew nearer and dearer to him.

They had sailed almost into the harbor; and a moment later the boat arrived. Svirski paid, and taking a seat in a carriage, gave directions to drive to his studio. On the street, amid the glare of lamps, the noise and the movement, he was carried away again by a yearning for that quiet, that endless spread of water, that calmness, that boundless truth of God, from which he had parted a moment before. At last, when he was near the studio, the following idea came to his head: "It is a marvellous thing that I, who feared women so much, and was so distrustful of them, have in the end of ends chosen one capable of rousing more fear than all the others."

There was in that a certain fatality, as it were; and Svirski would have found beyond doubt in that concourse of things material for meditation during a whole evening, had it not been that as he entered the servant gave him two letters. In one, was an invitation to the ball of the following day on board the "Formidable," the other was from Pani Lageat, the owner of the house.

She informed him of her departure in a couple of days for Marseilles, and at the same time told him that she had found a model who ought to satisfy his most extravagant taste, and who would come the next morning.

CHAPTER VI.

THE promised miracle came on the following morning at nine. Svirski was dressed and waiting with impatience and nervousness; happily his fears proved unfounded. The first glance satisfied him. The model was tall, slender, very graceful; she had a small head, a delicate face, a beautiful structure of forehead, long eyelashes, and great freshness of complexion. But, beyond all, Svirski was charmed by this, that she had "her own" style of face, and in her expression there was something girl-like. "She has noble movements," thought he; "and if she is formed as she seems, then 'Eureka!' I will engage her for a long time, and take her with me."

He was struck also by her timidity and a look, as it were, of fright. He knew, it is true, that models sometimes feign timidity. He admitted, however, that this one did not.

"What is thy name, my child?" asked he.

"Maria Cervi."

"Art thou from Nice?"

"From Nice."

"Hast ever been a model?"

"No, sir."

"Trained models know what is needed; with new ones there is trouble. Thou hast never been a model in thy life?"

"No, sir."

"How didst thou get the wish to be a model?"

She hesitated, and blushed somewhat.

"Pani Lageat told me that I should be able to earn something."

"True, but evidently thou art afraid. What dost thou fear? I will not eat thee! How much dost thou ask for a sitting?"

"Pani Lageat told me that you would pay five francs."

"Pani Lageat was mistaken. I pay ten."

Joy gleamed in the girl's face, and her cheeks grew still redder.

"When must I begin?" asked she, with a somewhat trembling voice.

"To-day, immediately," answered Svirski, pointing to the picture already begun. "There is the screen; go behind, undress to the waist only. Thou wilt sit for the head, the bosom, and a part of the stomach."

She turned to him an astonished face; her hands dropped slowly along her dress.

"How is that, sir?" asked she, looking at him with terrified eyes.

"My child," answered the artist, a little impatiently, "I understand that it may be difficult the first time. But either thou art a model, or thou art not. I need the head, the bosom, and a part of the stomach; I need these absolutely; dost thou understand? And be sure, at the same time, that there is nothing bad in me; but, first of all, think it over — and quickly; for, if thou art not willing, I shall look for another."

He spoke as a man somewhat vexed; for in his mind the point was that just she should be the model, and that he should not have to look for another. Meanwhile silence came. The model grew pale very evidently; still, after a while, she went behind the screen.

Svirski fell to pushing the easel toward the window, with a noise, thinking, meanwhile, —

"She will gain the habit, and in a week will laugh at her scruples."

Next, he arranged the sofa on which the model was to lie, took his brush, and began to grow impatient.

"Well, how is it? Art thou ready?"

Silence.

"Well, make up thy mind. What jokes are these?"

Just then from behind the screen came a trembling, imploring voice, with the prayer, —

"I have thought it over, sir. In our house there is poverty; but still — I — cannot! If you would be kind and take the head — for three francs, or even for two — if you would have the kindness."

And these words came with sobbing. Svirski turned toward the screen, dropped his brush, and opened his mouth. Unparalleled astonishment seized him, for the model was speaking in his own native tongue.

"Is the lady a Pole?" asked he at last, forgetting that a moment before he had said *thou* to her.

"Yes, sir. That is, my father was an Italian, but my grandfather is a Pole."

A moment of silence ensued. Svirski recovered, and said, —

"Arrange your dress; I will take only your head."

But evidently she had not begun to undress, for she came from behind the screen at once, confused, full of fear yet, and with traces of tears on her cheeks.

"I thank you," said she. "You are — I beg your pardon; but — "

"Be at rest," said Svirski. "Here is the chair; have no fear. You will pose for your head; I had no wish to offend you. You see that picture. I wanted a model for this figure here. But since it is so painful to you, the question is changed, especially as you are a Pole."

Tears began to flow over her cheeks again; but she looked at him through her blue eyes with gratitude; he found a bottle of wine, poured out half a glass, and, giving it to her, said, —

"Drink this. I have biscuits here somewhere, but deuce knows where they are. I ask you to drink. There, it is all right. Your hand trembles; but there is no danger here — I beg you to be calm."

And saying this he looked at her with the sympathy of his honest eyes, and said after a while, —

"Poor child!"

Then he stepped aside, and put the easel in its old place, saying while he did so, —

"There is no posing to-day. You are too much excited. To-morrow, we will begin work early; to-day, we will talk a little. Who could guess that Maria Cervi was a Pole! Your grandfather is a Pole then, is he not? Is he alive?"

"Yes; but he has not walked for the last two years."

"What is his name?"

"Orysevich," answered she, speaking somewhat with a foreign accent.

"I know that name. Has he been long in this country?"

"Grandfather has been sixty-five years out of Poland. First, he was in the Italian army, and then in the bank of Nice."

"How old is he?"

"Nearly ninety."

"Your father's name was Cervi?"

"Yes. My father was from Nice; but he served also in the Italian army."

"Then he is dead?"

"Five years."

"And your mother is alive?"

"She is. We live together in Old Nice."

"Very well. But now one more question. Does your mother know that you want to become a model?"

To this the girl answered in a hesitating voice, "No, mamma does not know. Pani Lageat told me that in this way I could earn five francs a day; and as there is poverty in our house, — very great poverty, — I had no other way."

Svirski took in the girl from head to foot with quick glance, and understood that he was listening to truth. Everything testified to poverty, — her hat, her dress, which was so worn, or rather consumed by age, that every thread in it was visible, her gloves, darned and faded.

"Go home now," said he, "and tell your mother that there is an artist named Svirski who wishes you to sit to him as a model for the head. Say also that this artist will come, at recommendation of Pani Lageat, to ask you to sit with your mother in his studio, for which he offers you ten francs a day."

Panna Cervi began to thank him, without knowing how to find speech, weeping and confusing her words, with a voice full both of tears and delight. He saw what was happening within her, and said, —

"Very well. I shall come in an hour. You seem to me a very honest girl. Have confidence in me. I am something of a bear, but I understand more things than one. We shall arrange this affair, and the trouble will pass. Ah! yes, one point more. I do not wish to give you money at once, for you would have to explain the matter; but in an hour I will bring all that is needed on account. I too had troubles formerly, and know what prompt aid means. You have nothing to give thanks for, a trifle! Till we meet again — in an hour."

So, after he had asked again for her address, he conducted the girl to the steps; and, when an hour had passed, he took his seat in a carriage and gave directions to drive to Old Nice.

All that had happened seemed to him so peculiar that he could think of nothing else. He felt too the delight which every honest man feels when he has acted as he ought, and when he may become a providence to some person.

"If that is not an honest and a good girl," thought he of Panna Cervi, "I am the dullest mule in Liguria."

But he did not admit that anything similar could

happen. On the contrary, he felt that he had struck a
very honest woman's soul, and at the same time he was
delighted that that soul was enclosed in such a young
and beautiful body.

The carriage stopped at last in front of an old and
battered house near the harbor. The woman at the gate
pointed contemptuously enough to Pani Cervi's apartments.

"Poverty indeed!" thought the artist, as he went up
the sloping steps. After a while he knocked at the
door.

"Come in!" answered a voice.

Svirski entered. A woman about forty years of age
received him; she was dressed in black; a brunette, sad,
thin, evidently broken by life: but she had nothing
common about her. At her side stood Panna Maria.

"I know all, and I thank you from my soul and
heart!" said Pani Cervi; "may God reward and bless
you."

Thus speaking, she caught his hand and bent her head
as if to kiss it; but he withdrew the hand quickly;
anxious to drive away ceremony at the earliest, and
break the ice of first acquaintance, he turned to Panna
Maria, and, shaking his finger at her, said, with the
freedom of an old acquaintance, —

"Ah, this little girl has let out the secret!"

Panna Maria smiled at him in answer, a little sadly,
a little perplexed. She seemed to him fair, more beautiful than in the studio. He noticed also that she had
around her neck a narrow, lily-colored ribbon which she
had not worn before; and this touched him still more
as a proof that evidently she did not consider him an
old grandfather, since she had dressed for him. Then
Pani Cervi said, —

"Yes, Maria told everything. God watched over her, and over us, so that she met such a man as you."

"Panna Maria told me of the difficult circumstances in which you are living," answered Svirski; "but, believe me, that even in those circumstances it is happiness to have such a daughter."

"Yes," said Pani Cervi, calmly.

"Meanwhile I owe gratitude to you; for I was looking, and looking in vain, till at last a head fell from heaven to me. Now I am sure of my picture. I must only make sure that my model does not run away!"

Meanwhile, he drew out three hundred francs and forced Pani Cervi to take them, assuring her that he would make a great profit, for he would receive much money, thanks to Panna Maria; and then he declared that he would like to make the acquaintance of the "grandfather," for he had always had a weakness for old soldiers.

Hearing this, Panna Maria ran to the adjoining chamber; soon the noise of a wheeled chair was heard, and the grandfather was rolled into the room. Evidently the old man had been prepared to receive the guest, for he was in uniform, with all his orders acquired in Italy. Svirski saw before him an old man whose face had grown small and wrinkled; his moustaches and hair were white as milk; his blue eyes opened widely, and looked something like the eyes of an infant.

"Grandfather," said Maria, bending over him in such fashion that the old man could see her lips, and speaking not in a loud voice, but slowly and precisely, "this is Pan Svirski, a fellow-countryman and an artist."

The old man turned his blue eyes toward the visitor, and looked at him persistently, meanwhile blinking as if summoning his mind.

"A fellow-countryman?" repeated he. "Yes!— a fellow-countryman."

Then he smiled, looked at his daughter, his granddaughter, and again at Svirski; he sought words for a time, and asked at last, with an aged, trembling voice, —

"And what will there be in spring?"

Evidently there remained to him some single thought, which had outlived all the others, but which he had not been able to express. So, after a while, he leaned his trembling head against the back of the chair, and began to look at the window, smiling, however, at that thought, and repeating, —

"Yes, yes! It will be!"

"Grandfather always acts that way," said Maria.

Svirski looked at him for a time with emotion; then Pani Cervi began to speak of her father and her husband. Both had taken part in the wars against Austria for Italian independence. They had lived some time in Florence; and only after the occupation of Rome did they return to Nice, where Cervi's family originated. There Orysevich gave his daughter to his young comrade in arms. Both men found places in the bank, thanks to relatives in Nice. All succeeded well till Cervi was killed in a railroad accident, a few years before, and Orysevich lost his place through old age. From that time their trouble began, for the only capital which the three persons had to support them was sixty lires, which the Italian government gave the old man. That was enough to keep them from dying, but not enough to give them life. The two women earned a little by sewing or teaching; but during summer, when life died away in Nice, when it was impossible to earn anything, their slender supplies were swallowed up. Two years before the old soldier had lost the use of his legs altogether; he was frequently sick, and had to be cared for; through this their condition grew worse and worse.

Svirski, while listening to this narrative, made note of two things. First, that Pani Cervi did not speak as good Polish as her daughter. Evidently the old man, in the years of his campaigning, could not devote himself to the education of his daughter in the same degree as he had afterward to the education of his granddaughter. But the second thing was more important for Svirski. "This granddaughter," thought he, " being such a beautiful girl, might, especially in Nice, on that shore where idlers squander millions every year, keep carriages, servants, and have a drawing-room finished in satin. But she wears a threadbare dress, and her only ornament is a faded lily-colored ribbon. There must be some strength which has kept her from evil. For this," said he to himself, " two things are requisite, — pure nature and honorable traditions; there is no doubt that I have found both."

And he began to have a pleasant feeling among those people. He noticed also that poverty had not destroyed in the two women traces of good-breeding, a certain elegance which comes from within and seems inborn. Both mother and daughter had received him as a providence; but in their words and manners one could notice more delight at making the acquaintance of an honest man, than at the aid which he brought them. It might be that the three hundred francs which he left with the mother saved the family from many cares and humiliations, but still he felt that mother and daughter were more thankful to him because he had acted in the studio like a man of true and tender heart, who understood the girl's pain, her modesty, and sacrifice. But to him the greatest pleasure came from noting that in Panna Maria's timidity, and in her charming glances, there was an anxiety which a young girl might experience before a man to whom she feels obliged with her whole soul, but who at the same time, according to Svirski's expression, " is not out of the current yet." He was forty-five years of age, but, in spite of a young heart, he began at moments to doubt himself, so that the lily-colored ribbon and this observation caused him real pleasure. Finally, he talked to them with the same respect and attention as with women of the best society, and, seeing that he entertained them more and more by this means, he felt satisfied. At parting, he pressed the hands of both; and when Panna Maria returned the pressure, with drooping eyelashes, but with all the strength of her warm young hand, he went out a little dazed, and with a head so full of the fair model that the driver of the carriage in which he took a seat had to ask him twice where he wished to go.

On the road he thought that it would not do to put the head of "Panna Maria" on a body naked to the waist, and he began to persuade himself that even for the picture it would be better to cast some light drapery over the bosom of the sleeping maiden.

"When I get back, I will bring in the first model I find, and work the picture over, so that to-morrow the thing will be ready," said he to himself.

Then it occurred to him that still he would not be able to hire such a model as Panna Cervi permanently and take her with him; at this thought he was sorry.

Meanwhile the carriage stopped at the studio. Svirski paid, and stepped out.

"A despatch for you," said the concierge.

The artist was roused as if from sleep.

"Ah! Very well, give it here!" And taking the despatch, he opened it impatiently.

But he had scarcely cast his eyes on it, when astonishment and terror were reflected on his face, for the telegram was as follows:—

Kresovich shot himself an hour ago. Come.
Helena.

CHAPTER VII.

PANI ELZEN met Svirski with a troubled and excited face; her eyes were dry, but reddened, as if from fever, and full of impatience.

"Have you received no letter?" inquired she, hurriedly.

"No. I have received nothing but your telegram. What a misfortune!"

"I thought that perhaps he had written to you."

"No. When did it happen?"

"This morning a shot was heard in his chamber. A servant ran in and found him lifeless."

"Was it here in the hotel?"

"No. Fortunately he moved to Condamine yesterday."

"What was the cause?"

"How am I to know?" answered she, impatiently.

"So far as I have heard he was not given to play."

"No. They found money on his person."

"You relieved him of his duties yesterday?"

"Yes; but at his own request."

"Did he take the dismissal to heart?"

"I cannot tell," answered she, feverishly. "If he had wished, he might have gone sooner. But he was a madman, and this explains everything. Why did he not go sooner?"

Svirski looked at her very attentively.

"Calm yourself," said he.

But she, mistaken as to the meaning of his words, answered, —

"There is so much that for me is disagreeable in this, and there may be so much trouble. Who knows but I shall have to give some explanation, some evidence — can I tell what? Oh, a fatal history! — besides there will be people's gossip. First, Vyadrovski's — But I wanted to beg you to tell among acquaintances, that that unfortunate lost at play, that he lost even some of my money, and that that was the cause of his act. Should it come to testifying before a court, it would be better not to say this, for it might be proved untrue; but before people, it is necessary to talk so. If he had gone even to Mentone, or to Nice! Besides, God only knows whether he has not written something before his death purposely to take revenge on me! Only let a letter of that sort reach the papers after his death! From such persons everything may be expected. As it was, I wished to leave here; but now I must—"

Svirski looked more and more attentively at her angry face, at her compressed lips, and said at last, —

"An unheard of thing!"

"Really unheard of! But would it not increase gossip were we to go from here to-morrow?"

"I do not think it would," said Svirski.

Then he inquired about the hotel in which Kresovich had shot himself, and declared that he would go there, get information from the servants, and occupy himself with the dead man.

She tried to stop him with uncommon stubborness; till at last he said, —

"Madame, he is not a dog, but a man; and it is necessary in every case to bury him."

"Somebody will bury him anyhow," answered she.

But Svirski took leave of her and went out. On the steps of the hotel he drew his hand across his forehead, then covered his head with his hat and said, —

"An unheard of thing!"

He knew from experience to what degree human selfishness may go; he knew also that women in selfishness, as well as in devotion, surpass the common measure of men; he remembered that during life he had met typical persons in whom, under an external crust of polish, was hidden an animal selfishness in which all moral sense ended exactly where personal interest began; still, Pani Elzen had been able to astonish him.

"Yes," said he to himself, "that unfortunate was the tutor of her children; he lived under the same roof with her; and he was in love with her. And she? Not even one word of pity, of sympathy, of interest — Nothing and nothing! She is angry at him for causing her trouble, for not having gone farther away, for having spoiled her season, for exposing her to the possibility of appearing in court and of being subjected to the gossip of people; but the question of what took place with that man has not entered her head; or why he killed himself, and if it were not for her sake. And in her vexation she forgot even this, that she was betraying herself before me; and if not for her heart's sake, for her reason's sake, she ought to have appeared before me differently. But what spiritual barbarism! Appearances, appearances, and under that French bodice and accent, absence of soul and a primitive African nature, — a genuine daughter of Ham. Civilization stuck onto the skin, like powder! And this same woman asks me to report around that he played away her money. Tfu! May a thunderbolt split her!"

With such thoughts and imprecations he reached Condamine, where he found easily the little hotel in which the event had taken place. There was a doctor in Kresovich's room, also an official of the tribunal, who rejoiced at the artist's arrival, hoping that he would be able to give some items concerning the dead man.

"The suicide," said the official, "left a letter directing to bury him in a common ditch so as to send the money on his person to Zürich, to a given address. Moreover, he has burned all papers, as is shown by traces in the chimney."

Svirski looked at Kresovich, who was lying on the bed with open, terrified eyes, and with lips pursed together, as if to whistle.

"The dead man considered himself an incurable," said the artist; "he mentioned that himself to me, and took his life very likely for that reason. He never entered the Casino."

Then he told all that he knew concerning Kresovich, and afterward left the money needed for a separate grave, and went out.

Along the road he recalled what Kresovich had said to him in Nice about microbes, as well as his answer to Vyadrovski, that he would enroll himself in the party of the "silent;" and he reached the conviction that the young student had really occupied himself for a long time with the project of taking his own life, and that the main cause of his act was the conviction that he was condemned to death in every case.

But he understood that there might be collateral causes, and among them his unhappy love for Pani Elzen, and the parting with her. These thoughts filled him with sadness. The corpse of Kresovich, with lips fixed as if for whistling, and with the terror before death in his eyes, did not leave the artist's mind. But he thought that no one would sink into that terrible night without dread, and that all life, in view of the inevitableness of death, is one immense, tragic absurdity; and he returned to Pani Elzen in great depression of spirit.

She drew a deep breath of relief when she learned that Kresovich had left no papers. She declared that she would send as much money as might be needed for his funeral; and only then did she speak of him with a certain regret. She strove in vain, however, to detain Svirski for a couple of hours. He answered that he was not himself that day, and must return home.

"Then we shall meet in the evening," said she, giving him her hand at parting. "I intended even to drop in at Nice and go with you."

"Where?" asked Svirski, with astonishment.

"Have you forgotten? To the 'Formidable.'"

"Ah! Are you going to that ball?"

"If you knew how weighed down I am, especially after such a sad event, you would weep over me. I am sorry, too, for that poor fellow; but it is necessary — it is necessary even for this reason, that people should not make suppositions."

"Is it? Till we meet again!" said Svirski.

And a moment later, while sitting in the train, he said to himself, —

"If I go with you to the 'Formidable,' or any other place, I am a dead crab!"

CHAPTER VIII.

BUT next morning, he received Pani Cervi and Panna Maria with a gladder heart. At sight of the fair, fresh face of the girl even delight seized him.

Everything had been prepared in the studio: the easel was in its place; the sofa for the model pushed forward and covered properly. Pani Lageat had received the strictest command not to admit any one, not even "Queen Victoria herself," should she come. Svirski now opened and now closed the curtains which hid the window of the skylight; but while drawing the cords he looked unceasingly at his charming model.

Meanwhile the ladies removed their hats, and Panna Maria inquired, —

"What must I do now?"

"First of all, it is necessary to let down your hair," said Svirski.

He approached her, and she raised both hands to her head. It was clear that this confused her somewhat, and seemed strange, but also nice. Svirski gazed at her confused face, at her drooping eyelashes, at her form bent backward, at her exquisite outline of hips, and said to himself that, in that great dust heap of Nice, he had discovered a genuine double pearl.

The hair fell, after a moment, on her shoulders. Panna Maria shook her head, wishing to spread her hair, which then covered her completely.

"Corpo Dio!" exclaimed Svirski.

Then came the turn for a more difficult task, — placing the model.

Svirski saw plainly that her heart was beating with more life in the maiden, that her breast was moving more quickly, that her cheeks were flushed, that she had to conquer herself and overcome an instinctive resistance, which she herself could not define, and at the same time she was yielding with a certain alarm which resembled an unknown delight.

"No! this is no common model," said Svirski to himself; "this is something else; and I am not looking on her merely as an artist." In fact, he also felt troubled, and his fingers trembled a little while he was placing her head on the pillow; but, wishing to save her and himself from embarrassment, he spoke to her jestingly, feigning temper.

"Lie quietly, in that way! Besides, we must do something for art. Oh, the position is perfect now! In this way the profile comes out beautifully on the red background. If you could see it! But that cannot be. You must not laugh! You must sleep. Now I will paint."

And he began to paint; but while painting he chatted, as his custom was, told stories, and asked Pani Cervi of past times. He learned from her that "Maria" had held a good position the year before as reader for a Polish countess, the daughter of a great manufacturer of Lodz, Atrament by name; but the position lasted only till the countess learned that Maria's father and grandfather had served in the Italian army. This was a great disappointment, for the dream of mother and daughter had been that Maria should hold such a place with some lady who passed every winter in Nice; for in that case they would have no need to separate.

The artist was roused in Svirski meanwhile. He wrinkled his brows, concentrated his mind, looked across the handle of the brush, and painted persistently. From time to time he laid down the pallet, approached the model, and, taking her lightly by the temples, corrected the position of her head. At such movements he bent toward her more nearly perhaps than was required by the interest of art; and, when the warmth from her youthful body struck him, when he looked at her long eyelashes and her lips slightly parted, a quiver went through his bones, his fingers began to tremble nervously, and in spirit he called to himself, —

"Hold up, old man! What the deuce is this? hold up!"

She simply pleased him with his whole soul. Her confusion, her blushes, her timid glances, which still were not devoid of maiden coquettishness, made him happy beyond expression. All this proved to Svirski that she did not look on him as too old. He felt that he pleased her also. The grandfather in his time must have told her wonderful things about his countrymen; he had roused her imagination, perhaps; and now at last one of them had come in her way — not some common man, but one honorable and famous, who, besides, had appeared as in a fairy tale, at the moment of direst need, with assistance and an honest heart. How could she help feeling sympathy for him and looking at him with interest and gratitude?

All this caused the time to pass for Svirski till midday in such a manner that he did not even notice it. But at midday Panna Maria was the first to declare that she must return, for her grandfather was alone, and it was time to think of lunch for him. Svirski then begged the ladies to come in the afternoon. If they could not leave the old man alone, perhaps they had an acquaintance who would consent to stay with him for two hours. Maybe the gatekeeper, or her husband, or some one else of the family would do so? It was a question of the picture. Two sittings a day would be an excellent thing! After that there might be some new work; meanwhile, two sittings a day would be useful for both sides. If there should be expense in finding some one to care for the old man, he, Svirski, would consider it a favor if he were permitted to bear it, for first of all he was anxious about the picture.

Two sittings were really too profitable to be refused by Pani Cervi in view of poverty at home. It was agreed, therefore, that they would come at two in the afternoon. Meanwhile the fortunate Svirski resolved to conduct them home. At the gate they were met by his hostess, who gave Svirski a bunch of moss roses, saying that they were brought by two handsome boys attended by a wonderfully dressed servant. The boys wanted absolutely to enter the studio; but she, remembering his command, did not permit them.

Svirski answered that she had done well, then, taking the roses, he gave them all to Panna Maria. After a while they were on the Promenade des Anglais. To Svirski, Nice seemed beautiful and animated in a way that he had never seen before. The variety and bustle on the "Promenade," which had angered him at other times, began now to amuse him. On the way he saw Vyadrovski and De Sinten, who halted at sight of him. Svirski bowed and went on, but in passing he noted how De Sinten put a monocle to his eye to look at Panna Cervi, and heard his "Prristi!"[1] full of astonishment. Both even followed them awhile, but opposite the "Jetée Promenade" Svirski called a carriage and took the ladies home.

On the way, he was seized by a desire to invite the whole family to lunch; but he thought that there would be trouble with the old man, and that, in view of their short acquaintance, Pani Cervi might be surprised at such a sudden invitation. But he promised himself that when the grandfather had some person to care for him he would, under pretext of saving time, arrange a lunch in the studio. Taking leave of the mother and daughter at the gate, he hurried into the first hotel he found and

[1] For the French *Sapristi*.

ordered lunch. He swallowed a few kinds of food, without knowing himself what he was eating. Pani Elzen, Romulus, and Remus, with the moss roses, shot through his mind repeatedly, but in a way which was really ghost-like. A few days before the beautiful widow and their relations were questions of prime importance for him, over which he had tortured his head not a little. He recalled also that internal struggle through which he had passed on the sea while returning to Villa Franca. Now he said to himself, "This has ceased to exist for me, and I will not think again of it." So he felt not the least alarm, not the least compunction. On the contrary, it seemed to him that a kind of oppressive burden had dropped from his shoulders, and all his thoughts ran to Panna Cervi. His eyes and his head were full of her; by the power of imagination he saw her again, with dishevelled hair and closed eyelids; and when he thought that in an hour he would touch her temples with his fingers, that he would bend over her again and feel the warmth radiating from her, he felt elated, as if by wine, and for the second time asked himself, —

"Hei, old man, what is happening thee?"

When he reached home, he found a telegram from Pani Elzen, "I expect you to dinner at six." Svirski crushed the paper and put it in his pocket; when Pani Cervi and her daughter arrived, he had forgotten it altogether, so that when his work was done at five he began to think where to dine, and was angry that he had nothing to do with himself that evening.

CHAPTER IX.

NEXT day when Pani Lageat brought a lunch for three persons to the studio, she stated that an hour before the same two handsome boys had come, this time, however, not with a strangely dressed servant, but with a youthful and beautiful lady.

"The lady wanted absolutely to see you; but I told her that you had gone to Antibes."

"To Toulon! to Toulon!" cried the artist, joyously.

Next morning there was no one to whom Pani Lageat could give that answer, for only a letter came. Svirski did not read it. That day it happened that while trying to correct Panna Cervi's "position," he put his hand under her shoulder, and raised her so that their bosoms almost met, and her breath struck his face. Meanwhile her face changed from emotion, and he said to himself that if such a moment lasted longer, it would be worth while to give life for it.

That evening he talked to himself as follows: "The senses are playing in thee, but not as at other times; now thy soul rushes forth after them, and rushes forth because this is a child who in this 'pudridero' of Nice has remained as pure as a tear. This is not even her merit, but her nature; where could such another be found? This time I am not deceiving myself, and I am not talking anything into myself, for reality is speaking."

And it seemed to him that a sweet dream was taking hold of him. Unfortunately, after sleep comes waking. To Svirski, it came two days later in the form of one more telegram, which, shoved in through an opening in the door intended for letters and newspapers, fell on the floor in presence of both women.

Panna Maria, while preparing to let down her hair, saw the telegram first, and, raising the envelope, handed it to Svirski.

He opened it unwillingly, looked; and confusion was evident on his face.

"Pardon me, ladies," said he, after a while. "I have received such news that I must go at once."

"I hope at least that it is nothing bad," said Panna Maria, with alarm.

"No, no! But perhaps I shall not be able to return to the afternoon sitting. In every case work is over for to-day; but to-morrow I shall be calm."

Then he took leave of them somewhat feverishly, but with exceeding cordiality, and next moment he was in a carriage which, at his command, was to go straight to Monte Carlo.

When he had passed the "Jetée Promenade," he took out the telegram and read it again. It was as follows: —

I expect you this afternoon; if you do not come by the four o'clock train, I shall know what to think, and how to act. MORPHINE.

Svirski was simply frightened at the signature, especially as he was under the recent impression of the event with Kresovich. "Who knows," said he in his mind, "to what a woman may be brought, not by genuine love, but by wounded vanity? I should not have acted as I have. It was easy to answer her first letter — and break with her. It is not proper to trifle with any one, whether good or bad. At present I must break with her decisively; but I must go without waiting for the four o'clock train."

And he urged on the driver. At moments he strengthened himself with the hope that Pani Elzen would not, in any case, attempt her own life. That seemed utterly unlike her. But at moments he was possessed by doubt. If that monstrous egotism of hers is turned into a feeling of offence, would it not urge her to some insane act?

He remembered that there was a certain stubbornness in her character, a certain decision, and no little courage. Regard for her children, it is true, ought to restrain her; but did she really care for those children? And at thought of what might happen, the hair rose on his head. Conscience moved in him again, and a profound internal struggle began. The picture of Panna Cervi passed before his eyes every moment, rousing bitter and immense regret. He repeated to himself, it is true, that he was going to break with Pani Elzen, that he would break with her decisively; at the bottom of his soul, however, he felt a great fear. What would happen if that woman, vain and malicious, as well as determined, should say to him, "Thee, or morphine"? And meanwhile, with the alarm and uncertainty, there was born in his mind a disgust; for it seemed to him that the question could be put that way only by some counterfeit heroine belonging to "vile literature." But still what would happen if she should put it so? In society, especially in the society of Nice, there are many women who belong to "vile literature."

In the midst of these thoughts, and in a cloud of gray dust, he arrived finally at Monte Carlo, and ordered the driver to stop in front of the Hôtel de Paris. But before he had time to alight he descried Romulus and Remus on the turf with netted clubs in their hands, throwing up balls under the care of a Cossack whom Pani Lageat had called the strangely dressed servant. They, when they saw him, ran up.

"Good-day, sir!"

"Good-day."

"Good-day! Is mamma upstairs?"

"No. Mamma has gone bicycling with M. de Sinten." Silence followed.

"Ah! mamma has gone bicycling with De Sinten?" repeated Svirski. "Well!"

And after a while he added,—

"True! she expected me only at four o'clock."

Then he began to laugh.

"The tragedy ends in a farce. But this, however, is the Riviera! Still what an ass I am!"

"Will you wait for mamma?" asked Romulus.

"No. Listen, my boys. Tell your mamma that I came to say good-bye to her, and that I am sorry not to find her, because I am going on a journey to-day."

Then he gave directions to return to Nice. That evening he received one telegram more, in which there was the single word, "Scoundrel!"

After reading it he fell into excellent humor, for the telegram was not signed this time, "Morphine."

CHAPTER X.

TWO weeks later the picture "Sleep and Death" was finished. Svirski began another which he intended to call "Euterpe." But his work did not advance. He said that the light was too sharp; and for whole sittings, instead of painting, he was looking at the bright face of Panna Cervi. He seemed to be seeking the proper expression for Euterpe. He gazed so persistently that the lady grew red under the influence of his eyes; he felt in his breast an increasing disquiet. At last, on a certain morning, he said suddenly, in a kind of strange, altered voice, —

"I notice that you ladies love Italy immensely."

"We and grandfather," answered Panna Cervi.

"I, too. Half my life passes in Rome and in Florence. There the light is not so sharp at present, and it would be possible to paint whole days. Oh, yes! Who could help loving Italy! And do you know what I think sometimes?"

Panna Maria lowered her head, and, opening her lips somewhat, began to look at him carefully, as she always did when listening to him.

"I think that every man has two fatherlands: one his own, the nearer, and the other Italy. Only think, all culture, all art, all science, everything came from there. Let us take, for instance, the Renaissance. . . . Really, all are, if not the children, at least the grandchildren of Italy."

"True," answered Panna Maria.

"I do not know whether I mentioned that I have a studio in the Via Margutta in Rome, and that when the light becomes too sharp in this studio I am yearning for that one. Here it is — if we should all go to Rome — that would be perfect! Afterward we could go to Warsaw."

"There is no way to carry out that plan," answered Panna Maria, with a sad smile.

But he approached her quickly, and, taking her two hands, began to speak, looking at her with the greatest tenderness in his eyes.

"There is a way, dear lady, there is a way! Do you not divine it?"

And when she grew pale from happiness, he pressed both her palms to his breast, and added,—

"Give me thyself and thine—"

THAT THIRD WOMAN

THAT THIRD WOMAN.

CHAPTER I.

THE rent for that studio in which Antek Svyatetski and I lived and painted, was unpaid, first, because we had about five rubles joint capital, and, second, because we felt a sincere repugnance to paying house-rent.

People call us artists squanderers; as for me, I would rather drink away my money than waste it in paying a house-owner.

Our house-owner was not a bad fellow though, and, moreover, we found means of defence against him.

When he came to dun us, which was usually in the morning, Antek, who slept on a straw bed on the floor, and covered himself with a Turkish curtain used by us as a background for portraits, would rise to a sitting posture, and say in sepulchral tones, —

"It is well that I see you, for I dreamed that you were dead."

The house-owner, who was superstitious, and dreaded death evidently, was confused at once and beyond measure. Antek would throw himself back on the straw bed, stretch his legs, fold his hands across his breast, and continue, —

"You were just like this; you had white gloves on your hands, the fingers were too long; on your feet patent-leather boots; for the rest, you were not changed much."

Then I would add, "Sometimes those dreams come true."

It seems that this "sometimes" brought the man to despair. At last he would fall into a rage, slam the door after him; and we could hear him rush downstairs four steps at a time, swearing by what the world stands on. Still the honest soul did not like to send the house-bailiff to us. In truth, there was not much to take; and he had calculated that were he to bring other artists to that studio, and the kitchen adjoining, the story would be the same, or still worse.

Our sharp method grew dull in time, however. The house-owner became accustomed to the thought of death. Antek had the idea to finish three pictures in the style of Würtz, "Death," "Burial," and "Waking from Lethargy." Naturally our man was to figure in all of them.

Such funereal subjects became a specialty for Antek, who, as he says himself, paints "corpses big, medium, and small size." This is the reason, of course, why no one buys his pictures; for, subjects aside, he has talent. He has sent to the Paris Salon two "corpses," and as I also sent my "Jews on the Vistula," which in the catalogue of the Salon are christened "Jews on the Babylon," we were both waiting impatiently for the decision of the *jury*.

Of course Antek foresaw that the worst would happen, that the *jury* would be made up of perfect idiots, and even if not made up of idiots, I am an idiot, he is an idiot, our pictures are idiotic, and reward for them would be the summit of idiocy!

How much blood that monkey has spoiled in me during the two years that we have lived in one studio, I cannot tell.

Antek's whole ambition is to pass for a moral "corpse." In company he poses as a drunkard, which he is not. He will pour down two or three tiny glasses of vodka, and turn to see if we are looking; if not sure that we are, he will punch one of us with his elbow frown and say, in subterranean tones,—

"Yes, how low I have fallen, that far! Is it possible?"

We answer that he is a fool. He falls into a rage then; nothing can bring him into worse humor than to show disbelief in his moral fall. Still, he is an honest fellow to the marrow of his bones.

Once he and I went astray in the mountains of Salzkammergut, near Zell am See. Since night had come it was easy to break one's neck.

"Dost hear," said Antek to me, "thou hast more talent than I, therefore life is a greater loss to thee. I will go ahead. If I fall, thou wilt stay on the spot till morning, and in the morning thou canst save thyself somehow."

"Thou wilt not go ahead; I will go, because I can see better."

"If I don't break my neck to-day," said Antek, "I'll finish in the canal—it's all one to me."

We fall to disputing. Meanwhile it has become as dark as in a cellar. In the end of ends we conclude to go at hazard. We advance cautiously.

The place is wide enough at first, but afterward narrower and narrower. As far as we can see, on the right and left are abysses, probably bottomless.

The ridge grows still narrower, and, what is more, pieces of stone, loosened by the wind, fall away from under our feet.

"I will go on my hands and knees; 't is impossible to go any other way!" said Antek.

In truth, 't is impossible to go any other way, so we go on our hands and knees, advancing like two chimpanzees.

But soon it appears that that too is impossible. The back of the cliff becomes as narrow as a horse's back. Antek sits astride of it, I also, and leaning on our hands put down before us we pushed forward with uncommon damage to our clothing. After a certain time I hear the voice of my comrade, —

"Vladek?"

"What is it?"

"The ridge has come to an end."

"And what is there beyond?"

"Emptiness — there must be a precipice."

"Take a stone and throw it, we will listen to hear if it is a long time falling."

In the darkness I hear Antek feeling to find a fragment of crumbling rock.

"I am throwing," said he, "listen."

I open both ears.

Silence!

"Haven't you heard anything?"

"No!"

"We have ended up nicely! The place must be a hundred fathoms deep."

"Throw once more."

Antek finds a larger stone, throws it.

No sound!

"What does this mean, no bottom, or what?" asked Antek.

"Hard to help it! We will sit here till morning."

We are sitting there. Antek throws a couple of

stones more; all in vain. An hour passes, a second, at last I hear my friend's voice, —

"Vladek, but don't go to sleep — hast a cigarette?"

It appears that I have cigarettes, but we have used up our matches. Despair! The hour may be one in the morning, or not even so late. Very fine rain begins to fall. Around us, darkness impenetrable. I come to the conclusion that people who live in towns or in villages have no idea of what silence is, — silence like that which surrounds us, silence which rings in our ears. I almost hear the blood coursing in my veins; I hear the beating of my own heart perfectly. At first the position interests me. To sit in the midst of the silent night on the back of a cliff, as on a horse, and right over a bottomless abyss, that could not be done by some shopkeeper of the city; but soon the air becomes cold, and, to crown everything, Antek begins to philosophize, —

"What is life? Life is just swinishness. People talk about art! art! May I and art be ——. Art is pure monkeying with nature, and meanness besides. Twice I have seen the Salon. Painters sent in so many pictures that one might have made canvas beds of them for all the Jews living; and what were these pictures? The lowest possible pandering to shopkeepers' tastes, painted for money, or the stuffing of stomachs. A chaos of art, nothing more! Were that art, I would that paralysis had struck it; luckily there is no real art upon earth — there is only nature. Maybe nature is swinishness also. The best would be to jump down here — and end everything quickly. I would do so if I had vodka; but as I have no vodka, I will not, for I have made a vow not to die sober."

I was used to this gabbling of Antek's; still, in that silence and bewilderment, in cold, in darkness, at the edge of a precipice, his words made even me gloomy. Fortunately he talked himself out and stopped. He threw a couple of stones more, repeated a couple of times more, "Not a sound," and then for three hours we were silent.

It seemed to me that daybreak would come before long, when suddenly we heard a calling and the sound of wings.

It was dark yet, and I could see nothing; I was certain, however, that eagles were beginning to circle over the precipice. "Kra! kra!" was heard with greater force above and in the darkness. It astonished me to hear such a multitude of voices, just as if whole legions of eagles were passing. But, happen what might, they were heralding daylight.

After a while, I saw my hands resting on the rocky edge; then Antek's shoulders were outlined in front of me, precisely like a dark object on a ground somewhat less dark. That ground grew paler each instant. Then a rich, light silver tone began to shine in on the rocks and on Antek's shoulders. This color filled the darkness more and more, just as if into that darkness some one were pouring a silver liquid which permeated it, mixed with it, and from black made it gray, from gray pearl-color. There was also a certain severity and dampness about us; not only the cliff but the air too seemed moist.

Now more light comes every moment. I am looking, trying to fix in my mind those changes in tone, and am painting a little in my soul, when all at once Antek's cry interrupts me,—

"Tfu! idiots!"

And his shoulders vanish from my eyes.

"Antek!" I cry, "what are thou doing?"

"Don't howl! look here!"

I bend over, look — what appears? I am sitting on a rocky cliff which slopes down to a meadow, lying perhaps a yard and a half below me. The moss deadened the sound of the stones, for the meadow is very level; at a distance the road is visible, and on it crows, which I took for eagles. To walk home with the greatest comfort it was merely necessary to take our legs off the rock.

Meanwhile, we had been sitting on that rock, our teeth chattering, through the whole of God's night.

I know not why, but while waiting in the studio with Antek for the house-owner, that adventure of a year and a half before came to my mind, as if it had happened the previous day. That recollection gave me great solace; therefore I said at once, —

"Dost remember, Antek, how we thought ourselves sitting on the edge of a precipice, and it turned out that there was a level road right before us? It may be the same to-day. We are as poor as church mice, as thou knowest; the house-owner wants to turn us out of the studio; meanwhile all things may change. Let some sluice of glory and money open out to us."

Antek was sitting just then on the straw bed, pulling on his boots, grumbling the while that life was made up of pulling boots on in the morning and pulling them off at night; that only the man had sense who had courage to hang himself, which, if he, Antek, had not done hitherto, it was simply because he was not only a supreme fool, but a low coward besides.

My outburst of optimism interrupted his meditation; so he raised his fishy eyes and said, —

"Thou, beyond all men, hast something to rejoice at; the other day Suslovski drove thee from his house and the heart of his daughter; to-day the house-owner will drive thee from the studio."

Alas! Antek told the truth. Three days before I was the betrothed of Kazia Suslovski, but on Tuesday morning — yes, on Tuesday, I received from her father the following letter: —

DEAR SIR, — Our daughter, yielding to the persuasion of her parents, has consented to break the tie which for her would have been a misfortune. She may find a refuge at all times on the bosom of her mother and under the roof of her father; but it pertains specially to us, her parents, to avoid this extremity. Not only your material position, but your frivolous character, which, in spite of every effort, you are unable to conceal, inclines us and our daughter to return you your word, and to break with you further relations, which, however, does not change our good will toward you. With esteem,

HELIODOR SUSLOVSKI.

Such was the letter; I agree more or less with this, that out of my material position dog's boots might be made; but what that pathetic gorilla knows of my character I, in truth, do not understand.

Kazia's head brings to mind types from the time of the Directory; and it would be finer if she would dress her hair, not in the fashion of to-day, but of that time. I tried even to beg her to do so, but in vain, since she has no mind for such things. But she has a complexion as warm as if Fortuni had painted it.

For that very reason I loved her sincerely; and the first day, after receiving the letter from her father, I went about as if poisoned. Only on the second day, and that in the evening, did I feel a little easier, and say to myself, "If not, then not." It helped me most to bear the blow that I had my head filled with the Salon and with my "Jews." I was convinced that the picture was a good one, though Antek predicted that it would be thrown, not only out of the Salon, but out of the antechamber. I began the picture the year before in this way: It is evening. I am walking alone for amusement by the Vistula. I look; I see a basket of apples lost in the river; street Arabs are fishing the apples out of the water; and on the bank are sitting a whole Jewish family in such despair that they are not even lamenting, they are clasping their hands, and looking into the water, as dumb as statues. There is an old Jew there, a patriarch, a poor devil; an old Jewess; a young Jew, a colossal creature as big as Judas Maccabæus; a maiden, freckled somewhat, but with immense character in the outline of her nose and mouth; finally two little Jews. Twilight is coming; the river has a bronze reflection which is simply miraculous. The trees on Saxon Island are all in the light of evening; beyond the island is water, widely spread, tones purple, ultra-marine, tones almost steel, then again tones passing into purple and violet. The aërial perspective, splendid! The transition from some tones to others so subtile and marvellous that the soul just pipes in a man; round about it is quiet, bright calm. Melancholy over all things so that there is a wish to weep; and that group in mourning, sitting as if each person in it had been posing in studios.

In a moment the thought flashed into my head: That is my picture!

I had my portfolio with me, and colors, for I never go walking without them; I begin to sketch on the spot, but I say to the Jews, —

"Sit as you are, don't move! — a ruble to each one at dark."

My Jews see the point, in a twinkle, and, as it were, grow to the ground. I sketch and sketch. The street Arabs crawl out of the water, and soon I hear behind me, —

"Painter! painter! When a man steals a thing, he says that he found it."

But I answer them in their jargon, and win them at once; they even stop throwing chips at the Jews, so as not to injure my work. But, as an offset, my group fall unexpectedly into good humor.

"Jews," cry I, "be sorrowful;" but the old woman answers, —

"With permission, Pan artist, how can we be sorrowful when you promise us each one a ruble? Let him be sad who has no profit."

I have to threaten them that I will not pay.

I sketched for two evenings; then they posed for me two months in the studio. Let Antek say what he pleases, the picture is good, for there is nothing cold in it; it has pure truth and a tremendous lot of nature. I left even the freckles on the young Jewess. The faces might be more beautiful; but they could not be truer or have greater character.

I thought so much of this picture that I bore the loss of Kazia more easily. When Antek reminded me of her, the subject seemed one of long ago. Meanwhile, my comrade pulled on his other boot, and I heated the samovar. Old Antonia came with cakes; Antek had been persuading this woman in vain for a year to hang herself. We sat down to tea.

"Why art thou so glad?" asked Antek, peevishly.

"Because I know that thou wilt see something of uncommon interest to-day."

At this moment we hear steps approaching the studio.

THAT THIRD WOMAN.

"Thy house-owner! There is thy 'something uncommon'!"

Saying this, Antek gulps down his tea, which is so hot that tears fill his eyes. Up he springs; and since our little kitchen is in the passage, he hides in the studio behind the costumes, and from his hiding-place cries, with a panting voice, —

"Thou! he loves thee immensely, talk thou to him."

"He is dying for thee!" answer I, flying to the costumes, "talk thou to him!"

Meanwhile the door opens, and who comes in? Not the house-owner, but the watchman of the house in which the Suslovskis are living.

We rush out from behind the costumes.

"I have a letter for you," says the watchman.

I take the letter. By Hermes! it is from Kazia! I tear open the envelope, and read as follows, —

I am certain that my parents will forgive us. Come at once; never mind the early hour. We have just returned from the waters in the garden.   KAZIA.

I have no idea what the parents really have to forgive me, but neither have I time to think of it, for I am losing my head from amazement. Only after a while do I give the letter to Antek, and say to the watchman, —

"Friend, tell the young lady that I will come right away — wait, I have no small money, but here are three rubles [all I have] change the bill, take a ruble for yourself, and bring me the rest."

Speaking in parenthesis, the monster took the three rubles, and did not show himself again. He knew, the abortion, that I would not raise a scandal at Suslovski's, and took advantage of the position most dishonorably. But at the time I didn't even notice it.

"Well, Antek, what?" ask I.

"Nothing! Every calf will find its butcher."

The haste with which I was dressing did not permit me to find an answer befitting this insult from Antek.

CHAPTER II.

A QUARTER of an hour later I ring at Suslovski's. Kazia herself opens the door. She is comely; she has about her yet the warmth of sleep, and also the freshness of morning, which she brought from the garden in the folds of her muslin robe, which is pale blue in color. Her hat, just removed, has dishevelled her hair somewhat. Her face is smiling; her eyes are smiling; her moist lips are smiling, — she is just like the morning. I seize her hands, kiss them, and kiss her arms to the elbows. She bends to my ear and inquires, —

"But who loves better?"

Then she leads me by the hand to the presence of her parents. Old Suslovski has the mien of a Roman who is sacrificing *pro patria* the life of his only child; the mother is dropping tears into her coffee, for both are at coffee. But they rise at sight of us, and Papa Suslovski speaks, —

"Reason and duty would command me to answer, no! but the heart of a parent has its rights — if this is weakness, let God judge me!"

Here he raises his eyes in proof that he will be ready to answer, if the tribunal of Heaven begins to write a protocol that moment. I had never seen anything more Roman in my life, unless macaroni sold on the Corso. The moment is so impressive that a hippopotamus might burst from emotion. The solemnity is increased by Pani Suslovski, who crosses her hands, and says in a tearful voice, —

"My children, should you have trouble in the world at any time take refuge here — here!"

While saying this, she pointed to her bosom.

She could not fool me! I was not to be taken for preservation there — there! If Kazia had offered me a similar refuge, it would have been different. Still I am amazed at the honesty of the Suslovskis, and my heart is filled with gratitude. I drink so many glasses of coffee from emotion that the Suslovskis begin to cast anxious glances at the coffee-pot and the cream. Kazia fills my cup continually; I try at the same time to press her foot under the table. But she draws it back always, shaking her head meanwhile, and smiling so roguishly that I know not how I escaped jumping out of my skin.

I sit an hour and a half; but at last I must go, for in the studio Bobus is waiting for me, — Bobus who takes drawing-lessons, and leaves me a note each time, with a coat of arms on it, but I lose those notes generally. Kazia and her mother conduct me to the entrance; I am angry at that, for I want Kazia alone to conduct me. What a mouth she has!

My road leads through the city garden. It is full of people coming from the waters. On the way I notice that all halt at sight of me. I hear whispers, "Magorski! Magorski! that's he —" Young ladies, dressed in muslin of every shade under which their forms are outlined wonderfully, cast glances at me which seem as if wishing to say, "Enter! the dwelling is ready!" What the devil, am I so famous, or what? I fail to understand.

I go on — always the same thing. At the entrance

of the studio, I come against the house-owner, as a ship against a rock. Oh, the rent!

But the man approaches me and says,—

"My dear sir, though I have annoyed you sometimes, believe me, I have so much — just permit me simply —"

With that he seizes me around the neck and hugs me. Ha! I understand, Antek must have told him that I am going to marry; and he thinks that in future I shall pay my rent regularly. Let him think so.

I thunder upstairs. On the way I hear a noise in our quarters. I rush in. The studio is dark from smoke. There I find Yulek Rysinski, Wah Poterkevich, Franek Tsepkovski, old Sludetski, Karminski, Voytek Mihalak, — all amusing themselves by driving the elegant Bobus around on a string; but seeing me, they let him go, barely alive, in the middle of the studio; then they raise an unearthly uproar.

"We congratulate! congratulate! congratulate!"

"Up with him!"

In one moment I am in their arms, and for a certain time they hurl me up, howling meanwhile in a way befitting a pack of wolves; at last I find myself on the floor. I thank them as best I can, and declare that they must all be at my wedding, especially Antek, whom I engage in advance as my best man.

Antek raises his hands and says,—

"That soap thinks that we are congratulating him on his marriage."

"But on what are you congratulating me?"

"How is that, don't you know?" asked every voice.

"I know nothing; what the hangman do you want?"

"Give him the morning number of 'The Kite,'" cries Poterkevich.

They give me the morning number of "The Kite," shouting, one interrupting the other, "Look among the despatches!"

I look at the despatches, and read the following,—

"Special telegram to the 'The Kite.' Magorski's picture, 'The Jews on the river of Babylon,' received the great gold medal of the Salon of the present year. The critics cannot find words to describe the genius of the master. Albert Wolff has called the picture a revelation. Baron Hirsch offers fifteen thousand francs for it."

I am fainting! Help! I have lost my senses to that degree that I cannot utter a word. I knew that my picture was a success, but of such a success I had not even dreamed. The number of "The Kite" falls from my hand. They raise it and read to me among current comments the following notes on the despatch,—

"Note I. We learn from the lips of the master himself that he intends to exhibit his picture in our garden of sirens.

"Note II. In answer to a question put by the vice-president of the Society of Fine Arts to our master, whether he intends to exhibit his masterpiece in Warsaw, he answered: 'I would rather not sell it in Paris than not exhibit it in Warsaw.' We hope that those words will be read by our posterity (God grant remote) on the monument to the master.

"Note III. The mother of our master, on receiving the despatch from Paris, fell seriously ill from emotion.

"Note IV. We learn at the moment of going to press, that the mother of our master is improving.

"Note V. Our master has received invitations to exhibit his picture in all the European capitals."

Under the excess of these monstrous lies, I return to my senses a little. Ostrynski, the editor of "The Kite," and at the same time an ex-suitor of Kazia's, must have gone mad, for this passes every measure. It is natural that I should exhibit the picture in Warsaw; but, I. I have not mentioned that matter to any one; II. the vice-president of the Society of Fine Arts has made no inquiry of me touching anything; III. I have given him no answer; IV. my mother died nine years ago; V. I have not received an invitation from any quarter to exhibit my picture.

Worse than all, it comes to my mind in one moment that if the despatch is as truthful as the five notes, then farewell to everything. Ostrynski, who half a year since, in spite of the fact that her parents were for him, received a basket [1] from Kazia, wished perhaps purposely to make a fool of me; if that is the case "he will pay me with his head, or something else," as says the libretto of a certain opera. My colleagues pacify me, however, by saying that Ostrynski might fabricate the notes, but the despatch must be genuine.

At the same time Stah Klosovich comes with a morning number of "The Courier." The despatch is in "The Courier." I recover breath.

Now congratulations in detail begin. Old Sludetski, false to the core, but in manner sweet as syrup, shakes my hand and says, —

"Beloved God! I have always believed in the genius of my colleague, and I have always defended him [I know that he used to call me an ass]; but — Beloved God, perhaps my colleague does not wish that such a *fa-presto* as I should call my colleague, colleague; in that event let my colleague forgive an old habit, Beloved God!"

In my soul I wish him hanged; but I cannot answer,

---
[1] Refusal.

for at that moment Karminski draws me aside and tells
me in an undertone, but so that all hear him, —
"Maybe my colleague needs money, if he does, let him
say the word, and then — "
Karminski is known among us for his professed willingness to oblige. Time after time he says to some of
us, "If my colleague needs aid, let him say the word;
and then — till we meet again!" In truth, he has
money. I answer that if I do not find it elsewhere, I
will apply to him. Meanwhile other men come, true
as gold; and they squeeze me till my sides ache. At
last Antek appears; I see that he is moved, but he conceals his emotion, and says roughly, —
"Though thou art becoming a Jew, as I see, I
congratulate thee!"
"Though thou art becoming a fool, as I see, I thank
thee," and we embrace with all our strength. Poterkevich mentions that it is dry in his throat. I haven't
a copper; but Antek has two rubles; others have as
much. A contribution follows, and punch. They drink
my health, throw me up again; and because I tell them
that the affair with the Suslovskis is settled, they drink
Kazia's health also. With that Antek comes to me and
says, —
"Dost think, youthful idiot, that they hadn't read the
despatch before the young woman wrote to thee?"
Oh, the monkey! how gladly I would give him a club
on the head. On one side the horizon was growing
bright for me; on the other, the devil was darkening it.
Anything might be expected of the Suslovskis; but that
Kazik[1] should be capable of such calculation!
Still it was very likely that they had read the despatch
at the waters in the morning, and invited me straightway.

[1] A form of endearment for Kazia.

At the first moment I want to fly to the Suslovskis, and stand before their eyes. But I cannot leave my company. Meanwhile Ostrynski comes, elegant, cold, self-confident, gloved as usual. Shrewdness is shining from him, as light from a fire, for he is a rogue in full armor. From the threshold he begins to wave his cane protectingly, and says, —

"Congratulations to the master; *I* too congratulate."

He uttered that "I" with an emphasis, as if congratulation from him meant more than from any other man. Perhaps it did really.

"How much you have invented!" cried I; "as truly as you see me here, I learned all about myself in 'The Kite.'"

"How does that concern me?" asked Ostrynski.

"I said nothing about exhibiting the picture either."

"But now you do," answered he, phlegmatically.

"And he has no mother, so his mother has not grown weak!" cried Voytek Mihalak.

"That concerns me little," repeated Ostrynski, with dignity taking off his second glove.

"But is the despatch true?"

"True."

That assurance pacifies me thoroughly. Through thankfulness I pour out punch for him. He puts his lips to the edge of the glass, drinks a sip, and says, —

"First to your health, and a second draught I drink you know to whom. I congratulate you doubly."

"Where do you get your information?"

Ostrynski shrugs his shoulders. "Suslovski was in the editorial rooms before eight o'clock this morning."

Antek begins to mutter something about mean people in general; I can restrain myself no longer; I seize my hat. Ostrynski follows me out; but I leave him on the street; and a couple of minutes later I am ringing at Suslovski's for the second time. Kazia opens the door; her parents are not at home.

"Kazia!" ask I, severely, "didst thou know of the despatch?"

"I knew," answered she, calmly.

"But, Kazik!"

"What was to be done, my dear? Do not wonder at my parents; they must of course have some reasonable cause to accept thee."

"But thou, Kazia?"

"I seized the first opportunity; dost take that ill of me, Vladek?"

The question grows clear, and it seems to me that Kazia is perfectly right. Speaking plainly, why did I rush hither like a madman? Kazia comes up and rests her head on my shoulder. I put my arm around her waist; she drops her face toward my arm, closes her eyes, pushes up her rosy mouth and whispers, —

"No, no, Vladek! not now — only after marriage, I implore thee."

In view of that request, I press her lips to mine, and we remain in that way as long as the process of breathing permits. Kazia's eyes become languishing. At last, she screens them with her arm, and says, —

"But I begged thee not to —"

The reproach and the look melt me to such a degree that I kiss her a second time. When you love some one, you have naturally a greater desire to give a kiss than a blow to that person. And I love Kazia beyond measure and wit, during life till death, after death! She, or none, and that's the end of it!

Kazia, with panting voice, expresses the fear that I have lost respect for her. Dearest creature, what nonsense she utters! I pacify her as best I can, and we begin to talk reasonably.

An agreement is made between us that if the parents pretend that they heard of the despatch only after my coming, I am not to let them know that I am aware how affairs stand. I bid farewell then to Kazia, promising to come in the evening.

In fact, I must rush to the office of the Society for Promoting Fine Arts; through it I can communicate most easily with the secretary of the Salon.

CHAPTER III.

I SEND a despatch stating that I accept Baron Hirsch's price; but stipulate, first, to exhibit the picture in Warsaw, etc.

For the sending of despatches and other needs I borrow money in the institution. It is given without hesitation. Everything goes as if on oil.

In "The Kite" and "The Courier" appears my biography, in which, however, there is not one word of truth; but as Ostrynski says, "How can that concern me?" I have received also a request from two illustrated papers; they wish to publish my portrait and reproduce my picture. Let them do so. Money will be as abundant as water.

CHAPTER IV.

A WEEK later I receive the earnest money from Baron Hirsch. The remainder will be paid when the purchaser obtains possession of the canvas. Meanwhile, the Bank of Commerce fires onto the table for me five thousand francs in louis d'or. In life I have not seen so much money. I come home laden down like a mule.

There is an assembly in the studio. I throw my coin on the floor; and since I have never wallowed in gold, I begin to wallow in it. After me Antek wallows. The house-owner comes in, and thinks that we have lost our senses. We amuse ourselves like cannibals.

CHAPTER V.

ONE day Ostrynski informs me that he feels happy that he got a basket from Kazia, for prospects are opening before him of which I cannot have the least idea.

I am very glad of this, or rather, it is all one to me; I believe meanwhile that Ostrynski will take care of himself in this life. When he was trying for Kazia, her parents were on his side, especially Father Suslovski; Ostrynski had even a complete preponderance over him, pushed to the degree that that Roman lost his statuesqueness in presence of this suitor. Kazia, however, could not endure him from the first moment of their acquaintance. It was some unconscious repugnance; as to other things I am perfectly sure that he did not offend her with that with which he offends me, and all who know his nature thoroughly. He is a wonderful man, or rather a wonderful man of letters. There are, of course, not only among us, but in all the greater centres of literature and art, men of whom, when you think, you ask involuntarily, Whence comes their importance? To this category belongs my friend of "The Kite." Who would believe that the secret of Ostrynski's significance and the reason of his mental position is this, that he does not love and does not respect talents,—especially literary talents,

— and that he simply lives by disregarding them? He has for them the contempt of a man to whom regularity of life, a certain incisive quickness and great shrewdness secure in society permanent victories over them.

One should see him at sessions, at artistic and literary meetings, at jubilee dinners; with what condescending irony he treats men who in the region of creativeness have ten times more power than he; how he pushes them to the wall; how he confuses them with his logic, with his judgment; how he overwhelms them with his literary importance!

Whenever Antek thinks of this, he calls for a slat from the bedstead with which to crack Ostrynski's skull; but Ostrynski's preponderance does not astonish me. People of genuine talent are frequently awkward, timid, devoid of marked quickness and mental equilibrium. It is only when genuine talent is alone with itself that wings grow out on its shoulders; Ostrynski in such a position could only go to sleep, for he has absolutely nothing to say to himself.

The future brings order, gives rank, and assigns to each man his own proper place. Ostrynski is too clever not to know this; but in his soul he laughs at it. For him, 't is enough that at present he has greater significance than others, and that people count more with him than with men better than he.

We painters stand less in his way. Still he advertises the talents of writers at times, but only when urged by the interest of "The Kite" and in opposition to "The Courier." For the rest, he is a good comrade, an agreeable person. I can say that I like the man; but — devil take him! — we've had enough of Ostrynski.

CHAPTER VI.

THEY will make me slam the door some day.

What a comedy! Since I have won reputation and money, Suslovski, in spite of my forethought, treats me simply with contempt; his wife, all Kazia's relatives, male and female, meet me frigidly.

On the first evening Suslovski announces that if I suppose that my new position has influenced their action, or if I suppose — which for that matter is evident in me — that I am doing them a favor, I am mistaken. Though ready to sacrifice much for the happiness of their child, still even that only child cannot ask them to sacrifice their human dignity. The mother adds, that, in case of need, the child will know where to seek refuge. The honest Kazia defends me at moments very angrily; but they are in wait for every word of mine.

Barely do I open my mouth when Suslovski bites his lips, looks at his wife and nods, as if to say, "I knew that it would come to this." Such a saw have they fixed for me from morning till evening.

And to think that all this is hypocrisy, that its special service is to keep me in their net, that at the bottom of the question they are after my fifteen thousand francs, and that they are as anxious for them as I am, though our motives are different.

It is time to finish.

They have brought me to this that I seem to myself to have committed really some scoundrelism in getting the gold medal and the fifteen thousand francs for my picture.

CHAPTER VII.

THE day of my betrothal is drawing near. I buy a beautiful ring in the style of Louis XV. which does not please the Suslovskis, nor even Kazia, for in that whole house there is no one who has an idea of real art.

I must work much yet over Kazia to destroy in her vulgar preferences and teach her to feel artistically; but since she loves me, I am hopeful.

I invited no one to the betrothal except Antek. I wanted him to visit the Suslovskis as a preliminary; but he declared, that though physically and morally bankrupt, he has not become so degraded yet as to go visiting. It cannot be helped! I forewarn the Suslovskis that my friend is an original beyond compare, but a painter of genius and the most honest man in the world.

Suslovski, learning that my friend paints "corpses," raises his brows, declaring that hitherto he has had to do with decent people, that his whole official career is unspotted, and that he hopes my friend will respect the manners prevailing in an honorable and decorous house.

I confess to myself that I am not free from fears touching Antek, and from the morning hours I am at war with him. He insists on wearing leggings. I persuade, I implore, I entreat.

At last he gives way, declaring that he sees no reason decisively why he should not remain a fool. It is a pity that his shoes remind one of explorers in Central Africa; for no blacking has touched them since they were brought from the shoemaker's on credit!

Still worse, Antek's head looks like the summit of the Carpathian Mountains, covered with forests, torn by columns of wind. I must put up with this, for there is no comb on earth which could conquer that forelock; but I force him to put on a frock coat, instead of the blouse which he wears every day. He does this, but has the look of one of his corpses, and falls into sepulchral humor.

On the street people turn to look at his knotty stick and his immense tattered hat; but I am accustomed to this.

We ring; we enter.

In the antechamber, the voice of Cousin Yachkovich reaches me; he is discoursing on overpopulation. Cousin Yachkovich is always discoursing on overpopulation; that is his hobby. Kazia looks in her muslin like a cloud, and pretty. Suslovski is in a dress-coat; the relatives are in dress-coats; the old aunts are in silk gowns.

Antek's entrance makes an impression. They look at him with a certain disquiet. He looks around gloomily, and informs Suslovski that in truth he would not have come "unless Vladek were getting married, or something of that sort."

This "something of that sort" is received most fatally. Suslovski straightens himself with dignity, and inquires what is meant by "something of that sort." Antek answers that it is all one to him; but "for Vladek" he might even knock his heels off, especially if he knew that Pan Suslovski cared anything about the matter. My future father-in-law looks at his wife, at me, at Kazia, with a look in which amazement is struggling with mortification.

Happily I save the position, and, with presence of mind rare with me, beg my future father-in-law to present me to those members of his family with whom I am still unacquainted.

The presentation follows; then we sit down. Kazia sits near me, and lets her hand stay in mine. The room is full of people; but all are stiff and silent. The atmosphere is heavy.

Cousin Yachkovich begins again at his talk on overpopulation. My Antek looks under the table. In the silence the voice of Yachkovich is heard with increasing shrillness; not having a front tooth, whenever he has to pronounce *sz*, he utters a prolonged hiss.

"The most dreadful catastrophe may arise from this for all Europe," said Yachkovich.

"Emigration," put in some one from aside.

"Statistics show, that emigration will not prevent overpopulation."

Suddenly Antek raises his head and turns his fishy eyes toward the speaker. "Then Chinese customs should be introduced among us," says he, with a gloomy bass.

"With permission, — what Chinese customs ?"

"In China parents have the right to smother imbecile children. Well, then, with us, children should have the right to kill imbecile parents."

It has come! The bolt has struck; the sofa groans under the aunts; and I am lost. Suslovski closes his eyes, and loses speech for a season.

Silence.

Then is heard the voice of my coming father-in-law, trembling with terror, —

"My dear sir, I hope, that as a Christian — "

"Why must I be a Christian?" interrupts Antek, shaking his head ominously.

Another thunderbolt!

The sofa with the aunts begins to tremble as if in a fever; it vanishes from my sight; I feel the earth opening beneath me. All is lost; all hope is vain.

Suddenly Kazia's laughter rings out, resonant as a bell; then Yachkovich bursts into laughter, not knowing why; after Yachkovich, I laugh, also not knowing why.

"Father!" cries Kazia, "Vladek forewarned father, that Pan Svyatetski [Antek] is an original. Pan Svyatetski is joking; he has a mother, I know that, and he is the best of sons to her."

A rogue, not a maiden, that Kazia! — not only does she invent, but she divines. In fact, Antek has a mother, and he is a good son to her.

Kazia's words make a certain diversion. The entrance of a servant with wine and cake makes a still greater diversion. That servant is the watchman who took my last three rubles; but now he is arrayed in a dress-coat, and comes out with the dignity of a waiting-man. He keeps his eyes fixed on the tray; the glasses rattle, and he moves forward as slowly as if he were carrying glasses filled with water. I begin to fear that he will drop them all to the floor; fortunately my fear proves barren.

After a while the glasses are filled. We proceed to the act of betrothal.

A little cousin holds a porcelain plate on which two rings are lying. The eyes are creeping out of her head with curiosity, and the whole ceremony causes her such evident pleasure that she is dancing together with the plate and rings. Suslovski rises; all rise; the noise of the chairs is heard as they are pushed back.

Silence follows. I hear one of the matrons remark in a whisper, how she had hoped that my ring "would be better." In spite of this remark there is such solemnity of feeling that flies are dropping from the wall.

Suslovski begins to speak, —

"My children, receive the blessing of your parents."

Kazia kneels; I kneel as well.

What a physiognomy Antek must have at this moment, what a face! I dare not look at him; I look at Kazia's muslin robe, which, on the faded red sofa, makes a very nice spot. The hands of Suslovski and of Pani Suslovski rest on our heads; then my future father-in-law says, —

"My daughter, thou hast had the best example at home of what a wife should be to a husband, therefore I need not teach thee thy duties, which moreover thy husband will indicate to thee." (I hope so.) "But I turn to thee, Pan Vladislav — "

Here begins a speech during which I count to one hundred, and having counted to a hundred, I begin again at one. Suslovski the citizen, Suslovski the official, Suslovski the father, Suslovski the Roman, had the opportunity of showing all his grandeur of soul. The words: child, parents, duties, future, blessing, thorns, pure conscience, buzz around my ears like a swarm of wasps, sit on my head, sting me on the above-mentioned ears as well as on my neck and forehead.

It must be that I tied my cravat too tightly, for it is suffocating me. I hear the weeping of Pani Suslovski, which affects me, for at heart she is an honest woman; I hear the sound of the rings, held on the plate by the dancing little cousin. O Lord Christ, what a face that Antek must have!

At last we rise. The little cousin thrusts the plate under my very eyes. Kazia and I exchange rings.

Uf! I am betrothed! I suppose this to be the end; but no, Suslovski calls us to go and beg a blessing of all the aunts.

We go. I kiss five hands which are like the feet of storks. All the aunts hope that I will not deceive their confidence.

What the devil confidence can they have in me?

Cousin Yachkovich seizes me in his embraces. Absolutely I must have tied my cravat too tightly.

But the worst is over. Tea is brought in. I sit near Kazia, and it seems to me all the time that I do not see Antek. The monkey, he frightens me once more; when the question whether he will have rum in his tea is asked, he answers that he drinks rum only by the bottle. At last the evening is ended successfully.

We go out. I draw in the air with full breast. Indeed, my cravat was too tight.

Antek and I walk on in silence. The silence begins to weigh on me and soon becomes unendurable. I feel that I must talk to Antek, tell him something of my happiness, how handsomely all has passed, how I love Kazia — I prepare, but it is of no use! At last when just near the studio I say, —

"Own up, Antek, that life is still beautiful."

Antek halts, casts a frowning glance at me, and says, —
"Poodle!"

That night we conversed no more with each other.

CHAPTER VIII.

A WEEK after the evening of betrothal my "Jews" arrive for exhibition. The picture is placed in a separate hall, and a special fee is charged for admission. One half of the net proceeds is for me. At the exhibition there is probably a throng from morning till evening

I see it only once; but as people look at me more than at the picture, I shall not go again, for why should I be angry for nothing. If my picture were a masterpiece, such as has never been seen in the world till this day, people would rather satisfy that curiosity in virtue of which they go to see "Krao" or the Hottentot who eats live pigeons.

Such a Hottentot am I at this moment. I should be satisfied were I really a poodle; but I am too much of a painter not to be enraged by such degradation of art before a fashionable peculiarity.

CHAPTER IX.

THREE weeks ago few persons knew of my existence, but now I begin to receive tens of letters, for the greater part love-letters. I may wager that of five four begin with these words: "It may be that when you have read this letter, you will despise the woman who, etc. —" I will not despise the woman, on condition that she will keep away from me.

Were it not for Kazia, perhaps, to tell the truth, I should n't shrug my shoulders so much at such a torrent of feeling.

How can such an "unknown" hope that a man who has never seen her will answer the invitation of an invisible woman? This makes me specially indignant. Remove first the curtain, O fair unknown! and when I behold thee, I will say to thee — Oi! I will say nothing, because of Kazia.

I receive also an anonymous missive, from some gray-haired friend*ess*, in which I am called master, and Kazia a little goose.

"Oh, master, is she a wife for thee?" inquires my gray-haired friend*ess*. "Is that a choice worthy of him on whom the eyes of the whole country are turned? Thou art a victim of intrigue, etc."

A wonderful supposition, and a still more wonderful demand, that I should marry not to please my heart but the public! And poor Kazia is already in their way!

There are greater crimes surely than anonymous letters, but there is no greater — how can I express myself justly? But never mind!

The end of my betrothal is not fixed yet, but it will come before long. Meanwhile I shall tell Kazia to array herself famously, and I will escort her to the exhibition. Let the world see us together.

Antek's two corpses have come also from Paris. The picture is called "The Last Meeting," and represents a young man and a young woman lying on the dissecting-table. At the first glance the idea is interpreted perfectly. It is clear that those two dead ones loved each other in life, that misery separated and death united them.

The students bending over the corpses have come out in the picture somewhat rigid; there are faults in the perspective of the dissecting-room; but the "corpses" are painted superbly. Such corpses that icy cold comes from them! The picture did not receive even mention, perhaps for the reason that the subject is wonderfully unpleasant; but critics praised it.

Among our "painters" there are beyond doubt many talents. For instance, at the side of Antek's corpses Franek Tsepkovski exhibited "The Death of Koretski." Immense strength in it, and immense individuality.

Antek calls Franek an idiot: first, because Franek has a forelock, and wears his beard wedge-form; second, because he dresses according to the latest fashion; and, third, because he is terribly well-bred and ceremonious, and mentions rather frequently his high-born relatives. But Antek is mistaken. Talent is a bird that builds its nest where it pleases, at one time in a wild desert, at another in a trimmed garden.

I have seen, in Monachium and Paris, painters who looked like laborers in a brewery, then others like barbers or dandies, you would not give three coppers for the men; still one and the other beast of them had in his soul such exaltation, such uncommon feeling of forms and colors, and such a power of projecting that feeling out of himself onto canvas! Ostrynski, who has a trite phrase for everything, would have written in mentioning them in his "Kite," *spiritus flat ubi vult* (the spirit bloweth where it listeth).

In Antek's opinion, historical painting is "obscure barbarism." I do not paint historical subjects, and personally the question is all one to me, but I hear this opinion on every side as being progressive. People have made a saw of it, and it begins to annoy me.

Our Polish painters have one defect: they become wedded to certain doctrines touching art, live under their slippers, look at everything with the eyes of these doctrines, force art to them, and are rather apostles than painters. In contrast to painters mentioned above (in connection with Monachium and Paris), I have known others whose lips were worn off in talking of what art is, and what it should be; but when it came to the brush they could not do anything

More than once I have thought that a theory of art should be framed by philosophers, and if they framed nonsense — let them answer; but painters should paint what the heart dictates to each man, and to know how to paint is the main thing. To my thinking, the most wretched talent is worth more than the most splendid doctrine, and the most splendid doctrine is not worthy to clean the boots of freedom.

CHAPTER X.

I WAS with Kazia and the Suslovskis at the exhibition.

There are crowds before my picture at all times. They began to whisper the moment we entered; and this time they looked mostly, not at the picture, and not at me, but at Kazia. The women especially did not take their eyes from her. I saw that she was pleased with this fabulously; but I did not take it ill of her. I take it worse that she said of Antek's corpses, "that is not a decent picture." Suslovski declared that she had taken the words out of his mouth; but I was raging. To think that Kazia too should have such a view of art!

From anger I took farewell of them at once, on pretence that I must see Ostrynski. I went to his office, it is true, but to induce him to dine with me.

CHAPTER XI.

I SAW a miracle, and that's the end of it.

Now for the first time I understand why a man has eyes.

Corpo di Bacco; what beauty!

I am walking with Ostrynski; I see on a sudden at the corner of Willow Street some woman passing quickly. I stand as if fixed to the earth; I become oak; I become stone; I stare; I lose consciousness; without knowing it I seize Ostrynski by the cravat; I loosen his cravat — and — save me, or I die!

What that she has perfect features? It is not the features, she is simply an artist's ideal, a masterpiece as outline, a masterpiece as coloring, a masterpiece as sentiment. Greuze would have risen from the dead in her presence, and hanged himself then for having painted so much ugliness.

I gaze and gaze. She is walking alone, — how alone? Poetry is walking with her; music, spring, splendor, and love are walking with her. I know not whether I should prefer to paint her immediately; I should rather kneel before her and kiss her feet, because such a woman was born. Finally, do I know what I would do?

She passes us as serenely as a summer day. Ostrynski bows to her; but she does not see him. I wake from my amazement and cry, —

"Let us follow her!"

"No," answers Ostrynski; "have you gone mad? I must tie my cravat. Give me peace! that is an acquaintance of mine."

"An acquaintance of yours? Present me."

"I do not think of it; look to your own betrothed."

I hurl a curse at Ostrynski and his posterity to the ninth generation; then I wish to fly after the unknown. To my misfortune, she has entered an open carriage. Only from a distance do I see her straw hat and red parasol.

"Do you know her really?" ask I of Ostrynski.

"I know all people."

"Who is she?"

"Pani Helena Kolchanovski of the house of Turno, otherwise Panna Vdova [Miss Widow], so called."

"Why Miss Widow?"

"Because her husband died at their wedding supper. If you have recovered, I will tell you her history. There was a rich, childless bachelor, Kolchanovski de Kolchanovo, a noble of the Ukraine. He had immensely honorable relatives who hoped to be his heirs, and an immeasurably short neck, which gave the greater hopes to the heirs. I knew those heirs. They were in truth perfectly honorable people; but what's to be done? The most honorable and the least interested of them could not refrain from looking at Kolchanovski's neck. This annoyed the old man so intensely that out of spite to the family he paid court to a neighbor's daughter, drew up a document, conveyed to her all his property, then married her; after the ceremony there was dancing; at the end of the dancing a supper; at the end of the supper apoplexy killed him on the spot. In that way Madame Helena Kolchanovski became Miss Widow."

"Was that long ago?"

"Three years. At that time she was twenty-two years of age. Since then she might have married twenty-two times; but she does n't want to marry. People supposed that she was waiting for a prince. It turned out that that was not true; for she fired a prince out a little while ago. Besides I know well that she has no pretensions; the best proof of which is that Pani Kolchanovski lives to this time in close friendship with our well-known, sympathetic, gifted, etc., Eva Adami, who was a friend of hers in the boarding-school."

Hearing this, I just jumped from joy. If that is true, no more of Ostrynski. My beloved, honest Evusia[1] will smooth the way for my acquaintance with Pani Helena.

"Well, then you won't take me to her?" asked I of Ostrynski.

"Decidedly not; if any man wishes to make the acquaintance of any one in the city, why, he will make it," answered Ostrynski; "but because you put me out with

[1] A form of endearment for Eva.

Kazia, I do not wish people to say in the present case that I caused — Do I know? Be in good health!"[1]

CHAPTER XII.

I WAS to dine with the Suslovskis, but I wrote them that I could n't come.

My teeth have never ached, it is true, but then they might ache.

Helena did not go from my eyes all day; for what sort of a painter would he be, who would not think of such a face? I painted in my soul ten portraits of her. To my mind came the idea of a picture, in which such a face as Helena's would make a splendid impression. It was only necessary to see her a couple of times more. I flew to Eva Adami's, but did not find her. In the evening I receive a card from Kazia with an invitation for the morning to waters in the garden, and then to coffee. Those waters and that coffee are a regular saw!

I cannot go; for if I do not find Eva at home in the morning, I shall not catch her all day.

Eva Adami (that is her stage appellation; her real name is Anna Yedlinski) is an exceptional maiden. I have enjoyed her friendship this long time, and we say "thou" to each other. This is her ninth year on the stage, and she has remained pure in the full sense of the word. In theatres, there are, it is true, plenty of women who are innocent physically; but if their corsets could betray all the desires of those women, I suppose that the most shameless baboon, on hearing the story, might blush at all points not covered with hair. The theatre spoils souls, especially female souls.

[1] This means farewell.

THAT THIRD WOMAN.

It is difficult even to ask that in a woman, who every evening feigns love, fidelity, nobleness, and similar qualities, there should not be developed at last an instinctive feeling that all these virtues belong to the drama, but have no connection with life. The immense difference between art and reality confirms her in this feeling; rivalry and envy roused by applause poison the heart's noblest impulses.

Continual contact with people so spoiled as actors excites lower instincts. There is not a white Angora cat which would not be soiled in such an environment. This environment can be conquered only by great genius, which purifies itself in the fire of art; or a nature so thoroughly æsthetic that evil does not pass through it, as water does not pass through the feathers of a swan. Of such impermeable natures is Eva Adami.

At night, at tea, and the pipe more than once, I have talked with my colleagues about people belonging to the world of art, beginning with the highest, that is, poets, and ending with the lowest, that is, actors.

A being who has imagination developed beyond ordinary mortals, a being impressionable beyond others, sensuous, passionate, a being who, in the domain of happiness and delight, knows everything, and desires with unheard of intensity, — that is an artist. He should have three times the character and will-power of others to conquer temptation.

Meanwhile, as there is no reason why a flower, beautiful beyond others, should have greater strength to resist wind, there is no reason why an artist should have more character than an ordinary person. On the contrary, there is reason why, as a rule, he has less, for his vital energy is wasted in that gulf which divides the world of art from the world of every-day reality.

He is simply a sick bird, in a continual fever, — a bird which at times vanishes from the eye beneath the clouds, and at times drags its wearied wings in the dust and the mire. Art gives him a disgust for dust and mire; but life takes strength of flight from him. Hence that discord which is so frequent between the external and the internal life of artists.

The world, when it asks more from artists than from others, and when it condemns them, is right perhaps; but Christ, too, will be right when He saves them.

Ostrynski maintains, it is true, that actors belong to the artistic world as much as clarionets and French horns belong to it.

But that is not true; the best proof is Eva Adami, who is a thorough artist, both by gifts and that feeling which has preserved her from evil as a mother would. In spite of all the friendship which I have for Eva, I had not seen her for a long time; when she saw me then, she was very glad, though she had a certain astonished look, which I could not explain.

"How art thou, Vladzio?"[1] asked she. "For a wonder I see thee."

I was delighted to find her. She wore a Turkish morning gown with split sleeves; it had red palm-leaves on a cream-colored ground, and was bordered with wide embroidery in old gold. The rich embroidery was reflected with special beauty in her pale face and violet eyes. I told her so, and she was greatly pleased. I came to the point then at once.

"My golden diva! thou knowest Pani Kolchanovski, that wonderful lady of the Ukraine?"

"I do; she was my schoolmate."

"Take me to her."

---

[1] A form of endearment for Vladek or Vladislav

Eva shook her head.

"My golden, my good one, as thou lovest me!"

"No, Vladek, I will not take thee!"

"See how bad thou art; but at one time I was almost in love with thee."

What a mimosa that Eva is! When she hears this, she changes, puts her elbow on the table (a miracle, not an elbow), puts her pale face on her palm and asks,—

"When was that?"

I was in a hurry to speak of Helena; but since on a time I had in truth almost fallen in love with Eva, and since I wish now to bring her into good humor, I begin the narrative,—

"We were going once, after the theatre, to the botanical garden. Dost thou remember what a wonderful night that was? We were sitting on a bench near the fountain; thou hadst just said, 'I should like to hear a nightingale.' I was sad for some reason, and took off my cap, for my head was aching; and thou, going to the fountain, moistened a handkerchief, and put it on my forehead with thy hand. Thou didst seem simply as good as an angel, and I thought to myself: If I take that hand and put my lips to it, all will be over! I shall be in love to the death."

"And then what?" asks Eva, in an undertone.

"Thou didst step aside quickly, as if divining something."

Eva sat a while in thought, then woke from it and said with nervous haste, "Let us not speak of this matter, I pray thee."

"Well, let us not speak of it. Dost thou know, Eva, I like thee too well to fall in love with thee? One feeling excludes the other. From the time that I made thy acquaintance, I have had for thee a real genuine feeling."

"But," said Eva, as if following her own thoughts, "is it true that thou art betrothed?"

"True."

"Why hast thou not told me of it?"

"Because the engagement was broken, and then rearranged not long since. But if thou tell me that as betrothed I should not become acquainted with Pani Helena, I will answer, that I was a painter before I was betrothed. However, thou hast no fear for her?"

"Do not imagine that. I will not take thee to her, for I do not wish to expose her to people's tongues. They say that for some weeks half Warsaw is in love with thee; they relate uncreated things of thy conduct. No longer back than yesterday, I heard a witticism, that thou hast made the ten commandments of God into one for thy own use. Knowest thou into what one?"

"What one?"

"Thou shalt not covet thy neighbor's wife — in vain."

"Thou, O God, seest my suffering! but the witticism is good."

"And surely pointed."

"Listen to me, Evus;[1] art thou willing to hear the whole truth? I have ever been timid, awkward: I have not had, and have not now success with women. People imagine, God knows what; and meanwhile they do not suspect how much truth there is in the cry, Thou, O God, seest my suffering!"

"Povero maestro!"

"Give peace to thy Italian; take me to Pani Helena."

"My Vladek, I cannot; the more thou art thought a Don Juan, the less does it beseem me, an actress, to take thee to a lone woman who attracts the attention that Hela[2] does."

[1] Eva.   [2] Helena.

"Then why dost thou receive me?"

"I am different. I am an actress, and can apply to myself the words of Shakespeare, 'Be thou as chaste as ice, as pure as snow, thou shalt not escape calumny.'"

"It is possible to lose one's senses in such a case. Every one may know her, may be at her house, may look at her; but I may not! And why? Because I have painted a good picture and have made some reputation."

"From thy point of view, thou art right," said Eva, smiling. "Thou dost not suspect that I knew beforehand why thou hast come to me. Ostrynski was here, and he persuaded me that it was 'better' not to take thee to Hela."

"Ha, I understand!—and thou hast promised him?"

"I have not; I was even angry; still I think it is 'better' not to take thee. Let us talk now of thy picture."

"Do not torment me with the picture and painting. But since things are so, let them be so! This is what I will tell thee: in the course of three days I will make the acquaintance of Pani Kolchanovski, even if I have to go in disguise to her."

"Dress up as gardener and take her a bouquet — from Ostrynski."

But at that moment an idea altogether different comes to me; this idea seems so splendid that I strike my forehead, forget my anger and the offence which a moment before I felt that Eva had committed, and say,—

"Give thy word not to betray me."

"I give it," says the curious Eva.

"Know, then, that I shall disguise myself as an old minstrel. I have a whole costume and a lyre; I have been in the Ukraine, and know how to sing songs. Pani

Helena is from the Ukraine; she will be sure to receive me. Dost thou understand now?"

"What an original idea!" cried Eva.

Eva is artistic to such a degree that the idea cannot but please her; besides, she has given her word not to betray me, and she has no objection to make.

"What an original idea!" repeats she. "Hela so loves her Ukraine that she will just sob when she sees a minstrel in Warsaw; but what wilt thou tell her? How wilt thou explain thy coming to the Vistula?"

My enthusiasm is communicated to Eva in spite of her. For a time we sit and conspire in the best fashion possible. We agree that I am to put on the disguise; and Eva is to take me in a carriage to avoid the curiosity of onlookers. Pani Hela is to know nothing till Eva betrays the secret herself, when she chooses. Eva and I amuse ourselves with this plan, perfectly; then I fall to kissing her hands, and she keeps me for lunch.

I spend the evening at the Suslovskis. Kazia is a little gloomy because I did not come in the morning; but I endure her humors like an angel, besides, I am thinking of my adventure of the morrow and — of Hela.

CHAPTER XIII.

ELEVEN o'clock in the forenoon.
Only somehow Eva is not visible.

I am wearing a coarse linen shirt, open at the breast, a coat somewhat worn, but fairly good, a girdle, boots, everything that is needed. The hair of a gray wig falls in my eyes; and he would have been a keen man who could have recognized that as a wig; my beard was a masterpiece of patience. From eight o'clock in the morning I had been fastening, by means of isinglass, white hair among my own, and I had become gray in such fashion that in old age I shall not grow gray more naturally; diluted sepia gave me swarthiness; and Antek made wrinkles with the power of a genius. I seemed to be seventy years old.

Antek insists that, instead of painting, I could earn my bread as a model, which would in truth be with greater profit to art.

Half-past eleven — Eva is coming.

I send to the carriage a bundle containing my usual clothing, since, for aught I know, I may be obliged to change costume; I take the lyre then, and go down; at the door of the carriage I cry, —

"Slava Bogu!"[1]

Eva is astonished and enchanted.

"A wonderful beekeeper, a wonderful grandfather!" repeats she, laughing. "Such a thing could only come to the head of an artist!"

Speaking in parenthesis, she herself looks like a summer morning. She is in a robe of raw silk and a straw hat with poppies. I cannot take my eyes from her. She came in an open carriage. Therefore people begin at once to surround us; but what does she care for that!

At last the carriage moves on; my heart beats with more animation; in a quarter of an hour I shall see the Helena dreamed of.

We have not driven a hundred yards when I see Ostrynski at a distance coming toward us. That man must be omnipresent! Seeing us, he halts, bows to Eva, then looks quickly at both of us, especially at me. I do not admit that he recognizes me; still, after we pass him

[1] This is Russian. Glory to God.

I look around, and see that he is standing there all the time, following us with his eyes. Only at the turn do we lose him from sight. The carriage moves on rather swiftly; still it seems to me that the ride lasts an age. At length we stop in the alley of Belvedere.

We are before Hela's house.

I fly to the door as if shot at it.

Eva runs after me, crying, —

"What a hateful old grandfather!"

The servant, in a very showy livery, opens the door; and the next instant opens his eyes very widely at sight of me. Eva allays his astonishment, saying that the grandfather came with her, and we go upstairs.

The waiting-maid appears in a moment, declares that the lady is dressing in the next chamber, and vanishes.

"Good-day, Hela!" cries Eva.

"Good-day, Evus!" answers a wonderful, a fresh voice, "right away! right away! I shall be ready in a moment."

"Hela, thou knowest not what is waiting for thee, nor whom thou wilt see. I have brought thee a 'grandfather,' — the most genuine 'grandfather-minstrel' that has ever walked over the steppes of the Ukraine."

A cry of joy is heard in the chamber; the door opens suddenly, and in rushes Hela, in her corsets, her hair hanging down.

"A grandfather! a blind grandfather! here in Warsaw!"

"He is not blind; he sees!" cried Eva, hurriedly, not wishing to carry the jest too far.

But it was late, for that instant I throw myself at Hela's feet, and cry, —

"Cherub of the Lord!"

I embrace her feet with both hands, raising my eyes the while: I see a little more than the form of those

THAT THIRD WOMAN. 527

feet. Nations kneel down! People come with censers! A Venus of Milo! a perfect one!

"Cherub!" I repeat, with genuine ecstasy.

My minstrel enthusiasm was explained by this, that after long wandering I had met the first Ukraine soul. Notwithstanding that, Hela withdraws her feet from my hands and hurries away. I see her bare shoulders during the twinkle of an eye, and her neck, which reminds me of Psyche in the Neapolitan Museum. She vanishes then through the doorway; but I remain kneeling in the middle of the room.

Eva threatens me with her parasol, and laughs, hiding her rosy face in a bouquet of reseda.

Meanwhile a dialogue is begun through the door in the most beautiful dialect ever spoken from the Pripet to Chertomelik.

I had prepared myself for every possible query, therefore I lie as if from notes. "I am a beekeeper, from near Chigirin. My daughter wandered after a Pole to Warsaw; and I, old man, was grieving, grieving on the beefarm, till I wandered on after her. Good people give me coppers for singing — and now what? I shall see my dear child, give her my blessing, then return home, because I yearn for Mother Ukraine. There I am to die among the beehives. Every man must die; and it is time for old Philip this long while."

What a thing the actor nature is! Evus knows who I am; but she is affected so much by my rôle that she begins to nod her beautiful head in a melancholy manner, and looks at me with sympathy. Hela's voice quivers from the other room, also with emotion.

The door opens a little; a wonderfully white arm appears through the opening; and, unexpectedly, I find myself in possession of three rubles, which I receive; I

cannot do otherwise, and what is more, I pour out on
Hela's head a torrent of blessings in the names of all the
saints.

I am interrupted by the waiting-maid with the announcement that Pan Ostrynski is downstairs, and
inquires if the lady will receive him.

"Don't let him in, my dear!" cries Eva, in alarm.

Hela declares that of course she will not receive him.
She even expresses astonishment at such an early visit.
I, to tell the truth, also do not understand how Ostrynski,
who boasts, and is celebrated for his knowledge of social
forms, should come at that hour.

"There is something in this," says Eva.

But time fails for further explanations, since Hela
appears at that moment already dressed, and breakfast is
announced.

Both ladies pass into the dining-room. Hela wishes to
seat me at the table; but I refuse, and sit with my lyre
at the threshold. Soon I receive a plate so filled with
food that if six grandfathers of the Ukraine were to eat
all of it, they might have a fit of indigestion. But I eat,
for I am hungry, and while eating I look at Hela.

In truth, a more beautiful head there is not in any gallery on earth. As I live, I have not seen such transparent
eyes; it is simply possible to see all thoughts through
them, just as the bottom of a clear stream is seen. Those
eyes possess this power also, that they begin to laugh before the mouth; by this the face is brightened, as if a sunray had fallen on it. What incomparable sweetness in the
form of the mouth! That is a head somewhat in the
style of Carlo Dolce, though the outline of the brows and
the eyes bring to mind Raphael in his noblest type.

At last I cease to eat; I gaze and gaze; I would gaze
till death.

"Thou wert not here yesterday," says Hela to Eva.
"I hoped all the afternoon to see thee run in."

"In the morning I had a rehearsal, and in the afternoon I wanted to see Magorski's picture."

"Didst see it?"

"Not well, for there was a crowd — and thou?"

"I went in the morning. What a poet! — one wishes to weep with those Jews."

Eva looks at me, and my soul rises.

"I will go again, and as often as I can," says Hela. "Let us go together; maybe we can go to-day? It was so agreeable to me not only to look at that picture, but to think that such power appeared among us."

And people do not glorify that woman!

Then I hear further, —

"It is a pity that such strange things are told of that Magorski. I confess that I am dying of curiosity to know him."

"Ah!" says Eva, carelessly.

"Thou knowest him, I suppose?"

"I can assure thee that he loses much on closer acquaintance; presumptuous, vain, oh, how vain!"

I have such a desire to show Eva my tongue that I can barely restrain myself; she turns her roguish violet eyes toward me, and says, —

"Somehow thou hast lost appetite, grandfather?"

I'll show her my tongue; I can't restrain myself!

But she spoke again to Hela, —

"Yes, Magorski is much worthier of admiration than of acquaintance. Ostrynski has described him as a genius in the body of a 'barber.'"

I should cut off Ostrynski's ears if he had said anything similar; I knew that Eva has the devil at her collar; but in truth she is exceeding the measure. Fortunately, breakfast comes to an end. We go out to the grounds, where I am to give my songs. This annoys me somewhat, and I should rather be with Hela as a painter than a minstrel. But it is hard to escape! I sit at the wall in the shade of chestnut-trees, through the leaves of which the sun penetrates, forming on the ground a multitude of bright spots. Those spots quiver and twinkle, vanish and shine out anew, just as the leaves move. The garden is very deep, so the sound of the city barely reaches it, especially since it is dulled by the noise of fountains in the garden. The heat is great. Among the thick leaves, the twittering of sparrows is heard; but it is faint and, as it were, drowsy. At last there is silence.

I see that a perfectly harmonious picture is forming: A garden, a background of trees, spots of sunlight, fountains, those two women with uncommonly beautiful faces one of them leaning against the other; and I see an old minstrel sitting with a lyre at the wall, — all this has its own charm which affects me as a painter. Meanwhile I remember my rôle, and begin to sing with feeling, —

"People say that I am happy;
I laugh at their saying,
For they know not how often
I am covered with tears!

"I was born in misfortune,
In misfortune I perish.
Why didst bear me, O mother,
In that evil hour?"

Eva is affected, for she is an artist; Hela because she is from the Ukraine; and I — because both are so beautiful that the sight of them enchants me.

Hela listens without exaggerated attention, without false enthusiasm; but in her transparent eyes I see that the listening gives her pure, genuine pleasure.

How different from those Ukraine women who come to Warsaw for the carnival, and during a contra-dance annoy partners with tales of homesickness for the Ukraine; while, in fact, as an acquaintance of mine puts it, no power could draw one of them with hooks from Warsaw and the carnival to her Ukraine!

Hela listens, keeps time with her exquisite head; at moments she says to Eva, "I know that," and sings with me; I surpass myself. I cast forth from my bosom and memory a whole stock of material from the steppe, beginning with hetmans, knights, and Cossacks, and ending with falcons, Sonyas, Marusyas, steppes, grave-mounds, and God knows what! I am astonished myself, whence so much comes to me.

Time passes as in a dream.

I return a trifle weary, but enchanted.

CHAPTER XIV.

IN the studio I find, most unexpectedly, the Suslovskis and Kazia. They have come to give me a surprise.

Why did Antek tell them that surely I should be back soon?

Neither Kazia nor the Suslovskis know me, because I am disguised. I approach Kazia and take her hand; she draws back, somewhat frightened.

"Kazia, dost thou not know me?" And laughter seizes me at sight of her astonishment.

"But it is Vladek," says Antek.

Kazia looks at me more carefully; at last she cries, —

"Tfu! what an ugly grandfather!"

I an ugly grandfather! I am curious to know where she saw a handsomer. But for poor Kazia, reared in the ascetic principles of her father, of course every minstrel is ugly!

I withdraw to our kitchen, and after a few minutes reappear in my natural form. Kazia and her parents inquire what this masquerade means.

"A very simple thing. You see, sometimes we painters render one another a friendly service, and pose to one another for pictures. As Antek, who posed to me for an old Jew. You did n't know him, Kazia, did you, in the picture? I am posing for Tsepkovski. Such is the custom among painters, especially as there is a lack of models in Warsaw."

"We have come to give thee a surprise," said Kazia; "besides, I have never visited a studio in my life. Oh, what disorder! Is it this way with all painters?"

"More or less, more or less."

Pan Suslovski declares that he would rather find a little more system; and in this respect he hopes for a change in the future. I want to break his head with my lyre. Meanwhile Kazia smiles with coquettishness, and says, —

"There is one painter, a great good-for-nothing, with whom it will be different; only let me take the matter in hand, all will be put in order, arranged, cleaned, fumigated."

Thus speaking, she raises her nose, which is in the air, looks at the festoons of spider-webs adorning the corners of our studio, and adds, —

"Such disorder might discourage a merchant even. Some one will come, and immediately find himself, as it were, in an old clothes shop. For example, look at that armor; terrible how rusty it is! Still, all that is needed is to call a servant, tell her to crush a little brick; and all will begin to shine like a new samovar."

THAT THIRD WOMAN. 533

Jesus Mary! She talks of merchants, and wants to clean with brick-dust my armor dug out of a tomb — O Kazia, Kazia!

Suslovski, now happy, kisses her on the forehead; and Antek gives out certain ominous sounds which call to mind the grunting of a wild boar.

Kazia threatens me with forefinger on her nose, and talks on, —

"I beg thee to remember that all will be changed." Then she concludes, "And if a certain gentleman will not come to us this evening, he will be bad, and people will not love him."

So saying, she closes her eyes. I cannot say that there was not much charm in those tricks of hers. I promise to come; and I conduct my future family to the ground-floor.

Returning, I find Antek looking awry and distrustfully on a whole package of hundred ruble notes which are lying on the table.

"What is that?"

"Dost know what has happened?"

"I do not."

"I, like a common thief, robbed a man."

"How?"

"I sold him my corpses."

"And is that the money?"

"It is; I am a low usurer."

I embrace Antek; I congratulate him from my whole heart; he begins to relate how it happened, —

"I sit here after your departure, till some gentleman comes and asks if I am Svyatetski. I answer, 'I am curious to know why I should not be Svyatetski!' Then he says, 'I saw your picture and I want to buy it.' I say, 'You are free to do so; but permit me to say that a man must be an idiot to buy a wretched picture.' 'I am not an idiot,' says he; 'but I have a fancy to buy pictures painted by idiots.' 'If that is so, very well,' I answer. He asks the price. I say, 'What is that to me?' 'I will give you so much and so much?' 'That is well! if you will give that price, then give it.' He gave it, and went away. He left his card with the name Byalkovski, M. D. I am a low usurer, and that's the end of the matter!"

"Long life to the corpses! Antek, get married."

"I would rather hang myself; I am a low usurer, nothing more."

CHAPTER XV.

IN the evening I am at the Suslovskis; Kazia and I are in the niche in which there is a small sofa. Pani Suslovski is sitting at a table lighted by a lamp, and is sewing on something for Kazia's trousseau. Pan Suslovski sits at a table reading, with dignity, the evening number of "The Kite."

Somehow I am not myself; I wish to dissipate that feeling by pushing up very near Kazia.

In the salon silence is supreme; it is interrupted only by Kazia's whisper. I beg to embrace her; she whispers,—

"Vladek, papa will see us."

With that "papa" begins to read aloud, "The picture of our well-known artist, Svyatetski, 'The Last Meeting,' was bought to-day by Dr. Byalkovski for fifteen hundred rubles."

"That is true," I add. "Antek sold it this morning."

Then I try to embrace Kazia, and again I hear her whisper, —

"Papa will see us —"

THAT THIRD WOMAN. 535

My eyes turn involuntarily to Pan Suslovski. I see on a sudden that his face is changing; he shades his eyes with his hands and bends over "The Kite."

What the devil can he find there of such interest?

"Father, what is the matter?" asks Pani Suslovski.

He rises, advances two steps toward us, then halts, transfixes me with a glance, and, clasping his hands begins to nod his head.

"What is the matter?" I ask.

"See how falsehood and crime come always to the surface," answers Suslovski, pathetically. "My dear sir, read to the end, if shame will permit."

Thus speaking, he makes a movement as if to wrap himself in his toga, and gives me "The Kite." I take the number, and my glance falls on an announcement entitled: "A Minstrel of the Ukraine." I am confused somewhat, and read hurriedly the following, —

"Some days since a rare guest came to our city in the person of a decrepit minstrel who visits Ukraine families resident among us, begging them for alms, and singing songs in return. It is said that our well-known and sympathetic actress, Eva Adami, is particularly occupied with him; he was seen with her in a carriage no longer ago than this morning. In the first days of the appearance of this guest from a distance, a wonderful report rose that under the coat of the minstrel is hidden one of the most famous of our artists, who, in this manner, without arresting the attention of husbands and guardians, finds easy access to boudoirs. We are convinced that this report has no foundation, even for this reason alone, that our diva would never consent to further an undertaking of that kind. The old man, according to our information, has wandered in here straight from the Ukraine. His intelligence is dulled somewhat; but his memory is perfect."

"Hell!"

Suslovski is so enraged that he cannot recover his voice; at last he casts forth his superabundance of indignation, —

"What new falsehood, what excuse will you find to justify your conduct? Have we not seen you to-day in that shameful disguise? Who is that minstrel?"

"I am that minstrel," I answer; "but I do not understand why you find that disguise shameful."

At that moment Kazia snatches "The Kite" from my hand and begins to read. Suslovski wraps himself still more closely in the toga of indignation and continues, —

"Scarcely have you passed the threshold of an honest house when you bring with you corruption; and before you are the husband of that unfortunate child, you, in company with women of light character, betray her; you trample already on her confidence and ours; you break your plighted word — and for whom? For a hetaira of the theatre!"

Anger carries me off at last.

"My dear sir," say I, "enough of those commonplaces. That hetaira is worth ten such false Catos as you. You are nothing to me yet; and know this, that you annoy me! I have enough of you with your pathos, with your —" Here words fail me; but I have no further need of them, for Suslovski is opening his waistcoat, as if wishing to say, —

"Strike! spare not, here is my breast!"

But I have no thought of striking; I declare simply that I am going, lest I might say something more to Pan Suslovski.

In fact, I leave without saying farewell to any one.

The fresh breeze cools my heated head. Nine o'clock in the evening, and the night is very calm. I must walk to regain my composure, therefore I fly to the Alley of the Belvedere.

The windows in Hela's villa are dark. Evidently she is not at home. I know not myself why that causes me immense disappointment.

If I could see even her shadow on the window-pane, I should grow calm; but as it is, anger bears me away again.

What I shall do with that Ostrynski at the first meeting — I know not. Fortunately, he is not a man who withdraws before responsibility.

But speaking precisely, what claim have I against him? The article is written with infernal dexterity. Ostrynski denies that the minstrel is a disguised painter; he stands up, as it were, for Eva; but at the same time betrays the whole secret to Hela. Evidently he is trying to compromise Eva in the opinion of Hela; he takes vengeance on me for Kazia, and covers me besides with ridicule.

If only he hadn't said that my intelligence is blunted! The deed is done. In Hela's eyes I am covered with ridicule. She reads "The Kite."

Oh, what a dish of hash, and what bitterness for Eva! How that Ostrynski must triumph! Surely I must do something; but if I know what, may I become a reporter for "The Kite"!

It occurs to me to take counsel with Eva. She plays to-day; I will fly to the theatre and see her after the play.

There is time yet.

Half an hour later I am in her dressing-room.

Eva will finish directly; meanwhile, I look around.

Our theatres are not distinguished, as is known, for luxury of furnishing. A chamber with white walls; two jets of gas quivering from the draught; a mirror; a washstand; a number of chairs; and in one corner a long chair, probably the private property of the diva, — this is her dressing-room. Before the mirror a multitude of toilet articles, a cup of black coffee partly drunk, boxes with rouge and white, lead for the brows, a number of pairs of gloves, still retaining the form of the hand, and among them two false tresses; at the side walls bunches of costumes, white, rose-colored, dark, light, and heavy; on the floor are two baskets full of things pertaining to female costumes. The room is full of odor of toilet powder. What a medley everywhere; how everything has been cast about in a hurry! How many colors and reflections; what shadows; what a play of light from the quivering gas-jets!

That is a picture of its own kind; there is character in it. Of course there is nothing here more than in an ordinary dressing-room of a woman, still there is something which causes that chamber to seem, not a dressing-room, but a sanctuary of some kind; there is a certain spell and charm there. Above this disorder, this medley and hurry, between these scratched walls, hovers the inspiration of art.

A thunder of applause is heard. Ha! it is finished. Through the walls come to my ears the sound of calling; "Adami! Adami!" A quarter of an hour passes; they are shouting yet.

At last Eva rushes in; she is in the character of "Theodora." She has a crown on her head; her eyes blackened underneath; on her cheeks a blush of rouge; her dishevelled hair falls like a storm on her naked neck and shoulders. She is feverish and exhausted to that degree that she speaks to me in a whisper barely audible.

"How art thou, Vladek?" and removing her crown hurriedly, she throws herself in her regal robes on the long chair. Evidently she cannot utter words; for she looks at me silently, like a suffering bird. I sit near her, place my hand on her head, and think only of her.

I see in those blackened eyes the flame of unquenched ecstasy; I see on that forehead simply the stigma of art. I see that the woman brings to the altar of that theatrical Moloch her health, blood, and life, that breath is lacking in her breast at that moment. Such pity embraces me, such sorrow, such sympathy, that I know not what to do.

We sit some time in silence; at last Eva points to a number of "The Kite" lying on the toilet table, and whispers,—

"What a vexation, what a vexation!"

Suddenly she bursts into nervous weeping, and trembles like a leaf.

I know that she is weeping from weariness, not because of "The Kite;" for that article is buffoonery which every one will forget to-morrow; and the whole of Ostrynski is not worth one tear from Eva; still my heart is straitened the more. I seize her hands and cover them with kisses. I take her; I press her to my breast. My heart begins to beat with growing violence; something amazing takes place in me. I kneel down at Eva's knees, not knowing myself what I am doing; a cloud covers my eyes; suddenly I seize her in my arms, without thinking what I do.

"Vladek, Vladek, pity!" whispers Eva.

But I press her to my stormy breast; I know nothing of anything. I have lost my wits! I kiss her on the forehead, mouth, eyes; I can only say,—

"I love thee! I love —"

With that Eva's head drops back; her arms enclose my neck feverishly, and I hear the whisper, —

"I have loved thee this long time."

CHAPTER XVI.

IF for me there is a dearer creature on earth, I am a pickled herring.

They say that we artists do everything under the first impression of the moment; that is not true! for it seems that I loved Eva long ago, only I was ass enough not to see it. God alone knows what took place in me while I attended her home that evening. We went hand in hand, without speaking. From moment to moment I pressed Eva's arm to my side, and she pressed mine. I felt that she loved me with all her power.

I conducted her upstairs, and when we were in her little drawing-room, the position became in some way so awkward for us that we didn't dare to look into each other's eyes. But when Eva covered her face with her hands, I removed them gently and said, —

"Evus, thou art mine, is it not true?"

And she nestled up to me.

"I am, I am."

She was so beautiful, her eyes were drowsy, and at the same time gleaming, there was such a sweet weariness in her whole posture that I could not break away from her.

And in truth she could not break from me; she wished, as it were, to reward herself for continued silence, and for such a long-concealed feeling.

I returned home late. Antek was not sleeping yet;

he was drawing by lamplight, on wood, for one of the illustrated papers.

"There is a letter here for you," said he, without raising his eyes from his work.

I take a letter from the table and feel a ring through the envelope. Good! that ring will do for to-morrow. I open the letter, and read as follows, —

I know that the return of this ring will cause pleasure, for you had this in view evidently. As to me, I do not think of rivalling actresses. KAZIA.

At least it is brief. From this letter anger alone is looking forth, nothing more. If any shade of charm surrounded Kazia in my eyes hitherto, that shade is blown away now beyond return.

A wonderful thing! all supposed that Eva was the cause of my disguise and of all those adventures; and in truth the cause of what follows will be Eva.

I crush the letter, put it in my pocket, and go to bed.

Antek raises his eyes from his work, and looks in expectation that I will say something; but I am silent.

"That scoundrel Ostrynski was here this evening after the theatre," said Antek.

CHAPTER XVII.

IN the morning about ten o'clock I wish to fly to Eva; but I cannot, for I have guests.

Baron Kartofler comes and engages a duplicate of my "Jews." He offers me fifteen hundred rubles; I want two thousand. The bargain is made at that price. After his departure I receive an order for two portraits from Tanzenberg. Antek, who is an Anti-Semite, reviles me as a Jewish painter; but I am curious to know who would buy productions of art, if not the "finance." If the "finance" is afraid of Antek's corpses, the fault is not mine.

I am with Eva at one o'clock. I give her the ring, and declare that we shall go to Rome after our marriage.

Eva consents with delight. We are as much given to talking to-day as we were to silence last evening. I tell her of the order which I have received, and we rejoice together. I must finish the portraits before our departure; but "the Jews" for Kartofler I will paint in Rome. When we return to Warsaw, I will fit up a studio, and we will live as in heaven.

While forming these projects, I tell Eva that we will keep the anniversary of yesterday as a holiday all our lives.

She hides her face on my shoulder, and begs me not to mention it. Then she winds the split sleeves of her gown round my neck, and calls me her great man. She is paler than usual; her eyes are more violet than usual, but they are beaming with gladness.

Ah! what an ass, that having near me such a woman I was seeking for happiness elsewhere, in a circle where I was a perfect stranger, and which was strange to me.

What an artistic nature that of Eva! She is my betrothed, accepts the rôle at once, and involuntarily plays the part of a young and happy affianced. But I do not take that ill of a beloved creature, after so many years in a theatre.

After dinner we go to Hela Kolchanovski's.

From the moment that Eva can present me as her betrothed, the minstrel trick becomes innocent and can cause no misunderstanding between those two ladies. In fact, when Hela heard of the engagement, she received us with open arms, and was delighted at Eva's happiness. We laugh like three maniacs at the "grandfather," and at that which the "grandfather" had to hear concerning the painter Magorski. Yesterday I wanted to put a stiletto into Ostrynski; to-day I am astonished at his cleverness.

Hela laughs so heartily that her transparent eyes are filled with tears. Speaking in parenthesis, she is marvellous. When she inclines her head at the end of the visit, I cannot take my eyes from it; and Eva herself is under its spell to such a degree that during the day she imitates unconsciously that bending of the neck and that look.

We agree that, after our return from abroad, I shall paint a portrait of Hela; but first I shall make my Eva in Rome, if I can reproduce those features, which are so delicate that they are almost over-refined, and that face, so impressionable that every emotion is reflected in it as a cloud in clear water.

But I shall succeed; why shouldn't I?

The evening "Kite" publishes uncreated tales of the orders which have come to me; my income is reckoned by thousands. That in a small degree is the reason, perhaps, that next day I receive a letter from Kazia, stating that she returned the ring under the influence of anger and jealousy, but if I come and we fall at the feet of her parents, they will let themselves be implored.

I have enough of that falling at the feet and those forgivenesses. I do not answer. Let him fall at Suslovski's feet who wants to; let Kazia marry Ostrynski! I have my Eva.

But my silence casts an evident panic on the Suslovski family; for a few days later the same messenger comes with a letter from Kazia, but this time to Antek.

Antek shows me the letter. Kazia prays him to come for a moment's conversation concerning an affair on which her whole future depends; she reckons on his heart, on that sense of justice which from the first glance of the eye she divined in him. She has the hope that he will not refuse the prayer of an unhappy woman. Antek curses, mutters something under his nose about low Philistines, and about the necessity of hanging both them and their posterity at the next opportunity; but he goes.

I divine that they wish to influence me through him.

CHAPTER XVIII.

ANTEK, who in reality has a soft heart, is won over evidently. For a week he goes to the Suslovskis regularly; for three days he walks around me, frowns, looks at me just like a wolf.

At last one day at tea he inquires peevishly, "Well, what dost thou think of doing with that girl?"

"With what girl?"

"With that Suslovski, or what is her name?"

"I don't think of doing anything with that Suslovski, or what is her name."

A moment of silence follows, then Antek speaks again, —

"She is whining whole days, till I cannot look at her."

What an honest soul! At that moment too his voice trembles with emotion; but he snorts like a rhinoceros and adds, —

"A decent man does not act in that fashion."

"Antek, thou art beginning to remind me of Papa Suslovski."

"I would rather remind thee of Papa Suslovski than wrong his daughter."

"I beg thee to drop me."

"Very well! I can even not know thee at all."

With this the conversation ends, and thenceforth I do not speak to Antek.

We pretend not to know each other, which is the more amusing since we live together. We drink tea together in the morning, and it never occurs to either of us to move out of the studio.

The time of my marriage is approaching. Through the intermediary of "The Kite" all Warsaw knows of that now. All look at us; all admire Eva. When we were at the exhibition, they surrounded us so that we could not push through.

My unknown friend*ess* sends an anonymous letter in which she warns me that Eva is not the wife for a man like me.

"I do not believe what is said of the relations between Panna Adami and Pan Ostrynski [writes my friend*ess*]; but thou, O master, art in need of a wife who would devote herself altogether to thy greatness; Panna Adami is an artist herself, and will always be drawing water to her own mill."

Antek goes continually to the Suslovskis, but surely as a comforter, for the Suslovskis must know of my intentions.

I have obtained an unlimited leave of absence for Eva. She begins to wear her hair as a village maiden; she dresses very modestly and wears robes closed to the neck. This becomes her very much. The scene in the dressing-room has not been repeated. Eva does not permit it. The utmost right I have is to kiss her hands. That makes me greatly impatient; but I flatter myself that it affects her in the same way.

She loves me madly. We spend whole days together. I have begun to give her lessons in drawing. She is swallowed up in those lectures, and painting in general.

CHAPTER XIX.

THUNDER hurling Zeus, at what art thou gazing from the summit of Olympus? Things are done of which philosophers have never dreamed.

On the eve of my marriage Antek comes to me, nudges me with his elbow, and, turning aside his dishevelled head, says gloomily, —

"Vladek, dost thou know I have committed a crime?"

"Well, since thou hast mentioned it," I answer, "what sort of a crime?"

Antek looks at the floor fixedly, and says, as if to himself, —

"That such a drunkard as I, such an idiot without talent, such a moral and physical bankrupt should marry such a maiden as Kazia is an out-and-out crime."

I do not believe my ears; but I throw myself on my friend's neck without regard to the fact that he pushes me away.

His marriage will be in a couple of days.

CHAPTER XX.

AFTER a residence of some months in Rome, Eva and I receive a splendid card inviting us to the wedding of Pan Ostrynski and Panna Helena Turno, *primo voto*, Kolchanovski.

We cannot go, for Eva's health does not permit.

Eva paints continually, and makes immense progress. I receive a gold medal in Pest. A certain rich Croat bought my picture. I have entered into relations with Goupil.

CHAPTER XXI.

A SON is born to me in Verona.

Eva herself says that she has never seen such a child.

Uncommon.

CHAPTER XXII.

FOR some months we are in Warsaw.

I have fitted up a splendid studio. We visit the Ostrynskis rather frequently. He has sold "The Kite," and is now "President of the Society for Distributing Barley Grits to Laborers out of Employment." Nothing can give an idea of his lordliness or the gratitude with which he is surrounded. He pats me on the shoulder and says to me: "Well, benefactor!" He patronizes literary talents also, and receives on Wednesdays.

She is as beautiful as a dream. They have no children.

CHAPTER XXIII.

OH, save me or I die of laughter. Antek and his wife have come home from Paris. She poses as the wife of an artist of golden Bohemia; he wears silk shirts, has a forelock, and wears his beard wedge-form. I understand all; I understand that she could overcome his habits, his character; but how did she conquer his hair? — that remains for me an endless puzzle.

Antek has not stopped painting "corpses;" but he paints also genre pictures of village life. He has great success. He paints portraits too; these, however, with less result, for the carnation always recalls the "corpse."

I asked him, through old friendship, if he is happy with his wife. He told me that he had never dreamed of such happiness. I confess that Kazia has disappointed me in a favorable sense.

I too should be perfectly happy, were it not that Eva begins to be a little weak, and, besides, the poor thing becomes peevish. I heard her crying once in the night. I know what that means. She is pining for the theatre. She says nothing, but she pines.

I have begun a portrait of Pani Ostrynski. She is simply an incomparable woman! Regard for Ostrynski would not restrain me, of course, and were it not that to this hour I love Eva immensely, I know not —

But I love Eva immensely, immensely!

TRANSLATOR'S NOTES.

CHARCOAL SKETCHES were written in the Pico House, Los Angeles, California, in 1878. Perhaps the hotel is in existence yet; in that case the register for the above year contains the signature of Sienkiewicz and the number of his room. These Charcoal Sketches, as the author informed me, are founded on facts observed by him, and give a picture of life in the district where he was born and where he spent his youth. Ignorance, selfish class isolation, and resultant social helplessness, are depicted in remarkable relief and unsparingly. There is not collective intelligence and strength enough in Barania-Glova to save Repa's wife from ruin and murder. Pan Floss is driven from his land of "Little Progress" and has to pay for Sroda's oxen, which the owner himself turned in on his neighbor's clover; since Pan Floss is a noble and Sroda a peasant, the latter thinks himself justified in taking what he can from the noble in the night or the daytime, by fair means or foul. Pan Skorabevski has no wish to annoy himself in aiding peasants; if he wants anything from them, or wishes to defend himself against them, he calls in Pan Zolzik. The great public forces of Barania-Glova are the vile Zolzik, and Shmul without conscience. Father Chyzik, the priest, considering that his whole business is with another world, has no thought for the temporal welfare of Repa's wife.

The following is a translation of most of the names in Charcoal Sketches:—

Barania-Glova	Sheep's Head.
Burak	Beet.
Krucha Wola	Brittle will.
Kruchek	A small raven, or rather a rook. It is a name given frequently to a dog.
Lipa	Basswood.
Maly Postempovitsi	Little Progress.
Oslovitsi	Asstown.
Repa	Turnip.
Shmul	Samuel.
Sroda	Wednesday.
White Crawfish	A phrase meaning eggs.
Zolzik	Strangler.
Zweinos	Two noses.

Tartar Captivity is a sketch preliminary to "With Fire and Sword." Though it appears as a fragment of a memoir, it is an original production written by Sienkiewicz in the style of the seventeenth century. Here the author uses for the first time the two main historical elements of Polish society: nobility and the Church. These two elements were raised to an ideal height in the Polish mind. Zdaniborski was a noble sincere and naïve, who considered the position and privileges of the nobility to be as sacred and inviolable as those of the Church; both he believed to be the direct product of God's will.

Mayors of the air, referred to in Chapter V., were men appointed to keep alive fires which would fill the air with a smoke disagreeable to the plague or pest, and prevent it, or rather her, from approaching. The plague or pest in the popular mind was represented as a female who went around killing people.

TRANSLATOR'S NOTES.

On the Bright Shore. All persons who have read "Children of the Soil" will remember Svirski, the sympathetic artist in that book; this same Svirski is the hero of the present narrative.

That Third Woman. In this narrative the only character needing explanation is, I believe, the minstrel. In Little Russia and the Ukraine the minstrel called "Kobzar," from kobza, the instrument on which he plays, and also "Did" (grandfather), because he is generally old and sometimes blind, is a prominent figure to this day. In centuries past he played a great part by rousing popular feeling and carrying intelligence from place to place. At present his rôle is to entertain people who wish to hear either what the minstrel himself improvises, or the ballads of that region. The Duma, or ballad of the Ukraine, is famous.

Let Us Follow Him was written somewhat earlier than "Quo Vadis," and was a tentative sketch in a new field, as was Tartar Captivity, which preceded "With Fire and Sword."

www.ingramcontent.com/pod-product-compliance
Lightning Source LLC
Chambersburg PA
CBHW011751220426
43671CB00017B/2941